Personal Finance For Canadians For Dummies, 3rd Edition

Cheat Sheet

W9-CDY-034

Eric and Tony's Keys to Personal Financial Success

- Take charge of your finances. Procrastinating is detrimental to your long-term financial health. Don't wait for a crisis or major life event to get your act together. Read this book and start implementing now!

- Don't buy consumer items (cars, clothing, vacations, and so on) that lose value over time on credit. Use debt only to make investments in things that gain value, such as real estate, a business, or an education.

- Use credit cards only for convenience, not for carrying debt. If you have a tendency to run up credit card debt, then get rid of your cards and use only cash, cheques, and debit cards.

- Live within your means and don't try to keep up with your coworkers, neighbours, and peers. Many who engage in conspicuous consumption are borrowing against their future; some end up bankrupt.

- Save and invest at least 5 to 10 percent of your income. Preferably, invest through an RRSP or other retirement savings plan to reduce your taxes and ensure your future financial independence.

- Understand and use your employee benefits. If you're self-employed, find out the best investment and insurance options available to you, and use them.

- Research before you buy. Never purchase a financial product on the basis of an advertisement or salesperson's solicitation.

- Avoid financial products that carry high commissions and expenses. Companies that sell their products through aggressive sales techniques generally have the worst financial products and the highest commissions.

- Don't purchase any financial product that you do not understand. Ask questions and compare what you're offered to the best sources recommended in this book.

- Invest the majority of your long-term money in ownership vehicles that have appreciation potential, such as stocks, real estate, and your own business. When you invest in bonds or bank accounts, you are simply lending your money to others and will earn a return that probably won't keep you ahead of inflation and taxes.

- Avoid making emotionally based financial decisions. For example, investors who panic and sell their stock holdings after a major market correction miss a buying opportunity. Be especially careful in making important financial decisions after a major life change such as a divorce, job loss, or death in your family.

...For Dummies®: Bestselling Book Series for Beginners

Personal Finance For Canadians For Dummies, 3rd Edition

Cheat Sheet

- Make investing decisions based upon your needs and the long-term fundamentals of what you are buying. Ignore the predictive advice offered by financial prognosticators — nobody has a working crystal ball. Don't make knee-jerk decisions based on news headlines.

- Own your home. In the long run, owning is more cost-effective than renting, unless you have a terrific rent-control deal. Don't buy until you can stay put for a number of years.

- Purchase broad insurance coverage to protect against financial catastrophes. Eliminate insurance for small potential losses.

- If you're married, make time to discuss joint goals, issues, and concerns. Be accepting of your partner's money personality; learn to compromise and manage as a team.

- Prepare for life changes. The better you are at living within your means and anticipating life changes, the better off you will be financially and emotionally.

- Read publications that have high-quality standards and that aren't afraid to take a stand and recommend what's in your best interests.

- Prioritize your financial goals and start working toward them. Be patient. Focus on your accomplishments and learn from your past mistakes.

- Hire yourself first. You are the best financial person that you can hire. If you need help making a major decision, hire conflict-free advisers who charge a fee for their time. Work in partnership with advisers — don't abdicate control.

- Invest in yourself and others. Invest in your education, your health, and your relationships with family and friends. Having a lot of money isn't worth much if you don't have your health and people with whom to share your life. Give your time and money to causes that better our society and world.

Copyright © 2001 Eric Tyson and Tony Martin
All rights reserved.

Cheat Sheet $2.95 value. Item 3-29-6.

For more information about John Wiley & Sons
Canada, Ltd call 1-800-567-4797.

...For Dummies®: Bestselling Book Series for Beginners

Personal Finance For Canadians

FOR DUMMIES®

3RD EDITION

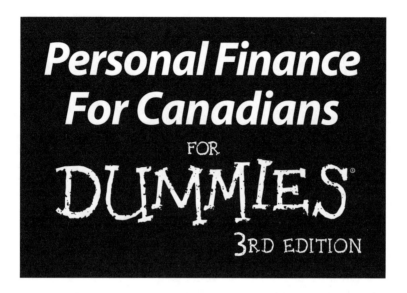

Personal Finance For Canadians For DUMMIES

3RD EDITION

by Eric Tyson and Tony Martin

John Wiley & Sons Canada, Ltd

Personal Finance For Canadians For Dummies, 3rd Edition®

Published by
John Wiley & Sons Canada, Ltd
22 Worcester Road
Etobicoke, ON M9W 1L1
www.wiley.ca

Canadian Cataloguing in Publication Data

Tyson, Eric (Eric Kevin)

Personal finance for Canadians for dummies

3rd ed.

Previously published under title: Personal finance for dummie$ for Canadians.

Includes index.
ISBN 1-894413-29-6

1. Finance, Personal – Canada. I. Martin, Tony (Tony M.). II. Title.
III. Title: Personal finance for dummie$ for Canadians.

HG179.T97 2001   332.024'00971   C00-933240-5

Printed in Canada

2 3 4 5 TRI 05 04 03

Distributed in Canada by John Wiley & Sons Canada, Ltd.

For general information on John Wiley & Sons Canada, Ltd, including all books published by Wiley Publishing, Inc., please call our warehouse, Tel: 1-800-567-4797. For reseller information, including discounts and premium sales, please call our sales department, Tel: 416-646-7992. For press review copies, author interviews, or other publicity information, please contact our marketing department, Tel: 416-646-4584; Fax: 416-236-4448.

For authorization to photocopy items for corporate, personal, or educational use, please contact Cancopy, The Canadian Copyright Licensing Agency, One Yonge Street, Suite 1900, Toronto, ON M5E 1E5; Tel: 416-868-1620; Fax: 416-868-1621; www.cancopy.com

About the Authors

Eric Tyson first became interested in money matters three decades ago. After toiling as a management consultant to Fortune 500 financial-service firms, Eric took his inside knowledge of the banking, investment, and insurance industries and committed himself to making personal financial management accessible to us all.

Today, Eric is an internationally acclaimed and best-selling personal finance book author, syndicated columnist, and speaker. He has worked with and taught people from all financial situations, so he knows the financial concerns and questions of real folks just like you. Despite being handicapped by an M.B.A. from the Stanford Graduate School of Business and a B.S. in Economics and Biology from Yale University, Eric remains a master at "keeping it simple."

An accomplished personal finance writer, his "Investor's Guide" syndicated column is read by millions, and he was an award-winning columnist for the San Francisco *Examiner*. He is the author of five national best-selling financial books in the *...For Dummies* series on personal finance and investing. Eric's work has been featured and quoted in hundreds of publications including *Newsweek*, *The Wall Street Journal*, *Forbes*, *Kiplinger's Personal Finance Magazine*, *Parenting*, *Money*, *Family Money*, and on NBC'S Today Show, ABC, CNBC, PBS Nightly Business Report, CNN, and on CBS national radio, NPR Sound Money and Bloomberg Business Radio.

Tony Martin, after graduating from Queen's University with a business degree, set off to see the world. (Best buy? A two-day "cruise" from Jakarta to Singapore for $8, including a place to unroll a sleeping bag on deck, and fish and rice three times a day!) He then joined CBC radio, and, from then on, has been involved in helping people understand the world of money. He excels at equipping individuals with the knowledge and tools they need to make better financial and investment choices for themselves and their families.

Tony is the co-author with Eric of *Investing For Canadians For Dummies*. His widely read column "Me and My Money" appears in the *Globe and Mail's* week-end *Net Worth* personal finance section. He has also written for many other leading publications, including *ROB Magazine*, *Reader's Digest*, and *IE:Money*. Tony is a frequent speaker on personal finance and investing, and appears regularly on television and radio, including RobTV, CBC Radio, and TVOntario.

Tony has also taken his talents on-line. He is currently developing a unique hands-on system that teaches people how to be better investors with Simvest Solutions, the leading global provider of on-line educational investing simulations. He was also the editor and major contributor to the personal finance Knowledge Base of imoney.com (now at www.canoe.ca).

Dedication

This book is hereby and irrevocably dedicated to our families and friends, as well as clients and customers, who ultimately have taught us everything that we know about how to explain financial terms and strategies so that all of us may benefit.

Authors' Acknowledgements

Being an entrepreneur involves endless challenges, and without the support and input of good friends and mentors Peter Mazonson, Jim Collins, and my best friend and wife, Judy, I couldn't have accomplished what I have.

I hold many people accountable for my perverse and maniacal interest in figuring out the financial services industry and money matters, but most of the blame falls on my loving parents, Charles and Paulina, who taught me most of what I know that's been of use in the real world.

I'd also like to thank Maggie McCall, David Ish, Paul Kozak, Chris Treadway, Sally St. Lawrence, K.T. Rabin, Will Hearst III, Ray Brown, Susan Wolf, Rich Caramella, Lisa Baker, Renn Vera, Maureen Taylor, Jerry Jacob, Robert Crum, Duc Nguyen, and Maria Carmicino and all the good folks at King Features for believing in and supporting my writing and teaching.

— *Eric*

There is no such thing as working on one's own, as the support, good humour, and advice of many are essential to success. I owe many thanks to my wife, Jane Howard, and my good friend Geoff Rockburn who have both been endlessly supportive and helpful over the years. I'm as grateful as always to my parents, Ruth and John, for teaching me so much about what really matters.

There are also many people in the personal finance industry who have kindly offered their help in assisting me in penetrating, understanding, and explaining money matters. Many thanks to everybody who has generously shared their insights and expertise over the years, including Peter Volpe, Gena Katz, Sandra McLeod, Anthony Layton, Paul Hickey, Jim Bullock, Alisa Dunbar, Alan Silverstein, and Janet Freedman.

In addition, I'd like to thank Karen Benzing, David Chilton, Patricia Davies, Carmela DiLalla, Douglas Goold, Don Hendry, Michael Lee, Dave Pyette, Peggy Wente, and Trish Wilson, for their support and encouragement over the years.

— *Tony*

Many thanks to all the people who provided insightful comments on this book, especially tax and financial planner extraordinaire Barton Francis, financial planner par excellence Warren Baldwin, and Mike van den Akker, Gretchen Morgensen, Craig Litman, Gerri Detweiler, Mark White, Alan Bush, Nancy Coolidge, and Chris Jensen. Thanks to Peter Volpe for his detailed and extremely helpful technical review of this book.

And thanks to all the wonderful people on the front line and behind the scenes — Joan Whitman, Melanie Rutledge, Rebecca Conolly, Kelli Howey, and Pam Erlichman — for putting this 3rd edition together.

Publisher's Acknowledgements

We're proud of this book; please send us your comments at canadapt@wiley.com.

Some of the people who helped bring this book to market include the following:

Acquisitions and Editorial

Editorial Director: Joan Whitman

Associate Editor: Melanie Rutledge

Copy Editor: Kelli Howey

Special Help

Michael Kelly

Production

Director of Production: Donna Brown

Production Editor: Rebecca Conolly

Layout and Graphics: Kim Monteforte, Heidy Lawrance Associates

Proofreader: Pamela Erlichman

Indexer: Belle Wong

John Wiley & Sons Canada, Ltd

Bill Zerter, Chief Operating Officer

Robert Harris, Publisher, Professional and Trade Division

Publishing and Editorial for Consumer Dummies

Diane Graves Steele, Vice President and Publisher, Consumer Dummies

Joyce Pepple, Acquisitions Director, Consumer Dummies

Kristin A. Cocks, Product Development Director, Consumer Dummies

Michael Spring, Vice President and Publisher, Travel

Brice Gosnell, Publishing Director, Travel

Suzanne Jannetta, Editorial Director, Travel

Publishing for Technology Dummies

Andy Cummings, Acquisitions Director

Composition Services

Gerry Fahey, Executive Director of Production Services

Debbie Stailey, Director of Composition Services

Contents at a Glance

Table of Contents

Part V: Where to Go for More Help...............................367

Chapter 19: Financial Planners 369

Introduction

*W*elcome to *Personal Finance For Canadians For Dummies,* 3rd Edition. For a number of years, we both dreamed of writing a personal finance book that would be different. The book would describe in a down-to-earth and friendly way the important concepts that you need to know in order to manage your money. It would give specific answers to financial questions where it could, and where it couldn't give the answers it would suggest the best resources to turn to.

As fate would have it, Eric's path crossed that of IDG Books, and Tony then bumped into them both. The *...For Dummies* approach is how we had both conceived our personal finance book; we just didn't know it at the time!

More than 70,000 copies of the first and second editions of this book are in print, and as you can see from the quotes in the front of this edition, readers and reviewers alike were pleased with the previous editions. However, we and the good folks at CDG — the Canadian publishing partner of IDG — don't rest on our laurels. So what you hold in your hands reflects more hard work to bring you the freshest material to address your personal financial quandaries.

Why This Book?

Many Canadians are financially illiterate. If you are, it's probably not your fault. Personal Finance 101 is not offered in our schools — not in high school, not even in the best universities and graduate schools. It should be. (Of course, if it were, we wouldn't be able to write fun and useful books such as this — or maybe they would use this book in the course!)

There are some common financial problems and mistakes — procrastinating and lack of planning, wasteful spending, falling prey to financial salespeople and pitches, failing to do sufficient research before making important financial decisions, and so on — and different people keep making those same mistakes over and over. This book, like a good friend, can whop you upside the head to keep you from falling into the same traps.

Unfair as it seems, many of these traps await you when you are actually seeking help. The world is filled with biased and bad financial advice. We regularly see and hear about the consequences of this poor advice. Of course, every profession has bad apples, but too many people calling themselves "financial planners" have conflicts of interest and inadequate competence.

All too often, financial advice ignores the big picture and focuses narrowly on investing. Because money is not an end in itself but part of your whole life, this book helps connect your financial goals and problems to the rest of your life. You need a broad understanding of personal finance to include all areas of your financial life: spending, taxes, saving, insurance, and planning for major goals like education, buying a home, and retirement.

Even if you understand the financial basics, thinking about your finances in a holistic way can be difficult. Sometimes you're too close to the situation to be objective. Like the organization of your desk or files (or disorganization, as the case may be), your finances may reflect the history of your life more than they reflect a comprehensive plan for your future.

You are likely a busy person and don't have enough hours in your day to get things done. Thus, you want to know how to diagnose your financial situation quickly (and painlessly) and determine what you should do next. Unfortunately, after figuring out which financial strategies make sense for you, choosing specific financial products in the marketplace can be a nightmare. You have literally thousands of investment, insurance, and loan options to choose from. Talk about information overload!

To complicate matters, you probably hear about most products through advertising that can be misleading, if not downright false. Of course, some ethical and useful firms advertise, but so do those that are more interested in converting your hard-earned income and savings into their profits. And they may not be here tomorrow when you need them.

You want to know the best places to go for your circumstances, so we filled this book with specific, tried-and-proven product recommendations. We also suggest how and where to turn next if you need more information and help.

Uses for This Book

You can use this book in one of three ways:

- If you want to find out about a specific topic, such as getting out of high-interest consumer debt, planning for major goals, or investing, you can flip to that section and get your answers quickly.

- If you want a crash course in personal finance, read this book cover-to-cover. Reading the whole book helps to solidify major financial concepts and gets you thinking about your finances in a more comprehensive way.

- If you're tired of picking up scattered piles of bills, receipts, and junk mail every time the kids chase the cat around the den, you can use this book as a paperweight!

Seriously, though, this book is basic enough for a novice to get his or her arms around thorny financial issues. But advanced readers will be challenged as well to think about their finances in a new way and identify areas for improvement. Check out the table of contents for a chapter-by-chapter rundown of what's in this book. You can also look up a specific topic in the index. Or you can turn the page and start at the beginning: Chapter 1.

The Big Picture

This book is organized into five parts, each covering a major area of your personal finances. The chapters within each part cover specific topics in detail. You can read each chapter and part without having to read what comes before, which is useful if you have better things to do with your free time. This book also makes for great reading anywhere you might be sitting for a length of time (perhaps the bathroom). You may be referred occasionally to somewhere else in the book for more details on a particular subject. Here is a summary of what you find in each part.

Part I: Where Do You Go from Here?

This part explains how to diagnose your current financial health and explores common reasons for any missing links in your personal finance knowledge. We all have dreams and goals, so in this part we also encourage you to think about what your financial aspirations are and to figure out how much you should be saving if you want to retire someday or accomplish other important goals.

Part II: Saving More, Spending Less

Most people don't have gobs of extra cash. Therefore, this part shows you how to figure out where all your dollars are going and how to reduce your spending. Chapter 5 is devoted to helping you get out from under the burden of high-interest consumer debt, such as credit card debt. We also provide specifics for reducing your tax burden.

Part III: Investing Crash Course

Earning and saving money is hard work, so you should be careful when it comes to investing what you have worked so hard to save (or waited so long to inherit!). Learning investment basics helps you pick investments wisely and understand investment risks, returns, and a whole lot more. We explain all the major and best investment options. We recommend specific strategies and investments for both inside and outside of tax-sheltered RRSPs and retirement plans. We also discuss buying, selling, and investing in real estate, as well as other wealth-building investments.

Part IV: Protecting What You've Got

Insurance is an important part of financial life. Unfortunately, for most people, it is a thoroughly overwhelming and dreadfully boring topic. But perhaps we can pique your interest in this esoteric topic by telling you that you're probably paying more than you should for insurance and you probably don't have the right coverages for your situation. This part tells you all you ever wanted to know (okay, fine — all you *never* wanted to know but probably should know anyway) about how to buy the right insurance at the best price.

Part V: Where to Go for More Help

As you build your financial knowledge, more questions and issues may arise. In this part, we discuss where to go and what to avoid should you be in the market for more financial information and advice. In this part, we also discuss hiring a financial planner as well as investigating resources in print, on the air, and online.

Part VI: The Part of Tens

These chapters of ten somethings can help you manage major life changes or help you keep money in its proper perspective with the rest of your life.

Glossary

The world of money is filled with jargon, so you'll be happy to know that this book includes a comprehensive glossary of financial terms that you'll often hear tossed around but seldom hear properly explained.

Icons Used in This Book

This nerdy guy (who is rumoured to bear some resemblance to a senior official at IDG Books!) appears beside discussions that aren't critical if you just want to learn basic concepts and get answers to your financial questions. You can safely ignore these sections, but reading them will deepen and enhance your personal financial knowledge. This stuff can also come in handy if you're ever on a game show or find yourself stuck on an elevator with a financial geek.

This target flags strategy recommendations for making the most of your money (for example, paying off your credit card debt with your lottery winnings).

This icon highlights the best financial products in investment, insurance, and so on to implement strategy recommendations (for example, calling the Ethical Bank for low-interest-rate loans).

This icon is a friendly reminder of information discussed elsewhere in the book or stuff you'll definitely want to remember.

This icon marks things to avoid and common mistakes people make in managing their finances.

This icon alerts you to scams and scoundrels that prey on the unsuspecting.

This icon highlights when you should consider doing some additional research. Don't worry — we explain what to look for and look out for.

Part I
Where Do You Go from Here?

The 5th Wave   By Rich Tennant

AT THE HOME OF BILL AND MELINDA GATES

©RICHTENNANT

"You bought what? You know we're on a budget. Now take Hughes Electric back to General Motors and see if you can get your money back."

In this part . . .

*W*e discuss the concepts that underlie sensible personal financial management. You also find out why you didn't know all these concepts before now (and who to blame). Here, you'll undergo a (gentle) financial physical exam to diagnose your current economic health. We also cover how to plan for and accomplish your financial goals.

Chapter 1

Figuring Your Financial Fitness

. . . .

In This Chapter

▶ Common financial problems

▶ Bad debt, good debt, and too much debt

▶ Assets, liabilities, and your (financial) net worth

▶ How much you really saved last year

▶ Investment and insurance checkups

▶ Fitting money into your life

. . . .

"I've made just about every financial mistake there is to make," laments a student in a personal finance course. The student, who has an anxious yet depressed look, seems to be asking the instructor for forgiveness.

It's incidents such as this that make you realize that as grown-up children — referred to as adults — we're not really allowed to make mistakes. If you mangle your car in an accident because you weren't paying attention or get fired from a job because of poor attendance and performance, you feel awful.

With financial matters, however, the fact that you've made a mistake may not be as obvious as twisted metal or a pink slip and no more paycheque. Some mistakes take months, years, even decades to manifest themselves. Even then, some people don't realize the foolishness of their ways.

Few people like to be made to feel stupid or be told that they're doing something wrong. And what you do with your money is a quite personal and confidential matter. We've endeavoured not to be paternalistic in this book but to provide guidance and advice that is in your best interest. You don't have to take it all — pick what works best for you and understand the pros and cons of your options. But from this day forward, please don't make the easily avoidable mistakes or overlook the sound strategies that we discuss throughout this book.

If you're young, congratulations for being so forward-thinking as to realize the immense value of investing now in your personal financial education. You'll reap the rewards for many decades to come. But even if you're not so young, you surely have many years to make the most of what money you currently have and will earn (and may even inherit!) in the future.

Throughout our journey together, we hope to challenge and even change the way you think about money, about making important personal financial decisions — sometimes even about the meaning of life. No, we're not philosophers, but we do know that money, for better but more often for worse, is connected to many other parts of our lives.

Common Financial Problems

How financially healthy are you? You may already know the bad news. Or perhaps things aren't quite as bad as they seem.

When was the last time you sat down surrounded by all of your personal and financial documents and took stock of your overall financial situation, including reviewing your spending, savings, future goals, and insurance? If you're like most people, you've either never done this exercise or did so a long time ago.

Financial problems, like many medical problems, are best detected early (clean living doesn't hurt, either). Here are some common personal financial problems we've seen in our work:

- **Not planning.** Human beings were born to procrastinate. That's why there are deadlines — and deadline extensions. With your finances, unfortunately, you have no deadlines, and you may think you have unlimited extensions! You can allow your credit card debt to accumulate or leave your savings sitting in lousy investments for years. You can pay higher taxes, leave gaps in your retirement and insurance coverage, and overpay for financial products. Of course, planning your finances isn't as much fun as planning a vacation, but doing the former will help you take more of the latter.

- **Overspending.** The average Canadian saves less than 5 percent of his or her after-tax income (in contrast to those in many other industrialized countries, where the savings rate is 13, 14, or even 15 percent). Simple arithmetic helps you determine that savings is the difference between what you earn and what you spend (assuming you're not spending more than you're earning!). To increase your savings, you either have to work more (yuck!), know a wealthy family who wants to leave its fortune to you, or spend less. For most of us, the thrifty approach is the key to building savings and wealth.

✔ **Buying with consumer credit.** Even with the benefit of today's lower interest rates, carrying a balance month-to-month on your credit card or buying a car on credit means that even more of your future earnings are earmarked for debt repayment. Buying on credit encourages you to spend more than you can really afford.

✔ **Delaying saving for retirement.** Most people say they want to retire by their mid-60s or sooner. But in order to accomplish this financially, most people need to save a reasonable chunk (10 percent or more) of their incomes starting sooner rather than later. The longer you wait to start saving for retirement, the harder it will be to reach your goal. And you'll pay much more in taxes to boot if you don't take advantage of the tax benefits of investing through particular retirement plans.

✔ **Falling prey to financial sales pitches.** Great deals that can't wait for a little reflection or a second opinion are often disasters waiting to happen. A sucker may be born every minute, but a slick salesperson is born every second! Steer clear of those who pressure you to make decisions, promise high investment returns, and lack the proper training and experience to help you.

✔ **Not doing your homework.** To get the best deal, you need to shop around, read reviews, and get advice from disinterested, objective third parties. You need to check references and track records so you don't hire incompetent, self-serving, or fraudulent financial advisers. But with all the different financial products available, making informed financial decisions has become an overwhelming task. We've done a lot of the homework for you with the recommendations in this book. We also explain what additional research you need to do and how to go about doing it.

✔ **Making decisions based on emotion.** You are most vulnerable to making the wrong moves financially after a major life change (a job loss or a divorce, for example) or when you feel under pressure. Maybe your investments have plunged in value. Or perhaps a recent divorce has you fearing that you won't be able to afford to retire when you had planned, so you pour thousands of dollars into some newfangled financial product. Take your time and keep your emotions out of the picture. In Chapter 21, we discuss how to approach major life changes with an eye to determining what changes you may need to make to your financial picture.

✔ **Not separating the wheat from the chaff.** In any field in which you're not an expert, you run the danger of following the advice of someone who you think is an expert but really isn't. This book teaches you to separate the financial fluff from the financial facts. If you look in the mirror, you'll see the person who is best able to manage your personal finances. Educate and trust yourself!

✔ **Exposing yourself to catastrophic risk.** You're vulnerable if you or your family don't have insurance to pay for financially devastating losses. People without a savings reserve and support network can end up homeless. Many people lack sufficient insurance coverage to replace their income. Don't wait for a tragedy to strike to learn whether you have the right insurance coverages.

✔ **Focusing too much on money.** Too much emphasis on making and saving money can warp your perspective on what's important in life. Money is not the first or even second priority in happy people's lives. Your health, relationships with family and friends, career satisfaction, and fulfilling interests should be more important.

Most problems can be fixed over time and with changes in your behaviour. That's what the rest of the book is all about.

The rest of this chapter puts you through a *financial physical* to help you detect problems with your current financial health. But don't get depressed and dwell on your "problems." View them for what they are — opportunities to improve your financial situation. In fact, the more areas for improvement that you can identify, the greater the potential you have to build real wealth and accomplish your financial and personal goals.

Bad Debt versus Good Debt

Why do you borrow money? Usually, it's because you don't have enough money to buy something you want or need — like a university education. If you want to buy a four-year university education, you could easily spend $50,000 to $60,000, and much more if you study in the United States. Not too many people have that kind of spare cash. So borrowing money to finance part of that cost enables you to buy the education.

How about a new car? A trip to your friendly local car dealer shows you that a new set of wheels will set you back around $20,000 or more. Although more people have the money to pay for that than, say, the university education, what if you don't? Should you finance the car the way you'd finance the education?

The auto dealers and bankers eager to make you an auto loan say you deserve to and can afford to drive a nice, new car, so borrow away.

We say, *No! No! No!*

Why do we disagree with the auto dealers and lenders? For starters, we're not trying to sell you a car or loan from which we derive a profit! More importantly, there's a *big* difference between borrowing for something that represents a long-term investment and borrowing for consumption.

If you spend, say, $1,500 on a vacation, the money is gone. Poof! You may have fond memories and even some Kodak moments, but you'll have no financial value to show for it. "But," you say, "vacations replenish my soul and make me more productive when I return. In fact, the vacation more than pays for itself!"

Great. We're not saying don't take a vacation. By all means, take one, two, three, or as many as you can afford yearly. But that's the point — *what you can afford.* In order to take the vacation, if you had to borrow money in the form of an outstanding balance on your credit card for many months, then you *could not afford* the vacation you took.

We refer to debt incurred for consumption as *bad debt.* Don't get us wrong — you're not a bad person for having the debt, but the debt is harmful to your long-term financial health.

You'll be able to take many more vacations during your lifetime if you save the cash in advance to afford them. If you get into the habit of borrowing and paying all that interest for vacations, cars, clothing, and other consumer items, you'll spend more of your future income paying back the debt and interest. So you'll have *less* money available for vacations and all your other goals.

One of the reasons you'll have less money using bad debt is because of the relatively high interest rates banks and other lenders charge for such debt. Money borrowed through credit cards, auto loans, and other types of consumer loans not only carries a relatively high interest rate but also is not tax-deductible.

We're not saying never borrow money and that all debt is bad. Good debt, such as that used to buy real estate and small businesses, is generally available at lower interest rates than bad debt and is tax-deductible in some cases. If properly and smartly managed, these investments should also increase in value. Borrowing to pay for educational expenses can also make sense. Education is generally a good long-term investment. It should increase your earning potential.

How Much Bad Debt Is Too Much?

A useful way to size up your debt load is to calculate how much debt you have relative to your annual income. Ignore, for now, good debt — the money you may owe on real estate, a business, an education, and so on. We're focusing on bad debt, the higher-interest stuff used to buy items that depreciate in value.

For example, suppose that you earn $30,000 per year. Between your credit cards and an auto loan, you have $15,000 of debt. In this case, your bad debt represents 50 percent of your annual income.

$$\frac{\text{bad debt}}{\text{annual income}} = \text{debt danger ratio}$$

The financially healthy amount of bad debt is zero. (Not everyone agrees with us. One major U.S. credit card company says in its "educational" materials, which it gives to schools to supposedly teach students about sound financial management, that it's just fine to carry consumer debt amounting to 10 to 20 percent of your annual income.)

When your *debt danger ratio* starts to push beyond 25 percent, that can spell real trouble. High-interest consumer debt on credit cards and auto loans is like cancer when it gets to those levels. As with cancer, the growth of the debt can snowball and get out of control unless something significant intervenes. If you have this much debt, see Chapter 5 to find out how to get out of debt.

How much good debt is acceptable? The answer varies. The key question is, are you able to save sufficiently to accomplish your goals? Later in this chapter we help you figure how much you are actually saving, and in Chapter 3 we help you determine what you should be saving to accomplish your goals. Take a look at Chapter 15 to find out how much mortgage debt is appropriate to take on when buying a home.

Avoid borrowing money for consumption (bad debt) — for spending on things like cars, clothing, vacations, and so on that decrease in value and eventually become financially worthless. Borrow money only for investments (good debt) — for purchasing things that retain and hopefully increase in value over the long term, such as an education, real estate, or your own business.

Your Financial Net Worth

Your financial net worth is an important barometer of your financial health. It indicates your capacity to accomplish major financial goals such as buying a home, retiring, and withstanding unexpected expenses or loss of income.

Before you crunch any numbers here and before you experience the thrill of bigness or the agony of nothingness or negativity, let's get one thing perfectly clear. Sit down. Take a deep breath. And repeat after us:

"My financial net worth has absolutely, positively, *no* relationship to my worth as a human being." This is not a test. You don't have to compare your number with your neighbour's. It's not the scorecard of life. So do we have an understanding? Good! We hate to see people get depressed about unimportant things that they have the power and ability to change.

Your *net worth* is your financial assets minus your financial liabilities.

```
Financial Assets - Financial Liabilities = Net Worth
```

Financial assets

A *financial asset* is worth real money or is something that you plan to convert to hard dollars that you can use to buy things now or in the future.

Financial assets generally include money in bank accounts, stocks, bonds, and mutual fund accounts (see Part III, which deals with investments). Also included is money that you have in retirement plans, including those with your employer. You should also include the value of any businesses or real estate that you own.

 We generally recommend that you exclude your personal residence. Include your home *only* if you expect to someday sell it or otherwise live off the money you now have tied up in it (perhaps by taking out a reverse mortgage, which we discuss in Chapter 15). If you plan on someday tapping into the equity (the difference between the market value and any debt owed on the property) in your home, add that portion of the equity that you expect to use to your list of assets.

Assets also include your future expected government benefits and pension payments if your employer has such a plan. These are usually quoted in dollars per month rather than in a lump-sum value. We show you in a moment how to account for these monthly benefits when tallying your financial assets.

Personal property such as your car, clothing, stereo, wine glasses, and straight teeth do *not* count as financial assets. We know adding these things to your assets makes your assets *look* larger (and some financial software packages and publications encourage you to list these items as assets), but you can't live off them unless you hock them at a pawn shop or otherwise sell them to meet your financial goals.

Financial liabilities

You must subtract your *financial liabilities* from your assets to arrive at your financial net worth. Liabilities include loans and debts outstanding, like credit card and auto loan debts. Include money you've borrowed from family and friends (unless you're not gonna pay it back — we won't tell). Include mortgage debt on your home as a liability *only* if you include the value of your home in your asset list. Be sure to include debt owed on other real estate, no matter what.

Your net worth calculation

Ready? Table 1-1 provides a place for you to figure your financial assets. Go ahead and write in the spaces provided, unless you plan to lend this book to someone and you don't want to put your money situation on display.

Important note: See Table 3-1 in Chapter 3 to estimate your government benefits.

Table 1-1	Your Financial Assets
Account	*Value*
Savings and investment accounts (including retirement plans):	
Example: Bank savings account	$ 5,000
_____	$_____
_____	$_____
_____	$_____
_____	$_____
_____	$_____
_____	$_____
Total =	$_____
Benefits earned that pay a monthly retirement income:	
Employer's pensions	$_____ / month
Government benefits	$_____ / month
	x 240*
Total =	$_____
Total financial assets =	$_____

In Table 1-1, to convert benefits that will be paid to you monthly into a total dollar amount, we assume that you will live 20 years in retirement. (Ah, think of two decades of lollygagging around — vacationing, harassing the kids, spoiling the grandkids, starting another career, or maybe just living off the fat of the land.) As a shortcut, multiply the benefits that you'll collect monthly in retirement by 240 (12 months in a year times 20 years). Inflation may reduce the value of your employer's pension if it doesn't contain a cost-of-living increase each year in the same way that government benefits do. Don't sweat this now — you'll take care of it in the section on planning for retirement (see Chapter 3).

Now comes the potentially depressing part — your debts and loans in Table 1-2:

Table 1-2	Your Financial Liabilities
Loan	*Balance*
Example: Gouge 'Em Bank credit card	$ 4,000
_____	$_____
_____	$_____
_____	$_____
_____	$_____
_____	$_____
_____	$_____
Total financial liabilities =	$_____

Now, you can subtract your liabilities from your assets to figure your net worth in Table 1-3:

Table 1-3	Your Net Worth
Find	*Write It Here*
Total financial assets (from Table 1-1)	$_____
Total financial liabilities (from Table 1-2)	– $_____
Net worth =	$_____

Interpreting your net worth results

Your net worth is important and useful only to you and your unique situation and goals. What is a lot of money to a person with a simple lifestyle may seem like a pittance to another with desires for an opulent lifestyle and high expectations.

In Chapter 3, you need to crunch some more numbers to determine your financial status more precisely for such goals as retirement planning. We also discuss saving toward other important goals in that chapter. In the meantime, if your net worth (excluding expected monthly retirement benefits such as those from the government and company pension plans) is less than half your annual income or even negative, take notice. You have lots of company — in fact, you're in here with many other folks. If you're in your 20s and just starting to work, this is less of a concern. It's most important to get rid of your debts — and the highest-interest ones first. Then you need to build a safety reserve equal to three to six months of living expenses. You should definitely learn more about getting out of debt, reducing your spending, and developing tax-wise ways to save and invest your future earnings.

Savings Analysis

In the past year, how much money have you actually saved? By savings, we mean the amount of new money you have added to your nest egg, stash, or whatever you like to call it.

Most people don't know or have only a vague idea of the rate at which they are saving money. The answer may sober, terrify, or pleasantly surprise you. In order to calculate your savings over the past year, you need to calculate your net worth as of today *and* as of one year ago.

The amount you actually saved over the past year is equal to the change in your net worth over the past year — in other words, your net worth today minus your net worth from one year ago. We know it may be a pain to find statements showing what your savings and investments were worth a year ago, but bear with us; it's a useful exercise.

If you own your home, ignore this in the calculations. (You can consider as new savings extra payments you make to pay off your mortgage principal faster.) And don't include personal property such as your car, computer, clothing, and so on with your assets.

Okay, now you have your two figures. Go ahead and plug them into Step 1 of Table 1-4. You may be anticipating the exercise and are already subtracting your net worth of a year ago from what it is today in order to determine your rate of savings. Your instincts are correct, but the exercise is not quite that simple. You need to do a few more calculations in Step 2 of Table 1-4. Why? Well, counting the appreciation of investments you owned over the past year as savings wouldn't be fair. Suppose that you bought 100 shares of a stock a year ago at $17 per share, and now the value is at $34 per share. Your investment increased in value during the past year by $1,700. Although you would be the envy of your friends at the next party if you casually mentioned your investments, the $1,700 of increased value of your shares is not really savings. Instead, it represents appreciation on your investments, so you must remove this appreciation from the calculations.

Note: Just so you know, we're not unfairly penalizing you for your shrewd investments — you also get to add back the decline in value of your less-successful investments.

Table 1-4	Your Savings Rate over the Past Year	

Step 1: Figuring your savings.

Today		*One Year Ago*	
Savings & investments	$_____	Savings & investments	$_____
– Loans & debts	$_____	– Loans & debts	$_____
= Net worth today	$_____	= Net worth 1 year ago	$_____

Step 2: Correcting for changes in value of investments you owned during the year.

Net worth today	$_____
– Net worth 1 year ago	$_____
– Appreciation of investments (over past year)	$_____
+ Depreciation of investments (over past year)	$_____
= Savings rate	$_____

If all this gives you a headache or you get stuck or if you just hate crunching numbers, try the intuitive, seat-of-the-pants approach: Do you save a regular portion of your monthly income? You may save it in a separate savings account or retirement plan.

How much do you save in a typical month? Get out your statements for accounts and plans that you contribute to or save money in monthly. It doesn't matter if it's a retirement plan that you can't access. Money is money. Savings is savings.

Note: If you're able to save, say, $200 per month for a few months but then spend it all on auto repairs, you're not saving. If you contributed $2,000 to a Registered Retirement Savings Plan (RRSP), for example, but depleted money that you had from long ago (in other words, it wasn't saved during the past year), you should not count the $2,000 as new savings.

As you'll see later, most people should be saving around 10 percent or more of their annual income for longer-term financial goals such as retirement. If you're not, be sure to read Chapter 6 to find out how to reduce your spending so that you can increase your savings.

How Is Your Investing Knowledge?

Congratulations! You've completed the hardest part of your financial physical. The physical is a whole lot easier from here on in!

Playing the credit card float

Given what we have to say about the vagaries of consumer debt, you might think that we are against using credit cards. Actually, we have credit cards and we use them. But the key with credit cards is to pay the balance in full each month. Besides the convenience credit cards offer in not having to carry around extra cash and cheques, they have another benefit. You have free use of the bank's money extended to you through your credit card charges. (Some cards offer other benefits such as frequent-flyer miles. Also, purchases made on credit cards may be contested if the seller of the product or service doesn't stand behind what it sells.)

When you charge on a credit card that does not have an outstanding balance carried over from the prior month, you typically have several weeks, known as the *grace period*, from the date of the charge to when you must pay your bill. Financial types call this *playing the float*. Had you paid for this purchase by cash or cheque, you would have had to shell out the money sooner.

If you have difficulty saving money and plastic tends to burn holes through your budget, forget the float game. You'd be better off not using your credit cards. The same applies for those who pay their bills in full but who spend more because it's so easy to do so with a piece of plastic.

Regardless of how much or how little money you have invested in bank, mutual fund, or other types of accounts, you, of course, want your money invested in the wisest way possible.

Knowing the rights and wrongs of investing is vital to your long-term financial well-being. Few people have so much extra money that they can afford major or frequent investing mistakes. Answering yes or no to the following questions can help you size up how much time you need to spend with our "Investing Crash Course" in Part III, which focuses on investing.

Note: The more *no* answers you reluctantly scribble, the more you need to learn about investing, and the faster you should turn to Part III.

_____ Do you understand the investments you currently hold?

_____ Is the money that you would need to tap in the event of a short-term emergency in an investment where the principal does not fluctuate in value?

_____ Do you know what marginal income-tax bracket (combined federal and provincial) you're in, and do you factor that into which investments you choose?

_____ For money outside of retirement plans, do you understand how those investments produce income and gains and whether these types of investments make the most sense from the standpoint of taxes?

_____ Do you have your money in different, diversified investments that aren't dependent on one or a few securities or one type of investment (that is, bonds, stocks, international investments, and so on)?

_____ Is the money that you will need for a major expenditure in the next few years invested conservatively rather than in riskier investments such as stocks, real estate, or pork bellies?

_____ Is the money that you have earmarked for longer-term purposes (more than five years) invested to produce returns well ahead of inflation?

_____ Is the bulk of your long-term money invested inside retirement plans, and have you exhausted possibilities for directing more money into these tax-sheltered accounts?

_____ Is your longer-term money, particularly what is inside of retirement plans, invested in quality, growth-oriented investments rather than preservation-of-principal-oriented investments?

_____ If you currently invest in or plan to invest in individual stocks, do you understand how to evaluate a stock, including reviewing the company's balance sheet, income statement, business strategy, competitive position, price–earnings ratio versus its peer group, and so on?

_____ If you work with a financial adviser, is that person compensated in a way that minimizes potential conflicts of interest in the strategies and investments he or she recommends?

Making and saving money is not a guarantee of financial success but rather a prerequisite. If you don't know how to choose quality investments that meet your needs you will more than likely throw money away, which leads to the same end result as never having earned and saved it in the first place. Worse still, you won't have derived any enjoyment from spending the lost money on things that you perhaps needed or wanted. Turn to Part III to learn the best ways to invest; otherwise, you'll spin your wheels working and saving.

How Insurance-Savvy Are You?

Now we're in the home stretch of your financial physical. In this section, you must deal with the prickly subject of protecting your assets and yourself with _insurance._ If you're like most people, reviewing your insurance policies and coverages is about as much fun as a root canal. Open wide!

_____ Do you understand the individual coverages and protection types and amounts of each insurance policy that you have?

_____ Does your _current_ insurance protection make sense given your current financial situation (as opposed to your situation when you bought the policies)?

_____ If you couldn't make it financially without your income, do you have adequate long-term-disability insurance coverage?

_____ If you have family members who are dependent on your continued income, do you have adequate life insurance coverage to replace that income should you die?

_____ Do you buy insurance through companies that sell directly to the public (bypassing agents) and through discount brokers and fee-for-service advisers?

_____ Do you carry enough liability insurance on your home, car (including umbrella/excess liability), and business to protect all your assets?

_____ Did you recently (in the last year or two) shop around for the best price on your insurance policies?

_____ Do you know whether your insurance companies have good track records regarding paying claims and keeping their customers satisfied?

What is your relationship to money?

In this chapter, we help you analyze your current financial situation and knowledge. You crunch some numbers with us and take some quizzes to help determine your investment and insurance wisdom.

Over the years in our work writing and speaking about personal finance, we've learned that how a person relates to and feels about money has a great impact on how good he is at managing his money and making important financial decisions. For example, knowing that you have a net worth of negative $13,200 because of credit card debt is useful but probably not enough information for you to do something constructive about your problem. A logical next step would be to examine your current spending and take steps to reduce your debt load.

Although we cover practical solutions to common financial quandaries later in this book, we also discuss the more touchy-feely side of money. For example, some people who continually rack up consumer debt have a spending addiction. Other people who jump in and out of investments and follow them like a hawk have psychological obstacles to getting on productive investment paths.

And then there are those somewhat philosophical and psychological issues relating to money and the meaning of life. Saving more money and increasing your net worth isn't always the best approach. In our work, we've come across numerous people who attach too much significance to personal wealth accumulation and neglect important human relationships in their pursuit of more money. Some retirees have a hard time loosening the purse strings and actually spending some of the money they worked so hard to save for their golden years.

Balancing your financial goals with other important life goals is key to your happiness. What's the point, for example, of staying in a well-paying job and admired profession if you don't care for the work and you're mainly doing it for the financial rewards? Life is far too short and precious to squander your days.

That wasn't so bad, was it? If you answered no more than once or twice don't feel dumb — more than nine out of ten people make major mistakes when buying insurance. Find your insurance salvation in Part IV. If you answered yes to all the preceding questions you can spare yourself from reading Part IV, but bear in mind that most people need help in this area as much as they do in other aspects of personal finance.

So, as you read through the various chapters and sections of this book, please consider your higher life goals and purposes. What are your non-financial priorities (family, friends, causes) and how can you best accomplish those with the financial resources you do have?

Chapter 2

Overcoming Obstacles to Personal Financial Success

• •

In This Chapter

▶ Understanding financial illiteracy and its causes

▶ Believing what you read, see, and hear

▶ Identifying and overcoming what's holding you back

• •

*W*e're barely acquainted, but we do know that you're not dumb. Real dummies don't read and educate themselves. And real dummies don't understand the value of investing in their education. Real dummies also can't deflate their egos enough to admit that they need help and guidance.

Here's what dumb is: Dumb is the man who walked into a convenience store, put a $20 bill on the counter, and asked for change. When the cashier opened the register, the man pulled a gun and demanded all the cash. The crook took the loot — $15 — and fled, leaving his $20 bill on the counter. Or how about the criminal who robbed a person who didn't have any cash? The victim offered the assailant a cheque, which the assailant later attempted to cash at the bank, where — surprise, surprise — he was arrested. These are both true stories!

So you are most definitely not dumb! But you may be financially illiterate.

Personal Financial Illiteracy

Sadly, most Canadians don't know how to manage their personal finances because, in most cases, they were never taught how to do so. Most of our high schools, universities, and colleges lack even one course to teach this vital, lifelong-needed skill.

For the handful of schools that do offer a course remotely related to a personal finance class, the class is typically an economics course — and an elective at that. "Archaic theory is being taught and it doesn't do anything for the students as far as preparing them for the real world," says one high school principal. Having taken more than our fair share of economics courses in university, we understand the principal's concerns.

Fortunate and lucky people learn the financial keys to success at home or from knowledgeable friends. Others never learn or learn the hard way: by making lots of costly mistakes. Lack of proficiency in personal financial management causes not only tremendous anxiety but also serious problems. Consider the following sobering statistics:

- ✔ Around 75,000 personal bankruptcies are filed in Canada annually. That's about one in every one hundred households. So in the next ten years, nearly one in every ten households in Canada — one of the most affluent countries in the world — will file bankruptcy.

- ✔ Studies show that only about half of Canadians even intend to make an RRSP contribution most years, and that only around 10 percent contribute the maximum they are allowed to their plan.

- ✔ One in two marriages end in divorce. Studies show that financial disagreement is one of the leading causes of marital discord. In a survey conducted by *Worth* magazine and the market research firm of Roper/ Starch, couples admitted fighting about money more than anything else, and more than three times more often than they fight about their sex lives. A staggering 57 percent of those surveyed agreed with the statement, "In every marriage, money eventually becomes the most important concern."

- ✔ Almost half of all Canadians think they can deduct the interest on their home mortgage (they can't!), and that they reduce their risk by only putting their money into Canadian investments (they don't!). Further, one survey found that almost 80 percent of people feel that the lowest-risk investments make the most sense when saving for retirement (yup, you guessed it . . . they usually don't).

- ✔ In a Princeton Survey Research Associates investing basics test, approximately a third of those quizzed answered fewer than 50 percent of the questions correctly. These results are all the more stunning when you consider that all the questions offered only two or three multiple-choice answers as options.

- ✔ Nearly 80 percent of consumers do not know how the grace period on a credit card works. An even greater percentage don't understand that interest starts accumulating *immediately* for new purchases on credit cards with outstanding debts.

The overall costs of personal financial illiteracy to our society are huge. The high rate of spending and low rate of saving in Canada lead to lower long-term economic growth and higher interest rates. Annually, billions of dollars are wasted in North America through the purchase of inferior and inefficient financial products.

Teaching personal finance in schools

As part of her fifth-grade math class, Nancy Donovan teaches personal finance as a way to illustrate how math can be used in the real world. "Students choose a career, find jobs, and figure out what their taxes and take-home paycheques will be. They also have to rent apartments and figure out a monthly budget," says Donovan, adding, "Students like it and parents have commented to me how surprised they are with how much financial knowledge their kids can handle." Donovan also has her students invest $10,000 (play money) and track the performance of their investments.

To urge that our schools teach the basics of personal finance is just common sense. We should be teaching our children how to manage a household budget, about the importance of saving money for future goals, and about the consequences and dangers of overspending. Unfortunately, few schools offer classes like Nancy Donovan's. In most cases, the financial basics aren't taught at all.

Some people argue that it's the parents' job to teach their children the financial basics. However, this well-meant sentiment is what we rely on now, and for all too many, it isn't working. In some families, financial illiteracy is passed on from generation to generation.

We must recognize that education takes place in the home, on the streets, *and* in the schools. Therefore, schools must bear some responsibility for teaching this very important life skill. And with more students holding down after-school jobs, teaching money-management know-how through the schools makes even more sense.

Lobby your schools! Make sure that financial basics are taught in schools at all levels. If you think you're powerless to change the situation, you're mistaken. Many changes to our education system started at the grassroots level.

Talking money at home

We were both fortunate in that our parents taught and instilled in us the importance of personal financial management. Our moms and dads taught us a lot of things that have been invaluable throughout life. Among the useful things our folks taught us were sound principles of earning, spending, and saving money. Our parents had to know how to do these things because they were raising large families on (usually) one modest income. They knew the importance of making the most of what you have and passing on that vital skill to your kids.

In many families, however, money is a taboo subject — parents don't level with their kids about the limitations, realities, and details of their budgets. Some parents we talk with believe that dealing with money is an adult issue that kids should be insulated from so that the kids can better enjoy being kids. In many families, kids may hear about money *only* when disagreements and financial crises bubble to the surface. Thus begins the harmful cycle of children having negative associations with money and financial management.

In other cases, some parents, with the best of intentions, do pass on their money-management habits. Unfortunately, some of those habits are *bad* habits. Now, we're not saying that you shouldn't listen to your parents. But in personal finance, as in any other area, family advice can be problematic. Think about where your parents learned about money management and consider whether they had the time, energy, or inclination to research choices before making their decisions. For example, your parents may mistakenly think that banks are the best places to invest money (you can find where the better places are in Part III of this book).

In still other cases, the parents have the right approach, but the kids go to the other extreme out of rebellion. For example, if your parents spent money carefully and thoughtfully, you may tend to do the opposite, such as buying yourself gifts the moment any extra money comes your way.

Although you can't change what the educational system and your parents did or didn't teach you about personal finances, you do have the ability to find out now what you need to know to manage your finances. And if you have children of your own, we're sure you'll agree that kids really are amazing. Don't underestimate their potential or send them out into the world without the skills they need to be productive and happy adults. Buy them some good financial books when they head off to university or to their first jobs.

Illiteracy and conflicts in financial publishing and advising

Some people are smart enough to realize that they're probably not financial geniuses. So they set out to take control of their finances by reading or consulting a financial adviser. Because the pitfalls are so numerous and the challenges are so mighty in choosing an adviser, we devote Chapter 19 to the financial planning business and what you need to know to avoid being fooled.

Reading is good. Reading is fundamental. But reading to learn about managing your money can be dangerous if you're a novice. Surprisingly, written misinformation can come from popular and seemingly reliable information sources.

Won't gurus make me rich?

One formerly best-selling personal finance book (*Wealth Without Risk* by Charles Givens) advises you to "Buy disability insurance only if you are in poor health or accident prone." Putting aside the minor detail that *no* insurance company (that's interested in making a profit) would issue you a disability policy *after* you fall into poor health, how do you know when you'll be accident-prone? Because health problems and auto accidents cause many disabilities, you can't see disabilities coming unless your horoscope happens to warn you!

That same book also purports to describe how to send your kids to university or college "free." A few months before your child begins school, you're supposed to buy a four-bedroom property near the campus. Then you're advised to rent out the house to students. The idea is that while your kid is completing a four-year degree, the value of your rental property will appreciate dramatically because of the shortage of off-campus housing in almost every university- or college-campus area.

You realize, we're sure, that students will give your property the same love and attention that people give to rental cars. And, on the financial side, a modestly priced property would need to *increase by 25 to 50 percent in value over a four-year period* for this education-financing scheme to work. This is about as common as triplets (yes, it happens, but rarely).

Furthermore, this risky strategy may cost more than junior's education. Some real estate markets *drop* in value over a four-year time period, and if that were to happen, your already substantial university or college costs would be added to, not paid off. Then you need to factor in the hassles and expenses of locating, buying, and selling the property. And another minor detail: How many parents paying tuition bills also have piles of extra cash lying around available for the down payment on a property?

Don't the media act as watchdogs?

You may be asking how Charles Givens became so popular despite the obvious flaws in his advice. He made the most of his talent for working the media and his great self-promotion through seminars. One of the problems of the mass media is that hucksters like Givens can get good coverage and publicity. Many members of the media are themselves financially illiterate. And they love a good story. So Givens got all sorts of free publicity, being quoted in the press and invited on a number of popular programs such as *The Today Show, Oprah, Donahue,* and *Larry King Live.*

Thousands of people went to seminars conducted by Givens, partly because of the credibility Givens built through media appearances. As has now been well documented by some of those same media, many unsuspecting investors were sold commission-laden products, including risky limited partnerships, through his organization.

One example is the case of Helen Giszczak, a 69-year-old retired secretary. She invested nearly two-thirds of her modest life savings in limited partnerships, which she said were described to her as "probably the most conservative investments we know of." But some of her limited partnerships ended up in bankruptcy, and the others lost much of their value.

Helen Giszczak appeared on the *Donahue* show with John Allen, a former investment broker-turned-securities lawyer who helped her sue Givens's organization to get her money back. After a lengthy dialogue with Giszczak and Allen, Phil Donahue asked Helen how a smart person like her could get sucked in like that. She replied, "He was on your show and Oprah's. You gave him credibility. You gave him free advertising."

Just as at the circus, oddities sell with the media. Over recent years, we've done some work with different parts of the media and observed how and what the media follows and ignores. As anyone who followed the O.J. Simpson trial knows, some members of the media love an unusual story. The financial media, when at its worst, is no different than the news media that fawned all over the O.J. trial. The more bizarre and novel something is, the more attention it gets — never mind if it's good for the readers and viewers.

With financial "guru" Charles Givens, the appeal was that people believed they could get rich without taking risks. Recent years have seen a flood of "we can beat the market" investing books written by, among others, a 17-year-old high school student and an investment club. One such book was written by a couple of Generation Xers who, despite failing at publishing a print newsletter, soared to fame by claiming that, using the online world to research stocks, anybody can easily and with low risk make 25 to 35 percent or more in returns per year. As you see in Part III, such returns are unrealistic, but they play well with some of the media.

Don't assume that someone with something to sell who is getting good press will take care of you. That "guru" could just be good at press relations and self-promotion. Certainly, talk shows and the media at large can and do provide useful information on a variety of topics, but be aware that sometimes bad eggs turn up on them. And the bad eggs don't always smell upfront.

Don't the financial media know what's going to happen next?

Scores of widely read financial publications offer predictive advice and commentary about investment markets. But such commentary can often be wrong or misguided.

For example, on October 16, 1987, just three days before the infamous (modern-day) Canadian and U.S. stock market crash, a widely read daily U.S. business paper had this to say about the prior day's relatively minor stock market decline: "But it is not yet time to pry the rubber seals out of the office windows. . . . On September 22nd, it should be remembered, the market had a record 75-point one-day rise. The underlying economic news is mostly good, not bad."

On the next trading day — Monday, October 19 — stock markets plummeted. The New York Stock Exchange, for instance, plunged 508 points, or nearly 23 percent! Remember, that loss occurred in one trading day!

Although most financial publications shy away from making predictions, many love to quote predictions made by the "experts." The monthly, weekly, and daily barrage of conflicting crystal ball visions causes many investors — perhaps even you — to be paralyzed and fearful. As you can clearly see in Part III of this book, you don't need a working crystal ball or a guru telling you when to buy and sell. The best investments for growth are not difficult to identify, but, once bought, are generally best held for the long haul.

Don't writers know what they're writing about?

Writers are people, too — some good, some bad; some full of hot tips, some full of hot air. During the 1980s, one of the most widely read personal finance magazines ran a piece that purported to tell you where to get "safe, high yields." In addition to utility stocks and junk bonds, the article recommended real estate and oil and gas *limited partnerships* (LPs) sold through brokers. Such LPs are not safe investments. Over the past decade, many people who bought these problematic investment vehicles lost huge portions of their money.

Another popular business magazine ran an article that touted life insurance as one of the best investments. The piece advocated the purchase of *cash-value insurance* — which contains an investment account as well as life insurance protection. The article went on to claim that life insurance should be the first consideration in most responsible investment programs. As you see in Parts III and IV of this book, this advice is *wrong* for the vast majority of working people who need life insurance. (They should buy *term insurance,* which is pure life insurance protection.) Any number of investment options would make a better first consideration than buying cash-value insurance, but you wouldn't have learned that from reading the article.

More than a few writers and talk-show hosts claim to be personal finance experts but hardly ever address spending and debt issues. Instead, they focus almost exclusively on investments. For example, they may make you feel like an undisciplined failure for not saving through your employer's retirement savings program to reduce your taxes, when other considerations may also apply.

Don't book publishers exercise due diligence?

Book publishers are businesses first and, like most businesses, their business practices vary. Some have a reputation for care and quality; some just want to push a product out the door with maximum hype and minimum effort.

For instance, you may think that book publishers check out an author before they sign him or her to write an entire book. Well, you may be surprised to learn that some publishers don't do their homework.

What most publishers care about first is how marketable an author is. Some authors are marketable because of their well-earned reputation for sound advice. Others are marketable because of stellar promotional campaigns built on smoke and mirrors. Still others may have the potential for marketability if a publisher takes a chance on them, but most publishers like a sure thing.

Even more troubling, few publishers require that the many advice guides on the market be technically reviewed for accuracy by an expert in the field other than the author, who sometimes may not be an expert. You, the reader, are expected to be your own technical reviewer. But do you have the expertise to do that? (Don't worry; this book has been checked for accuracy.)

As authors and financial commentators, we know that financial ideas and strategies can differ considerably. Different is not necessarily wrong. When a technical reviewer looks at our text and tells us that another, better way is out there, we take a second look. Maybe we even see things in a new way. That's not possible if we're the only experts who see our book before publication. How do you know whether a book's been technically reviewed? Check the credits page or the author's acknowledgments.

Authors write books for many reasons other than to teach and educate. The most common reason financial book authors write books is to further their own business interests. That may not always be a bad thing, but it's not the best thing for you when you're trying to educate yourself and better manage your own finances. For example, some investment books are written by investment newsletter sellers. Rather than teaching you how to make good investments, the authors make the investment world sound complicated so that you'll feel the need to subscribe to their ongoing newsletters.

Saving through your employer's retirement program is all well and good, but the truth is many people live paycheque-to-paycheque. So unless you *first* learn how to reduce spending and get out from under high-cost consumer debt, the "experts" can talk until they're blue in the face about terrific investment strategies. If you don't have anything to invest in the first place, then they're not really helping you.

There are some good writers and smart writers at most financial publications. But there are also some people who would have been better off covering politics. Come to think of it, some of them *do* also cover politics, and therein lies the problem — you're getting financial advice from people who don't focus on the field, have little if any training in it, and have no experience with people like you.

Pandering to advertisers

Newspapers, magazines, Internet sites, radio, television — you name it — thousands of publications and media outlets dole out personal financial advice and perspectives. Although many of these "service providers" collect revenue from subscribers, virtually all are dependent — in some cases, fully dependent (especially on the Internet, radio, and television) — on advertising dollars. Although advertising is a necessary part of capitalism, unfortunately and sadly, advertisers can taint and, in some cases, dictate the content of what you read, listen to, and view.

Consider this case from a non-financial publication — *Modern Bride* magazine. *Harper's* magazine got hold of an apologetic letter, which it humorously entitled "To Love, Honor And Obey Our Advertisers," that *Bride's* fashion advertising director sent to its advertisers. Here's an excerpt:

> *Bride's* recommends that its readers (your customers) negotiate price, borrow a slip or petticoat, and compare catalog shoe prices, and tells its readers that the groom's tuxedo may be free. It is difficult to understand why *Bride's* was compelled to publish this information. With 57 years of publishing experience and support to the bridal industry, *Bride's* could and should have been more sensitive to the retailers that it purports to serve. All of us in the bridal business must concentrate on projecting full-service bridal retailing in a positive light.

We don't find it difficult to understand why the writer of the criticized *Bride's* article revealed cost-saving strategies to its readers — she was trying to give them useful information and advice! Now, revealing letters like this one are hard to come by, so how can you, a consumer of financial information, separate the good from the advertiser-biased publications? We've developed some ideas on the subject from having written and worked for a number of publications and from observing the workings of even more.

First, consider how dependent a publication or media outlet is on advertising. We see the most conflicts of interest in the pandering to advertisers done by "free" publications and radio and television, which derive all of their revenue from advertising. Much of what is on the Internet is advertiser-driven as well. Many of the investing sites on the Internet cater to offering advice about individual stocks. Interestingly, such sites derive much of their revenue from online brokerage firms seeking to recruit customers who believe that selecting their own stocks is the best way for them to invest (see Part III for more information about your investment options).

Next, as you read various publications, watch TV, or listen to the radio, note how consumer-oriented these media are. Do you get the feeling that they're looking out for your interests? Or are they primarily creating an advertiser-friendly broadcast or publication? For example, if lots of auto manufacturers advertise, does the media outlet ever tell you how to save money when shopping for a car and the importance of buying a car within your means?

Real and Imaginary Hurdles

Perhaps you know that you should be living within your means, buying and holding sound investments for the long term, and securing proper insurance coverage. However, you can't bring yourself to do these things. Everywhere you turn lurks temptation to spend money. Ads show attractive and popular people enjoying the fruits of their labours — a new car, exotic vacation, and lavish home.

Maybe you felt deprived as a youngster by your tightwad parents or you're bored with life and like the adventure of buying new things. If only you could hit it big on one or two investments, you think, you could get rich quick and do what you really want with your life. As for disasters and catastrophes — well, those things happen to other people, don't they? Not to you. Besides, you'll probably have advance warning of pending problems and can prepare accordingly.

Your emotions and temptations can get the better of you. Certainly part of successfully managing your finances involves coming to terms with your shortcomings and the consequences of your behaviours. If you don't, you may end up enslaved to a dead-end job to keep feeding your spending addiction. Or you can spend more time with your investments than you do with your family and friends. Disasters and catastrophes can happen to anyone at any time.

Discovering the real hurdles holding you back

A variety of personal and emotional hurdles get in the way of people making the best financial moves. As we discuss earlier in this chapter, most people's lack of financial knowledge (which stems from a lack of personal financial education) stands in the way of making good decisions.

However, we have seen some people get caught in the psychological trap of blaming something else for their financial problems. For example, some people believe that all our adult problems can be traced back to our childhood and how we were raised. Behaviours ranging from substance abuse to credit card addiction to sexual infidelity are supposedly caused by our roots.

We don't want to diminish the negative impact particular backgrounds can have on some people's tendency to make the wrong choices during their lives. Exploring your personal history can certainly yield clues to what makes you tick. That said, we are adults making choices and engaging in behaviour that affects ourselves as well as others. We shouldn't blame our parents for our own inability to plan for our financial futures, live within our means, and make sound investments.

Another common tendency is for some people to blame their financial short-comings on not earning more income. Such people believe that if they only earned more income, their financial (and personal) problems would melt away.

Our experience speaking with people from diverse economic backgrounds has taught us that achieving financial success — and, more importantly, personal happiness — has virtually nothing to do with how much income a person makes but rather with what she makes of what she does have. We know financially wealthy people who have all the material goods they want yet are emotionally poor. Likewise, we know people who are struggling financially yet are quite happy, contented, and emotionally wealthy. If you think of the people in your own life, you can probably find plenty of evidence that how much money a person does — or doesn't — have often has little to do with their psychological and emotional well-being and outlook on life.

Canadians — even those who have not had an "easy" life — should be able to come up with things to be happy about and grateful for: a family who loves them; friends who laugh at their stupid jokes; the freedom to catch a movie or play or read a good book; a great singing voice or sense of humour; or the fact that they live in a country that's not at war with any other country.

Financially speaking, Canadians are pretty spoiled. Most of the people in the world have a standard of living that is a fraction of the Canadian average.

Practising good habits

Once you learn the basic concepts and know where to buy the best financial products when you need to buy them, you'll soon see that managing your personal finances well is not much more difficult than other things you do regularly, like tying your shoelaces and getting to and from work each day.

Regardless of your income, you can make your dollars stretch farther if you learn good financial habits and avoid mistakes. In fact, the lower your income, the more important it is that you make the most of your income and savings (because you don't have the luxury of falling back on your next fat paycheque to bail you out).

More and more industries are subject to global competition, and you need to be on your financial toes now more than ever. Job security is on the wane. Layoffs and retraining for new jobs are on the increase. Putting in 20 or 30 years for one company and retiring with the gold watch and lifetime pension are becoming as rare as never having computer problems.

Speaking of company pensions, odds are increasing that you work for an employer that has you save toward your own retirement rather than providing a pension for you. Not only do you need to save the money, you must also decide how to invest it.

Managing your personal finances involves much more than just managing and investing money. It also includes making all the pieces of your financial life fit together. It means lifting yourself out of financial illiteracy. Like planning a vacation, managing your personal finances means formulating a plan to make the best use of your limited time and dollars.

Here are a few areas you likely need to tackle:

- ✔ **Tracking and reducing spending.** If, like most people, you're not saving sufficiently to meet your future financial goals, then sound financial management also involves tracking and reducing your spending. See Part II.

- ✔ **Investing wisely.** Investing your savings is, of course, an important part of your financial puzzle. So, too, are understanding and making the best use of tax incentives, tax breaks, and your employer's benefits.

- ✔ **Making informed real estate and insurance purchases.** You need to ensure that you invest in real estate intelligently, that you have the right types of insurance coverage, and that you're not paying more than necessary.

Intelligent personal financial strategies have little to do with your gender, ethnicity, or marital status. We *all* need to manage our finances wisely. Some aspects of financial management become more or less important at different points in your life, but for the most part the principles remain the same for all of us.

Knowing the right answers isn't enough. You have to practise good financial habits just as you practise other habits, such as brushing your teeth. Don't be overwhelmed. As you read this book, make a short list of your financial marching orders and then start working away. Throughout this book, we highlight ways you can overcome temptations and keep control of your money rather than letting your emotions and money rule you.

Chapter 3

Establishing and Accomplishing Goals

● ●

In This Chapter

▶ Defining your own happiness

▶ Establishing and prioritizing your financial goals

▶ Saving for a rainy day, a home purchase, a small business, or educational needs

▶ What you need to get through retirement and ways to make up for lost time

● ●

*I*n our work, we regularly ask people what their short- and long-term personal and financial goals are. Quite a large portion of people report that reflecting on this question is incredibly valuable because they haven't considered it for a long time — if ever.

In this chapter, we help you dream about what you want to get out of life. Although our expertise is in personal finance, we wouldn't be doing our job if we didn't get you to consider your non-financial goals and how money fits in with the rest of your life. So before we jump into how to establish and save toward common financial goals, we'd like to take a moment to discuss how you think about making and saving money and how to best fit your financial goals into the rest of your life.

Creating Your Own Definition of "Wealth"

Pick up just about any major financial magazine or newspaper or scan stories on the Internet, and you will quickly see our culture's obsession with financial wealth. The more money financial executives, movie stars, or professional athletes make and have, the more publicity and attention they seem to get. In fact, many publications go so far as to regularly rank those people who earn the most or have amassed the greatest wealth!

Bill Gates, founder and CEO of Microsoft, for example, has in recent years been in the No. 1 position among the world's wealthiest people. We have to shake our heads as we watch reporters and others continually follow him around like he's some sort of hero or cult figure.

We're frankly perplexed at why many of the most affluent and highest-income earners maintain workaholic schedules despite being married and having kids. From what we observe, our society seems to define "wealth" as the following:

- Fat paycheques

- Huge investment account balances

- The ability to hire full-time people to raise your children

- Being too busy at your career to maintain friendships or take an interest in your neighbours, community, or important social problems and environmental issues

- The freedom to be unfaithful to your spouse and to dump your mate when you're no longer pleased with him or her

What money can't buy

Recall the handful of moments in your life that you wouldn't trade for anything. Odds are, those moments don't include the time you bought a car or found a sweater that you liked for 50 percent off at your favourite retailer. The old saying is true: The most enjoyable and precious things of value in your life can't be bought.

What we are about to say should go without saying, but we must say it because too many people act as if it weren't so: Money can't buy happiness. It is tempting to think that if you could make only 10 or 20 percent more money, you'd be happier. You'd have more money to travel, eat out, and buy that new car you've been eyeing, right? Not so fast. A great deal of thoughtful research suggests that little relationship exists between money and happiness.

"Wealth is like health: Although its absence can breed misery, having it is no guarantee of happiness," summarizes Dr. David Myers, professor of psychology at Michigan's Hope College, in his book *The Pursuit of Happiness: Who Is Happy and Why*. (This guy has it good! Imagine studying happiness for a living.)

Despite cheap air travel, VCRs, compact discs, microwaves, computers, voice mail, and all the other stuff that's supposed to make our lives easier and more enjoyable, people aren't any happier than they were four decades ago. For example, according to research conducted in the United States by the National Opinion Research Center, 35 percent of Americans in 1957 said that they were "very happy," whereas in the 1990s fewer said the same. These unexpected results occurred even though incomes in the United States, after adjusting for inflation, more than doubled during that time.

As Dr. Myers observes in *The Pursuit of Happiness*, ". . . if anything, to judge by soaring rates of depression, the quintupling of the violent crime rate since 1960, the doubling of the divorce rate, and the tripling of the teen suicide rate, we're richer and less happy."

The balancing act

Believe it or not, some people save too much. In our work, we've certainly seen plenty of people who fell into that category. If making and saving money is a good thing, then the more the merrier, right?

Well, take the admittedly extreme case of Anne Scheiber, an American who, on a modest income, started saving at a young age and allowed her money to compound in wealth-building investments such as stocks over many years. The result was that she was able to amass $20 million U.S. by the time that she passed away at the age of 101.

Scheiber lived in a cramped studio apartment and never used her investments. She didn't even use the interest or dividends — she lived solely on her Social Security benefits and the small pension from her employer. Scheiber was extreme in her frugality and obsessed with her savings. As reported by James Glassman in the *Washington Post*, "She had few friends . . . she was an unhappy person, totally consumed by her securities accounts and her money."

Most people, ourselves included, would not choose to live and save the way that Scheiber did. She saved for the sake of saving: no goal, no plan, no reward for herself. Saving should be a means to an end, not something that makes you mean *to* the end.

Even those who are saving for an ultimate goal can become consumed by their saving habits. We see some people pursuing higher-paying jobs and pinching pennies in order to retire early. But sometimes they make too many personal sacrifices today while chasing after some vision of their lives tomorrow. Others get consumed by work and then don't notice or understand why their family and friends feel neglected.

Another problem with seeking to amass wealth is that tomorrow might not come. Even if all goes according to plan, will you know how to be happy when you're not working if you spend your entire life making money? More importantly, who will be around to share your leisure time? One of the costs of an intense career is time spent away from friends and family. You may indeed realize your goal of retiring early, but you may be putting off too much living today in expectation of living tomorrow.

As Charles D'Orleans said in 1465, "It's very well to be thrifty, but don't amass a hoard of regrets."

Of course, at the other extreme are spendthrifts who live only for today. A friend once said, "I'm not into delayed gratification." Shop 'til you drop seems to be the motto of this personality type. "Why bother saving when I might not be here tomorrow?" reasons this type of person.

The danger of this approach is that tomorrow may come after all, and most people don't want to spend all their tomorrows working for a living. The earlier neglect of saving, however, handicaps the possibility of not working when you are older. And if for some reason you can't work and have little money to live on, much less live enjoyably, the situation can be tragic. The only difference between a person without savings or access to credit and some homeless people is a few months of unemployment.

Making and saving money is like eating food. If you don't eat enough, you may suffer. If you eat too much, the overage may go to waste or make you overweight. The right amount, perhaps with some extra to spare, affords you a healthy, balanced, peaceful existence. Money should be treated with respect and acknowledged for what it is — a means to an end and a precious resource that shouldn't be thoughtlessly squandered and wasted.

As Dr. David Myers, whom we discuss earlier in this chapter, says: "Satisfaction isn't so much getting what you want as wanting what you have. There are two ways to be rich: one is to have great wealth, the other is to have few wants." Find ways to make the most of the money that does pass through your hands, and never lose sight of all that is far more important than money.

Prioritizing Your Savings Goals

Many people who we know have financial goals. The rest of this chapter discusses the most common ones and how to work toward accomplishing them:

- ✔ **Become part of the landed gentry.** Renting and dealing with landlords can be a financial and emotional drag, so most folks want to buy into the Canadian dream and own some real estate — the most basic of which is to own your own home.

- ✔ **Retire.** No, retiring does not imply sitting on a rocking chair watching the world go by while hoping that some long-lost friend, your son's or daughter's family, or the neighbourhood dog comes by to visit. *Retiring* is a catch-all term for discontinuing full-time work or perhaps not even working for pay at all.

✔ **Educate the kids**. No, all those diaper changes, late-night feedings, and trips to the zoo aren't enough to get junior out of your house and into the real world as a productive, self-sufficient adult. You may want to help your children get a university or college education, and, unfortunately, that can cost a truckload of dough.

✔ **Own your own business.** Many employees want to become employers so that they can face the challenges and rewards that come with being the boss. The primary reason that many people continue to dream without actually plunging into their own small businesses is that they lack the money to do so. Although many businesses don't require gobs of start-up cash, almost all require that you withstand a substantial reduction in your income in the early years.

Because each of us is unique, each of us can have goals other than those above and unique to our own situation. No matter — accomplishing such goals almost always requires saving money. As one of our favourite Chinese proverbs says, "Do not wait until you are thirsty to dig a well."

Know what's most important to you

Unless you earn really big bucks or have a large family inheritance to fall back on, your personal and financial desires will probably outstrip your resources. Thus, you must prioritize your goals if you want to accomplish them.

One of the biggest mistakes that we see people make is to rush into financial decisions without considering what is really important to them. Because many of us get caught up in the responsibilities of our daily lives, time for reflection often never happens.

From the experience we've had studying personal financial management, we can tell you that the people who accomplish their goals aren't necessarily smarter or higher-income earners than those who don't. People who accomplish their goals identify their goals and work toward them.

The advantages of retirement plans

Where possible, you should try to save and invest in plans that offer you a tax advantage. That's precisely what registered plans do for you. These accounts — known by such enlightening acronyms as *RRSP* (Registered Retirement Savings Plan) and *RPP* (Registered Pension Plan) — offer tax breaks to people of all economic means (the different types of retirement plans are detailed in Chapter 11):

✔ **Contributions are usually tax-deductible.** Retirement plans should really be called *tax-reduction plans*. If they were, people might be more excited about contributing to them. For many, avoiding higher taxes is the motivating force that opens the plan and starts the contributions.

By putting money in a retirement plan, you not only plan wisely for your future, but you also get an immediate financial reward: lower taxes — and lower taxes mean more money available for saving and investing. Retirement savings plan contributions are generally not taxed at either the federal or provincial income tax levels until withdrawal. If you're paying, say, 40 percent in federal and provincial taxes (refer to Chapter 7 to determine your tax bracket), a $5,000 contribution to a retirement plan would lower your taxes by $2,000.

✔ **Returns on your investment compound over time without taxation.** After money is in an RRSP or other retirement plan, any interest, dividends, and appreciation add to your account without being taxed. Of course,

TIP

Avoiding RRSP early withdrawal penalties

There are times and ways to avoid the early withdrawal penalties that the tax gods normally apply.

You can now make penalty-free withdrawals from an RRSP for either a first-time home purchase (limit of $20,000 per person) or expenses for higher education for you or your spouse (up to $10,000 a year with a total maximum of $20,000), your children, or your grandchildren. Note, though, that in both cases you have to repay the money over time to your plan.

If you lose your job and withdraw RRSP money simply because you need it to live on, that money has to be included in your annual income, and taxed accordingly. However, if you're not working and earning so little income that you need to raid your retirement plan, you are surely in a low tax bracket. The lower income taxes you pay as compared to the taxes you would have paid on that money had you not sheltered it in a retirement plan in the first place should make up for most or all of the penalty.

When you do make a withdrawal from your RRSP, the plan administrators are required by the government to hold back some of the money as a sort of tax down payment. The withholding tax rates (unless you live in Quebec) are 10 percent on the first $5,000, 20 percent on the next $10,000, and 30 percent on any amount beyond $15,000. In Quebec, the rates are 25 percent on the first $5,000, 33 percent on the next $10,000, and 38 percent on any amount over $15,000. These tax rates are calculated on each individual transaction. If you need to withdraw a large amount, consider breaking the amount you need into separate withdrawals of no more than $5,000 each. This will *minimize* the amount of tax held back, and *maximize* the amount of money you can get your hands on. However, don't forget that the withholding tax may not be sufficient to cover all the tax you'll owe, given that the withdrawals will be included in that year's annual income come tax time. Plan ahead.

there's no such thing as a free lunch — these accounts don't allow for complete tax avoidance. Yet, you can get a really great lunch at a discount — you get to defer taxes on all of the accumulating gains and profits until you withdraw the money down the road. Thus, more money is working for you over a longer period of time.

Dealing with competing goals

Unless you enjoy paying higher taxes, why would you save money outside of an RRSP or Registered Pension Plan? The reason is that accomplishing some financial goals are not easily achieved through saving in these retirement plans.

If you're accumulating down-payment money for a major purchase or to start or buy a business, for example, you'll probably need to save that money outside of an RRSP. Why? Because if you withdraw funds from an RRSP, you have to include that money in your income and pay tax on it. (See the sidebar "Avoiding RRSP early withdrawal penalties," where we discuss exceptions to this rule.)

Because you're constrained by your financial resources, you must prioritize your goals. Before funding your retirement plans and racking up those tax breaks, read on to consider your other goals.

Building Emergency Reserves

No one can predict the future. There is simply no reliable way to tell what may happen with your job, health, or family. Because you don't know what the future holds, preparing for the unexpected is financially wise. Even if you're the lucky sort who sometimes finds $5 bills on street corners, you can't control the sometimes chaotic world in which we live.

Conventional wisdom says that you should have approximately six months of living expenses put away for an emergency. This particular amount may or may not be right for you because it depends, of course, on how expensive the emergency is. Why six months, anyway? And where should you put it? Unfortunately, no hard and fast rules exist. How much of an emergency stash you need depends on your situation.

We recommend saving the following emergency amounts under differing circumstances (in Chapter 12, we recommend good places to invest this money):

 ✔ **Three months' living expenses** if you have other accounts such as a registered retirement savings plan or family members and close friends that you could tap for a short-term loan. This minimalist approach makes sense when you're trying to maximize investments elsewhere (for example, in retirement plans) or have stable sources of income (employment or otherwise).

 ✔ **Six months' living expenses** if you don't have other places to turn for a loan and/or have some instability in your employment situation or source of income.

 ✔ **Up to one year's living expenses** if your income fluctuates wildly from year to year or if your profession involves a high risk of job loss and it could take you a long time to find another job and you don't have other places to turn for a loan.

In the event that your only current source of emergency funds is a high-interest credit card, you should first save at least three months' worth of living expenses in an accessible account before funding a retirement plan or saving for other goals.

Saving to Buy a Home or Business

When you're starting out financially, deciding whether to save money to buy a home or to put money into a retirement plan presents a dilemma. In the long run, owning your own home is a wise financial move. On the other hand, saving sooner for retirement makes achieving your goal easier.

The bottom line is this: Presuming both goals are important to you, you should be saving toward both buying a home *and* for retirement. If you're eager to own a home, then you can throw all of your savings toward achieving that goal and temporarily put retirement savings on hold. Save for both purposes simultaneously if you're not in a rush.

To save money for starting or buying a business, most people face the same dilemma as when deciding to save to buy a house: If you fund your retirement plans to the exclusion of building money for your small-business dreams, your entrepreneurial aspirations may never become a reality. Generally, we advocate hedging your bets by saving some money in your tax-sheltered retirement plans as well as some toward your business venture. As we discuss in Part III, an investment in your own small business can produce great rewards, so you may feel comfortable focusing your savings there.

Don't buy cash-value life insurance plans

Life insurance salespeople are often eager to sell you cash-value life insurance policies, which combine life insurance protection with a type of savings account. You may very well be suckered into buying a cash-value life insurance policy as a savings vehicle for accomplishing goals such as retiring or paying for a child's educational costs. Don't fall for this sales trap.

Cash-value life insurance policies give you no immediate tax deduction. By contrast, a retirement savings plan such as an RRSP allows you to deduct your contributions from your taxable income. Most people are far better off buying term life insurance (see Chapter 17 for more details). Because agents earn far larger commissions selling cash value policies, those policies generally get pitched.

Saving for Kids' Educational Expenses

Wanting to provide for your children's future is perfectly natural. But doing so before you've saved adequately toward your own goals can be a major financial mistake.

It may sound selfish, but you need to take care of your future first. You should consider first taking advantage of saving through your tax-sheltered retirement plans before you set aside money in custodial savings accounts or education savings plans for your kids. This practice isn't selfish — do you really want to have to leech off your kids when you're old and frail because you didn't save any money for yourself?

See Chapter 14 for a complete explanation of how to save for educational expenses.

Saving for Big Purchases

If you want to buy a car or a canoe or a plane ticket to France, do not — we repeat, *do not* — buy such things with consumer credit. As we explain in Chapter 5, cars, boats, vacations, and the like are consumer items, not investments that build wealth, such as real estate or a small business. A car begins to depreciate the moment you drive it off the sales lot. A plane ticket to France is worthless the moment you arrive back home. (We know your memories will be priceless, but they won't pay the bills.)

Paying for high-interest consumer debt can cripple your ability not only to save for long-term goals like retirement or a home but also to make major purchases in the future. Interest on consumer debt is exorbitantly expensive — up to 18 percent or higher for most credit cards. When contemplating the purchase of a consumer item on credit, add up the total interest you end up paying on your debt and call it the price of instant gratification.

Don't deny yourself gratification; just learn how to delay it. Get into the habit of saving for your larger consumer purchases to avoid paying for them over time with high-interest consumer credit. When saving up for a consumer purchase like a car, a money market account (see Chapter 13) is a good place to store your short-term savings.

Preparing for Retirement

Many people toil away at work, dreaming about a future in which they can stop the daily commute grind; get out from under that daily deluge of faxes, voice mails, and e-mails; and do what they want when they want. People often assume that this magical day will arrive either on their next true day off or when they retire or win the lottery, whichever comes first.

We've never cared much for the term *retire*. It seems to imply idleness or the end of usefulness to society. But if retirement means not having to work at a job (especially one you don't enjoy) and having financial flexibility and independence, then we're all for it.

One of most people's dreams is to be able to retire sooner rather than later. But this idea has some obvious problems. First, you set yourself up for disappointment. If you want to retire by your mid-60s, you'll need enough money to live for an additional 20 years, maybe longer. Two decades is a long time to live off your savings. You're going to need a good-sized chunk — more than most people realize. The earlier you hope to retire, the more money you need to set aside and the earlier you have to start saving — unless you plan to work part-time in retirement to earn more income!

Most people we speak to say that they do want to retire, and most say the sooner, the better. Yet only about half of Canadians even plan to put money into their RRSP each year, and just 10 percent put in the maximum they're allowed to contribute. One sardonic middle-aged person we know who had saved little for retirement, when asked when he would like to retire, dead-panned, "Sometime before I die." If you're in this group, and even if you're not, determine where you stand financially regarding retirement. If you're like most working people, you need to increase your savings rate for retirement.

What you need for retirement

If you hope to someday cease working or reduce the time you spend working for an income, you will need sufficient savings to support yourself. Many people — particularly young people and those who don't work well with numbers — underestimate the amount of money needed to retire. To figure out how much you should be saving per month given your retirement goals, you can't avoid crunching a few numbers (but don't worry, this number-crunching is easier than doing your taxes).

Luckily for you, you don't have to start cold. Studies have shown how people typically spend money before and during retirement. Most people need about 70 to 80 percent of their pre-retirement income throughout retirement to maintain their standard of living. For example, if your household earns $40,000 per year before retirement, you're likely to need $28,000 to $32,000 (70 to 80 percent of $40,000) per year during retirement to live the way that you're accustomed to living. The 70 to 80 percent is an average. Some people may need more simply because they have more time on their hands to spend their money. Others adjust their standard of living and can live on less.

You, of course, are not average in any way — you're unique! So how do you estimate what you will need? The simplest method to estimate what you need is for us to tell you what percentage you need. (We know we've only known you a short time, but let us offer some friendly counselling.) The following three profiles provide a rough estimate of the percentage of your pre-retirement income that you need during retirement. Pick the one that most accurately describes your situation. If you fall between two descriptions, pick a percentage in between.

To maintain your standard of living in retirement:

- You need **65 percent of your pre-retirement income** if you
  - save a large amount (15 percent or more) of your annual earnings
  - are a high-income earner
  - will own your home free of debt by retirement, and
  - do not anticipate leading a lifestyle in retirement that reflects your current high income.

  If you're an especially high-income earner who lives well beneath his or her means, you may be able to do with even less than 65 percent. Try picking an annual dollar amount or percentage of your current income that should allow the kind of retirement lifestyle you desire.

- You need **75 percent of your pre-retirement income** if you
  - save a reasonable amount (5 to 14 percent) of your annual earnings

- will still have some mortgage debt or a modest rent to pay by the time you retire, and

- anticipate having a standard of living in retirement that is comparable to what you have today.

✔ You need **85 percent of your pre-retirement income** if you

- save little or none of your annual earnings (less than 5 percent)

- will have a significant mortgage payment or sizeable rent to pay in retirement, and

- anticipate wanting or needing to maintain your current lifestyle throughout retirement.

Of course, you can use a more precise approach to figure out how much you need per year in retirement. Be forewarned, though, that this more personalized method is far more time-consuming, and because you're making projections into an uncertain future, it may not be any more accurate than the simple method we just explained. Those who are more data-oriented may feel comfortable tackling this method: You need to figure out where you're spending your money today (worksheets are located in Chapter 4) and then work up some projections for your expected spending needs in retirement (the information in Chapter 20 may help as well).

Retirement building blocks

Did you play with Lego blocks or Tinker Toys when you were a child? You start by building a foundation on the ground, and then you build up. Before you know it, you're creating bridges, castles, and panda bears. Although preparing financially for retirement isn't exactly like playing with blocks, the concept is the same: You need a basic foundation for your necessary retirement reserves to grow.

If you have been working steadily, you may already have a foundation, even when you haven't been actively saving toward retirement. In the pages ahead, we walk you through the probable components of your future retirement income and how to figure out how much you should be saving to reach a particular retirement goal.

Government benefits

It's old news that no one should depend on the *Canada Pension Plan (CPP)* or *Quebec Pension Plan (QPP)* and other programs such as *Old Age Security (OAS)* if they want anything but a bare bones existence when they retire. One poll found that around two-thirds of Canadians believe that government programs won't provide them with a secure income in their retirement years.

Don't neglect non-financial preparations for retirement

Investing your money is just one, and not even the most important, aspect of preparing for your retirement. In order to enjoy the lifestyle that your retirement savings will provide you, you need to invest energy into other areas of your life as well.

✔ Few things are more important than your health. Without your health, enjoying the good things in life is hard. Unfortunately, many people are not motivated to care about their health until after they discover problems. By then, it may be too late.

Although exercising regularly, eating a balanced and nutritional diet, and avoiding substance abuse cannot guarantee you a healthful future, they go a long way toward preventing many of the most common causes of death and debilitating disease. Regular medical exams also are important in detecting problems early.

✔ In addition to your physical health, invest in your psychological health. It is well documented that people live longer and are happier and healthier when they have a circle of family and friends around them for support.

Unfortunately, as they grow older, many people become more isolated as they lose regular contact with business associates, friends, and family members.

Happy retirees tend to be active and involved in volunteer organizations and in new social circles. They may travel to see old friends or to visit younger relatives who may be too busy to visit them.

Treat retirement life like a bubbly, inviting hot tub. You want to ease yourself in, nice and slow; taking a hasty plunge can take most of the pleasantness out of the experience. Abruptly leaving your job without some sort of plan for spending all that free time is an invitation to boredom and depression. Everyone needs a sense of purpose, a sense of routine. Establishing hobbies, volunteer work, or a sideline business while gradually cutting back your regular work schedule can be a terrific way to ease the transition into retirement.

Lower yourself into the tub slowly. Take some time to get used to the temperature change. Ahhh . . . nice, isn't it?

Contrary to widespread cynicism, some form of government-provided income should be there for you when you retire, no matter how old you are today. The CPP, for instance, is one of the sacred cow political programs. Imagine what would happen to the group of politicians that voted not to pay any more benefits!

If you think you can never retire because you have no money saved, we're happy to inform you that you're probably wrong. You've likely got some CPP (or QPP) and Old Age Security benefits coming to you. But they generally won't be enough to live on comfortably.

The Canada Pension Plan, for instance, is intended to provide you with a subsistence level of retirement income for the basic necessities: food, shelter, and clothing. It is not intended to be your sole source of income. Few people could maintain their current lifestyles without supplementing CPP payments with personal savings and company retirement plans.

How much will I get from CPP?

The Canada Pension Plan is designed to replace about a quarter of your pre-retirement income — but only up to a certain limit. The retirement pension you'll receive from the Canada Pension Plan is determined by two factors. The first is the number of years you contribute to the plan. The second is how much you contribute to the plan. When you're working, you pay a percentage of your earnings above $3,500, up to a maximum, which in 2000 was $37,600. Just how much you have to contribute is determined by the contribution rate. This was set at 7.8 percent in 2000, and is set to rise each year, reaching 9.9 percent by 2003. If you are earning a salary, you pay half of your required CPP contributions and your employer pays half. If you are self-employed, you pay the full amount yourself. However, you don't make CPP contributions if you are receiving disability or retirement payments from the CPP. Also, even if you are still working and haven't yet started receiving your CPP retirement benefits, you stop paying into the plan when you turn 70.

In 2000, the average monthly benefit was $412.27. The maximum was $762.92. The payments are set for life, and are fully indexed to inflation. An adjustment is made to reflect the change in the cost of living once a year, in January.

If you qualify for CPP/QPP and are no longer able to work due to a disability, you may be eligible for a disability pension. The maximum is slightly higher than regular CPP/QPP benefits. In 2000, the average disability benefit was $676.33, while the maximum was $917.43.

If you make CPP contributions, you should receive a statement summarizing your contributions every few years. If you want to get an estimate of the size of benefits you can expect, contact Health and Welfare Canada. (If you live in Quebec, contact the Quebec Pension Plan.)

You can start collecting as early as age 60 or as late as age 70. The amount of your monthly benefits will be permanently reduced by half a percent for every month before age 65 that you start drawing your pension. This works out to 6 percent a year. The reduction continues for the rest of your life. On the other hand, if you choose to delay receiving your CPP/QPP, your benefits will be increased by the same 0.5 percent a month for each month beyond your 65th birthday.

If you are a member of the CPP and die, there are three different types of survivor benefits your family may be eligible to receive, depending on how long you have been making CPP contributions.

The first is a death benefit, a one-time lump-sum payment to your estate. This is six times the retirement figure, to a maximum of $2,500.

The second death benefit is a pension paid to your surviving spouse or common-law partner. The amount of the payment is the combination of a flat sum and a percentage of what your retirement benefit is, or would be if you had been 65 at the time you died. Your spouse's age and whether they are disabled are also factored in. For a spouse under age 65, the average monthly payment in 2000 was $303.08 and the maximum was $420.80. For a surviving spouse aged 65 or older, the average for 2000 was $240.29 and the maximum was $457.75. However, if your surviving spouse is also eligible to receive retirement benefits from their own CPP contributions, the total they will receive will usually be less than the sum of the two benefits.

Finally, there is a children's benefit. This is paid to your natural or adopted children, or children in your care and control at the time you die. The benefits continue until your child turns 18. The benefits may continue up to age 25 as long as your child is going to school full-time at a recognized institution. If the benefits are stopped and then your child goes back to school and is still between the ages of 18 and 25, the benefits can be reinstated. The average and maximum benefit in 200 was about $172 a month. This benefit is a flat rate, which is adjusted annually.

How much will I get from Old Age Security?

Old Age Security is paid out to all Canadians who are 65 and older. The only problem is that, depending on your other income, you may have to give some or even all of it back!

The rules as to who is eligible and how much you receive are very complex. In general, to receive the maximum (which in 2000 was $424.12 a month) you must have lived in Canada for at least 40 years since you turned 18. To earn at least the minimum OAS monthly benefit you must have lived in Canada for at least 10 years. However, there are further and different eligibility rules for those who immigrated to Canada after 1977, people who were under the age of 25 in 1977, and those who have lived outside the country for extended periods since turning 18. For the specifics, contact the Income Securities Program Branch of Human Resources Development Canada at 800-277-9914, or visit the government Web site at www.hrdc-drhc.gc.ca/isp/oas/oasind_e.shtml.

OAS payments are adjusted four times a year for inflation. Your payments don't start automatically when you hit the big 65. You have to fill out a formal application. Be sure to send it in well ahead of time.

The big question for many people, though, isn't how much they'll receive from OAS, but how much of it they'll be able to hang on to. The government will recoup or *claw back* some or all of your OAS payments if your net income is over a certain level. In 2000, for instance, the threshold was $53,960 of 1999 net income. If your net income was higher than that, you had to repay a portion of your OAS benefits. The repayment rate is 15 percent of the amount that your net income exceeds the threshold amount. So if you made $60,500, you would have $81.75 of your monthly OAS payments clawed back every month. Because of this formula, if your net income exceeds a certain level you end up repaying every single cent of OAS benefits. If your net income in 1999 was $87,025 or higher, for example, than you would have had all of your 2000 OAS payments clawed back.

If you have a very low retirement income, you may be eligible to receive a form of top-up to the OAS, known as the *Guaranteed Income Supplement*, or *GIS*. To receive the GIS, you must be getting Old Age Security pension benefits and must also meet the income requirements. If you are married or in a common-law relationship, the income used to judge your eligibility is the combined income of you and your spouse. In 2000 the average monthly GIS payment for a single person was $351.81 and the maximum was $504.05. To qualify, your income had to be no greater than $12,120. The figure includes all income — including CPP payments — except for Old Age Security. For households where both spouses are receiving OAS benefits, the average monthly GIS benefit in 2000 was $193.80 and the maximum was $328.32. To qualify, the total household income had to be below $15,792.

Personal savings and investments

Money that you are saving toward retirement can include money under the mattress as well as money in a retirement plan such as a Registered Retirement Savings Plan (see Chapter 11). You may have also earmarked investments in non-retirement plans toward your retirement.

Equity in rental real estate can be counted as well. Deciding whether to include the equity in your primary residence (your home) is trickier. If you don't want to count on using this money in retirement, then don't include it when you tally your stash. You may want to count a portion of your home equity in your total assets for retirement. Many people do sell their homes when they retire to move to a cheaper region of the country, to move closer to family, or to downsize to a more manageable household. And increasing numbers of older retirees are tapping their homes' equity through reverse mortgages.

Pensions

Pension plans are a benefit offered by some employers — mostly larger organizations and government agencies. Even if your current employer does not offer a pension, you may have earned pension benefits through a previous job.

The plans we're referring to are known as *defined-benefit plans.* You qualify for a monthly benefit amount to be paid to you in retirement based on your years of service.

Although each company's plan differs, all plans calculate and pay benefits based on a formula. A typical one might credit you with 1.5 percent of your salary for each year of service (full-time employment). For example, if you work ten years, you earn a monthly retirement benefit worth 15 percent of your monthly salary.

This type of benefit is quite valuable. In the better plans, an employer puts away the equivalent of 5 to 10 percent of your salary to pay your future pension. This money is not quoted as part of your salary — it's in addition to your salary. You never see it in your paycheque, and it is not taxed. What the employer is doing is putting money away in an account for your retirement.

To qualify for pension benefits, you don't have to stay with an employer long enough to receive the 25-year gold watch. Depending on your province, an employee must generally be fully *vested* (entitled to receive full benefits based on years of service upon attaining retirement age) after either two or five years of full-time service.

Defined-benefit pension plans are becoming rarer for two major reasons:

- ✔ First, they are costly for employers to maintain. Many employees don't understand how these plans work and why they're so valuable, so companies don't get mileage out of their pension expenditures — employees don't see the money, so they don't appreciate how generous the company is being.
- ✔ Second, most of the new jobs being generated are with small companies that typically don't offer these types of plans.

More employers are offering plans in which employees elect to save money out of their own paycheques. Known as *defined-contribution plans,* these plans allow you to save toward your retirement at your own expense rather than at your employer's expense. (To encourage participation in these plans, some employers "match" a portion of their employees' contributions.) More of the burden and responsibility for investing for retirement falls on your shoulders with these plans. You must be educated about how these plans work. Most people are ill equipped to know how much to save and how to invest the money. The retirement planning worksheet in the next section should help get you started with figuring out the amount you should be saving. The "Investing Crash Course" in Part III can help you understand how to invest.

Retirement planning worksheet

Now that you've toured the components of your future retirement income, we'd like you to take a shot at tallying where you stand in terms of retirement preparations. Don't be afraid to do this exercise — it's not difficult, and you may find that you're not in such bad shape. We even explain how to catch up if you find that you are behind in saving for retirement.

Note: The following worksheet (Table 3-1 and the Growth Multiplier Minitable) assumes that you will retire at age 66 and that your investments will produce an annual rate of return that's 4 percent per year higher than the rate of inflation. (For example, if inflation averages 3 percent, this table assumes you will earn 7 percent per year on your investments.)

Table 3-1	Retirement Planning Worksheet
1. Annual retirement income needed in today's dollars (see earlier in this chapter).	$ _____ / year
2. Annual government benefits.	–$ _____ / year
3. Annual pension benefits (ask your benefits department). Multiply by 60% if your pension won't increase with inflation during retirement.	–$ _____ / year
4. Annual retirement income needed from personal savings (subtract lines 2 and 3 from line 1).	= $ _____ / year
5. Savings needed to retire at age 66 (multiply line 4 by 15).	$ _____
6. Value of current retirement savings.	$ _____
7. Value of current retirement savings at retirement (multiply line 6 at by Growth Multiplier in following minitable).	$ _____
8. Amount you still need to save (line 5 minus line 7).	$ _____
9. Amount you need to save per month (multiply line 8 by Savings Factor in following minitable).	$ _____ / month

Growth Multiplier Minitable		
Your Current Age	*Growth Multiplier*	*Savings Factor*
26	4.8	.001
28	4.4	.001
30	4.1	.001
32	3.8	.001
34	3.5	.001
36	3.2	.001
38	3.0	.002
40	2.8	.002
42	2.6	.002
44	2.4	.002
46	2.2	.003
48	2.0	.003
50	1.9	.004
52	1.7	.005
54	1.6	.006
56	1.5	.007
58	1.4	.009
60	1.3	.013
62	1.2	.020
64	1.1	.041

How to make up for lost time

If the amount that you need to save per month to reach your retirement goals seems daunting, don't despair. All is not lost. In fact, here are our top recommendations to make up for lost time — none of which requires you to work for the rest of your life!

✔ **Question your spending.** There are only two ways to boost your savings: Earn more money or cut your spending (or do both). Most people don't spend their money nearly as thoughtfully as they earn it. Refer to Chapter 6 for spending reduction suggestions and strategies.

✔ **Be more realistic about your retirement age.** If you extend the age at which you plan to retire, you get a double financial benefit. You're earning and saving money for more years and spending your nest egg over fewer years. Of course, if your job is making you crazy, this option may not be too appealing. Try to find work that makes you happy and consider working, at least part-time, during the years typically considered the retirement years.

✔ **Use home equity.** Psychologically, the prospect of tapping the cash in your home can be troubling. After getting together the down payment, you probably worked for many years to pay off that sucker. You're delighted not to have to mail a mortgage payment to the bank anymore. But what's the use of owning a house free of mortgage debt when you lack sufficient retirement reserves? All that money tied up in the house can help to increase your standard of living in retirement.

There are a number of ways to tap your home's equity. You can sell your home and either move to a lower-cost property or rent. Any profit that you made on the sale of your home is yours to keep, tax free, as long as the property was your principal residence. Another option is a *reverse mortgage* — where you get a monthly income cheque as you build a loan balance against the value of your home. The loan is paid when your home is finally sold (see Chapter 15 for more information about reverse mortgages).

✔ **Get aggressive with your investments.** The faster the rate at which your money grows and compounds, the less you need to save each year to reach your goals. Earning just a few extra percentage points per year on your investments can dramatically slash the amount you need to save. The younger you are, the more powerful the effect. For example, if you're in your mid-30s and your investments appreciate 6 percent per year faster than the rate of inflation rather than 4 percent, the amount you need to save each month to reach your retirement goals drops by about 40 percent!

✔ **Turn a hobby into supplemental retirement income.** Even if you've earned a living in the same career over many decades, you have skills that are portable and can be put to profitable use. Pick something you enjoy and are good at, develop a business plan, and get smart about how to market your services and wares. Remember, as people get busier, more specialized services are being created to support their hectic lives. A demand for quality, homemade goods of all varieties also exists. Be creative! You never know — you may wind up profiled in a business publication!

✔ **Invest in a tax-wise way.** A free way to boost the effective rate of return on your investments without taking on additional risk is to insulate more of your money from taxation. Many people who are able to save money do not do so in a way that minimizes their taxes.

Direct your savings into a tax-favoured retirement plan like an RRSP. You get an immediate tax deduction for your contribution. For a typical person, a third or more of your contribution represents money you would have had to pay in federal and provincial income taxes. This money gets to work for you, rather than for the government, in the years ahead. Plus, the money compounds over the years without taxation.

As for money outside of tax-sheltered retirement plans, if you're in a relatively high tax bracket you may earn more by investing in tax-free investments and other vehicles that do not make a great amount of taxable distributions. (We discuss tax-friendly investments and retirement plans in detail in Chapters 11 and 12.)

✔ **Take a look at jobs that offer retirement plans.** When you're evaluating employers, cash is usually king. As long as the position includes health insurance, most people are concerned only about the salary. But having access to a pension plan, which pays you a monthly retirement benefit based on your years of service (a completely pain-free way to build wealth for retirement) is very valuable. If you're lucky enough to have choices, check out these plans when considering a job offer.

What's an RRSP worth in the long run? A lot. Suppose that a person who is 40 years old earns $40,000 per year and pays 41 percent in federal and provincial taxes on her last dollars of income. If she can contribute 10 percent of her salary, or $4,000, to an RRSP, she reduces her current year's taxes by $1,640. Assume further that the money she contributes this year grows at the rate of 8 percent per year until she withdraws the money at age 65. Even if she pays taxes at the same rate she is paying today when she withdraws the money at age 65, she'll have about $16,161 left. If she hadn't saved this money through a retirement plan, she would start off with just $2,360, since she would have paid $1,640 in taxes on the $4,000 of income. If she invested the money and earned an average annual compound return of 6 percent after tax, she would have only $10,128 at 65. In other words, on *just one year's contribution* of $4,000, she nets $6,033 more in retirement because of the tax-deferred compounding allowed in the retirement account.

You tax gurus might feel that the previous comparison isn't completely fair. After all, when investing outside of a retirement plan, not all of your investment return would likely be taxed annually since some of it would reflect not-yet-taxed appreciation on investments that you continue to hold. Nonetheless, a retirement plan investor still comes out substantially ahead, even factoring these issues in. Also consider that if our mythical investor in the previous example is like most people, she probably would have been tempted to spend the money if she had access to it, so she might not have saved even the $10,128 if she hadn't used the RRSP!

✔ **Think about inheritances.** Although you should never count on an inheritance to support your retirement, in reality you may someday inherit money. If you want to see what impact an inheritance has on your retirement calculations, simply add the amount (use a conservative estimate) that you expect to inherit to your current total savings in Table 3-1.

Overcoming objections to retirement plans

Despite all the great tax benefits of investing through RRSPs and other retirement plans, many people aren't jumping at the opportunity to take advantage of them. Everyone has unique priorities. Maybe you're saving for a home purchase or paying off student loans. Some reasons, however, stem from a lack of knowledge and understanding. The following are the objections to contributing to tax-favoured plans that we hear most frequently. Some of these objections can be overcome, whereas others are legitimate reasons to not fund retirement plans.

Retirement's a long way away

When you're in your 20s or 30s, age 65 seems like the distant future. For many people, it's not until middle age that some warning bells start to stimulate thoughts about one's golden years.

Delaying the age at which you start to sock away money is usually a financial mistake. The sooner you start to save, the less painful it is to save each year because your contributions have more years to compound. Each decade you procrastinate approximately doubles the percentage of your earnings you should save to meet your goals. For example, if saving 5 percent per year in your early 20s would get you to your retirement goal, waiting until your 30s may mean socking away 10 percent; your 40s, 20 percent; and so on.

When should you start saving toward retirement? Ideally, you should start saving a small portion of your employment earnings with your very first paycheque. Start your kids' saving habits while they're young!

Only losers who don't know how to have fun save for retirement

Some people really believe this statement. But we also know losers who don't save for retirement and still don't know how to have a good time.

This attitude is just a rationalization. The reality is that if you manage your finances efficiently and start working toward your goals sooner, you can spend more *and* have more fun in the long run. Besides, who says spending all your money is the only way to have fun?

My taxes probably won't decrease in retirement

Some people feel that there's little point in contributing to retirement savings plans if their tax rate will be the same or even higher in retirement. Although your taxes could increase when you retire, the following simple example shows you why your time is better spent worrying about more important issues.

Earlier in this chapter, we create the scenario of a woman earning $40,000 per year who pays 41 percent in federal and provincial taxes on her last dollars of income. She contributes 10 percent, or $4,000, per year to an RRSP, thereby decreasing her current year's taxes by $1,640. Assume that the money she contributes grows at the rate of 8 percent per year until she withdraws the money at age 65. If she is still in the same tax bracket when she starts withdrawing money at age 65, her $4,000 contribution is worth $16,161. If she had saved this money through a non-retirement plan, she would have had only $10,128 at age 65.

Suppose that her career takes off and she earns more money (and pays more taxes) as she gets closer to retirement. How high would her retirement tax rate have to be before she should regret having saved in the retirement account? Answer: She would have to pay about 63 percent in taxes on the RRSP withdrawals to be worse off, a very unlikely occurrence. Remember, she was paying 41 percent in taxes during her working years. It's highly unlikely that your tax rate would increase this much.

You may actually be in a lower tax bracket in retirement, because most people have less income when they're not working. Thus, you get an added bonus from deferring taxes on your RRSP and other retirement plan assets if you are in a lower tax bracket when you withdraw the money.

There are greener investment pastures elsewhere

Real estate is a good example. Some people find RRSPs and pension plans boring and believe that they can get a better return in the real estate market. Rental real estate can appreciate in value and produce increasing rental income over the years. Investing in real estate is a legitimate reason for not maximizing retirement plan contributions.

Although real estate provides some tax breaks, consider its drawbacks:

- First, while you accumulate the down payment, you may pay higher income taxes if you're sacrificing contributions to retirement plans that are tax-deductible.

- Second, rental real estate produces income that is taxable and is added to all your other income during the year, which may push you into a higher tax bracket. Even if the extra real estate income doesn't push you into a higher tax bracket, this income is taxable at the ordinary income tax rates, which are higher than the tax rates on long-term capital gains (see Chapter 7).

In an RRSP, the earnings continue to compound without taxation, and *you* decide when you want to start drawing on the money.

There may be a way for you to invest in what you want and gain tax relief, too. Many types of investments — stocks, bonds, mutual funds, precious metals, and even real estate — can be held in RRSPs. (See Chapter 12 for more details.)

I have no money left over to save

The more you spend, the less able you will be to fund retirement savings plans. Thus, the extra taxes that you pay because you can't afford retirement plan contributions are an additional cost of overspending today. So if you can reduce your expenditures (refer to Chapter 6), you can more easily meet your retirement goals. You'll have more money to contribute to retirement plans, and you'll save on your taxes to boot!

In some cases, people have a pile of money not earmarked for specific future needs that's invested outside of tax-sheltered RRSPs. They may use all of their monthly employment income to meet their ongoing living expenses. As a result, they believe they can't afford to save in a retirement plan.

If you think this way, you're compartmentalizing your finances. Look at the big picture. For example, what if you save $300 per month through your tax-deductible RRSP? Suppose that doing so reduces your taxes by $100 and thus really costs you only $200 a month. You then can take $200 from your savings outside the RRSP and put it toward living expenses.

What you're effectively doing is transferring your savings from outside an RRSP (or other tax-favoured plan) to inside an RRSP. You're not really saving new money, but you're getting terrific tax savings by playing this perfectly legal investing shell game. Just be careful not to drain your emergency savings reserve down too far.

I love my job and will work forever

Are you one of those people who loves your work? You don't plan to retire and therefore don't need to amass a pile of money to live on for 20-plus years? If so, you can get away with saving a lot less than your eager-to-retire friends.

You may not, however, be able to work at your current job forever. What if you lose your job? What if something happens to your health? You can't assume that you will always be able to work — plan ahead for these what-ifs.

I've saved enough already

Congratulations! This is the single best excuse for not saving more for retirement. If you have a lot of money outside of tax-sheltered retirement plans, you may still want to contribute to retirement plans anyway for the tax deductions.

Part II
Saving More, Spending Less

The 5th Wave
By Rich Tennant

In this part . . .

We show you how to identify where your hard-earned dollars are going. We detail numerous ways to make those dollars go toward helping you build up your savings rather than going to wasteful spending. What? You're buried in debt with little to show for it? Well, it's never too late to start digging out. Here you'll find out how to reduce your debt burden. We also devote an entire chapter to discussing taxes and legally minimizing them, since too much of your money may be going to pay taxes.

Chapter 4

Where Did Your Money Go?

*I*n order for most people to accomplish their financial goals, they must live within their means. This means spending less than you earn and then taking that "savings" and hopefully investing it intelligently.

Many folks earn just enough to make ends meet. And some can't even do that; they simply spend more than they make. The result of such spending habits is, of course, accumulation of debt — witness the Canadian government and its 577 billion dollars or so worth of debt accumulation.

Whatever your financial dreams, you need to save and invest (unless you plan on winning the lottery or gaining a large inheritance). To put yourself in a position that allows you to start saving, you need to take a close look at your spending habits.

Why You Overspend

Most of the influences on you in society encourage you to spend, and credit is widely and easily available to help you do just that. Think about it. In the media and in the hallowed halls of our government, more often than not, you're referred to as a *consumer.* Not a person, not a citizen, not a human being — but a consumer.

In fact, we know some people who feel unpatriotic or inadequate if they don't spend enough. "Saving too much and not spending enough could hurt the economy," they say. "People could be thrown out of work, and it could be a friend or family member. My favourite politician might not get re-elected if I don't do my part and spend."

Bunk! Ultimately, you are the one who suffers the consequences of spending more than you can afford.

Here are some of the adversaries you're up against as you attempt to control your spending. In Chapter 5, we explain detailed strategies for getting out of debt, and in Chapter 6, we share practical tactics for slimming your spending.

Access to credit

As you probably already know, spending your money is easy. Thanks to credit cards and innovations like automated bank machines and debit cards, your money is available for spending 24 hours a day, 365 days a year (except during leap years, when your money is available 366 days a year). Every little outlet in the mall is pitching its own credit card, including the gas station across the street and the convenience store down the road. It certainly won't surprise us when those two little kids on your block start taking credit cards at their lemonade stand. We can hear it now: "We take VISA, but we don't take American Express."

Sometimes, it may seem as though lenders are trying to give away money by making credit so easily available. But this is a dangerous illusion. When it comes to consumer debt (credit cards, auto loans, and the like), lenders aren't giving away anything except the opportunity for you to get in over your head, rack up high interest charges, and delay your progress toward your financial and personal goals.

Credit is most dangerous when you make consumption purchases that you can't afford in the first place.

Using credit cards

The modern-day bank credit card was invented by Bank of America near the tail end of the baby boom. The credit industry has been booming along with the boomers ever since.

If you pay your bill in full every month, credit cards offer a convenient way to buy things with an interest-free, short-term loan. But if you carry your debt over month to month at high interest rates, credit cards encourage you to live beyond your means. Credit cards make spending money that you don't have easy and tempting.

If you have a knack for charging up a storm and spending more than you should with those little pieces of plastic, only one solution exists: Get rid of them. Put scissors to the plastic. Go cold turkey. Except in rare circumstances, you *can* function without them (see the next chapter for details if you think you can't live without credit cards).

Making minimum monthly payments

You'll *never* get your credit card debt paid off if you keep charging on your card and make only the minimum monthly payment. Interest continues to pile up on your outstanding debt. Paying only the minimum monthly payment is like using a Dixie cup to bail water from a sinking boat that has a basketball-sized hole in its bottom.

Taking out car loans

It's too easy to walk onto a car lot and go home with a new car that you could never afford if you had to pay cash. The dealer gets you thinking in terms of monthly payments that sound small compared to what that four-wheeler is *really* gonna cost you. Auto loans are easy for just about anyone to get (except maybe a recently paroled felon).

Suppose that you're tired of driving around in the old clunker. The car is battle-scarred and boring, and you don't like to be seen in it. Plus, the car is likely to need more repairs in the months ahead. So off you go to your friendly local car dealer.

You start looking around at all the shiny, new cars and then — like the feeling you experience when spotting a water fountain on a scorching hot day — there it is: the replacement for your old clunker. It's sleek and clean and — oooh, look! — it has A/C, stereo, and power everything.

Before you have an opportunity to read the fine print on the sticker page on the side window, the salesperson moseys on up next to you. He gets you talking about how nice the car is, the weather, anything but the price of that car.

"How," you begin to think to yourself, "can this guy afford to spend time with me without knowing if I can afford this thing?" After a test drive and more talk about the car, the weather, and your love life, or lack thereof, comes your moment of truth.

The salesperson, it seems, doesn't care about how much money you have. If in fact you have lots of money, that doesn't matter either. Either way, it's no problem!

The car is only $299 a month.

That's not bad, you think. Heck, you were expecting to hear that the car cost at least 20 grand. Before you know it, the dealer runs a credit report on you, has you sign a few papers, and minutes later you're driving home — the proud owner of a spanking new car.

See, the dealer wants you to think in terms of monthly payments because the cost *sounds* so cheap: $299 for a car. But, of course, that's $299 per month, every month, for many, many months. You're gonna be payin' forever — after all, you just bought a car that cost a huge chunk (perhaps 100 percent or more) of your yearly take-home income!

But it gets worse. What does the total sticker price come to when interest charges are added in? And how about insurance and registration and maintenance over the seven or so years that you'll own it? Now you're probably up to *more* than a year's worth of your income. Ouch! (See Chapter 6 for how to spend what you can afford on a car.)

Bending to peer pressure

You go out with some friends to dinner, a ballgame, or a show. Try to remember the last time one of you said, "Let's go someplace (do something) cheaper. I can't afford to spend this much."

On the one hand, you don't want to be a stick in the mud. But on the other hand, some of your friends have more money than you do — and the ones who don't may be running up debt fast.

Spending to feel good

Life is full of stress, obligations, and demands. "I work hard," you say. "And darn it, I deserve to indulge!" Especially after your boss took the credit for your last great idea or blamed you for his last major screw-up. So you buy something expensive or go to a fancy restaurant. Feel better? You won't when the bill arrives. And the more you spend, the less you save, and the longer you'll be stuck working — and working for jerks like that!

Becoming addicted to spending

Just as people can become addicted to alcohol, tobacco, television, and the Internet, some become addicted to the high they get from spending. A number of psychological causes can be identified for spending addiction, some of which may date back to how your family handled money and spending. (And you thought you'd identified all the problems you can blame on Mom and Dad!)

If your spending and debt problems are chronic, Debtors Anonymous, a 12-step support group program patterned after Alcoholics Anonymous, can help. See Chapter 5 for more information.

Trying to keep current

You just have to see the latest hit movie or wear the latest designer clothes or get the new, superimproved, oversized tennis racquet with shock absorbers, double-wishbone suspension, and polyxylitol handgrips. All your friends are getting one, so you'd better get one, too. Right?

Wrong. Besides, many new technologies or products don't live up to their billing. Be smart and wait until a product is proven and you can afford it.

Ignoring your financial goals when buying

When was the last time you heard someone say that he decided to forgo a purchase because he was saving toward retirement or a home purchase? Doesn't happen often, does it? Just dealing with the here-and-now and forgetting your long-term needs and goals are tempting. That's why people toil away for too many years in jobs they dislike.

Living for today has its virtues: Tomorrow *may* not come. But odds are good that it will. Will you still feel the same way tomorrow about today's spending decisions? Or will you feel guilty that you again failed to stick to your goals?

Of course, this assumes that you have financial goals to stick to. Most people haven't yet set goals and don't know how much they should be saving to accomplish them. Chapter 3 helps you to kick-start that process.

Wanting the "best" for your children

For children, many of the best things in life are free, just as they are for you. Junior *can* live without the latest $100 sneakers. Later on in life, your children will thank you: Better to pass on sound judgment and wise thriftiness than the worship of material goods.

Education can cost good money, we know. However, education experts are the first to dissuade you of the assumption that you're doing the best for your children if you spend lots of money to live in a town with a supposedly top-of-the-line school district or to fund private-school tuition from preschool through high school if you can't be home enough to take care of your children's other wants and needs.

Education begins in and is best done in the home. We see some parents spend so much time running around working, working, working to afford all the supposedly best things for their kids that they neglect to spend *time* with their kids — the most important ingredient to their children's long-term happiness and success.

Analyzing Your Spending

Washing your face, brushing your teeth, and exercising regularly are good habits. The financial equivalents of these habits are spending less than you earn and saving enough to meet your future financial objectives.

Despite relatively high incomes compared with the rest of the world, most Canadians have a hard time saving a good percentage of their incomes. Why? We spend too much — often far more than is necessary.

The first step to saving more of the income that you work so hard for is to figure out where that income typically gets spent; that's what the spending analysis in the next section helps you determine.

You should do the spending analysis if any of the following apply to you:

✔ You aren't saving enough money to meet your financial goals (should you not know whether this is the case, please see Chapter 3).

✔ You feel as if your spending is out of control or you don't really know where all your income goes.

✔ You're anticipating a significant life change (for example, marriage, leaving your job to start a business, having children, retiring, and so on).

In the event that you're a good saver already, you may not need to complete the spending analysis. If you're saving enough to accomplish your goals, we don't see much value in continually tracking your spending. You've already established the good habit — saving. The good habit is *not* tracking exactly where you spend your money month after month. As long as you're saving enough and simply spending what's left over, we say, who cares where the money is being spent!

The immediate goal of a spending analysis is to figure out what you typically spend your money on. The long-range goal is to establish a good habit: to maintain a regular, automatic savings routine.

Notice the first four letters in the word *analysis.* (You may never have noticed, but we felt the need to bring it to your attention.) Knowing where your money is going each month is useful. It's terrific to make changes in your spending behaviour and to cut out the fat so that you can save more money and meet your financial goals. But you'll perhaps make yourself and those around you unhappy campers if you try to be anal-retentive about documenting precisely where you're spending every single dollar and cent.

Remember: What matters is that you save what you want and need to achieve your goals.

Tracking your spending on paper

Doing your spending analysis is a little bit like being a detective. Your goal is to reconstruct the crime of *spending.* You probably have some major clues at your fingertips or piled somewhere on your desk or on the table where you plop yourself down to pay bills.

Unless you keep meticulous records that detail every dollar you spend, you won't have perfect information. Don't sweat it! A number of available sources should allow you to reconstruct where you have been spending the bulk of your money.

Get out your

- ✔ Recent pay stubs
- ✔ Tax returns
- ✔ Chequebook register or cancelled cheques
- ✔ Credit- and charge-card bills

Ideally, you should assemble the documents needed to track one year's spending (12 months). But, if your spending patterns don't fluctuate greatly from month to month (or if your dog ate some of the old bills), you can reduce your data gathering to one six-month period or to every other or every third month for the past year. If you take a major vacation or spend a large amount on gifts during certain times of the year, make sure you include these months in your analysis.

The hardest transactions to track are cash transactions, because they don't leave a paper trail. Over the course of a week or perhaps even a month, you *could* keep track of everything you buy with cash. Tracking cash can be an enlightening exercise — it can also be a hassle. If you're lazy like we sometimes are or lack the time and patience, try *estimating.* Think about a typical week or month — how often do you buy things with cash? For example, if you eat lunch out four days a week at work, paying around $5 a shot, that's about $80 a month. You might also add up all the cash withdrawals from your chequing account statement and then work backward to try to remember where you might have spent that cash.

Try to separate your expenditures into as many useful and detailed categories as possible. Table 4-1 gives you a suggested format — you can tailor it to fit your needs. Remember, if you lump too much of your spending into broad, meaningless categories like *Other,* you'll end up where you started: wondering where all the money went. (*Note:* When completing the tax section in Table 4-1, you should report the total tax you paid for the year as tabulated on your annual income tax return, rather than the tax withheld or paid during the year.)

Table 4-1	Detailing Your Spending	
Category	*Monthly Average ($)*	*Percentage of Total Gross Income (%)*
Taxes, taxes, taxes (income)		_____
Federal	_____	
Provincial and local	_____	
The roof over your head		_____
Rent	_____	
Mortgage	_____	
Property taxes	_____	
Gas/electric/oil	_____	
Water/garbage	_____	
Phone	_____	
Cable TV	_____	
Furniture/appliances	_____	
Maintenance/repairs	_____	

Category	Monthly Average ($)	Percentage of Total Gross Income (%)
Food, glorious food		_____
Supermarket	_____	
Restaurants and take-out	_____	
Getting around		_____
Gasoline	_____	
Maintenance/repairs	_____	
Provincial registration fees	_____	
Tolls and parking	_____	
Bus or subway fares	_____	
Style		_____
Clothing	_____	
Shoes	_____	
Jewellery (watches, earrings)	_____	
Dry cleaning	_____	
Debt repayments (excluding mortgage)		_____
Credit/charge cards	_____	
Auto loans	_____	
Student loans	_____	
Other	_____	
Fun stuff		_____
Entertainment (movies, concerts)	_____	
Vacation and travel	_____	
Gifts	_____	
Hobbies	_____	
Pets	_____	
Other	_____	
Personal care		_____
Haircuts	_____	
Health club or gym	_____	
Makeup	_____	
Other	_____	

(continued)

Table 4-1 (continued)

Category	Monthly Average ($)	Percentage of Total Gross Income (%)
Personal business		_____
Accountant/lawyer/financial adviser	_____	
Other	_____	
Health care		_____
Physicians and hospitals	_____	
Drugs	_____	
Dental and vision	_____	
Therapy	_____	
Insurance		_____
Homeowner's/renter's	_____	
Auto	_____	
Health	_____	
Life	_____	
Disability	_____	
Umbrella liability	_____	
Educational expenses		_____
Tuition	_____	
Books	_____	
Supplies	_____	
Children		_____
Daycare	_____	
Toys	_____	
Child support	_____	
Charitable donations	_____	_____
Other		_____
_____	_____	
_____	_____	
_____	_____	
_____	_____	
_____	_____	
_____	_____	

Don't waste time on financial administration

Tom is the model of financial organization. All his financial documents are neatly organized into colour-coded folders. Every month, he enters all his spending information into his computer. He even carries a notebook to detail his cash spending so that every penny is accounted for.

Tom also balances his chequebook, "to make sure that everything is in order." He can't remember the last time his bank made a mistake, but he knows a friend who once found a $50 error.

If you spend seven hours per month as Tom does, balancing your chequebook and detailing all your spending, you may be wasting nearly two weeks' worth of time per year — the equivalent of two-thirds of your vacation time if you take three weeks annually.

Suppose that you're "lucky" enough, every other year, to find a $100 error the bank made in its favour. If you spend just three hours per month tracking your spending and balancing your chequebook to discover this glitch, you'll spend 72 hours over two years to find a $100 mistake. Your hourly pay: a wafer-thin $1.39 per hour. You could make more flipping burgers at a burger joint if you wanted to moonlight. (*Note:* If you make significant-sized deposits or withdrawals, be sure that those are captured on your statement.)

To add insult to injury, after working a full week and doing all your financial and other chores, you may not have the desire and energy left to do the more important stuff. Looking at your big personal financial picture — establishing goals, choosing wise investments, securing proper insurance coverage — may continue to be shoved to the back burner. As a result, you may lose thousands of dollars annually. Over the course of your adult life, this could translate into tens or even hundreds of thousands of lost dollars.

Tom, for example, didn't know how much he should be saving to meet his retirement goals. He hadn't reviewed his employer's benefit materials to understand his insurance and retirement plan options. He knows he pays a lot in taxes, but he hasn't educated himself about how to reduce his taxes.

You want to make the most of your money. Unless you truly enjoy dealing with money, you need to prioritize the money activities that you work on. Time is limited and life is short. Working harder on financial administration doesn't earn you bonus points. The more time you spend dealing with your personal finances, the less is available to gab with friends, watch a good movie, read a good novel, and do other things you really enjoy.

Don't get us wrong — nothing is inherently wrong with balancing your chequebook. In fact, if you regularly bounce cheques because you don't know how low your balance is, the exercise might save you a lot in returned cheque fees. However, if you keep enough money in your chequing account to rarely reach $0.00, balancing your chequebook is probably a waste of your valuable time, even if your hourly wages aren't lofty.

If you're busy, consider ways to reduce the amount of time spent on mundane financial tasks like bill paying. Increasing numbers of companies, for example, allow you to have your monthly bills paid to them electronically via your bank chequing account or your credit card (do this only if you pay your credit card bill in full each month). The fewer bills you have to pay, the fewer separate cheques and envelopes you must process each month. That translates into more free time for you — and fewer paper cuts!

Tracking your spending on the computer

Plenty of software packages exist to assist you with paying bills and tracking your spending. The main advantage of these software packages is that they continually track your spending as long as you keep entering the information. And, after you learn how to use these packages (not always an easy thing to do), they can speed the process of writing cheques.

But you don't need a computer and fancy software packages to figure where you're spending money and to pay your bills. Many software purchasers we know give up entering the data after a few months. If tracking your spending is what you're after, you're likely to have information in the software only for bills you pay by cheque. Expenses you pay by credit card and cash need to be entered specially into the software if you want to capture that data, too.

Like home exercise equipment and exotic kitchen appliances, such software often ends up in the consumer graveyard. Paper, pencil, and a calculator work just fine.

The Secret to Growing Rich on Your Income

We've dealt with people who bring in tiny incomes, incomes of hundreds of thousands of dollars or more, and everything in between. At every income level, people fall into one of the following three categories:

- People who spend more than they earn (accumulate debt)
- People who spend all that they earn (save nothing)
- People who save 2, 5, 10, even 20 percent (or more!)

We've seen $30,000 earners who save 20 percent of their income ($6,000), $60,000 earners who save just 5 percent ($3,000), and people earning well into six figures annually who save nothing or are accumulating debt.

Suppose that you currently earn $35,000 per year and spend all of it. You wonder: "How can I save money?"

Good question!

Rather than knocking yourself out at a second job or hustling for that next promotion, you could try living below your income — in other words, spend less than you earn. (We know spending less than you earn is hard to imagine, but you can do it.) Consider that for every discontented person earning and spending $35,000 per year, someone else is out there making do on $29,000.

A great many people live on less than you make. If you spent as they do, you could save and invest the difference.

Chapter 5

Dealing with Debt and Credit Problems

. . . .

. . . .

*A*s we discuss in Chapter 1, some debt is good, and some is bad. When debt is used for investing in your future, we call it *good debt*. Borrowing money to afford an education, buy real estate, or invest in a small business is like eating foods rich in calcium for strong bones or eating fruits and vegetables for their vitamins.

But accumulating *bad debt* (consumer debt) is like living on a diet of sugar and caffeine: a quick fix with no long-term nutritional value. Borrowing on your credit card to afford that vacation to Mexico is costly and detrimental to your long-term financial health.

In this chapter, we help you battle the increasing problem of consumer debt. Getting rid of your bad debts may be even more difficult than giving up the sugar-laden foods you love. But in the long run, you'll be glad you did; you'll be financially healthier and emotionally happier. And once you get rid of your high-cost consumer debts, practise the best way to deal with credit problems: *Don't borrow with bad debt.*

To decide which debt reduction strategies make sense for you, you first must consider your overall financial situation and assess your alternatives.

Using Savings to Reduce Your Debt

Many people have built up a psychological brick wall between their savings and investment accounts and their debt accounts. Failing to view their finances holistically, they have simply gotten into the habit of looking at these accounts individually. The thought of putting a door in that big brick wall has never occurred to them.

How you gain

Using savings to pay down debts may seem like you're losing money. You're *not* losing; you're gaining. Remember that the growth of your money is determined by your *net worth* — the difference between your assets and your liabilities (see Chapter 1). Hopefully, your savings and investments are earning decent returns, but if you have consumer debts, odds are that the interest on those debts is high.

Having consumer loans on a credit card at, say, 12 percent and paying them off is like finding an investment with a guaranteed return of 12 percent — *tax-free*. You would actually need an investment that yielded even more — anywhere from around 16 percent to 24 percent — to net 12 percent after paying taxes in order to justify not paying off your 12 percent loans. The higher your tax bracket (see Chapter 7), the higher the return you need on your investments to justify keeping high-interest consumer debt.

If you have the savings to pay off high-interest credit card and auto loans, do so. You diminish your savings, true, but you also reduce your debts. You benefit financially because the interest on your savings is far less than the interest your debt accrues. Make sure to pay off the loans with the highest interest rates first.

Even if you think you're an investment genius and can earn more on your investments, swallow your ego and pay down the debts anyway. In order to chase that higher potential return from investments, you need to take substantial risk. You *may* earn more investing in that hot stock tip or that bargain real estate located on a toxic waste site, but it's more than likely you won't.

If you use your accessible savings to pay down consumer debts, be careful to leave yourself enough of an emergency cushion. You want to be in a position to withstand an unexpected large expense or temporary loss of income. On the other hand, if you use savings to pay down credit card debt, unless your card gets cancelled, you can run your credit card balances back up in a financial pinch (or turn to a family member or wealthy friend for a low-interest loan).

Money you may be overlooking

Have you ever reached into the pocket of an old winter parka and found a rolled-up $20 bill you forgot you had? Stumbling across some forgotten funds is always a pleasant experience. But before you root through all your closets in search of stray cash to help you pay down that nagging credit card or other costly consumer debt, check out some of these financial jacket pockets that you may have overlooked:

- ✔ **Borrow against your cash-value life insurance policy.** If you were approached by a life insurance agent, odds are good that this is the type of policy you were sold, because it pays high commissions to its agents. Or perhaps your parents bought one for you when you were a little gremlin. Borrow against the cash value to pay down your debts. (*Note:* Continuing with such a policy may not be the best thing to do — see Chapter 18 for more details.)

- ✔ **Sell investments held outside of RRSPs.** Maybe you have some shares of stock or a Canada Savings Bond gathering dust in your safety deposit box. Consider cashing in these investments to pay down your loan balances. Just be sure to consider the tax consequences of selling and, if possible, sell only those investments that won't generate a big tax bill.

- ✔ **Borrow against the equity in your home.** If you're a homeowner, you may be able to tap into your home's *equity,* which is the difference between the property's market value and outstanding loan balance. You can generally borrow against real estate at a lower interest rate.

- ✔ **Borrow from friends and family.** They know you, love you, realize your shortcomings, and — heck — probably won't be as cold-hearted as some bankers we know. Money borrowed from family members can have strings attached, of course. Treating the obligation seriously is important. It's also best to write up a simple agreement listing the terms and conditions of your loan to avoid misunderstandings. Unless your family members are like the worst bankers we know, you'll probably get a fair interest rate, and your family will have the satisfaction of helping you out — just don't forget to pay them back.

Decreasing Debt When You Lack Savings

"I don't have savings, you nincompoops!" you exclaim. "That's why I have all this debt!"

If you read the preceding section, thank you for patiently waiting; we just wanted to make sure that you didn't have any money that you forgot about. (The number of people with consumer debt who can pay it down with savings but haven't done so always surprises us.)

But on to your quandary: You lack savings to pay off your high-interest consumer debt. Well, not surprisingly, you have some work to do. If you're currently spending all your income (and more!), you need to figure out how you can decrease your spending (see Chapter 6 for lots of great ideas) and/or increase your income. In the meantime, you need to slow the growth of your debt.

Transfer to lower-interest-rate credit cards

Different credit cards charge different interest rates. Why in the world should you pay 14, 16, 18 percent or more when you can pay less? The credit card business has become quite competitive. Gone are the days when all banks charged 18 percent or more for VISA and MasterCard.

Here's one of the few times in your life when you should want to be below average! Until you get your debt paid off, make it more difficult for your debt to grow. You may be able to accomplish this slowing process by reducing the interest rate you're paying on your debt. Here are some ways to do that:

- ✔ **Apply for a lower-rate credit card.** If you are earning a decent income, are not *too* burdened with debt, and have a clean credit record, qualifying for lower-rate cards is relatively painless. Some persistence (and clean-up work) may be required if you have nicks in your credit report or have income and debt problems. Once you are approved for a new, lower-interest-rate credit card, you can simply transfer your outstanding balance from your higher-rate card.

  A number of financial institutions offer low-interest-rate credit cards, including all of the big-name banks. However, you will usually have to inquire about them, as they generally aren't promoted — if you don't ask, you'll typically be signed up for the higher-rate card. If you have access to the Web, you can find out the latest rates by looking in the consumer information area at www.strategis.gc.ca, a federal government Web site.

  Call the bank(s) that issued your current high-interest-rate credit card(s) and say that you want to cancel your card(s) because you found a competitor that offers no annual fee and a lower interest rate. Your bank may choose to match the terms of the "competitor" rather than lose you as a customer.

- ✔ **While you're paying down your credit card balance(s), stop making new charges on cards that have outstanding balances.** Many people don't realize that interest starts to accumulate *immediately* when they carry a balance. *You have no grace period* — the 20-odd days you normally have to pay your balance in full without incurring interest charges — if you carry a credit card balance month-to-month.

6.9-percent-interest-rate credit cards!

Buyer beware if you're lured into applying for a credit card that hypes its low interest rate — such as those offering a 6.9 percent rate. One such card advertises a 6.9 percent rate, but you have to dig into the fine print for the rest of the story.

First, any card that offers such a low interest rate inevitably will only honour that rate for a short period of time — in this case, six months. Then, the interest rate skyrockets to nearly 15 percent.

And there's more. Make just one late payment or exceed your credit limit, and the company raises your interest rate to 17.9 percent — in addition to whacking you for $29 for each such infraction. Need a cash advance on your card? You'll get socked with a fee equal to 3 percent of the amount advanced.

Now, we're not saying that everyone should avoid this type of card. Such a card could make sense for you if you want to transfer an out-standing balance and plan to pay off that balance within a matter of months, cancel the card, and avoid getting socked with the high fees on the card.

If you hunt around for a low-interest-rate credit card, be sure to check out all the terms and conditions. Start by reviewing the uniform rates and terms disclosure, which details the myriad fees and conditions. Also, be sure that you understand how the future interest rate is determined on cards that charge variable interest rates.

Cut 'em up, cut 'em all up

If you have a pattern of living beyond your means through buying on credit, get rid of the culprit — the credit card, that is. To kick the habit, a smoker needs to toss all the cigarettes, and an alcoholic needs to get rid of all the booze. Cut up all of your credit cards and call the issuers of the cards to cancel your accounts. And when you buy consumer items such as cars and furniture, do not apply for E-Z credit.

The world worked fine back in the years *B.C.* (Before Credit). Think about it: Just a couple of generations ago, credit cards didn't even exist. People paid with cash and cheques — imagine that! You can function without buying anything on a credit card. In certain cases, you may need a card as collateral — like when you rent a car. When you bring back the rental car, however, you can pay with cash or cheque. Leave the card at home in the back of your sock drawer or freezer and pull (or thaw) it out only for the occasional car rental.

If you can trust yourself, keep a separate credit card *only* for new purchases that you know you can absolutely pay in full each month. No one needs three, five, or ten credit cards! You can live with one (and actually none), given the wide acceptance of most cards. Count 'em up, including retail store and gas cards, and get rid of 'em. Retailers such as department stores and gas stations just love to give you their cards. Not only do these cards charge outrageously high interest rates, they duplicate VISA and MasterCard. Virtually all retailers accept VISA and MasterCard. More credit lines mean more temptation to spend what you can't afford.

Should you decide to keep one widely accepted credit card instead of getting rid of them all, be careful. You may be tempted to let debt accumulate and roll over for a month or two, and you'll start the whole horrible process of running up your consumer debt again. Rather than keeping one credit card, consider getting a debit card.

Debit cards: The best of both worlds

Credit cards are the main reason that today's consumers are consuming more than they can afford. So logic would say that one way you can keep your spending in check is to not use your credit cards. But in a society used to flashing the widely accepted VISA and MasterCard plastic for purchases, changing habits is hard. And you may be legitimately concerned that carrying your chequebook or cash can be a hassle or costly if you're mugged.

Well, *debit cards* truly offer the best of both worlds. The beauty of the debit card is that it offers you the convenience of making purchases with a piece of plastic without the temptation and ability to run up credit card debt. Debit cards keep you from spending money you don't have and help you live within your means.

A debit card looks a lot like a credit card. The big difference between debit cards and credit cards is that debit card purchase amounts are deducted electronically from your account the moment the transaction is approved. If you've ever used an automated banking machine (ABM) card, you likely already have a debit card. Through the miracle of modern technology, most financial institutions have programmed their bank cards to do double duty as debit cards.

If you keep your chequing account balance low and don't ordinarily balance your chequebook, you may need to start balancing your chequebook if you switch to a debit card. Otherwise, you could be facing unnecessary bounced-cheque charges.

You should also know about other differences between debit and credit cards.

> ✔ If you pay your credit card bill in full and on time each month, charging on your credit card gives you free use of the money you owe until it's time to pay the bill; debit cards take the money out of your bank account almost immediately. (Note that some credit cards charge a fee even if you pay your balance in full each month. You didn't think the banks would let you use the float forever, did you?)

✔ Also, credit cards more easily allow you to dispute charges for problematic merchandise through the issuing bank. Most banks allow you to dispute charges for up to 60 days after purchase and will credit the disputed amount to your account pending resolution. Most debit cards offer a much shorter window, typically less than one week, to make disputes.

Filing for Bankruptcy

For consumers in over their heads, the realization that their monthly income is increasingly exceeded by their bill payments is usually a painful one. In many cases, years can pass before drastic measures like bankruptcy are considered. Both financial and emotional issues come into play in one of life's most difficult and painful yet potentially beneficial decisions.

When Helen, a mother of two and a sales representative, contacted a professional to handle her bankruptcy, her total credit card debt of about $20,000 equalled her annual gross income of $20,000. Due to the crushing debt load, she couldn't meet her minimum monthly credit card payments. Rent and food gobbled up most of her earnings. What little was left over went to the squeakiest wheel.

Creditors were breathing down Helen's back. "I started getting calls from collection departments at home and work — it was embarrassing," relates Helen. Helen's case is typical in that credit card debt was the prime cause of her bankruptcy. "If credit card debt didn't exist, I wouldn't have a job," says one bankruptcy professional.

Helen's case is typical in other regards. Her debt accumulated over a number of years. A former homeowner with a master's degree from a prestigious university, Helen had good credit until a couple of years before. After divorcing, Helen rented an apartment with her two children while holding down a job. Unfortunately, she was laid off when her employer encountered tough times.

At first, bills to her dentist went unpaid. Then, when Helen went into business for herself, she used her credit cards to purchase office furniture and pay other start-up expenses. "I would have done more corner cutting, but the credit cards were easily available cash and allowed me to think in terms of monthly payments," says Helen.

As the debt load grew, partly exacerbated by the double-digit interest rates on the cards, more and more purchases got charged — from the kids' clothing to repairs for the car. Finally, out of cash, she had to take a large cash advance on her credit cards to pay for rent and food.

Despite trying to work out lower monthly payments to keep everyone happy, most of the banks to which Helen owed money were inflexible. "When I asked one bank's VISA department if it preferred that I declare bankruptcy because it was unwilling to lower my monthly payment, the representative said yes," Helen says. Out of options, Helen filed for personal bankruptcy.

Bankruptcy benefits

Every year, more than 50,000 Canadian households (that's about 1 in every 200 households) file for personal bankruptcy.

The value or benefit of bankruptcy is that certain types of debts can be completely eliminated or *discharged*. Debts that typically can be discharged include credit card, medical, auto, utilities, rent, and taxes. Debts that may not be cancelled include child support, alimony, and court-ordered fines and penalties (for example, traffic tickets). Student loans are also generally not cancelled if bankruptcy is filed within ten years of finishing your studies.

Helen was an ideal candidate for bankruptcy because her debts (credit cards) were dischargeable. Helen also met another important criterion: Her level of high-interest consumer debt relative to her annual income was high. When this ratio exceeds more than 25 percent, filing for bankruptcy may be your best option.

Eliminating your debt also allows you to start working toward your financial goals. Depending on the amount of debt you have outstanding relative to your income, you may need a decade or more to pay it all off. In Helen's case, at the age of 48 she had no money saved for retirement to supplement government benefits, and she was increasingly unable to spend money on her children.

In addition to the financial benefits are the emotional benefits in filing for bankruptcy. "I was horrified at filing, but it is good to be rid of the debts and collection calls — I should have filed six months earlier. I was constantly worried. When I saw homeless families come to the soup kitchen where I sometimes volunteer, I thought that someday that could be me and my kids," she said.

Bankruptcy drawbacks

There are, needless to say, a number of drawbacks to filing for bankruptcy. First, bankruptcy appears on your credit report for seven years — six years after you are discharged from bankruptcy, which happens nine months after you go bankrupt. As a result, you will have difficulty obtaining credit, especially in the years immediately following your filing.

If you already have problems on your credit report, however, because of late payments or failure to pay previous debts, damage has already been done. And, without savings, you probably won't make major purchases, such as a home, in the next several years anyway.

If you do file for bankruptcy, getting credit in the future is not impossible. You'll probably be able to obtain a *secured credit card,* which requires you to deposit money in a bank account equal to the credit limit on your credit card. If you can hold down a stable job, most creditors are willing to give you loans within a few years of your filing for bankruptcy. Almost all lenders ignore bankruptcy after five to seven years.

Another bankruptcy drawback is that it costs money. We know this seems terribly unfair. You're already in financial trouble — that's why you're filing for bankruptcy! Nevertheless, filing for bankruptcy will probably set you back from several hundred dollars up to several thousand in court filing and legal fees.

Finally, most people find that filing for bankruptcy causes emotional stress. Admitting that your personal income can't keep pace with your debt obligations is a painful thing to do. Although filing for bankruptcy clears the decks of debt and gives you a fresh financial start, feeling a profound sense of failure is only human. Despite the increasing frequency of bankruptcy, bankruptcy filers are reluctant to talk about it with others, including family and friends.

Another part of the emotional side of filing bankruptcy is that you must open your personal financial affairs to court scrutiny and court control during the several months it takes to administer a bankruptcy. A court-appointed bankruptcy trustee oversees your case and tries to recover as much of your property as possible to satisfy the *creditors* — those to whom you owe money.

Some people also feel that they're shirking responsibility by filing for bankruptcy. One client Eric worked with who should have filed couldn't bring herself to do it. She said, "I spent that money, and it's my responsibility to pay it back."

Most banks make gobs and gobs of money from their credit card businesses. We can tell you that credit cards are one of the most profitable lines of business for banks. If you don't believe us, consider that, at a banking conference sponsored by the investment bank Salomon Brothers, CEO John Reed referred to the credit card business for banks as a "high-return, low-risk" business. Now you know why your mailbox is always filled with solicitations for more cards even though you're already up to your eyeballs in solicitations.

So if you file for bankruptcy, don't feel too bad about not paying back the bank. The nice merchants where you bought the merchandise have already been paid. *Charge-offs* — the banker's term for taking the loss on debt that you discharge through bankruptcy — are part of the business. This is another reason why the interest rate is so high on credit cards and why you shouldn't borrow on credit cards.

What you can keep if you file for bankruptcy

In every province, you can retain certain property and assets even though you're filing for bankruptcy. In most cases, you're allowed to keep a few thousand dollars' worth of clothing and personal effects. You likely will also be able to keep a few thousand dollars' worth of the tools of your trade if such items are necessary for you to earn a living. Depending on the province that you live in, you may also be able to hang on to a vehicle worth no more than $3,000 to $5,000, and possibly a small amount of equity in your home.

"Light" and "full" bankruptcy

You can file one of two forms of personal bankruptcy:

- ✔ **A consumer proposal** allows you to try to work out a deal with your creditors without having to go the route of actually filing for bankruptcy. A trustee assists you in assessing your assets and income, organizes a budget for you, and provides a few counselling sessions. Your trustee then presents a detailed plan to your creditors detailing how much and when you'll pay them, to which the creditors have 30 days to respond. If your plan is accepted, you'll still have to teach yourself to live on a lot less.

  In order to take the consumer proposal option, your debts must generally total less than $75,000, excluding your mortgage. In addition, alimony, child support, and legal fines aren't covered by the proposal. They remain payable in full. This is often a sensible route to take, especially if you have a lot of assets and a regular income. In a regular bankruptcy, almost all your assets are sold. Under a consumer proposal, that may not be necessary if your creditors are willing to settle for a piece of your paycheque.

- ✔ **Full bankruptcy** is your only other alternative if your consumer proposal is turned down or if your debts are too high to allow you to try the proposal route. The trustee takes control of your assets, sells them, and distributes the proceeds to your creditors. After the paperwork is filed, you're officially "bankrupt" for nine months.

Bankruptcy advice

Be very careful where you get advice about whether to file for bankruptcy. Lawyers who earn a legal fee from doing bankruptcy filings, for example, have a conflict of interest. All things being equal, their bias is to — you guessed it — *recommend bankruptcy,* which generates their fees.

If you want to learn more about the pros, cons, and details of filing for bankruptcy, pick up a copy of *Buy Now, Pay Later? What You Should Know about Credit, Debt, and Bankruptcy: A Legal Guide* by Allan A. Parker (published by Self-Counsel Press).

Regardless of how you deal with paying off your debt, you're in real danger of falling back into old habits. Backsliding happens not only to people who file bankruptcy but also to those who use savings or home equity to eliminate their debt. If history has shown that you're likely to fall into this trap, the best and only solution is to go cold turkey. Eliminate your access to credit and pay for everything with cash, cheques, and debit cards.

Ending the Spend-and-Debt Cycle

Regardless of how you deal with paying off your debt, you're in real danger of falling back into old habits. Backsliding happens not only to people who file for bankruptcy but also to those who use savings or home equity to eliminate their debt. This section speaks to that risk and what to do about it.

Identifying and treating an addiction

As hard as they try to break the habit, some people become addicted to spending and debting. It becomes a chronic problem that starts to interfere with other aspects of their lives. Financial problems can lead to problems at work and with family and even friends.

Officially started in 1976, Debtors Anonymous (DA) is a non-profit organization that provides support, primarily through group meetings, to people trying to break their debting and spending habits. DA is modelled after the 12-step Alcoholics Anonymous program.

Like AA, Debtors Anonymous works with people from all walks of life and socioeconomic backgrounds. It's typical to find people who are financially on the edge, $100,000-plus income earners, and everybody in between at a DA meeting. Even former millionaires join the program.

DA has a simple questionnaire that helps determine whether you are a problem debtor. If you answer yes to at least 8 of the following 15 questions, you may be developing or already have a compulsive debting habit:

1. Are your debts making your home life unhappy?

2. Does the pressure of your debts distract you from your daily work?

3. Are your debts affecting your reputation?

4. Do your debts cause you to think less of yourself?

5. Have you ever given false information in order to obtain credit?

6. Have you ever made unrealistic promises to your creditors?

7. Does the pressure of your debts make you careless of the welfare of your family?

8. Do you ever fear that your employer, family, or friends will learn the extent of your total indebtedness?

9. When faced with a difficult financial situation, does the prospect of borrowing give you an inordinate feeling of relief?

10. Does the pressure of your debts cause you to have difficulty sleeping?

11. Has the pressure of your debts ever caused you to consider getting drunk?

12. Have you ever borrowed money without giving adequate consideration to the rate of interest you are required to pay?

13. Do you usually expect a negative response when you are subject to a credit investigation?

14. Have you ever developed a strict regimen for paying off your debts, only to break it under pressure?

15. Do you justify your debts by telling yourself that you are superior to the "other" people, and when you get your "break," you'll be out of debt?

To find a Debtors Anonymous support group in your area, check your local phone directory (in the "Business" section). Or write to DA's national headquarters for meeting locations in your area and a literature order form at the following address: Debtors Anonymous, P.O. Box 400, Grand Central Station, New York, NY 10163-0400. The organization also has a Web site at www.debtorsanonymous.org.

Resisting the credit temptation

Getting out of debt is usually challenging, but we have confidence that you can do it with this book by your side and us as your guide. In addition to the ideas discussed earlier in this chapter (eliminating all your credit cards, getting a debit card), the following are some additional tactics you can use to limit the influence credit cards hold over your life in the future:

✔ **Reduce your credit limit.** If you're not going to take our advice earlier in this chapter and get rid of all of your credit cards or secure a debit card, be sure to keep a lid on your credit card's credit limit (the maximum balance allowed on your card). Just because your bank keeps raising your credit limit to reward you for being such a profitable customer doesn't mean that you have to accept the increase. Call your credit card service's toll-free number and lower your credit limit to a level you're comfortable with.

✔ **Replace your credit card with a charge card.** A charge card (such as the American Express card) requires you to pay your balance in full each billing period. You have no credit line or interest charges. Of course, spending more than you can afford to pay when the bill comes due is possible. But, you'll be much less likely to overspend if you know you have to pay in full monthly.

✔ **Never buy on credit anything that depreciates in value.** Meals out, cars, clothing, and shoes all depreciate in value. Never buy these things on credit. Borrow money only for sound investments — education, real estate, or your own business, for example.

✔ **Think in terms of total cost.** Everything sounds cheaper in terms of monthly payments — that's how salespeople lure you into buying things you don't have the money to afford. Take a calculator along if necessary to tally up the sticker price, interest charges, and upkeep. The total cost will scare you. *It should.*

✔ **Stop the junk mail avalanche.** Look at your daily mail — we bet half of it is solicitations and mail-order catalogues. Save some trees and your time sorting junk mail by removing yourself from most mailing lists. Write to the Canadian Direct Marketing Association, 1 Concord Gate, Suite 607, Don Mills, Ontario, M3C 3N6. Also, be sure to tell any credit card companies you keep cards with that you want your account marked to indicate that you do not wish to have any of your personal information shared with telemarketing firms.

✔ **Limit what you can spend.** Go shopping with a small amount of cash and no plastic or cheques. That way you can only spend what little cash you have with you!

Consider Using the Credit Counselling Service (CCS)

If you having trouble with debt, one source you can turn to for information and advice is the Credit Counselling Service. Most major centres have at least one CCS branch. The offices are all non-profit. Some are run by the government, some are attached to Family Services departments, and some are independent.

(To help consumers better differentiate between the CCS and other credit counselling companies, a new organization called Credit Counselling Canada has been set up. Accreditation is just getting underway in Ontario and other provinces will soon follow. To be a member, a CCS office must be non-profit, and must also have a volunteer board of directors.)

Funding for CCS offices comes from a variety of different sources, including provincial governments, the United Way, local government, and creditors. Different offices have different funding arrangements.

The goal of the CCS is to offer no-cost (or low-cost) credit counselling. Depending on your situation, the CCS may simply give you some ideas for free about how to manage your savings better, and assist you in budgeting. The CCS also puts a strong emphasis on education to assist people in not continuing in debt-happy habits. The CCS can also contact creditors for you, set you up with a third-party mediator, or assist you in obtaining a consolidation loan.

Another way in which the CCS can help out is by working out a debt-management program. This would typically be recommended only if you were so deeply in debt you were unable to meet your minimum monthly payments and the interest was ballooning your outstanding debt. In such cases, the CCS would work out your monthly living costs, which would include your mortgage, and determine what was left over. The CCS then negotiates with creditors to see if it can get them to stop any further interest charges or perhaps even reduce your debt. You then make one monthly payment to the CCS, which distributes the money to your various creditors. Depending on your situation, you may also be asked to pay a fee that can range up to 10 percent of your payments to the CCS for its services in this case.

The usual maximum length of time you can take to repay your debts under such an arrangement is four years. If that isn't possible, bankruptcy may be a better choice. While enrolling in a debt-management program will affect your credit rating, your history is wiped clean two years after it is completed. By contrast, bankruptcy remains on your credit rating for seven years.

Dealing with Credit Mistakes

You may not know (or care), but you probably have a personal credit report. Creditors that are considering loaning you money generally examine your credit report before granting you a loan or credit line.

Many people don't realize that they have a blemish on their credit report until they are turned down for a loan or questioned by the creditor about the glitch. Although dealing with credit report problems takes up some of your time, it needn't be difficult if you know what and what not to do.

Obtain a copy of your credit report

If you're turned down for rental housing, employment, or a loan because of derogatory information on your credit report, ask the credit reporting bureaus to give you a copy of the report.

If you're applying for a mortgage or other major loan, most lenders will give you a copy of your credit report if you simply ask. And why shouldn't they if you're paying them to obtain the copy!

Reading a credit report is a challenge given all the abbreviations and jargon, so we recommend that, in addition to getting the report, you ask the lender what specific information on the report led to the denial of credit.

To get a copy of your credit rating, contact the following credit bureaus. You'll need to send them signed photocopies of two pieces of identification along with your name, address, and social insurance number.

- ✔ Equifax Canada Inc.
  Box 190, Jean-Talon Station
  Montreal, QC, HIS 2Z2
  1-800-465-7166
  www.equifax.ca
  (Equifax will fax you an application to obtain your report.)

- ✔ Trans Union Consumer Relations Centre
  P.O. Box 338, LCD1
  Hamilton, ON, L8L 7W2
  1-800-663-9980
  1-905-525-4420
  www.tuc.ca

Get others to correct their mistakes

If you obtain your credit report and find a boo-boo on it that you do not recognize as being your mistake or fault, do *not* assume that the information is correct and is simply another indicator of your faulty memory. Credit reporting bureaus and the creditors who report information to these bureaus often make mistakes.

You would hope and expect that, if a credit bureau has negative and incorrect information in your credit report and you phone them to bring the error to their attention, they would graciously and expeditiously fix the mistake. If you believe that, then you're the world's greatest optimist; perhaps you also believe that you won't have to wait in line at the post office or your local bank around noon on paydays.

Odds are you're going to have to make more phone calls or write a letter or two to fix the problems. Here's how most errors that aren't your fault are corrected:

✔ **It's someone else's credit problem.** A surprising number of personal credit report glitches are the result of someone else's negative information getting on your credit report. If the bad information on your report is completely foreign-looking to you, tell the credit bureau and also explain that you need more information because you don't recognize the creditor.

✔ **It's the creditor's mistake.** Creditors make mistakes, too. You need to write or call the creditor to get them to correct the erroneous information that they sent to the credit bureau. Phoning first usually works best (the credit bureau should be able to tell you how to reach the creditor if you don't know how). If necessary, follow up with a letter.

Whether you're speaking with a credit bureau or an actual lender, make notes of your conversations. If representatives say they can fix the problem, get their names and extensions and follow up with them if they don't deliver as promised. If you're ensnared in bureaucratic red tape, escalate the situation by speaking with a department manager.

Tell your side of the story

With a minor credit infraction, some lenders may simply ask for an explanation. Eric once had a credit report glitch that was the result of being away for several weeks and missing the payment-due date for a couple of small bills. When his proposed mortgage lender saw his late payments, all he had to do was provide a written explanation.

Chapter 6

Reducing Your Spending

- -

- -

A highly paid professional man, whom we'll call Bart, lived in one of the most prestigious communities in America. He owned his own business, drove top-of-the-line cars outfitted with all the latest toys and gadgets, and belonged to the most expensive country club in the area.

Problem was, however, that he was a workaholic and seemed to be so in order to support his spending habits. Over time, his wife tired of the life they were leading and filed for divorce. Bart called Eric for a consultation soon after his divorce was finalized. He looked beaten and depressed. Although he said he needed help making some financial decisions, what he appeared to need more than anything else was a good, long vacation and some personal counselling.

At the other spending extreme there was Justin, a young man in his mid-20s who, like Bart, was well-educated and intelligent. Justin lived a spartan lifestyle despite living in the same costly metropolitan area as Bart. Justin took a leave from his work to sail partway around the world with some friends. He was passionate about music and played in a band outside of work and found time to produce a CD. Justin was happy yet spent very little money.

Too often, especially in movies and in the media, people who make more money and have more toys are portrayed as being happier and more powerful. In our experience, we have come across far more Barts than Justins. In part because of his high income, Bart took no interest in learning how to spend smarter — as a result, he had little savings to show for all of his earnings. Justin, on the other hand, viewed living well beneath his means as both a welcome challenge and a means to an end. The better use he made of his money, the more freedom he felt he had.

No matter where you are or where you go today, you're bombarded with advertising and spending temptations. It's no surprise that the vast majority of us could spend our money more wisely.

Telling people how and where to spend their money is a risky undertaking because most people like to spend money, and most people hate to be told what to do. You'll be glad to hear that we're *not* going to tell you exactly where you must cut spending. We're simply going to give you strategies that have worked for other people. The final decision for what to cut rests solely with you. Only you can decide what's important to you and what's dispensable — should you cut out your weekly poker games or cut back on your shoe collection?

We assume throughout these recommendations that you value your time. Therefore, we're not going to tell you to scrimp and save by doing things like cutting open a tube of toothpaste so that you can use every last bit of it. And we won't tell you to have your spouse do your ironing to reduce your dry-cleaning bills (no point in having money in the bank if you lose your significant other).

Part of the reason you spend money the way you do is probably that you're busy. Therefore, the recommendations in this chapter focus on methods that don't involve a lot of time but produce significant savings. In other words, these strategies provide bang for the buck. We believe in saving wherever possible, but small change is awfully heavy to cart around — better to save the big bucks.

Four Keys to Successful Spending

For most people, spending money is a whole lot easier and more fun than earning it. Far be it for us to tell you to stop having fun and to turn into a penny-pinching, stay-at-home miser. Of course you can spend money. But there's a world of difference between spending money *carelessly* and spending money *wisely.*

Spending too much and not spending wisely puts pressure on your income and your future need to continue working. Savings dwindle, debts may accumulate, and you can't achieve your financial goals.

Sometimes, when you dive into details too quickly, you miss the big picture. So before we jump into the specific areas where you can trim your budget, here are the four overall keys to successful spending. These four principles run through most of the recommendations coming up in this chapter.

Live within your means

Spending too much is a *relative* problem. Two people can each spend $30,000 per year yet have drastically different financial circumstances. How? Suppose that one of them takes home $40,000 annually, and the other takes home $25,000. The $40,000 after-tax earner saves $10,000 each year. The $25,000 earner accumulates $5,000 of new debt (or spends that amount from prior savings). Spend within your means.

Don't let others and their spending habits dictate yours. Certain people — you know who they are — bring out the big spender in you. Do something else with them besides shopping. If you can't find any other activity to share with them, try shopping with limited cash and no credit cards. That way, you can't overspend on impulse.

How much you can safely spend while still working toward your financial goals depends on what your goals are and where you are financially. Chapter 3 assists you with figuring how much you should be saving and, therefore, what you can afford to spend to accomplish your financial goals.

Find the best values

You can find high quality and low cost in the same product. Conversely, paying a high price is no guarantee that you're getting high quality. Cars are a good example. Whether you're buying a subcompact, sports car, minivan, or luxury four-door sedan, some cars are more fuel-efficient and cost less to maintain than rivals that carry the same sticker price.

And when you evaluate the cost of a product or service, you need to think in terms of total, long-term costs. Suppose that you're comparing the purchase of two used cars: the Solid Sedan, which costs $15,000, and the Clunker Convertible, which weighs in at $12,000. On the surface, the convertible appears cheaper. However, the price that you pay for a car is but a small portion of what a car ultimately costs you. If the convertible is more costly to operate, maintain, and insure over the years, it could end up costing you much more. Sometimes paying more upfront for a higher-quality product or service ends up saving you money in the long run.

Those who are selling particular products and services may initially appear to have your best interests at heart if they steer you toward buying something that isn't costly. However, you may be in for a rude awakening once you discover the ongoing service, maintenance, and other fees you'll face in the years ahead. Salespeople are generally trained to pitch you a lower-cost product if you indicate that's what you're after.

We urge you to be especially careful when shopping via the Internet for the supposed purpose of saving money. You won't have much difficulty finding relatively low advertised prices on the Internet. However, many people overlook shipping costs and the cost of their computer equipment and monthly Internet service fees when weighing how great a deal they're really getting by shopping online. Also, what about the possibility that you're not going to be happy with the product once it's delivered? Then, you're probably stuck with paying the shipping costs back to the online retailer, which you hope is still in business, not to mention the hassle and inconvenience of returning the product.

Don't waste money on brand names

Don't compromise on quality, especially where the quality is important to you. But don't be snookered into believing that brand-name products are better or worth a substantially higher price. Be suspicious of companies that spend gobs on image-oriented advertising. Why? Heavy advertising costs many dollars, and, as a consumer of those companies' products and services, you're paying for all that advertising.

All successful companies do some advertising — advertising is cost-effective and good business if it brings in enough new business. But consider the products and services and the claims that companies make.

Does a cola beverage really taste better if it's "The real thing" or "The choice of a new generation"? Consider all the silly labels and fluffy marketing of colas. Blind taste testing demonstrates little if any difference between the expensive brand-name products and the cheaper, less heavily advertised ones.

Now, if you can't live without your Coca-Cola or Pepsi and think that these products are head and shoulders above the rest, drink them to your heart's content. But question the importance of the name and image in the products you buy. Companies spend a lot of money creating and cultivating an image, which has zero real impact on how their products taste or perform. Remember that the pundit who quipped "A good ad makes your beer taste better" was joking!

"Branding" is used in many fields to sell overpriced, mediocre products and services to consumers. Take the lowly can of paint. Tests show some differences among different brands of paint. However, when you can buy high-quality paints for about $20 to $30 a gallon, do you really think that spending $50 or more per gallon on a can of paint blessed with the name of Ralph Lauren or Martha Stewart makes it better?

D/L Laboratories, a testing firm, compared these snooty paints to $20-per-gallon high-quality alternatives and found little difference, at least no difference that was worth paying for. In fact, one of the "gourmet" paints splattered more, had a less uniform sheen, didn't cover the surface as well, was more prone to run when applied, and emitted a high level of volatile organic compounds! Some other snooty brands didn't fare much better. As people in the trade can tell you, if you find a particular colour of paint you like in a highbrow line, thanks to computer-based matching you can match it and buy it in a high-quality but far less costly line.

Get your money back

Take a look around your home for items you've never used. Odds are you have some, perhaps many. Returning such items to their retail origin can be cathartic. Doing so reduces your home's clutter and puts more money in your pocket.

Also, consider the last several times that you bought a product or service and didn't get what was promised. What did you do about it? Most people do nothing and let the derelict company off the hook. Why? We think there are several common reasons:

- **Low standards.** We've come to expect shoddy service and merchandise due to the common lousy experiences we've had.

- **Conflict avoidance.** Most people shun confrontation. It makes us tense and anxious and churns our stomachs.

- **Most companies don't make it easy for complainers to get their money back or obtain other satisfaction.** To get restitution from some companies, you need the tenacity and determination of a pit bull.

You can increase your odds of getting what you expect when you spend your money by doing business with companies that:

- **Have fair return policies.** Don't purchase any product or service until you understand the company's return policy. Be especially wary of buying from companies that charge hefty "restocking" fees for returned merchandise or that simply don't allow returns at all. Reputable companies will offer full refunds and won't make you take store credit (although taking credit is fine if you're sure you'll use it soon and the company will still be around).

- **Can provide good references.** Suppose you're going to install a fence on your property and will for the first time be speaking with fencing contractors. You can sift out many inferior firms by asking each contractor you interview for at least three references of people in your local area who have had a fence installed in the past year or two.

- **Are committed to the type of product or service.** Suppose your chosen fencing contractor does a great job, and now that you're in the market for new gutters on your home, that same contractor says no problem, he does gutters, too. Although the path of least resistance would be for you to simply hire the same contractor for your gutters, you should inquire about how many gutters the contractor has installed and also interview some other firms that specialize in such work. Your fencing contractor might have only done a handful of gutter jobs and may not know as much about such work.

The Better Business Bureau is not objective or independent

The Better Business Bureau (BBB) states that its mission is "to promote and foster the highest ethical relationship between businesses and the public." The reality of a typical consumer's experience dealing with the BBB doesn't live up to the BBB's marketing.

"They don't go after local established businesses — they are funded by these same businesses. The BBB certainly has a good public relations image, better than what is warranted. They don't do all that much for consumers," says consumer advocate Ralph Nader.

"It's a business trade organization and each local BBB is basically independent like a franchise. By and large, when somebody has a problem with a company and they fill out a complaint form with the BBB, if the company is a member of the BBB, there's ample evidence that consumers often end up not being satisfied. The BBB protects their members," says John Bear, an author of consumer advocacy books, including *Send This Jerk the Bedbug Letter: How Companies, Politicians, and the Mass Media Deal With Complaints and How to Be a More Effective Complainer* (Ten Speed Press).

Particularly problematic among the BBB's pro-business practices are the company reports the BBB keeps on file. Even when a legitimate complaint like yours comes in, the BBB will consider it satisfactorily resolved even though you're quite unhappy and the company is clearly not working to satisfy the problems for which it is responsible.

Bear also cites examples of some truly troubling BBB episodes. In one case, he says, a diploma mill (Columbia State University) was being run in Louisiana, and the company was a member of the local BBB. "When complaints started coming in, the BBB's response was always that the company met their standards and that the complaints were resolved. The reality was that the complaints weren't satisfactorily resolved and it took about two years until complaints reached into the hundreds for the BBB to finally cancel the diploma mill's membership and give out a bland statement about complaints. Two months later, the FBI raided the company. Millions of consumers' dollars were lost because the BBB didn't do its job," says Bear.

The president of a South Florida BBB, the fifth largest in the U.S., according to Bear, was ultimately imprisoned for taking bribes from companies in exchange for maintaining favourable reports on file.

The truth about the BBB is sad, because as consumer protection agencies are being cut back and dissatisfied consumers are being shunted to the BBB, more people are in for unsatisfactory experiences dealing with an organization that does not go to bat for them.

Following the guidelines should greatly diminish your chances of having unhappy outcomes with products or services you buy. And here's another important tip: Whenever possible, pay with a credit card. Doing so enables you to dispute a charge within the first 60 days and gives you more leverage for getting your money back.

Should you find yourself not making progress trying to get compensation for a lousy product or service, here's what we recommend that you do:

- **Document.** Taking notes whenever you talk to someone at a company makes good sense to validate your case down the road should problems develop. However, how realistic is it for any of us to take notes every time we buy a product or service? Obviously, the bigger the purchase and the more you have at stake, the more carefully you should document what you've been told and promised. In many cases, though, you probably won't start carefully noting each conversation until a conflict develops. Keep copies of companies' marketing literature, because such documents often make promises or claims that companies fail to live up to in practice.

- **Escalate.** Some front-line personnel either aren't capable of resolving disputes or lack the authority to do so. No matter the cause, speak with a department supervisor and continue escalating from there. If you're still not making progress, lodge a complaint to whatever government regulatory agency (if any) oversees such companies. Also, be sure to tell your friends and colleagues not to do business with the company (and let the company know that you're doing this until your complaint is resolved to your satisfaction).

- **Litigate.** Okay, we're half joking here — after all, you're not a big corporation with deep pockets! However, if all else fails and it's worth your time, consider taking the matter to small claims court if the company continues to be unresponsive. The maximum dollar limit that you may recover varies by province but is usually a few thousand dollars. For larger amounts than are allowed in small claims court in your province, you could, of course, hire a lawyer and pursue the traditional legal channels. You could end up throwing away more of your time and money. Mediation and arbitration are generally better for you than following through on a lawsuit.

Eliminate fat

If you want to reduce your overall spending by, say, 10 percent, you could just cut all of your current expenditures by 10 percent. Or you can reach your 10 percent goal by cutting some categories a lot and others not at all. You need to set priorities and make choices about what you can and can't live without.

What you spend your money on is sometimes a matter of habit rather than what you really want or value. For example, some people shop at whatever stores are closest because they know where the stores are; they never bother to look elsewhere.

Eliminating fat doesn't necessarily mean cutting back on your purchases. Buying in bulk is a good example. Some stores specialize in selling larger packages or quantities of a product at a lower price because they save money on the packaging and handling. You save money by buying in bulk. And even though that 10-kg bag of rice means more cash upfront than the little box of Uncle Ben's, every meal from now on that you make from the 10-kg bag will be a great deal cheaper than the meal out of the box would have been. (If you're single, shop with a friend and split the bulk purchases.)

Avoid buying on credit

As we discuss in Chapters 4 and 5, buying items that depreciate — such as cars, clothing, and vacations — on credit is hazardous to your long-term financial health. Buy today only what you can afford today. If you'll be forced to carry a debt for months or years on end, then you can't really afford what you're buying on credit today.

Without a doubt, "renting to own" is the most expensive way to buy. Here's how it works. You see a huge ad blaring "$12.95 for a VCR!" Well, there's a big hitch: That's $12.95 per week, for many weeks. When all is said and done and paid, buying a $200 VCR through a rent-to-own store costs a typical buyer more than $750!

Welcome to the world of rent-to-own stores, which offer cash-poor consumers the ability to lease consumer items and, at the end of the lease, an option to buy. Many items can be bought on this basis. Although this may be more of a troubling sign of the times, increasing numbers of stores are reported to offer rent-to-own engagement rings! One rent-to-own store manager said, "We do get some people with cold feet."

If you think paying an 18-percent interest rate on a credit card is expensive, imagine what you'll think of renting to own when we tell you that the effective interest rate charged on many purchases exceeds 100 percent and in some cases is 200 percent or more! Renting to own makes buying on a credit card look like a deal.

We're not sharing this information with you to encourage your buying on credit cards but to point out what a rip-off renting to own is. Such stores prey on cashless consumers who either can't get credit cards or don't understand how expensive renting to own really is.

Consumer credit is expensive and reinforces a bad habit: spending more than you can afford.

Strategies for Reducing Your Spending

Please keep in mind as you read through the following ideas that some of these strategies will make sense for you, and some of them won't. Start your spending reduction plan with the ones that come easily first. Work your way through them. Keep a list of the options that are more challenging for you — ones that require more of a sacrifice but that you can make work if necessary to achieve your spending and savings goals.

No matter which of the ideas in this chapter you choose for yourself, rest assured that keeping your budget lean and mean pays enormous dividends. After you implement a spending reduction strategy, you'll reap the benefits for

TIP

Budgeting to save more money

When most people hear the word *budgeting*, they usually think unpleasant thoughts — and, much like the word *dieting*, rightfully so. But budgeting can help you move from knowing how much you spend on various things to successfully reducing your spending.

The first step in the process of budgeting, or planning your future spending, is to analyze where your current spending is going (refer to Chapter 4). After you do that, calculate how much more you'd like to save each month. Then comes the harder part: deciding where to make cuts in your spending.

Suppose that you're currently not saving any of your monthly income and that you want to save 10 percent. If you can save and invest money through a tax-sheltered Registered Retirement Savings Plan, you don't actually need to cut your spending by 10 percent to reach a savings goal of 10 percent (of your gross income).

When you make a tax-deductible contribution to an RRSP or other tax-sheltered retirement plan, you reduce your federal and provincial taxes. If you're a moderate-income earner paying, say, 40 percent in federal and provincial taxes on your marginal income, you actually need to

reduce your spending by only 6 percent to save 10 percent. The "other" 4 percent of savings comes from the lowering of your taxes. (The higher your tax bracket, the less you need to cut your spending to reach a particular savings goal.)

So to boost your savings rate to 10 percent, go through your current spending, category by category, until you come up with enough proposed cuts to reduce your spending by 6 percent. Make your cuts in those areas that will be the least painful and where you're getting the least value from your current level of spending. Even if you don't have access to a tax-deductible retirement plan, budgeting still involves the same process.

Rather than examining your current expenses and making cuts from that starting point, another method of budgeting involves starting completely from scratch. Ask yourself how much you'd like to be spending on different categories. The advantage of this approach is that it doesn't allow your current spending levels to constrain your thinking. You'll most likely be amazed at the discrepancies between what you think you should be spending and what you actually are spending in certain categories.

years to come. Take a look at Figure 6-1: For every $1,000 that you can shave from your annual spending (that's just $83 per month), see how much more money you'll have down the road. (This chart assumes that you are in a 40 percent marginal tax bracket, that you invest your new-found savings in a tax-favoured Registered Retirement Savings Plan, and that you average 10 percent on your investments. You've stopped spending $1,000 in after-tax dollars, so that frees up $1,667 of your pre-tax income that can be diverted into your RRSP without being taxed — see Chapter 7 for information on tax brackets.)

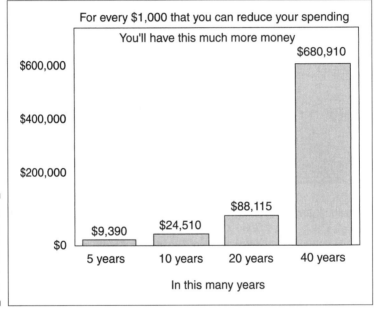

Figure 6-1: Reducing your spending can yield large investment sums.

Food

One way to reduce your food expenditures is to stop eating. However, this tends to make you weak and dizzy, so it's probably not a viable long-term strategy. The following culinary strategies will keep you on your feet — and perhaps even improve your health — for less money.

Buy from wholesale superstores

Superstores such as Costco, The Great Canadian Superstore, and the Great Canadian Wholesale Club enable you to buy groceries in bulk at wholesale prices. And, contrary to popular perception, you *don't* have to buy 1,000 rolls of toilet paper at once — just 24.

We've done price comparisons between these kinds of stores and retail grocery stores and have found that wholesalers sometimes charge 20 to 40 percent less for the exact same stuff — all without the hassle of clipping coupons or hunting for which store has the best price on crackers this month!

In addition to saving you lots of money, buying in bulk means that you make fewer shopping trips. You'll have more supplies around your humble abode — so there is less need to eat out (which is costly) or make trips to the local corner grocer, who may be really nice but who charges you out the wazoo.

Perishables run the risk of living up to their name, so don't buy what you can't use. Repackage bulk packs into smaller quantities for the freezer if possible. If you're single, shop with a friend or two and split the order.

Be careful shopping at the warehouse clubs — you might be tempted to buy things you don't really need. These stores carry all sorts of items, including wide-screen TVs, computers, furniture, clothing, complete sets of baseball cards, and giant canisters of M&Ms and biscotti — beware! Try not to make impulse purchases, and be especially careful when you have kids in tow.

Some of these stores charge a small membership fee and are, frankly, somewhat of a hassle to join. Costco, for example, charges $40 per year and asks for proof that you're a small-business owner or manager or that you work for a non-profit health-care organization, utility, bank, trust company, airline, the government, or the media. You can also join if you hold a professional licence or are a member of a credit union.

The reason you need to jump through these hoops is that if *anyone* could join the warehouse stores, retailers who sell similar merchandise would be upset. Anyone could get the better deals that the warehouse clubs pass on from manufacturers. That's why people with a potential business reason can join.

The reality, though, is that if you really want to join, you can. Many community organizations that you may belong to, such as the YMCA/YWCA or Big Brothers/Big Sisters, can often get you a membership. A small-business owner whom you know well can sponsor you. Or you can shop with a friend who's a member.

Eat out more frugally

Eating meals out or getting take-out can be a time-saver but can rack up big bills if done too often and lavishly. Eating out is a luxury — think of it as hiring someone to shop, cook, and clean up for you. Of course, some people hate to cook or don't have the time, space, or energy to do much in the kitchen. If this is you, choose restaurants carefully and order from the menu selectively. Here are a couple of tips:

✔ **Avoid beverages, especially alcohol.** Most restaurants make big profits on beverages. Drink water instead. (Water is also healthful and reduces the likelihood of your wanting a nap after a big meal.)

 ✔ **Order vegetarian.** Vegetarian dishes, including pasta and rice dishes, generally cost less than meat-based entrees (and are generally healthier for you).

We don't want to be killjoys. We're not saying that you should live on bread and water. You can have dessert — heck, have some wine, too! But perhaps not every time. Try eating appetizers and dessert at home, where they're a lot less expensive (especially if you follow our advice on shopping for food).

Shelter

Housing and all the costs associated with it (utilities, furniture, appliances, and, if you're a homeowner, maintenance and repairs) can gobble a large chunk of your monthly income. We're not suggesting that you live in an igloo (even though they're probably less costly and more energy-efficient), but people often overlook common opportunities to save money in this category.

Mom was right about eating those vegetables

Not only is meat expensive, but it is also coming under increasing scrutiny as being bad for your health. In a landmark report titled "The Surgeon General's Report on Nutrition and Health" (produced under former U.S. Surgeon General C. Everett Koop, M.D.), reliance on a meat- and dairy-based diet — with its fat and cholesterol — was found to be the cause of the majority of premature deaths in the United States. In fact, five out of the top ten causes of death — heart disease, certain types of cancer, stroke, diabetes, and arteriosclerosis — are caused largely by poor diets.

In developing countries that are poorer economically, people eat mainly grains, beans, and vegetables and have significantly lower rates of heart disease and diet-related cancers, such as cancer of the prostate and colon.

Meat is expensive, so the less meat you eat, the more money you save. Even if you choose to merely reduce your meat consumption rather than eliminate it, you can still save significant dough. Should you decide to eliminate meat from your diet, don't try to shift from burgers, pork chops, and meat loaf to tofu and sprouts overnight. Make changes in your diet gradually.

Besides saving you money and bolstering your health, a vegetarian diet is also friendlier to the environment. Raising cattle requires a great deal more land and water than growing vegetables does. Here's a tidbit sure to liven up a dull cocktail party conversation: Livestock also produce a great deal of flatulence, which adds more methane to the atmosphere. 100 million tons of the world's annual methane emissions — 20 percent of the total — are from cattle!

Don't take rent for granted

Rent can take up a sizeable chunk of your monthly take-home pay. Many people consider rent to be a fixed and inflexible part of their expenses. It's not. Here are some things you can do to cut it down in size:

- ✔ **Move to a lower-cost rental.** Of course, a lower-cost rental may not be as nice — it may be smaller or lack a private parking spot or be in a less popular locale. Make the trade-off and shave $50 to $100 or more off your monthly rent. Don't forget: The less you spend renting, the more you can save toward buying your own place. Just be sure to factor in all the costs of a new location, including possibly higher commuting costs.

- ✔ **Share a rental.** Living alone has some benefits, but financially speaking, it's a luxury. Rent a larger place with roommates. Your rental costs should go way down, and you'll get more home for your rental dollars. You have to be in a sharing mood, though. Roommates can be a hassle at times but can also be a plus — you meet all sorts of new people and have someone else to blame if the kitchen's a mess.

- ✔ **Negotiate your rental increases.** Every year, like clockwork, your landlord bumps up your rent a certain percentage. If your local rental market is soft or your living quarters are deteriorating, stand up for yourself! You have more leverage and power than you probably realize. A smart landlord doesn't want to lose good tenants who pay rent on time. Filling vacancies takes time and money. State your case: You've been a responsible tenant, and your research shows comparable rentals going for less. Crying poor may help, too. At the very least, if you can't stave off the rent increase, maybe you can wrangle some improvements to the place.

- ✔ **Buy rather than rent.** Purchasing your own place can be costly, yes, but in the long run, owning should be cheaper than renting, and you'll have something to show for it in the end. If you purchase real estate with a mortgage spread — *amortized* — over 25 years, your mortgage payment (which is your biggest ownership expense) will bounce around a certain level, depending on interest rates each time you renew. Only your property taxes, maintenance, utilities, and insurance costs are likely to steadily rise due to inflation.

  As a renter, your entire monthly housing cost can rise with increases in the cost of living (unless you are the beneficiary of a rent-controlled dwelling). See Chapter 15 to learn about buying real estate, even if you're short on cash.

Save on homeowner expenses

As every homeowner knows, houses suck money. You should be especially careful to watch your money in this area of your budget.

Saving on your phone bill

Telephone expenses are a good example of not needing to reduce your usage to save money. Just adjust when you place your calls. In most areas, the most expensive time to place long-distance calls is weekdays between 8 a.m. and 6 p.m. From 6 p.m. to 11 p.m. is cheaper, and the cheapest time to call is late at night (usually 11 p.m. to 8 a.m.), which can save you 50–70 percent (and as a bonus, you may get the thrill of waking up the other party). This bargain rate is also available all weekend, usually beginning after 11 p.m. Friday night and ending Sunday at 6 p.m.

You may be able to save money on your toll calls by switching companies. Despite (or perhaps because of) the millions of dollars that Bell and the other traditional phone companies pour into advertising to persuade you that their quality is better and prices are comparable, consider moving to Primus (800-670-2266), Sprint (800-980-5464) or Distributel (310-1112) if you live in Ontario or Quebec. Quality is virtually the same from company to company. Check with your long-distance provider to be sure that you're on the lowest-cost calling program given the patterns of your calls.

Sometimes sending a thoughtful letter is cheaper, more appreciated, and longer lasting than placing a phone call. Just block out an hour, grab a pen and paper, and rediscover the lost art form of letter writing. Formulating your thoughts on paper can be clarifying and therapeutic to boot. Computer users may find that they save money as well by sending e-mail.

✔ **Know what you can afford.** Don't make the mistake of overstretching when buying a home. Whether you're on the verge of buying your first home or trading up to a more costly property, crunch some realistic numbers before you jump. When too little money is left over for your other needs and wants — such as taking trips, eating out, enjoying hobbies, or saving for retirement — your new dream house may become a financial prison.

Calculate how much you can afford to spend monthly on a home by figuring your other needs first. (Doing the exercises in Chapter 4 about where you're spending your money and in Chapter 3 about saving for retirement will help.)

Although real estate can be a good long-term investment, you can end up pouring a large portion of your discretionary dollars into your home. In addition to decorating and remodelling, some people feel the need to trade up to a bigger home every few years. Of course, after they're in their new home, the remodelling and renovation cycle simply begins again, which costs even more money. Appreciate what you have and remember that homes are to live in, not museums for display. If you have children, why waste a lot of money on expensive furnishings that take up valuable space and require you to constantly nag your kids to tread carefully? And don't covet — the world will always have people with bigger, nicer houses and toys than you have.

✔ **Rent out a room.** Since selling your home to buy a less expensive place can be a big hassle, consider taking in a tenant to reduce your housing expenses. Check out the renter thoroughly: Get references, run a credit report, and talk about ground rules and expectations before sharing your space. Don't forget to check with your insurance company to see whether your homeowner's policy needs adjustments to cover potential liability from renting.

✔ **Appeal your property-tax assessment.** You may be able to save money by appealing your assessment if you bought during a period when housing prices were higher in your area than they are now. Also, if you live in a region of the country where your assessment is based upon how the local assessor valued the property (rather than what you paid for your home), your home may be over-assessed. Check with your local assessor's office for the appeals procedure to follow. You may be able to get a reduction by proving that your property is worth less today than when you bought it or that the assessor incorrectly valued your property. In the first case, an appraiser's recent evaluation of your property will do — you may already have one if you took out a mortgage with a new lender or refinanced your mortgage recently. In the latter case, review how the assessor valued your property compared with similar ones nearby — mistakes happen.

✔ **Reduce utility costs.** Sometimes you have to spend money to save money. Old refrigerators, for example, can waste a lot of electricity. Insulate to save on heating and air-conditioning bills. Install water flow regulators in showerheads and toilet bowls. When planting your yard, don't select water-guzzling plants, and keep your lawn area reasonable. Even if you don't live in an area susceptible to droughts, why waste water (which isn't free)? If you water your lawn, install a barrel that saves run-off water from your roof. Recycle — recycling means less garbage, which translates into lower trash bills and benefits the environment by reducing landfill.

Transportation

Canada is a car-driven society. In most other countries, cars are a luxury. More than 90 percent of the people in the rest of the world can't afford a new car. If more people in Canada thought of cars as a luxury, Canadians might have far fewer financial problems (and accidents). Cars not only pollute the air and clog the highways but also cost you a bundle. Purchasing the best car you can and using it wisely can save you big dollars. So can using other transportation alternatives.

Contrary to advertising slogans, cars are not built to last — car manufacturers don't want you to stick with the same car year after year. New models are constantly introduced with new features and styling changes. Getting a new set of wheels every few years is an expensive luxury.

Don't try to keep up with the Joneses as they show off their new cars every year — for all you know, they're running themselves into financial ruin just trying to impress you. Let your neighbours admire you for your thriftiness and wisdom instead.

Research before you buy a car

When you buy a car, not only do you pay the initial sticker price, but you're also on the hook for gas, insurance, registration fees, maintenance, and repairs. Don't compare simple sticker prices; think about total, long-term costs of ownership.

Speaking of total costs, remember that you are also trusting your life to the car. With about 3,500 Canadians killed in auto accidents annually, safety should be an important consideration as well.

The Consumer Reports Buying Guide summarizes all the latest information on cars and includes a list of the most reliable used cars in various price categories. For a detailed assessment of defects, repair costs, and safety ratings, check out the annual *Lemon-Aid* books put out by Phil Edmonston. He has separate books dealing with new cars, used cars, new trucks and vans, and used trucks and vans (including minivans). The books also detail average resale prices by model and year. For you data jocks, *The Complete Car Cost Guide* (published by Intellichoice) is packed with information about all categories of ownership costs, warranties, and dealer costs (costs are in U.S. dollars, however). The guide rates new cars based on total ownership costs. But can you *really* afford a new car?

Buy your car with cash

The main reason people end up spending more than they can afford on a car is that they finance it. As we discuss in Chapter 1 and elsewhere in this book, you should avoid borrowing money for consumption purchases, especially for items that depreciate in value like cars. A car is most definitely *not* an investment.

In most situations, leasing is even more expensive than borrowing money to buy a car. Leasing is like a long-term car rental. We all know how well rental cars get treated — well, leased cars are treated just as well, which is one of the reasons leasing is so costly.

Unfortunately, the practice of leasing cars or buying them on credit is increasingly becoming the norm in our society. This is certainly attributable to a lot of misinformation spread by car dealers and, in some cases, the media. Consider the magazine article entitled "Rewards of Car Leasing." Compared to buying, the article claims, leasing is a great deal. Placed immediately next to the article were ads for auto dealers advertising auto leasing. The magazine, by the way, is *free* to subscribers — which means that 100 percent of its revenue comes from advertisers such as auto dealers. Also be aware that because of the influence of advertising (and ignorance), leasing is widely endorsed on Internet sites that purport to provide information on cars.

Besides those "low monthly payments," one of the main reasons many people end up leasing is because doing the math to compare the cost to buying with cash or a loan is confusing! If you want to do the numbers, there are programs available to help you through the comparison. One user-friendly piece of software we've looked at is called the CarCalculator. You can check it out on-line at `www.b4usign.com`, or by calling 1-877-248-7446.

Replace high-cost cars

Maybe you've realized by now that your car is too expensive to operate because of insurance, gas, and maintenance costs. Or maybe you bought too much car — people who lease or borrow money to buy a car frequently buy a far more expensive car than they can realistically afford.

But I can't buy a new car for cash!

"Come on!" you may be thinking, "How can I and most wage earners today afford to buy a new car for cash — who has that kind of dough sitting around?!"

Some people feel that it's unreasonable to expect them to buy a new car using cash. After all, many publications, which not uncoincidentally derive great advertising revenue from auto dealers and lenders, effectively endorse and encourage loaning and leasing to buy a car.

If you knew us, you'd know that we're reasonable kinda guys. Believe us, we're trying to look out for your best long-term financial interests. Please consider the following:

✔ **If you lack sufficient cash to buy a new car, we say *"don't buy a new car!"*** Most of the world's population can't even afford a car, let alone a new one! Buy a car that you can afford — which for most people is not a new one.

✔ **Don't fall for the new-car-buying rationalization that says that buying a used car means lots of maintenance, repair expenses, and problems.** Do your homework and buy a good, used car and have the best of both worlds. A good used car costs less to buy and should cost you less to operate thanks to lower insurance costs.

✔ **A fancy car is not needed to impress people for business purposes.** Some people we know say that they absolutely must drive a brand-spanking nice new car to set the right impression for business purposes. We're not going to tell you how to manage your career, but we will ask you to consider that if clients and others see you driving an expensive new car, they may think that you spend money wastefully or that you're getting rich off of them!

Nothing says that you're stuck with it until the bitter end. *Dump* your expensive car and get something more financially manageable. The sooner you switch, the more money you'll save. Getting rid of a car on a lease is more of a challenge, but it can be done. We know of one person who, when he lost his job and needed to slash expenses, convinced the dealer (by writing a letter to the owner) to take the leased car back.

Keep cars to a minimum

We've seen households that have one car per person — four people, four cars! Some people have a "weekend" car that they use only on days off! Maintaining two or more cars for most households is an expensive extravagance. Try to find ways to make do with fewer cars.

One of the ways to move beyond the confines of a car is to ride buses or trains or carpool to work. Some employers give incentives for taking public transit to work, and some cities and regions offer assistance in setting up vanpools or carpools along popular routes. By leaving the driving to someone else, you can catch up on reading or just relax on the way to and from work. And you're doing your share to cut down on pollution.

When you're considering where to live and the cost of living in different areas, don't forget to consider commuting costs. One advantage of living close to work, or at least close to public transit systems, is that you may be able to make do with fewer cars in your household or with no car at all.

Buy commuter passes

In many areas, you can purchase train, bus, or subway passes to reduce the cost of commuting. Many toll bridges also have booklets of tickets that you can buy at a discount. Some booths don't advertise that they offer these plans — maybe as a strategy to keep revenues up.

Buy regular unleaded gas

A number of studies have shown that "superduperultrapremium" gasoline is not worth the extra expense. Also, don't use credit cards to buy your gas if you have to pay a higher price to do so.

Service your car regularly

Sure, servicing your car (for example, changing the oil every 8,000 kilometres) costs money, but it saves you dough in the long run by extending the operating life of the car. Servicing your car also reduces the chances that your car will crap out in the middle of nowhere, which requires a humongous towing charge to a service station. Even worse is stalling on the highway during peak rush hour and having thousands of angry commuters stuck behind you.

Clothing and accessories

Given the amount of money that some people spend on clothing and related accessories, we've come to believe that people in nudist colonies must be great savers! But you probably live among the clothed mainstream of Canadian society, so here's a short list of economizing ideas:

- **Avoid dry-cleanables.** When you buy clothing, try to stick with cottons and machine-washable synthetics rather than wools or silks that require dry cleaning. Check labels before you buy stuff. Despite his tremendous business success, Jack Bogle, founder of the thrifty U.S. Vanguard Group of mutual funds, wore wool ties to work. He proudly declared that his ties were more *efficient,* and he is right. They last longer and require less cleaning than silk ties!

- **Don't chase the latest fashions.** Fashion designers and retailers are constantly working to tempt you to buy more. Don't do it. Ignore publications that pronounce this season's look. In most cases, you simply don't need to buy racks of new clothes or an entire new wardrobe yearly. If your clothes are not lasting at least five or even ten years, you're probably tossing them before their time or buying low durability clothing.

  Fashion, as defined by what people wear, changes quite slowly. In fact, the classics don't ever go out of style. If you want the effect of a new wardrobe every year, store last year's purchases away next year and then bring them out the year after! Or rotate your clothing inventory every third year. Set your own fashion standards. Buy basic, buy classic — don't let fashion gurus be your guide, or you'll have the biggest wardrobe in the poorhouse.

- **Minimize accessories.** Shoes, jewellery, handbags, and the like can gobble large amounts of money. Again, how many of these accessory items do you really need? The answer is probably very few, and each one should last many years.

Go to your closet or jewellery box and tally up the loot. What else could you have done with all that cash? See things you regret buying or forgot you even had? Don't make the same mistake again. Have a garage sale if you have a lot of stuff that you don't want.

Debt repayment

In Chapter 5, we discuss strategies to reduce the cost of carrying consumer debt. The *best* way to reduce the costs of such debt is to avoid it in the first place when you're making consumption purchases. You can avoid consumer debt by eliminating your access to credit or by limiting your purchase of consumer items that you can pay off each month. Remember, borrow only for long-term investments. (Refer to Chapter 1 for more information.)

Don't keep a credit card that charges you an annual fee, especially if you pay your balance in full each month. Many no-fee credit cards exist — and some even offer you a benefit for using them:

- ✔ **Bank of Montreal MasterCard (800-263-2263)** gives you two choices. You can earn Air Miles, or opt to bank up to 5 percent of your purchases — to a maximum of $500 a year for five years — to put towards the purchase of a first home.

- ✔ **CIBC Classic (800-465-4653**) is a "dividend" card that offers a credit of 0.25 percent on the first $1,500 you spend annually, 0.5 percent on the next $1,500, and 1.0 percent on any amount beyond $3,000. The Club Z card lets you earn points that can be used for discounts at Zellers stores.

- ✔ **TD VISA (800-983-8472)** offers a GM VISA card lets you earn 5 percent of your charges towards the purchase of a GM-manufactured vehicle. There's a limit of $500 in credits a year, and a total maximum of $3,500. The TD Green VISA is a basic no-fee card.

- ✔ **Royal Bank (800-668-9700) and Scotiabank (800-387-6556)** both offer different versions of the Classic VISA. One option is a low-interest-rate card, which usually comes with an annual fee. If you're able to regularly pay off your balance, you're likely better off with the no-annual-fee card that comes with a higher interest rate.

Only consider most of the above cards if you pay your balance in full each month, because these cards levy high interest rates for balances carried month to month. There's not much point in earning a small reward only to have it negated by greater interest charges.

If you have a credit card that charges an annual fee, try calling the company and saying that you want to cancel the card because you can get a competitor's card without an annual fee. Some banks will agree to waive the fee on the spot. Some require you to call back yearly to cancel the fee — a hassle that can be avoided by getting a true no-fee card.

Some cards that charge an annual fee and offer credits toward a purchase, such as a car or airline ticket, may be worth your while if you pay your credit card bill in full each month and charge $10,000 or more annually. *Note:* Be careful, however, because some people are tempted to charge more on a card that rewards them for more purchases. Spending more than you would otherwise to rack up bonuses defeats the purpose of getting the credits.

Indulgences

Having fun, taking time out for R & R, and lavishing gifts on those you love can be money well spent. But in these areas, financial extravagance can wreck an otherwise good budget.

Gifts

Think about how you approach buying gifts throughout the year — and especially during the holidays. We know people who spend so much money on credit cards during the winter holidays that it takes them until late spring or summer to pay their debts off!

Although we don't want to deny your loved ones gifts from the heart — or you the pleasure of giving them — spend wisely. Homemade gifts are less costly to the giver and may be dearer to recipients. Many children actually love durable, classic, basic toys that aren't necessarily advertised on Saturday morning TV. If the TV commercials dictate your kids' desires, maybe it's time to toss the TV or set better rules for what the kids are allowed to watch.

Perhaps because we don't like to feel cheap when buying a gift, some people forget their thrifty shopping habits when gift buying. As with other purchases you make, however, careful attention to where and what you buy can save you significant dollars. And don't make the mistake of equating the value of a gift with its dollar cost.

And, here's a good suggestion for getting rid of those old, unwanted gifts — a "white elephant" gift exchange: Everyone brings a wrapped, unwanted gift from the past and exchanges it with someone else. Once the gifts are opened, trading is allowed.

Entertainment

Entertainment doesn't have to cost a great deal of money if you adjust your expectations. Especially in metropolitan areas, many movies, theatres, and museums offer discount prices on certain days and times. Same goes for restaurants.

Cultivate some interests and hobbies that are free or low-cost. Seeing friends, reading, hiking, and playing sports can be good for your finances as well as your health.

Vacations

For many people, vacations are a luxury. For others, regular vacations are essential parts of their routine. Regardless of how you recharge your batteries, remember that vacations are not investments, so you shouldn't borrow through credit cards to finance your travels. After all, how relaxed will you feel when you have to pay all those bills?

Try vacations that are shorter and closer to home. Have you been to a provincial or national park recently? Take a vacation at home and see the sights in your local area. Great places probably exist within 300 kilometres of you that you've always wanted to see but haven't visited for one reason or another. Or just block out some time and do what your average cat does: Take lots of naps and just hang out around your home.

When you do travel far and are heading for a popular destination, travel during the off-season for the best deals on airfares and hotels. Keep an eye out for discounts and "bought-but-unable-to-use" tickets advertised in your local paper. A number of Internet sites — including those of the airlines themselves — can help you find low-cost travel options as well. Seniors generally qualify for special fares at most airlines — ask the airline what programs it offers.

Also, be sure to shop around even when working with a travel agent. Travel agents work on commission, so they may not work hard to find you the best deals. Tour packages, when they meet your interests and needs, can also save you money. If you have flexible travel plans, doing contract work for courier services can cut your travel costs significantly (but make sure that the company is reputable).

Personal care

You have to take care of yourself, but as with anything else there are ways to do it that are expensive, and there are ways that can save you money.

- ✔ **Hair care.** One way to save money in this category is to go bald. In the meantime, if you have hair to be trimmed, a number of no-frills, low-cost hair-cutting joints can do the job. Supercuts is one of the larger chains. We know that some of you will insist that your stylist is the only one who can manage your hair the way you like it. At the prices charged by some of the trendy hair places, you have to really adore what they do to justify the cost. Consider going periodically to a no-frills stylist for maintenance after getting a fabulous cut at a more expensive place. If you're daring, you could try getting your hair cut at a local training school. For parents of young children, a great time and money saver is to buy a simple-to-use home electric shaving kit — no more agonizing trips with little ones to have their hair cut by a "stranger," and the kit pays for itself after just a couple of cuts!

- ✔ **Other personal-care services.** As long as we're on the subject of outward beauty, we have to say that in our personal opinion, the billions spent annually on cosmetics are a waste of money (not to mention all the time spent applying and removing it). Women look fine and in many cases better without makeup. And having regular facials, pedicures, and manicures can add up quickly.

- ✔ **Health club expenses.** Expenditure on exercise is almost always money well spent. But you don't have to belong to a trendy club to get benefits. If you belong to a gym or club for the social scene, whether it's for dating or business purposes, you have to judge whether it's worth the cost.

  Low-cost exercise facilities are everywhere — look for them anywhere you see children and young adults. Local schools, colleges, and universities almost always have tennis courts, running tracks, swimming pools, basketball courts, and exercise rooms and often provide instruction.

Look for value in your subscription publications

Everyone has a favourite and not-so-favourite publication. Some people don't realize how much they spend on publications, partly because they've never tallied up the cost.

As we discuss elsewhere in this book, "free" publications are often driven by advertisers, so we don't encourage you to load up on them. But take a close look at the total amount you spend on publications and how much each one costs. Keep the ones that you're getting sufficient value from and cancel the rest. You can always read them at your local library.

If you took the money that you're spending on one of your regular papers — say, $23 a month, or $276 a year — and invested it in your RRSP and earned a mere 10 percent per year, in 25 years you'd have more than $27,000! And this assumes that they don't increase the price of their paper, which they always do. Knowing these figures, you'd really have to believe you're getting good value from the paper to keep subscribing!

Community centres offer fitness programs and classes, too. Metropolitan areas that have lots of health clubs undoubtedly have the widest range of options and prices. *Note:* When figuring the cost of membership, be sure to factor in the cost of travel to and from these clubs and any parking costs (and the realistic likelihood of going there regularly to work out).

Don't forget that lots of healthy exercise can be done indoors or out, free of charge. Isn't biking in the park at sunset more fun than pedalling away on a stationary bike, anyway? You may want to buy some basic gym equipment for use at home. Be careful though: Lots of rowing machines and free weights languish in a closet beside that old fondue set and crockpot after their first week at home.

Personal business

Accountants, lawyers, and financial advisers can be worth their expense if they're good. But be wary of professionals who create or perpetuate work and have conflicts of interest in their recommendations.

The best way to use professionals for tax, legal, or financial advice is to get organized before you meet with them. Do some background research to evaluate their strengths and biases. Make sure that you set goals and estimate fees in advance so that you know what you're getting yourself into.

Computer and printed resources (see Chapter 20) can be useful, low-cost alternatives to hiring professionals.

Medical care

Health care is a big topic nowadays, and the cost of it is going up fast. Your health insurance — if you have health insurance, that is — probably covers most of your health-care needs (Chapter 16 explains how to shop for health insurance). But many plans require you to pay for certain expenses out of your own pocket.

Medical care and supplies are like any other services and products — price and quality vary. And, like any other profession, medicine in Canada is a business, and a conflict of interest exists whenever the person recommending treatment benefits financially from providing that treatment. Many studies have documented unnecessary surgeries and other medical procedures.

When seeking health insurance, remember — as with any other service or product that you buy — shop around. And don't take any one physician's advice as gospel. Always get a second opinion for any major surgery.

Therapy can be useful and even lifesaving. Have a frank talk with your therapist about how much total time and money you can expect to spend and what kind of results you can expect. As with any professional service, a competent therapist should be able to give you a straight answer if he or she is looking out for your psychological *and* financial well being.

Alternative medicine (holistic, for example) is gaining attention because of its focus on preventive care and treatment of the whole body or person. Although alternative medicine can be dangerous to undertake if you are in critical condition, alternative treatment for many forms of chronic pain or disease may be worth your investigation. Alternative medicine may lead to better *and* lower-cost health care.

If you must take certain drugs on an ongoing basis and pay for them out-of-pocket, ordering through a mail-order company can bring down your costs and be more convenient for refilling prescriptions. Your health plan may be able to provide more information about this. The following mail-order companies also offer generic drugs, which are medically equivalent to brand-name drugs but cost a lot less:

- ✔ MediTrust (800-263-8999 or www.meditrust.com)
- ✔ Pharmacy.ca or Central Medical Pharmacy (800-727-5048 or www.pharmacy.ca)
- ✔ Pharmex Direct (800-663-8637 or www.pharmexdirect.com)

Insurance

Insurance is a vast minefield. Part IV explains the different coverages, suggests what to buy and avoid, and reveals how to save on policies. The following are the most common ways people waste money on insurance.

✔ **Keeping low deductibles.** The *deductible* is the amount of a loss that must come out of your pocket. On an auto insurance policy, for example, if your collision deductible is $100 and you get into an accident, you pay for the first $100 of damage, and your insurance company picks up the rest. Low deductibles, however, translate into much higher premiums for you. In the long run, you should save money with a higher deductible, even factoring in the potential for greater out-of-pocket costs to you when you do have a claim. Insurance should protect you from economic disaster. Don't get carried away with a really high deductible, though, which could cause financial hardship if you do have a claim and lack savings.

If you have a lot of claims, your insurance premiums will escalate, so you still don't come out ahead with lower deductibles. Plus, low deductibles mean more claim forms to file for small losses (creating more hassle). Filing an insurance claim is usually not an enjoyable or quick experience.

✔ **Covering small potential losses or unnecessary needs.** You shouldn't buy insurance for anything that wouldn't be a financial catastrophe if you had to pay for it out of your own pocket. Although the postal service isn't perfect, insuring inexpensive gifts sent in the mail is not worth the price. Buying dental or home warranty plans also doesn't make financial sense for the same reason. And, if no one is dependent on your income, then you don't need to buy life insurance either (who will be around to collect when you're gone?).

✔ **Failing to shop around.** Rates vary *tremendously* from insurer to insurer. In Part IV, we recommend the best companies to call first for quotes and other cost-saving strategies.

Taxes

Taxes probably represent one of the largest — if not *the* largest — of your expenditures. (So why is it listed next-to-last here? You will soon see.)

Retirement savings plans are one of the best and simplest ways to reduce your tax burden. We explain more about retirement savings plans in Chapter 11. Unfortunately, most people can't take full advantage of these plans because they spend everything they make. So not only do they have less savings, they also pay higher income taxes — a double whammy.

We've attended many presentations where a fast-talking investment guy in an expensive suit lectures about the importance of saving for retirement and explains how to invest your savings. Yet details and tips about finding the money to save (the hard part for most people) are left to the imagination.

In order to take advantage of the tax savings that come through retirement savings plans, you must first spend less than you earn. Only then can you afford to contribute to these plans. That's why the first part of this chapter is all about strategies to reduce your spending.

Another benefit of spending less and saving more is reduced sales tax. When you buy most consumer products, you pay sales tax. Therefore, the less money you spend and the more you save in retirement plans, the more you reduce income *and* sales taxes. (See Chapter 7 for other tax-reduction strategies.)

Costly addictions

Human beings are creatures of habit. We all have habits that we wish we didn't have, and breaking those habits can be very difficult. Costly habits are the worst. The following tidbits may nudge you in the right direction toward breaking your own financially draining habits.

- **Kick the smoking habit.** Despite the decline in smoking over the past few decades, about 30 percent of all Canadians still smoke. Using smokeless tobacco, which also causes long-term health problems, is on the increase. Canadians spend around $6 billion annually on tobacco products. If you smoke just a pack a day, you're spending around $1,500 a year to damage your health. The increased medical costs and lost work time costs are even greater, estimated at anywhere from $3 billion to $7 billion every year. Of course, if you continue to smoke, you may eliminate the need to save for retirement.

  Check with local hospitals for smoking-cessation programs. The Canadian Cancer Society (check your local phone directory) offers a helpful brochure, *How to Be a Happy Ex-Smoker*, and maintains an up-to-date list of smoking cessation programs in your area. Branches of the Canadian Lung Association often offer group quit-smoking programs. Look in your phone book for the branch nearest you.

- **Stop abusing alcohol and other drugs.** Thousands of Canadians seek treatment annually for alcoholism or drug abuse. These addictive behaviours, like spending, transcend all educational and socioeconomic lines in our society. Even so, studies have demonstrated that only one in seven alcoholics or drug abusers seek help. Three of the ten leading causes of death — cirrhosis of the liver, accidents, and suicides — are associated with excessive alcohol consumption.

In Ontario, the Centre for Addiction and Mental Health runs a drug, alcohol, and mental health information line (800-463-6237). In other provinces, call your provincial Department of Health. To find a local Alcoholics Anonymous chapter, look in your telephone book or visit www.alcoholics-anonymous.org on the Internet.

✔ **Don't gamble.** The house *always* comes out ahead in the long run. Why do you think so many governments run lotteries? Because governments make money on people who gamble, that's why.

Casinos, horse and dog racetracks, and other gambling establishments are sure long-term losers for you. So, too, is the rapidly growing practice of day-trading stocks, which isn't investing but gambling. Getting hooked on the dream of winning is easy and tempting. And sure, occasionally you win a little bit (just enough to keep you coming back). Every now and then, a few folks win a lot. But it's built into the odds that your hard-earned capital mostly winds up in the pockets of the casino owners.

If you go just for the entertainment, take only what you can afford to lose. Gamblers Anonymous (213-386-8789 or www.gamblersanonymous.org) can help those for whom gambling has become an addiction.

Chapter 7

Taking the Trauma out of Taxes

· ·

In This Chapter

▶ Dealing with the baffling tax system

▶ Figuring your marginal income tax rate

▶ Reducing the taxes on your employment income

▶ Lowering the taxes on your investment income

▶ Increasing your deductions and credits

▶ Preparing your return with and without help

▶ What to do if you get an audit notice

· ·

*Y*ou pay a lot of money in taxes — probably more than you realize. Believe it or not, few people even know how much they pay in taxes each year. Most remember only whether they got a refund or owed money on their return. But when you file your tax return, all you're doing is settling up with the tax authorities over the amount of taxes you paid during the year versus the total tax that you owe based on your income and deductions.

Understanding the Taxes You Pay

Some people feel lucky when they get a refund, but really all a refund indicates is that you overpaid in taxes during the year. You should have had this money in your own account all along. If you're consistently getting big refunds, you should be paying less tax throughout the year.

Instead of caring about whether you get a refund when you complete your annual tax return, you *should* care about the *total* taxes you pay. The only way to know the total taxes you pay is to get out your tax return. On line 435 on the recent federal T1 General form, find your total federal and provincial tax payable. Subtract from this sum any credits deducted from your total tax payable, except for tax that you've already had deducted (line 437) or tax you paid in instalments (line 476). The end result? You'll probably see one of the single largest expenses of your financial life (unless you have an expensive home or a huge gambling habit).

The goal of this chapter is to help you legally and permanently reduce the total taxes you pay. The key to reducing your tax burden is to understand the tax system — if you don't, you will surely pay more in taxes than necessary. And your tax ignorance can lead to mistakes, which can be costly if Revenue Canada (now formally known as the Canada Customs and Revenue Agency) catches errors in their favour. With the proliferation of computerized information and data tracking, discovering mistakes has never been easier for the tax authorities.

The tax system, like other public policy, is built around incentives to encourage *desirable* behaviour and activity. Home ownership, for example, is considered desirable in part because it encourages people to take more responsibility for maintaining buildings and neighbourhoods. Clean, orderly neighbourhoods are supposed to be the result of home ownership. Home ownership is also seen as a way to help keep the construction industry working away. Therefore, the government offers all sorts of tax perks, which we discuss later in this chapter, to encourage people to buy and own homes.

To understand the tax system is to understand what your government thinks you should be doing. Naturally, not all people follow the path the government encourages — after all, it's a free country. You've spent years rebelling against your parents. Why should the government get better treatment?

However, the difference between rebelling against your parents and being a rebellious taxpayer, of course, is that as a taxpayer, the cost of defiance comes out of your pocket (we haven't heard of many parents who penalize their kids' unruliness in cash). The *fewer* desirable activities that you engage in, the more you will pay in taxes. If you understand the options, you can choose those that meet your needs as you approach different stages of your financial life.

Many people resent the taxes they pay — they feel that they pay too much and get too little in return. Therefore, another potential benefit to understanding the tax system is that you can become a more informed voter and citizen in the democratic process.

The importance of your marginal tax rate

"What's marginal about my taxes?" we hear you asking. "They're huge! They're not marginal in my life at all!" *Marginal* is a term often applied to those things that are small or minimally acceptable — sort of like getting a C– on a school report card (or an A– if you're from an overachieving family).

Marginal tax rates are a powerful concept. Once you understand them, you can understand the implications of many financial strategies that affect the amount of taxes you pay. And because you pay taxes on your income from employment as well as on your investments held outside of RRSPs and other registered retirement plans, a lot of personal financial decisions are at stake.

First, you must understand that when it comes to taxes, *not all income is treated equally*. This fact is far from self-evident. If you work for an employer and have a constant salary during the course of a year, a steady and equal amount of federal and provincial taxes is deducted from each paycheque. Thus, it appears as though all that earned income is being taxed equally.

In reality, however, you pay less tax on your *first* dollars of earnings and more tax on your *last* dollars of earnings. For example, if you're single and your *taxable income* (a term we define in the next section) totals $40,000 during 2001, you would pay federal tax at the rate of 16 percent on the first $30,754 of taxable income and 22 percent on income from $30,755 up to $40,000. In addition, you would also pay provincial income tax. Some provinces calculate this as a percentage of your federal tax, so your provincial tax rates also rise along with your income bracket. Other provinces calculate their taxes using their own graduated rates applied directly to your taxable income.

Table 7-1 gives approximate combined federal and provincial tax rates. Your actual marginal bracket may be somewhat higher or lower, depending on the province you live in.

Table 7-1	Approximate 2001 Combined Federal and Provincial Income Tax Brackets and Rates
Taxable Income	*Tax Rate (Bracket)*
Up to $30,754	24%
$30,754–$61,509	33%
$61,509–$100,000	42%
Over $100,000	47%

Your *marginal tax rate* is the rate of tax that you pay on your *last* or so-called *highest* dollars of income. In the example of a person with taxable income of $40,000, that person's combined federal and provincial marginal tax rate is approximately 33 percent. In other words, she effectively pays 33 percent tax on her last dollars of income — those dollars in excess of $30,754.

Your marginal tax rate allows you to quickly calculate additional taxes that you would pay on additional income. Conversely, you can delight in quantifying the amount of taxes that you save by reducing your taxable income, either by decreasing your income or by increasing your deductions.

Provincial taxes

As you are probably painfully aware, you pay not only federal income taxes but also provincial income taxes. Until recently, all provinces except Quebec simply used a percentage of your federal tax bill to arrive at your provincial taxes. This is known as the *tax-on-tax* method.

The rules have now been changed, and the provinces and territories can choose to calculate income taxes as a percentage of your income instead of as a percentage of your federal tax bill. This *tax-on-income* system will have been adopted in all provinces by 2001. B.C., Manitoba, Ontario, New Brunswick, and Nova Scotia implemented tax-on-income in 2000. In 2001, Alberta, Saskatchewan, P.E.I., and Newfoundland and Labrador will change over.

While they must still use the federal government's definition of taxable income, the provinces can establish their own tax brackets as well as set their own rates. And you thought the system was complicated enough already!

Taxable income defined

Taxable income is the amount of income on which you actually pay taxes. In the sections that follow, we explain strategies for reducing your taxable income. First, we'll define what we mean. You don't pay taxes on your total income for the following two reasons:

✔ **Not all income is taxable.** For example, any profit you make when you sell the home you live in — your *principal residence* — generally isn't taxable.

✔ **You get to subtract deductions from your income.** Some deductions are available just for being a living, breathing human being. In 2000, every taxpayer resident in Canada received an exemption — known as the *basic personal exemption* — on their first $7,231 of income in the year. You also don't have to pay income tax on allowable RRSP contributions that you deduct from your income in any year.

Trimming Employment Income Taxes

You are supposed to pay taxes on income you earn from work. Countless illegal ways are available to reduce your employment income — for example, not reporting it — but you could very well end up with a heap of penalties and extra interest charges on top of the taxes you owe. And you might even get tossed in jail. Because we don't want you to lose even more money by paying unnecessary penalties and serving jail time to boot, in this section we focus on the many *legal* ways to reduce your taxes.

RRSP and retirement plan contributions

An RRSP or your employer's pension plan is one of the few painless and completely legal ways to reduce your taxable employment income. Besides reducing your taxes, you build up a nest egg so that you don't have to work for the rest of your life.

From your taxable income you can deduct money that you tuck away into an RRSP or employer-based retirement plan. Therefore, if you contribute $1,000 to one of these plans and your combined federal and provincial marginal tax rate is 42 percent, you reduce your federal and provincial taxes by $420. Like the sound of that? How about this: Contribute another $1,000, and your taxes drop *another* $420 (as long as you're still in the same marginal tax rate). And, once inside a retirement plan, your money can compound and grow without taxation.

This process is a great tax-reducing device. You benefit both in the short term *and* the long term. So why don't more people take advantage of this tax break?

Many people miss this opportunity to reduce their taxes because they *spend* all (or too much) of their current employment income and, therefore, have nothing (or little) left to put into an RRSP or their employer's pension plan. Should you be in this predicament, you need to reduce your spending first in order to be able to contribute money to a retirement plan. Take an immediate tour through Chapter 6, which explains how to decrease your spending.

Alternative minimum tax (say what?)

As if the tax system weren't already complicated enough, there's actually a *second* tax system. Called the alternative minimum tax, or AMT, this second system may raise your taxes higher than they would have been. Let us explain while you reach for some Aspirin.

The AMT was introduced in 1986 in response to reports of wealthy individuals who purportedly using loopholes and deductions to reduce their tax bills to next to nothing.

The problem with the AMT is that it hits many more people than just those making excessive use of tax shelters and other sophisticated tax-planning strategies. For example, anyone who receives a very large capital gain — such as a farmer who sells off land — may also be thrown in with all the supposed robber barons.

If there's a chance that the rule will affect you, you must calculate your tax both the normal way *and* through the AMT calculations — and then pay the higher tax bill of the two! (The reason it's called the "alternative" minimum tax is *not* because you have a choice in the matter!)

If you think you might be a good AMT candidate, call up Revenue Canada and request the one-page AMT Calculations Sheet. The sheet walks you through recalculating your taxable income. You can also find the form online by searching for "Alternative Minimum Tax" at www.ccra-adrc.gc.ca.

If your employer does not offer a retirement savings plan to which they contribute, an RRSP is your next best bet. In many cases, you may be able to contribute to an RRSP after putting the maximum you can into your employer's pension plan and have it matched by a company contribution in your name. Chapter 11 can help you determine how much you can contribute to an RRSP and how to make the most out of registered retirement plans.

Income shifting

Income shifting, which has nothing to do with money laundering, is a more esoteric tax-reduction technique and is an option only to those who can control *when* they receive their income.

For example, suppose that your employer tells you in late December that you're eligible for a bonus. You are offered the option to receive your bonus in either December or January. Looking ahead, if you're pretty certain that you will be in a higher tax bracket next year, you should choose to receive your bonus in December.

Or suppose that you run your own business and think that you'll be in a lower tax bracket next year. Perhaps you plan to take time off to be with a newborn or take an extended trip. You may choose to push a big contract off until January so the income is earned and taxed in the next tax year.

Reducing Investment Income Taxes

For investments that you hold in *tax-sheltered* retirement plans — RRSPs, RRIFs (Registered Retirement Income Funds), and company pension plans, for example — you don't need to worry about taxes. This money is generally not taxed until you actually withdraw funds from the retirement account.

For investments that you hold outside of tax-sheltered retirement plans, the distributions and profits on those investments are exposed to taxation when you receive them. Interest, dividends, and profits (called *capital gains*) from the sale of an investment at a price higher than the purchase price are all taxed.

Taxes on investment income should definitely concern you if you are in a relatively high tax bracket. If you're in the 42 percent or higher bracket (see Table 7-1), you should pay especially close attention to the rest of this section.

Although this section explains some of the best methods to reduce the taxes on investments exposed to taxation, Chapter 13 discusses in detail how and where to invest money held outside of tax-sheltered retirement plans.

Fill up those retirement plans

The distributions and profits from investments outside retirement plans are exposed to taxation. Unless you have earmarked that money for some specific non-retirement account purpose, such as buying a home, and as long as hefty taxes aren't involved from selling those investments at a great profit, the money will probably serve you better in a tax-sheltered retirement plan.

Taking advantage of opportunities to direct money into retirement plans gives you two possible tax bonuses. First, your contributions to the retirement plan may be immediately tax-deductible (see Chapter 11 for details). Second, the distributions and growth of the investments in the retirement plans aren't generally taxed until withdrawal.

Select other tax-friendly investments

Too often, when selecting investments, people mistakenly focus on past rates of return. We all know that the past is no guarantee of the future. But an even worse mistake is choosing an investment with a reportedly high rate of return without considering tax consequences. What you get to keep — after taxes — is what matters in the long run.

Mutual funds are a good example. When comparing two similar funds, most people prefer a fund that averages returns of 14 percent per year to a fund earning 12 percent. But what if the 14-percent-per-year fund causes you to pay a lot more in taxes? What if, after factoring in taxes, the 14-percent-per-year fund nets just 9 percent, while the 12-percent-per-year fund nets an effective 10 percent return? In such a case, you'd be unwise to choose a fund solely on the basis of the higher (pre-tax) reported rate of return.

We call investments that appreciate in value and don't distribute much in the way of taxable income *tax-friendly* (some in the investment business use the term "tax efficient"). Examples include growth stocks, which pay low taxable dividends, and mutual funds that invest in such stocks. See Chapter 13 for more information.

Dividends

One tax-friendly way to earn investment returns is dividends paid out on Canadian equities. Dividends are paid out of a company's after-tax profits. So the same profits aren't taxed twice, shareholders get a credit for the tax already paid on the earnings that companies distribute as dividends.

The *dividend tax credit* is arrived at through a convoluted formula. The estimated effect of the dividend tax credit means that, after all the numbers have been crunched, dividends are taxed at a lower rate than your salary. See Table 7-2 for the approximate rate at which dividends are taxed:

Table 7-2	Approximate Dividend Tax Rates	
Income Level	**Salary Tax Rate**	**Dividend Tax Rate**
Up to $31,000	22%	16%
$31,000 up to $61,000	33%	24%
$61,000 up to $100,000	42%	30%
$100,000 and up	47%	32%

Capital gains

In 2000, the federal government dropped the amount of any taxable gains you have to include in your taxable income twice. (A *capital gain* is simply the profit you make when you sell an investment for more than you paid for it.) Instead of having to include the traditional three-quarters of your capital gains, for any gains realized after October 17, 2000, you need to include only half of your profit in your taxable income. The result is that where once dividends were the least-taxed type of investment income, that honour now belongs to capital gains.

Table 7-3 shows the approximate effective tax rates compared to tax on your employment income, given that only one-half of your capital gains are now taxed:

Table 7-3	Approximate Capital Gains Effective Tax Rates	
Income Level	**Salary Tax Rate**	**Capital Gains Effective Tax Rate**
Up to $31,000	22%	13%
$31,000–$61,000	33%	18%
$61,000–$100,000	42%	21%
$59,181 and up	50%	25%

Due to the changes to the way capital gains are taxed, there are special rules that apply to the way you calculate your capital gains or losses for the year 2000. The complication is that there are three different periods with different rates for the year. For the period January 1 to February 27, 2000, you include three-quarters of your capital gains or losses. For any gains or losses incurred between February 28 and October 17, 2000, you include two-thirds. Finally, for capital gains or losses realized from October 18, 2000 onward, you include just 50 percent.

Your principal residence

Any profits you make when you sell your principal residence generally aren't taxed. However, married couples (and, since 1992, common-law couples) are allowed to have only one principal residence between them. This means, for example, that you can no longer make tax-free gains on both your home and a cottage.

Strategies to Increase Your Deductions

Deductions are just that: You subtract them from your income after totalling your income and before calculating the tax you owe. To determine just what a deduction is worth, multiply it by your marginal tax rate. In the sections that follow, we detail some of the more common deductions you may be able to take advantage of. The dollar figures we use are for the 2000 year — many will likely have been revised for subsequent years.

Child care expenses

Many of the costs of having others take care of your children can be deducted from your income. Babysitters, day nurseries, daycare, day camps, and boarding school expenses all qualify. However, the expenses must be incurred either to enable you to work or to take an occupational training course.

You can deduct $7,000 for each child who is under age 7 at the end of the year, and $4,000 for each child age 7 to 16. Your total deduction can't be greater than two-thirds of your salary or net business income (technically your *earned* income). Quebec residents, however, can choose to allow either spouse to claim the deduction, which is capped at 100 percent of the earned income of the spouse with the lower income. In a two-parent family, child care expenses must generally be claimed by the spouse who earns the lower income. A single parent can deduct the expense from her or his own income.

Alimony and maintenance payments

Alimony or maintenance payments you make to an ex-spouse can be deducted, as long as they are made following a decree, order, judgment, or written agreement. To be deductible, they must be an allowance that is paid out in regular, predetermined payments. You can't deduct any transfers of property or one-time payments you make as part of a settlement.

Annual union and professional fees

Regular annual dues are deductible, but you can't claim initial fees or special assessments. (These dues are generally deducted from your paycheque.) Fees paid to professional organizations are deductible only if they must be paid to maintain a professional standing recognizable by law. If you are self-employed, however, you can generally deduct dues you pay to voluntarily belong to work-related organizations.

Business losses

If you work *and* run your own unincorporated business or professional practice, you can use business losses from the other businesses you're involved in to reduce your employment or professional income.

Say that you have a salaried job in a car plant, and you start up a contracting business. If your business expenses are greater than the income it brings in, you can subtract your losses from your other income.

Interest on investment loans

Any interest you pay on money you borrow to buy investments or to earn income from a business may be deducted. (*Note:* This rule doesn't apply to money borrowed to make an RRSP contribution.) You'll need to keep a record of any money you borrow and use to invest and the interest you pay during the year.

Married versus common-law partners

Your mother likely won't agree, but you're as good as married in the eyes of the tax authorities if you are living in a common-law relationship. If so, you are subject to the same tax rules that apply to legally married couples. For instance, if you are living common-law, you can't claim the "equivalent-to-married" credit for a child. On the other hand, you can take advantage of planning opportunities including setting up a spousal RRSP and pooling some expenses to take the most advantage of various credits.

You are considered to be common-law spouses if you and your partner "cohabit in a conjugal relationship," and either have had a child together or have been living together continuously for at least 12 months. You are deemed to have "separated" — or lost your common-law status — only if you are separated for more than 90 days due to the relationship breaking down.

Beginning in the year 2001, same-sex couples who have lived together for at least one year will be treated by the tax authorities in the same way as opposite-sex common-law couples.

Moving expenses

Eligible moving expenses are often overlooked, but they can be a very valuable deduction. The rules are straightforward. If you start a business or start working at a new location and move to a home that is at least 40 kilometres closer by road to your new business or job location than your old home, you can generally deduct most of the associated costs. However, moving to Canada from another country doesn't qualify.

Expenses that are eligible include the travelling costs to move you and your family (including food and lodging along the way) and your household belongings, as well as any related storage costs. In addition, you can deduct the cost of selling your old home, including the real estate commissions, and the legal bills on purchasing your new home. Expenses can be deducted only against income that is earned in the new location. If you are unable to deduct all the expenses in the year of the move, the remainder can be deducted in future years. So don't forget to carry that deduction forward.

Students who move so they can attend university or another post-secondary institution full time can also deduct moving expenses. The expenses must be deducted against taxable scholarships, bursaries, research grants, or fellowships. Students can also claim moving expenses if the move is in order to take a job — including a summer job — or to start a business.

Strategies to Increase Your Credits

Tax credits are *credited* to you as if you've already paid that amount in taxes. Once your tax bill has been calculated from your taxable income, any tax credits reduce your taxes by the full amount of the credit. A $500 credit is worth the same amount to everybody — it reduces the tax payable by $500. Most credits are *non-refundable,* which means that they can't be used to make your tax liability less than zero. If you have $1,500 in credits left over after wiping out your federal tax payable, that's as good as it gets. The government won't send you a cheque for $1,500.

Credits are usually deducted from your federal tax bill before your provincial taxes and surtaxes are calculated. Until 1999, provincial taxes were calculated as a percentage of your federal tax. Under this *tax-on-tax* system, a credit is worth anywhere from around 50 to 70 percent more than the straight federal credit, because by cutting your federal taxes you also reduce your provincial taxes and surtaxes.

However, by 2001 most provinces will be calculating their piece of your tax bill by applying their marginal rates directly to your taxable income, rather than as a percentage of your federal tax bill. However, the provinces are required to maintain the basic credits that are offered at the federal level, meaning federal credits will still be worth 1.5 to 1.7 times their value.

In the following sections are some common credits that may be available to you and your family, and some tips on how to maximize them. *Note:* Most of the dollar figures are from the 2000 tax year. Check your tax guide for the specific amounts for the year you're filing for.

Personal tax credit

Everyone gets a basic federal credit of $1,229. (When you're going through the form, you claim a "basic personal amount" of $7,231, which is then multiplied by 17 percent to work out to $1,229.)

Spousal credit

You can claim a federal credit of $1,044 if your spouse (including a common-law spouse) earned less than $614 during the year, and a smaller credit if he or she made between $614 and $6,754. If the spouse makes more than the cut-off amount of $6,754, the lower-earning partner may be able to get under the threshold by making an RRSP contribution.

Equivalent-to-married credit

You can claim this credit if you're single, separated, divorced, or widowed and you support a relative who lives with you. The most common example of this is a single mother. However, whether you're a man or a woman you can claim this credit if you're financially responsible for supporting a child, parent, or other relative. The only conditions are that the dependant must be related to you, completely financially dependent on you, living in Canada, and, except in the case of a parent or grandparent, under 18 years old at some point in the tax year. (The age limit doesn't apply if the person is dependent on you because of a mental or physical disability.)

Charitable donations credit

As long as you get an official tax receipt, you can earn credits from most contributions made to charities. In addition to cash contributions, you can often gain tax credits if you donate items of significant value, such as a used computer. The amount of the receipt must reflect the item's fair market value. However, you can't get a receipt for your time or the expenses you ring up while doing charitable work.

The first $200 you donate earns you a 17 percent federal tax credit in 2000 (which works out to about 25 percent once your savings on provincial taxes are accounted for). Once you're past the $200 level, though, your donations give you a 29 percent federal tax credit, worth about 50 percent once the savings on provincial taxes are counted. That makes your donations above $200 worth as much as a deduction if you're in the top (50 percent or so) tax bracket. (*Note:* The rates and subsequent savings will fall along with the marginal tax rates in 2001.)

Shifting or bunching expenses

Because you can control when you make some expenditures that earn you a credit, you can *shift* or *bunch* more of them into selected years to boost your tax savings. Take medical expenses: You're allowed to claim a deduction for medical bills for any 12-month period, as long as it ends within the tax year. If you anticipate a large medical bill, perhaps for some major dental work, and your 12-month period runs October to September, try to pay for the work in September rather than October. By having the expense included in the earlier 12-month period, you're able to get a credit for the expense a full year earlier.

Charitable donations is another expense category where grouping and timing your claims makes sense. You and your spouse are allowed to pool your contributions on one return. You can also group donations from up to six years together. The credit for your first $200 of donations each year earns you a combined federal/provincial tax credit of about 27 percent in 2000. For donations above a $200 total, the credit is worth about 50 percent.

You're also allowed to pool charitable contributions from up to five consecutive years. If you regularly make donations that are smaller than $200, hold on to your receipts and claim them every few years. Again, this puts more of your donations over the $200 level, earning you a credit at a higher percentage.

Tuition fees credit

You receive a credit worth 17 percent of tuition fees in 2000 (as long as they total more than $100) paid to a Canadian university, college, or other post-secondary institution during the year. Fees paid to an institution certified by Employment and Immigration Canada are also eligible. Tuition paid to universities outside Canada may also be eligible, but fees paid to private elementary schools or high schools don't earn you a tax credit. If you study full time, you also get to claim a federal educational status credit that in 2000 was $34 per month, rising to $64 a month in 2001.

Organizing to deduct

The hard part for most people is locating the forms, receipts, and all the other scraps of paper you need when you're completing your tax return. Setting up a filing system like one of the following can be a *very* big time-saver:

✓ **One receptacle.** If you have limited patience for setting up neat file folders and you lead an uncomplicated financial life (that is, you haven't needed to save receipts throughout the year for tax purposes), you can confine your filing to January and February. During those months, you should receive tax summary statements on wages paid by your employer (T4), taxable dividend income from Canadian corporations (T5), income from profit-sharing plans (T4PS), and interest income (T5 for bank account and regular-interest Canada Savings Bond "R" bonds, T5008 for T-bills). If you're older, you may also get a slip for Old Age Security income (T4AOAS) and the Canada Pension Plan or

Quebec Pension Plan (T4A(P)). Set up a folder that's labelled with something easy to remember ("2001 Taxes" is a brilliant choice) and dump these papers as well as your tax booklet into it. When you're ready to crunch numbers, you should have everything you need to complete the form.

✓ **Many receptacles.** A more thorough approach is to organize the bills you pay into individual folders during the entire year. This method is essential if you own your own business and need to tabulate your expenditures for office supplies. No one is going to send you a form totalling your office expenditures for the year — you're on your own.

✓ **Software as receptacle.** Software programs can help organize your tax information during the year and can save you time and accounting fees come tax-preparation time.

Tuition fees cover much more than just the standard admission charges. You can also claim library and lab costs, exam fees, and mandatory computer service fees. As well, you can include mandatory associated fees such as those for health services and athletics.

Sometimes the student in the family doesn't need to use all — or any — of the tuition fee tax credit or the education credit to bring her federal tax bill to zero. In this case, the credits don't go to waste. Up to $850 of the unused portion of either — or both — credits generally can be transferred to a parent, grandparent, or spouse. Unused tuition and education amounts can also be carried forward and claimed against your income in future years.

Medical expenses credit

The problem with this credit is that it's worth something only if your medical expenses exceed certain minimum amounts. But you can get a much bigger tax break by moving and grouping your medical bills.

After totalling your expenses, you can claim only the amount that exceeds 3 percent of your net income. Your credit for 2000 is 17 percent of that allowable amount. If your net income is $53,800 or more, you can claim 17 percent of any expenses exceeding $1,637. (The credit decreases to 16 percent beginning in 2001.)

To maximize the benefit of this credit, one spouse can and should claim the entire family's medical expenses. The claim generally should be made by the spouse with the lowest income, to get over the 3 percent floor as quickly as possible. Further, in any tax year you can claim your expenses for any 12 months ending in that particular year. If you have a lot of bills in the fall and spring, for example, make your claim run from August 1 to July 31.

You can include a fairly broad range of medical costs in calculating this credit. Add up any payments to doctors, nurses, dentists, and public or licensed private hospitals for medical or dental care. In addition, you can include payments for any prescription drugs and medications, eyeglasses, and therapy for speech or hearing problems. You can also include any premiums for private health insurance plans. (That includes the cost of travel insurance for your vacations out of the country; see Chapter 17 for more information.) You can't claim any expenses that you are reimbursed for from, say, a company dental plan, but any deductibles you pay do qualify.

Low-income earners who have high medical bills may also be able to take advantage of the *medical expense supplement.* The supplement is 25 percent of the medical expenses that are used to calculate your medical expenses credit — those beyond 3 percent of your income. The maximum this is worth is $507, and it gets reduced by 5 percent of your family's net income over $17,664.

Disability credit

If you have a severe and prolonged mental or physical impairment, you get a federal credit. The credit was $730 for the 2000 tax year, rising to $960 for 2001. Your disability must be certified by a medical doctor or, in the case of a vision impairment, by an optometrist.

Starting in 2000, families that care for children with severe disabilities can also receive a supplementary credit of up to $500. This will be reduced by child care expenses and attendant care expenses in excess of $2,000 claimed with respect to that child.

If you're unable to use the disability credit because you haven't earned enough, this credit can be used by your spouse or parent if they support you. If a parent supports a disabled child who is over 18 years old, the parent is allowed an additional federal credit. This credit was $406 for the 2000 tax year, and $560 for 2001. However, this credit for 2000 is reduced by 17 percent of the income the dependant earns beyond $4,845. The credit rises to $560 for 2001, and for that year will be reduced by 16 percent of the dependant's income over the threshold amount.

A *caregiver's credit* is also available to caregivers who provide in-home care for elderly or infirm relatives living in the same house. In 2000, the maximum credit was $406; it was raised to $560 for the 2001 tax year. However, you cannot claim this credit if you have claimed the equivalent-to-married credit or dependant tax credits in relation to that person.

Pension income credit

If you earn pension income, you can claim a credit of 17 percent on the first $1,000 of this income, which generally means money paid out by a life annuity. (This credit falls to 16 percent for 2001.) Income from Old Age Security or the Canada Pension Plan isn't eligible. If you're unable to use the credit, it may be transferred to your spouse.

If you're 65 or older or are receiving benefits due to your spouse's death, the pension income definition expands to include annuities from an RRSP or deferred profit-sharing plan, or an RRIF payment.

Age 65 or older

Another credit is for those over 65: If this means you, you can claim a federal tax credit of up to $600 for 2000. However, this credit is reduced if your net income is more than $26,284, and is completely eliminated if your income is more than $49,824.

Self-employment expenses

When you are self-employed, you can deduct a multitude of expenses from your income before calculating the tax that you owe. If you buy a computer or office furniture, you can deduct those expenses (sometimes they need to be gradually deducted or *depreciated* over time). Salaries for your employees, office supplies, rent or mortgage interest for your office space, and phone expenses are also generally deductible.

Some self-employed folks don't take all the deductions they should. In some cases, people simply aren't aware of the wonderful world of deductions. Others are worried that large deductions will raise the risk of an audit. Spend some time learning more about tax deductions; you will be convinced that taking full advantage of your eligible deductions makes sense and saves you money.

The following are common tax-related mistakes made by people who are their own bosses:

- ✔ **Being an island unto yourself.** When you're self-employed, going it alone is usually a mistake when it comes to taxes. You must educate yourself to make the tax laws work for you rather than against you. It's worth the money to hire tax help — either in the form of a tax adviser or other resources we recommend later in this chapter.

- ✔ **Making administrative tax screwups.** When you are self-employed, you are responsible for the correct and timely filing of all taxes owed on your income. You need to make estimated tax payments on a quarterly basis. And if you have employees, you also need to withhold taxes on their income from each paycheque they receive and make timely payments to Revenue Canada. In addition to taxes, you also need to withhold and send in Canada Pension Plan (or Quebec Pension Plan) contributions and Employment Insurance premiums.

- ✔ **Not documenting expenses.** When you pay with cash, following the paper trail for all the money you spent is hard for you (and for Revenue Canada, in the event you're ever audited). At the end of the year, how are you going to remember how much you spent for parking or client meals if you keep no record? How would you survive a Revenue Canada audit without proper documentation? Develop a system for recording a record of your daily petty cash purchases. Most pocket calendars or daily organizers include ledgers that allow you to track these small purchases. If you can't be that organized, at least get a receipt for cash transactions and stash them in a file folder in your desk. Or keep receipts in envelopes labelled with the month and year.

- ✔ **Choosing the wrong entity or form of organization.** When you set up your own business, you can structure its legal and tax organization in a variety of ways. To incorporate or not to incorporate is the first question you need to answer. Those motivated to incorporate do so not out of a love of paperwork (which can be considerable) but out of the desire to shield themselves from liabilities and lawsuits that might be brought against the business. A corporation may also offer opportunities for tax savings.

  A *corporation* is a separate legal entity from you, the individual. For example, if a customer slips on a stray banana peel at your office and decides to sue, the customer can sue your company if you're incorporated but usually can't go after your personal assets. Incorporating makes more sense if you have employees, customers who visit the office, or if you do business with many vendors.

Incorporating isn't always the right answer. For professional services, such as self-employed lawyers, physicians, or tax advisers, incorporating may not necessarily be useful as protection against professional negligence suits related to their work. In such cases, the law may treat the business and the professional as one and the same. The answer for these folks is *professional liability insurance*. Check with the professional associations in your field for information on insurers that offer such policies.

✔ **Not funding a retirement plan.** You should be saving money toward retirement, and you can't beat the tax break RRSPs offer. People who are self-employed are allowed to save up to 18 percent of their net income on an annual basis (less a "pension adjustment" if they also belong to a Registered Pension Plan) up to a set maximum. To learn more about RRSPs, see Chapter 11.

✔ **Not using numbers to help manage business.** If you are a small-business owner and you don't track your income, expenses, staff performance, and customer data on a regular basis, your tax return may be the one and only time during the year when you take a financial snapshot of your business. After you go to all the time, trouble, and expense to file your tax return, make sure that you reap the rewards of all your work: Use those numbers to help analyze and manage your business.

Some bookkeepers and tax preparers can provide you with management information reports on your business from the tax data they compile for you. Just ask! Likewise, software packages can help. See our recommendations later in this chapter.

✔ **Not paying family help.** If your children, spouse, or other relatives help with some aspect of your business, consider paying them for the work. Besides showing them that you value their work, this practice may reduce your family's tax liability. For example, a child is usually in a lower tax bracket than you are. So by shifting income to the child, you cut your tax bill.

Tax Resources

All sorts of ways to prepare your tax return exist. Which approach makes sense for you depends on the complexity of your situation and your level of interest in and knowledge of taxes.

Regardless of which approach you take, you should be making financial moves during the year to reduce your taxes. By the time you actually file your return in the following year, it's usually too late for you to take advantage of many tax-reduction strategies.

Revenue Canada assistance

If you have a simple, straightforward tax return, filing it on your own using only the Revenue Canada instructions is fine. This approach is as cheap as you can get. The main costs are time, patience, photocopying expenses (you should always keep a copy for your files), and postage to mail the completed tax return.

Revenue Canada publications don't, in general, have Tip or Warning icons like this book has. Another danger of relying on Revenue Canada is that it has been known to give wrong information on a more-than-infrequent basis. (That may not be the fault of the person you are speaking with. The tax system is so complicated that you need to be very precise about your questions and all the circumstances that may affect your situation.) When you call Revenue Canada with a question, be sure to take notes about your conversation to protect yourself in the event of an audit. Date your notes and include the name of the tax employee you talked to, what you asked, and the employee's responses. File your notes in a folder with a copy of your completed return.

In addition to the standard instructions that come with your tax return, Revenue Canada offers a number of free and helpful tax guides that you can pick up at your nearest taxation centre, or you can call to request them. These guides serve as useful references and provide more detail and insight than the basic Revenue Canada publications. For the self-employed, many booklets are available depending on your occupation, including *Business and Professional Income, Farming Income, Fishing Income,* and *Rental Income.* Other guides deal with specific circumstances, including *Alimony or Maintenance, Are You Moving?, Canadian Residents Going Down South,* and *Home Buyers' Plan.* For retirement planning, you can read *RRSPs and Other Registered Plans for Retirement, How to Calculate Your RRSP Contribution Limit,* and *When You Retire.* To request these documents, call 1-800-959-2221, or 905-712-5813 in the Toronto area. You can also visit the Revenue Canada Web site at www.ccra-adrc.gc.ca.

Preparation and advice guides

Books about tax preparation and tax planning that are written in clear, simple English and that highlight common problem areas are invaluable. They supplement the official instructions not only by helping you to complete your return correctly but also by showing you how to save as much money as possible.

Quite a few preparation guides are on the market. Our favourites are

> ✔ *Taxes For Canadians For Dummies* (ok, excuse our shameless promoting, but this book has everything you need to prepare and save on your tax return)

> ✔ *Winning the Tax Game* (written by Tim Cestnick and published by Prentice Hall)
>
> ✔ *How to Reduce the Tax You Pay* (prepared by Deloitte & Touche and published by Key Porter Books)

Software and online help

If you have access to a computer, good tax-preparation software can be helpful. We like QuickTax, Cantax, and GriffTax.

If you are on the Web, there are many helpful tax-related sites. The federal government has lots of good information available. Two good starting points are the Canada Customs and Revenue Agency (formerly known as Revenue Canada) site at www.ccra-adrc.gc.ca and www.strategis.gc.ca. The major accounting houses all have good sites. In addition to providing general concepts and strategies, they are also a good place to look for comments and perspective on recent changes and new regulations. Among the sites we frequent are those belonging to BDO Dunwoody (www.bdo.ca), Deloitte and Touche (www.deloitte.ca), Ernst & Young (www.ey.com/global), and KPMG (www.kpmg.ca).

Hiring help

Competent tax preparers and advisers can save you money — sometimes more than enough to pay their fees — by identifying tax-reduction strategies you may overlook. They can also reduce the likelihood of an audit, which can be triggered by blunders you might make. Mediocre and lousy tax preparers, on the other hand, may make mistakes and not be aware of sound ways to reduce your tax bite.

Tax practitioners come with varying backgrounds, training, and credentials. One credential is not necessarily better than another. The four main types are preparers, certified general accountants (CGAs), chartered accountants (CAs), and tax lawyers (tricked ya — no acronym!). The more training and specialization a tax practitioner has (and the more affluent his or her clients), the higher the hourly fee usually is. Fees and competence at all levels of the profession vary significantly. If you do hire a tax adviser and you're not sure of the quality of work performed and the soundness of the advice, try getting a second opinion.

Preparers

Among all the tax practitioners, preparers generally have the least amount of training and a greater proportion of them work part time. As with financial planners, no national regulations apply to preparers, and no licensing is required.

The appeal of preparers is that their services are relatively inexpensive — they can do most basic returns for around $100 or so. The drawback, of course, is that you may hire a preparer who doesn't know much more than you do.

Preparers make the most sense for folks who have relatively simple financial lives, who are budget minded, and who hate doing their own taxes. If you're not good about hanging on to receipts or don't want to keep your own files with background details about your taxes, you should definitely look for a tax preparer who's going to be around for a few years. You may need all that stuff someday for an audit, and many tax preparers keep and organize their clients' documentation rather than returning everything each year. Also, going with a firm that is open year-round may be safer (some small shops are open only during tax season) in case questions or problems arise.

Certified general accountants

CGAs are often a sound, economical choice for tax advice. Many certified general accountants have large personal-income-tax practices.

CGAs are best for people with moderately complex returns who don't necessarily need complicated tax-planning advice throughout the year. Many CGAs also have expertise in preparing returns for small businesses. A professional who is familiar with the peculiarities of your industry may be able to give you more complete advice on opportunities for saving and how to organize your business to minimize your tax bill. What's more, he or she will likely be able to do your return more quickly, meaning a lower bill.

CGAs don't close down when the tax season ends. That means you can go to them for advice and help on *your* schedule, and you'll be able to get help if you have problems after filing your return. Fees for a straightforward return should be about $100, while more complex situations (for example a part-time business or investment income) might mean a bill for several hundred dollars.

Chartered accountants (CAs)

CAs are the folks who audit public companies. They tend to have specialties in specific industries or types of businesses. Many CAs work for large firms, such as KPMG, Ernst & Young, PricewaterhouseCoopers, and Deloitte & Touche, that have international operations in both accounting and consulting, so they have the expertise to prepare complicated returns involving investments and earnings in different countries.

CA fees vary tremendously. Most charge around $100 per hour, but CAs at large companies and in high-cost-of-living areas tend to charge somewhat more. The cost of having a CA prepare your return can range anywhere from $150 to several thousand dollars.

Free filing advice

If your return is straightforward, you usually have a way to get some basic advice at no charge on how to prepare your return. And — surprise of surprises — it's all made possible by those helpful folks at Revenue Canada.

Under its long-running Community Volunteer Income Tax program, each year Revenue Canada trains volunteers to know how to prepare simple returns (those without rental income, business expenses, capital gains, and so on). The volunteers come from all walks of life but are often members of charitable organizations and com-munity groups. Advice is usually given in group sessions at local libraries, seniors' homes, and community centres.

Although the program focuses on people who might have special difficulty dealing with their returns — such as new immigrants, the elderly, and the disabled — the program can benefit anybody. And many Canadians do take advantage of the program. To find out whether a volunteer is giving a tax information session in your area, call your local district office of Revenue Canada, your library, or a local volunteer association.

CAs are of greatest value to people completing some of the more unusual and less user-friendly schedules, or who have to file in several countries. A typical CA user might be a Canadian who, because she works a portion of the year in the United States, has to file in both countries and who has numerous tax shelters and real estate investments.

If your return is uncomplicated and your financial situation is stable, hiring a high-priced CA year after year to fill in the blanks is a waste of money. Sometimes you'll be granted an initial interview with a partner, who then has a less qualified — and lower-paid — associate carry out the work. However, the bill you receive for the associate's advice often will reflect the CA's rate.

Paying for the additional cost of a CGA or CA on an ongoing basis makes sense if you can afford it and if your situation is reasonably complex or dynamic. If you're self-employed and/or file lots of other schedules, it may be worth hiring a CGA or CA. But you needn't do so year after year. If your situation grows complex one year and then stabilizes, consider getting help for the perplexing year and then using preparation guides, software, or a lower-cost preparer in the future.

Tax lawyers

Tax lawyers are hired guns who can tackle major tax problems and issues. In fact, many tax lawyers don't prepare returns as a normal practice. Often, their role is to interpret tax regulations and rules and advise accountants and clients on what strategies are acceptable or risky.

Unless you're a super-high-income earner with a complex financial life, it's prohibitively expensive to hire a tax lawyer to prepare your annual return. Because of their level of specialization and training, tax lawyers tend to have the highest hourly billing rates — $200, $300, or even $400 per hour isn't unusual. The total bill to have a tax lawyer prepare a return that includes complex offshore investments will be in the thousands, if not the *tens* of thousands of dollars.

The more training and specialization a tax practitioner has (and the more affluent his or her clients), the higher the hourly fee is. Select the one that best meets your needs. Fees and competence at all levels of the profession vary significantly. If you're not sure of the quality of work performed and the soundness of the advice, try getting a second opinion.

Dealing with an Audit

On a list of real-life nightmares, most people would rank tax audits right up there with rectal exams and court appearances. The primary trauma of an audit is that many people feel like they're on trial and are being accused of a crime. Take a deep breath and don't panic.

You might be getting audited simply because a business that reports tax information on you, or someone at Revenue Canada, made an error regarding the data on your return. In the vast majority of cases, Revenue Canada conducts its "audit" by corresponding with you through the mail. You may also simply work in an industry or run a type of business that Revenue Canada has targeted in a particular year. Revenue Canada regularly focuses on certain types of employees and professions. Finally, your return may have been red-flagged because of abnormally large deductions or credits.

The most feared type of audit is when you have to schlep to the local Revenue Canada office. Unfortunately, you'll most likely be one of the majority of audit survivors who end up owing more tax money. The amount of additional tax that you owe in interest and penalties hinges on how your audit goes.

Audit preparation

Preparing for an audit is sort of like preparing for a test in school. Revenue Canada informs you of which sections of your tax return the agency wants to examine.

The first decision you face when you get an audit notice is whether to handle it yourself or to turn to a tax adviser to represent you. Hiring representation costs money out-of-pocket but may save you time, stress, and dollars.

If you normally prepare your own return and are comfortable with your understanding of the areas being audited, then do it yourself. When the amount of tax money in question is small in comparison to the fee you'd pay the tax adviser to represent you, self-representation is probably the answer. However, if you're likely to turn into a babbling, intimidated fool and are unsure of how to present your situation, hire a tax adviser to represent you (see the "Hiring help" section in this chapter for information about whom to hire).

If you decide to handle the audit yourself, get your act together sooner rather than later. Don't wait until the night before to start gathering receipts and other documentation. You may discover, for example, that you can't find certain documents and need to contact others to get copies.

You need to document and be ready to speak with the auditor only about the areas the audit notice says are being investigated. Organize your various documents and receipts into folders. You want to make it as easy as possible for the auditor to review your materials. *Don't* show up, dump shopping bags full of receipts and paperwork on the auditor's desk, and say, "Here it is — *you* figure it out."

Whatever you do, *don't ignore your audit request letter.* Revenue Canada is the ultimate bill-collection agency. And if you end up owing more money (the unhappy result of most audits), the sooner you pay the less interest and penalties you'll owe.

The day of reckoning

Two people with identical situations can walk into an audit and come out with very different results. The loser can end up owing much more in taxes and have the audit expanded to include other parts of the return. The winner can end up owing less tax money than he or she really should pay under the tax laws.

Here's how to be a winner:

- ✔ **Treat the auditor as a human being.** Obvious advice, yes, but very often not practised by taxpayers. You may be resentful or angry about being audited. You may be tempted to gnash your teeth and tell the auditor how unfair it is that an honest taxpayer like you had to spend hours getting ready for this. You might feel like ranting and raving about how the government wastes too much of your tax money or that the party in power is out to get you. Bite your tongue.

  Believe it or not, most auditors are decent people just trying to do their job. They are well aware that taxpayers don't like seeing them. Don't suck up, either — just relax and be yourself. Behave as you would around a boss whom you like — with respect and congeniality.

✔ **Stick to the knitting.** Your audit is to discuss *only* the sections of your tax return that are in question. The more you talk about other areas or things that you're doing, the more likely the auditor will probe into other items. Don't bring documentation for parts of your return not being audited. Besides creating more work for yourself, you might be opening a can of worms that needn't be opened. Should the auditor inquire about areas not covered by the audit notice, politely say that you're not prepared to discuss those other issues and that another meeting should be scheduled.

✔ **Don't argue when you disagree.** State your case. When the auditor wants to disallow a deduction or otherwise increase the taxes you owe and you don't agree, state once why you don't. If the auditor won't budge, don't get into a knock-down, drag-out confrontation. He or she may not want to lose face and is inclined to find additional tax money — that's the auditor's job. *Remember:* When necessary, you can plead your case with several layers of people above your auditor. If that fails and you still feel wronged, you can take your case to tax court.

✔ **Don't be intimidated.** Most auditors are not tax geniuses. The work is stressful — being in a job in which people dislike seeing you is not easy. Turnover is quite high. The basic Revenue Canada tax boot camp that auditors go through can't and doesn't come close to covering all the technical details and nuances in the tax code. So you may not be at such a disadvantage in your tax knowledge after all, especially if you work with a tax adviser.

Part III
Investing Crash Course

The 5th Wave   By Rich Tennant

"Hey, Luke, I was just thinking — why don't we try investing some of the stolen loot in some mutual funds, bonds, maybe check out some international fund, or real estate,... shoot, what am I talking about? Let's just stash it in the old mine shaft like before."

In this part . . .

We lay out the basics of investing and show you how to choose your investments wisely. Earning and saving are hard work, so you should be careful where you invest the fruits of your labour. This part is where you find out the real story on such things as stocks, bonds, mutual funds, the differences between investing in retirement and non-retirement plans, how to invest for university, and how to buy a home.

Chapter 8

Important Investment Concepts

*M*aking wise investments need not be complicated. However, many investors get bogged down in the morass of the thousands of investment choices out there. This chapter helps you grasp the important, "bigger picture" issues that will ensure that your investment plan meshes with your needs and the realities of the investment marketplace.

First, Establish Your Goals

Before you select a specific investment, you should first determine your investment needs and goals. Why are you saving this pile of money? What are you going to use it for? You can't and don't need to earmark *every* dollar, but you should set some major objectives. Doing so is important because the expected use of the money determines how much time it's going to be invested. And that, in turn, helps determine which investment you choose.

Suppose the money you plan on using for Uncle Louie's sure-win deal is all the liquid cash you have available. What if Louie's deal goes bust? What are you going to tap into in the event of an emergency? Bad things don't just happen to "other" people. You need a safety net in case you lose your job or are hit with unexpected expenses.

The risk level of your investments should factor in your time frame *and your comfort level.* There's no sense investing in high-risk vehicles if you're going to spend all your profits on ulcer-induced medical bills. For example, suppose you've been accumulating money for a down payment on a home that you'd like to buy in a few years. You can't afford much investment risk with that money. You're going to need that money sooner rather than later. Putting that money in the stock market, then, is probably not a wise move. As you see later in this chapter, the stock market can drop a lot in a year or over several consecutive years. So stocks are probably too risky a place to invest home-down-payment money you plan on using soon.

Perhaps you're saving toward a longer-term goal, such as retirement, that is 20 or 30 years away. In this case, you're in a position to make riskier investments because your holdings have more time to bounce back from temporary losses or setbacks. A retirement savings plan that you leave alone for 20 years or longer may be where you should consider investing in growth investments like stocks. You can tolerate year-to-year volatility in the market — you have time on your side. If you haven't yet done so, take a tour through Chapter 3, which helps you contemplate and establish your financial goals.

The Major Investment Flavours

Jumping right into picking a particular investment is the fun and exciting part for most people. Or, perhaps you're tired of thinking about where to invest and watching others make profits while you sit on the sidelines. You may have an idea from some reading you've done or from some entertaining investment type touting investments on television or online. Or maybe Uncle Louie is whispering in your ear that he's gonna get you in on the ground floor of a great new opportunity — a real sure thing.

Lending investments

For a moment, forget all the buzzwords and jargon and product names you've heard tossed around in the investment world — in many cases, they're only meant to obscure what an investment really is and to hide the hefty fees and commissions it charges. Imagine a world with only two investment flavours — chocolate and vanilla ice cream (or low-fat, non-dairy frozen dessert for you health-minded folks). Just two choices. Might make the ice cream shop a lot less interesting, but it would sure simplify your decision.

The investment world is really just as simple. You have only two major investment choices: You can be either a lender or an owner.

You're a *lender* when you invest your money in a guaranteed investment certificate (GIC), a treasury bill (T-bill), or a bond issued by a company like Bombardier, for example. In each case, you lend your money to an organization — a bank, the federal government, or Bombardier. You are paid an agreed-upon rate of interest for lending your money. You are also promised to have your original investment (the *principal*) returned to you on a specific date.

The best that can happen with a lending investment is that you are paid all of the interest in addition to your original investment — the *principal* — as promised. Given that the investment landscape is littered with carcasses of failed investments, this is not a result to take for granted.

The worst that can happen is that you don't get everything you were promised. Promises can be broken under extenuating circumstances. When a company goes bankrupt, for example, you can lose all or part of your original investment.

 Another risk is that you get what you were promised, but because of the ravages of inflation, your money is worth less — it has less purchasing power than you thought it would. Back in the 1960s, for example, high-quality companies issued long-term bonds that paid approximately 4 percent interest. At the time, buying a long-term bond seemed like a good deal because the cost of living was increasing only 2 percent per year.

When inflation rocketed to 6, 8, 10 percent and higher, those 4 percent bonds didn't seem so attractive any longer. The interest and principal didn't buy nearly the amount they did years earlier when inflation was lower. Table 8-1 shows the reduction in the purchasing power of your money at varying rates of inflation after just ten years.

Table 8-1	Reduction in Purchasing Power Due to Inflation
Inflation Rate	**Reduction in Purchasing Power after 10 Years**
6 percent	–44 percent
8 percent	–54 percent
10 percent	–61 percent

A common mistake that some conservative-minded investors make is that they think they are diversifying their long-term investment money by buying several bonds, some GICs, T-bills, and an annuity. The problem, however, is that all these investments pay a relatively low fixed rate of return that is exposed to the vagaries of inflation.

 A final drawback to lending investments is that you do not share in the success of the organization to which you lend your money. If the organization doubles or triples in size and profits, neither your principal nor your interest rate doubles or triples in size along with it; they stay the same. Of course, such success should ensure that you will get your promised interest and principal back.

Ownership investments

You're an *owner* when you invest your money in an asset, such as a company or real estate, which has the ability to generate earnings or profits. In the first case, suppose that you own 100 shares of Nortel stock. With hundreds of millions of shares of stock outstanding, Nortel is a mighty big company — your 100 shares represent a tiny piece of it.

What do you get for your small slice of Nortel? As a shareholder, you share in the profits of a company in the form of annual dividends as well as an increase (you hope) in the stock price if the company grows and becomes more profitable. That's when things are going well. The downside is that if Nortel's business declines, your stock can become worth less (or even worthless!).

Although much of this part of the book is devoted to stocks, we are surprised by how many investors we talk with these days haven't considered other financially rewarding ownership investments such as real estate. Real estate can produce profits by being rented out for income (profits come when rental income exceeds the expense of owning the property) or by being sold at a higher price than what you paid to buy it. We know numerous successful real estate investors who have earned excellent long-term profits.

As with other ownership investments, the value of real estate depends not only on the particulars of the individual property but also on the health and performance of the local economy. When the local economy is growing and more jobs are being produced at higher wages, real estate should do well. When companies in the community are laying people off left and right and excess housing is sitting vacant because of previous overbuilding, then rents and property values are likely to fall.

A third way many investors have built substantial wealth is through small business. According to *Forbes* magazine, more of the U.S. and the world's wealthiest individuals have built their wealth through their stake in small businesses than through any other vehicle. Small business is the engine that drives much of North America's economic growth. Although firms with fewer than 20 employees account for about one-quarter of all employees, such small firms in the past two decades were responsible for nearly half of all new jobs created.

You can participate in small business in a variety of ways. You can start your own business, buy and operate an existing business, or simply invest in promising small businesses.

In the chapters ahead, we explain each of these major investment types in detail.

Shun gambling instruments and behaviours

Although investing is often risky, it's not gambling — at least not the way that we advocate you invest. *Gambling* is putting your money into schemes that are sure to lose you money over time. That's not to say that everyone loses or that you lose every time you play. However, the deck is stacked against you. The house wins most of the time.

In some cases, as with horse racing, gambling casinos, and lotteries, the system is set up to pay out 50 to 60 cents on the dollar. The rest goes to administration of the system and — don't forget that these are businesses — profits. Sure, your chosen horse may win a race or two, but in the long run you're almost guaranteed to lose about 40 to 50 percent of what you bet. Would you put your money in an "investment" where your expected return was negative 40 percent?

Gambling in the investment world is *speculation* — these opportunities are found in sales and trading of futures, options, and commodities. Futures, options, and commodities are *derivatives*, financial investments with value derived from the performance of another security such as a stock or bond.

You may have heard the radio ad by the firm of Fleecem, Cheatem, and Leavem, advocating that you buy heating oil futures because the cold-weather months lead to the use of more heating oil. You call and are impressed by the smooth-talking vice-president who spends so much time with little ol' you. His logic makes sense, and he's spent a lot of time with you, so you send him a cheque for $10,000.

Provincial governments pushing gambling?

The provinces have gotten into the gambling business in a big way as a way to bring in tax revenue. This is wrong for many reasons. First, it's been well documented that lotteries and casinos obtain most of their business from those least able to afford them — primarily middle- and low-income earners. They end up creating an additional tax on the less economically well off and operate on the basis of false hopes.

Second, government endorsement of gambling promotes the get-rich-quick mentality. Why get an education and work hard over the years when you can solve all your financial concerns with the next ticket you buy or slot you pull? Gambling also contributes to our nationally low personal savings rate.

Finally, gambling, like alcohol and tobacco, can be addictive and destructive. In the worst cases, gambling and gambling debts can split up families and lead to divorce or even suicides and murders.

It's bad enough that legalized gambling exists. It's even worse that, in the pursuit of short-term profits and a quick fix, local governments are piling into this business. Government is fostering an irresponsible attitude toward money.

Doing so isn't much different from blowing $10,000 at the craps tables in Las Vegas. Futures prices depend on short-term, highly volatile price movements. As with gambling, you occasionally win when the market moves the right way at the right time. But in the long run, you're gonna lose. In fact, you can lose it all.

Options are the same — you're betting on short-term movements of a specific security. If you have inside information, as Ivan Boesky did, such that you know in advance when a major corporate development is going to occur, you can get rich. But don't forget one minor detail — insider trading is illegal. You may end up in the slammer like Boesky.

Honest brokers who help their clients invest in stocks, bonds, and mutual funds tell you the truth about commodities, futures, and options. A former broker who used to work for Merrill Lynch and Shearson Lehman over a period of 12 years had this to say about these types of investments: "I had one client who made money in options, futures, or commodities, but the only reason he came out ahead was because he was forced to pull money out to close on a home purchase just when he happened to be ahead. The commissions were great for me, but there's no way a customer will make money in them." Remember these words if you're tempted to gamble with futures, options, and the like.

Day trading — which is the rapid buying and selling of securities online — is a newer and equally foolish vehicle for most individual investors to pursue. While placing trades via the Internet is far cheaper than the older methods of trading (such as telephoning a broker), the more you trade the more trading costs will eat into your investment capital. During a rising stock market, day traders can certainly make some profits. However, over an extended period of time, the great majority of day traders inevitably underperform the broad market averages. In those rare instances where a day trader does a little better, it's rarely worth the time and personal sacrifices that the day trader and his family and friends endure.

Investment Returns

You know the difference between ownership and lending investments. We hope you can also distinguish gambling and speculation from true investments.

"That's all well and good," you say, "but how do I choose which type of investments to put my money into? How much can I make, and what are the risks?"

Good questions. We'll start with the returns you *might* make. We say "might" because we're looking at history, and history is a record of the past. Using history to predict the future, especially the near future, is dangerous. History may repeat itself, but not always in exactly the same fashion and not necessarily when you expect it to.

Ownership investments like stocks and real estate have returned around 10 percent per year on average in North America, handily beating lending investments such as bonds (around 5 to 7 percent) and savings accounts (roughly 3 to 4 percent) in the investment performance race. Inflation has averaged 3 percent per year.

If you already know that the stock market can be risky, perhaps you're wondering why it's worth the anxiety and potential losses to invest in stocks. Why bother for a few extra percent per year? Well, over many years, a few extra percent per year can really magnify the growth of your money (see Table 8-2). The more years you have to invest, the greater the difference a few percent makes in your returns.

If you invest $10,000 for 25 years or 40 years (and are able to defer any taxes):

Table 8-2	The Difference a Few Percent Makes	
At This Rate of Investment Return on $10,000	*You'll Have This Much in 25 Years*	*You'll Have This Much in 40 Years*
4% (savings account)	$26,658	$48,010
6% (bond)	$42,918	$102,857
10% (stocks and real estate)	$108,347	$452,592

Investing is not a spectator sport. You can't earn good returns in stocks and real estate if you keep your money in cash and sit on the sidelines. When you do invest in growth investments such as stocks and real estate, don't chase one new investment after another trying to beat the market average returns. *The biggest value is to be in the market, not to beat it.*

Investment Risks

Many investors have a simplistic understanding of what risk means and how to apply it to their investment decisions. For example, when compared to the yo-yo motions of the stock market, a bank savings account may seem like a less risky place to put your money. Over the long term, however, the stock market usually beats the rate of inflation; money in a savings account does not. Thus, if you are saving your money for a long-term goal like retirement, a savings account can be a "riskier" place to put your money.

Before you invest, ask yourself these three questions:

- ✔ What am I saving and investing this money for? In other words, what's my goal?
- ✔ What is my timeline for this investment?
- ✔ What is the historical volatility of the investment I'm considering, and does that suit my comfort level and timeline for this investment?

With answers to these questions you will have a better understanding of *risk,* and you will be able to match your savings goals to their most appropriate investment vehicles. In Chapter 3, we help you to consider your savings goals and timeline. We address investment risk and returns in the sections that follow.

Stock and bond risks

Given the relatively higher historic returns we mention for ownership invest- ments in the last section, some people think they should put all of their money in stocks and real estate. So what's the catch?

Investments with a potential for higher returns carry greater risks. Risk and return go hand in hand. If you're not willing to accept more risk, you're not going to be able to achieve higher rates of return.

The risk with ownership investments is the short-term fluctuations in their value. On average during this century, for example, stocks in North America have declined by more than 10 percent in a year every five years. Drops in stock prices of more than 20 percent occurred, on average, once every ten years. Real estate prices suffer similar periodic setbacks.

Thus, to earn those generous long-term returns from ownership investments like stocks and real estate, you must be willing to tolerate volatility. That's why you absolutely should not put all your money in the stock or real estate market. At a minimum, you should not invest your emergency money or money you expect to use within the next five years in such volatile investments.

The shorter the time period that you have, the less likely that growth-oriented investments like stocks will beat out lending-type investments like bonds. Table 8-3 illustrates the historical relationship between U.S. stock and bond returns based on number of years held.

Table 8-3	Stocks versus Bonds
Number of Years Investment Held	*Likelihood of Stocks Beating Bonds*
1	60%
5	70%
10	80%
20	91%
30	99%

Some types of bonds have higher yields than others, but the risk-reward relationship remains intact. A bond generally pays you a higher rate of interest as compared to other bonds when it is:

- ✔ Lower credit — to compensate for the higher risk of default and higher likelihood of losing your investment

- ✔ Longer-term maturity — to compensate for the risk that you'll be unhappy with the bond's interest rate if interest rates move up

Focus on the risks that you can control

If asked what they would like to learn about money, many people would reply with something similar to what one personal finance student had to say: "I want to learn what to invest my money in now as the stock market is over-valued and interest rates are about to go up, so bonds are dicey and banks give lousy interest — *help*!"

This student recognizes the risk of price fluctuations in her investments, but she also seems to believe, like too many people, that there's a way to expect or predict what's going to happen. How does *she* know that the stock market is overvalued, and why hasn't the rest of the world figured it out? How does *she* know that interest rates are about to go up, and why hasn't the rest of the world figured that out, either?

When you invest in stocks and other growth-oriented investments, you must accept the volatility of these investments. Invest the money that you have earmarked for the longer term in these vehicles. Minimize the risk of these investments through diversification. Don't buy just one or two stocks; buy a number of stocks. Later in this chapter, we discuss what you need to know about diversification.

Investing lump sums via dollar cost averaging

Whether through accumulation of funds over the years, an inheritance, or a recent windfall from work that you've done, you have a problem when you have a large chunk of cash to invest. Many people, of course, would like to have your problem. (You're not complaining, right?) You want to invest your money, but you're a bit skittish, if not outright terrified, at the prospect of investing the lump of money all at once.

If the money is residing in a savings or money market account, you may feel like it's wasting away. You want to put it to work!

Our first words of advice: Don't rush. Nothing is wrong with earning only a few percentage points on your money in a money market account or high-interest savings account (see Chapter 13 for recommendations of the best money market funds and high-interest accounts). Remember that a money market fund or high-interest savings account beats the heck out of rushing into an investment in which you might lose 20 percent or more. We've spoken with people in a state of near-panic. Typically, these folks have GICs coming due and feel that they must decide exactly where they want to invest the money in the 48 hours before the GIC matures.

Take a deeeep breath. You have absolutely no reason to rush into an important decision. Instruct your friendly banker that when the GIC matures, you'd like the proceeds to be put in the bank's highest-yielding savings or money market account. Alternatively, arrange to have the funds automatically transferred to a high-interest savings account. That way, your money still earns interest while you buy yourself some breathing room.

One approach to investing is called *dollar cost averaging* (DCA). DCA is a process in which you invest your money in equal chunks on a regular basis, such as once a month.

For example, if you have $60,000 to invest, you can invest $2,500 per month until it's all invested, which takes a couple of years. The money that's awaiting future investment isn't lying fallow. You keep it in a money market–type account earning a bit of interest while it's waiting its turn.

The attraction of DCA is that it allows you to ease into riskier investments instead of jumping in all at once. The benefit may be that if the price of the investment drops after some of your initial purchases, you can buy some later at a lower price. Had you instead dumped all your money into the "sure win" investment at once and then it dropped like a stone, you'd kick yourself for not waiting.

The flip side of DCA is that when your investment of choice appreciates in value, you may wish that you had invested your money faster. Another possible drawback of DCA is that you may get cold feet continuing to pour money into an investment that's dropping in value. Many people who are attracted to DCA out of fear of buying before a price drop end up bailing out of what feels like a sinking ship.

DCA can also cause headaches with your taxes when the time comes to sell investments held outside retirement plans. When you buy an investment at many different times and prices, accounting is muddied as you sell blocks of the investment.

DCA is most valuable when the money you want to invest represents a large portion of your total assets and you can stick to a schedule. Make DCA automatic so that you're less likely to chicken out should the investment fall after your initial purchases. Most investment firms recommended in the next few chapters provide automatic exchange services.

Low-risk, high-return investments

Despite what professors teach in the nation's leading business and finance graduate school programs, low-risk investments that almost certainly will lead to high returns *are* available.

We can think of at least four such investments:

- **Pay off consumer debt.** If you're paying 10, 14, or 18 percent interest on an outstanding credit card or other consumer loan, pay it off before investing. To get a comparable return through other investment vehicles (after the government takes its share of your profits), you would have to start a new career as a loan shark. If between federal and provincial taxes you're in a 40-percent tax bracket, and you're paying 10 percent interest on a consumer loan, you'd need to annually earn a whopping 17 percent on an interest-earning investment pre-tax to justify not paying off the debt. Good luck!

  When your only source of funds to pay off debt is a small emergency reserve equal in size to a few months' living expenses, paying off debt may involve some risk. Tap into your emergency reserves only if you have a backup source — for example, the ability to borrow from a willing family member.

- **Invest in your health.** Eat healthy, exercise, and relax.

- **Invest in friends and family.** Improve your relationships with loved ones. Invest the time and effort in making them better.

- **Invest in personal and career development.** Learn a new hobby, improve your communication skills, or read widely. Take an adult education course or go back to school for a degree. Your investment will surely pay off in higher paycheques and greater happiness.

Diversification

Diversification is one of the most powerful investment concepts. All it really means is that you save and place your eggs (or investments) in different baskets.

Diversification requires you to place your money in different investments with returns that are not completely correlated. This is a fancy way of saying that, with your money in different places, when some of your investments are down in value odds are that others are up.

To decrease the odds of all of your investments getting clobbered at the same time, you must put your money in different types or classes of investments such as bonds, stocks, real estate, and small business (we cover all these investments and more in Chapter 9). You can further diversify your investments by investing in domestic as well as international markets.

Within a given class of investments, such as stocks, to diversify by investing in different types of stocks that perform well under various economic conditions is important. For this reason, mutual funds, which are diversified portfolios of securities such as stocks or bonds, are a highly useful investment vehicle. You buy into the mutual fund, which in turn pools your money with that of many others to invest in a vast array of stocks or bonds.

You can look at the benefits of diversification in two ways:

✔ Diversification reduces or dampens the volatility in the value of your whole portfolio. In other words, you can achieve the same rate of return that a single investment can provide with reduced fluctuations in value.

✔ Diversification allows you to obtain a higher rate of return for a given level of risk.

Keep in mind that no one, no matter whom he works for or what credentials he has, can guarantee returns on investments other than bonds that you hold until they mature or other interest-earning investments such as GICs. You can do good research and you can be lucky, but no one is free from the risk of losing money outside of truly guaranteed investments. Diversification allows you to hedge the risk of your investments. See Figures 8-1, 8-2, and 8-3 to get an idea of how diversifying can reduce your risk (figures in these charts use the longer historical data available in the U.S., and are adjusted for inflation).

Figure 8-1:
Value of $10,000 invested from 1928–1937.

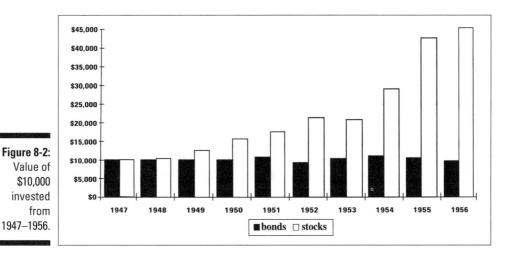

Figure 8-2:
Value of
$10,000
invested
from
1947–1956.

Figure 8-3:
Value of
$10,000
invested
from
1972–1980.

Notice that different investments did better during various time periods.
Because the future can't be predicted, you are safer diversifying your money
into different investments. (In case you're wondering what the 1990s looked
like, stocks appreciated greatly and bonds did pretty well, too, while gold and
silver did poorly.)

Asset allocation: Spreading it around

How you spread your investing dollars among different investment options (stocks, bonds, money market accounts, and so on) is known as *asset allocation*. Before you can intelligently decide how to allocate your assets, you should consider a number of issues, including your present financial situation, your goals and priorities, as well as the pros and cons of various investment options.

Although stocks and real estate offer investors attractive long-term returns, they can and do suffer significant declines in value from time to time. Thus, these investments are not suitable for money that you think you may want or need to use within, say, the next five years.

 Money market and bond investments are good places to keep money that you expect to use sooner. Everyone should have a reserve of money — about three to six months' worth of living expenses — in a money market fund or high-interest savings account that they can access in an emergency. Shorter-term bonds or bond mutual funds can serve as a higher-yielding, secondary emergency cushion (refer to Chapter 3 for more on emergency reserves).

 Bonds can also be useful for some longer-term investing for diversification purposes. For example, when investing for retirement, placing a portion of your money in bonds helps to buffer stock market declines. The remaining chapters in this part of the book detail your various investment options and how to select those that best meet your needs.

Allocating money for the long term

Investing money for retirement is a classic long-term goal that most of us have. Your current age and the number of years until you retire should be the biggest factors in allocating money for long-term purposes. The younger you are and the more years you have before retirement, the more comfortable you should be with growth-oriented (and more volatile) investments, such as stocks and investment real estate.

 One useful guideline for dividing or allocating your money between longer-term-oriented growth investments such as stocks and more conservative lending investments such as bonds is to subtract your age from 100 (or 120 if you want to be aggressive) and invest the resulting percentage in stocks. Invest what's left over in bonds.

For example, if you're 30 years old, that would mean that you could invest from 70 (100 minus 30) to 90 (120 minus 30) percent in stocks. What's left over — 10 to 30 percent — would be invested in bonds.

Table 8-4 lists some guidelines for allocating long-term money. All you need to figure out is how old you are and the level of risk you're comfortable with.

Table 8-4	Allocating Long-Term Money	
Your Investment Attitude	*Bond Allocation (%)*	*Stock Allocation (%)*
"Play it safe"	= Age	= 100–age
"Middle of the road"	= Age–10	= 110–age
"Aggressive"	= Age–20	= 120–age

For example, if you're the conservative sort who doesn't like a lot of risk but recognizes the value of striving for some growth and making your money work harder, you're a *middle-of-the-road* type. Using Table 8-4, if you're 40 years old you might consider putting 30 percent (40–10) in bonds and 70 percent (110–40) in stocks.

In most employer retirement plans, mutual funds are the typical investment vehicle. If your employer's retirement plan includes more than one stock mutual fund as an option, you may want to try discerning which options are best by using the criteria outlined in Chapter 10.

Historically, most employees haven't had to make their own investing decisions with retirement money. Pension plans, in which the company directs the investments, were more common in previous years. It's interesting to note that in a typical pension plan, companies choose to allocate the majority of money to stocks (about 60 percent), with a bit less in bonds (about 35 percent) and other investments. For more information on investing in retirement accounts, please see Chapter 11.

Stick with your allocations: Don't trade

Your allocation of your investment dollars should be driven by your goals and desire to take risk. As you get older, for most investors, it makes sense to gradually scale back on the riskiness (and therefore growth potential) of your portfolio.

Don't tinker with your portfolio daily, weekly, or monthly. (Every year or two, you may want to "rebalance" your holdings to get your mix to a desired asset allocation, as discussed in the previous section.) You should not engage in trading in the hopes of buying into a hot investment and selling your losers. Although hopping onto a "winner" and dumping a "loser" may provide some short-term psychological comfort, in the long term such an investment strategy can produce below-average returns.

By the time an investment gets front-page coverage and everyone is talking about its stunning rise, it's definitely time to take a reality check. The higher the value of an investment rises, the greater the danger that it's overpriced. Its next move may be downward. Don't follow the herd.

In recent years, some technology (especially Internet) stocks have had spectacular rises, thus attracting a lot of attention. Although the Canadian and U.S. economies are increasingly becoming technologically based, that doesn't mean that any price you pay for a technology stock is fine. Some investors who neglected to do basic research and who bought into attention-grabbing, high-flying technology stocks recently have lost 50 percent or more of their investments — and this during a time period when the overall stock market was moving higher. Ouch!

Conversely, when things look bleak, giving up hope is easy — who wants to be associated with a loser? However, investors who panicked and sold *after* the October 1987 stock market crash missed out on a tremendous buying opportunity. Ditto for those who dumped stocks after the smaller declines in the stock markets in 1990, 1994, and 1998.

Most people like buying everything from clothing to cars to ketchup on sale — yet whenever the stock market has a clearance sale, most investors stampede for the exits instead of snatching up great buys. Demonstrate your courage; don't follow the herd. After all, lemmings die that way. (By the way, how is it that lemmings aren't extinct?)

Investment Firms Are Not Created Equal

Thousands of firms sell investments and manage money. Banks, mutual fund companies, securities brokerage firms, and even insurance companies all vie for your hard-earned dough.

Just to make matters more complicated, each industry plays in the others' backyards. You can find banks that offer securities brokerage, insurance firms that are in the mutual fund business, and mutual fund companies that offer mortgages and even insurance through related trust companies. You benefit somewhat from all this competition and one-stop shopping convenience. On the other hand, some firms are novices at particular businesses and count on the fact that some people shop by brand-name recognition.

Where to focus

You should do business with firms that:

- ✔ **Offer the best-value investments in comparison to their competitors.**
Value combines performance and cost. Given the level of risk that you're
comfortable with, you'd like investments that offer higher rates of return,
but you don't want to have to pay a small fortune for them. Commissions,
management fees, maintenance fees, and other charges can turn a
high-performance investment into a mediocre or poor one.

- ✔ **Employ representatives who do not have an inherent self-interest in
steering you into a particular type of investment.** This criterion has
nothing to do with whether an investment firm hires polite, well-educated,
or well-dressed people. The most important factor is the way the
company compensates its employees. If the investment firm's personnel
are paid on commission, it's tough for employees not to focus on their
compensation. Give preference to investing through firms that do not
tempt their employees to push one investment over another in order to
generate more fees.

No-load (commission-free) mutual fund companies

Mutual funds are an ideal investment vehicle for most investors. You can invest
in mutual funds without paying sales commissions through *no-load mutual
fund companies*. In other words, every dollar you invest goes to work in the
mutual funds you choose — nothing is siphoned off to pay sales commissions.
See Chapter 10 for details on investing in mutual funds.

Discount brokers

Just over a generation ago, when investors bought or sold stocks, bonds, and
other securities, they were charged fixed commissions. In other words, no
matter which brokerage firm an investor did business with, the cost of the
firm's services was set. And the level of commissions was high.

In one of the most beneficial changes for investors, the Securities and Exchange
Commission (SEC) deregulated the U.S. retail brokerage industry, effective
May 1, 1975. In 1983, The Toronto and Montreal stock exchanges followed
suit. Brokerage firms could then charge people whatever their little hearts
desired. You may think that this change opened the door to exorbitantly high
rates. In fact, it did the opposite. A fair and open free market is good for
consumers. Competition inevitably resulted in more and better choices.

Most firms that were in business before that time continued doing business
as usual: That is, they continued to pay their brokers based on the amount of
trading their customers did and which investments they sold.

Fortunately, many new brokerage firms opened that did not do business the old way. They were dubbed *discount brokers* because the fees they charged customers were substantially lower than what brokers charged under the old fixed-fee system.

Even more important than saving the customer money, discount brokers established a vastly improved compensation system that greatly reduced conflicts of interest. Discount brokers generally pay their brokers salaries. The term *discount broker* is actually not an enlightening one. It is certainly true that this new breed of brokerage firm saves you lots of money when you invest. You can easily save 50 to 80 percent through the major discount brokers. But these firms' investments are not "on sale" or second-rate. Discount brokers are simply brokers without major conflicts of interest. Of course, like any other for-profit enterprise, they want your business and they are in business to make money. The more often you buy and sell investments, the more they make on commissions.

Places to consider avoiding

The worst places to invest are those that charge you a lot, have mediocre or poorly performing investments, and have major conflicts of interest. The prime conflict of interest comes with investment firms that pay their brokers commissions on the basis of how much and what they sell. The result: Some investment firms sell lots of stuff that pays fat commissions and churn your account (because each transaction has a fee, the more you buy and sell, the more money they make).

 Many folks who call themselves *financial planners* or *financial consultants* work on commission. In addition to working at the bigger brokerage firms, many of them belong to so-called *broker-dealer networks,* which provide back-office support and investment products to sell. When a person claiming to be a financial planner or adviser is part of a broker-dealer network, odds are quite high you're dealing with an investment salesperson. See Chapter 19 for more background on the financial planning industry and questions to ask an adviser you might hire.

Commissions and their impact on human behaviour

Investment products bring in widely varying commissions. The products that bring in the highest commissions tend to be the ones that money-hungry brokers push the hardest.

Table 8-5 lists the commissions that you pay and that come out of your investment dollars when you work with brokers, financial consultants, and financial planners working on commission.

Table 8-5	Investment Sales Commissions	
Investment Type	*Average Commission on $20,000 Investment*	*Average Commission on $100,000 Investment*
Annuities	$1,400	$7,000
Initial public offerings (new stock issue)	$1,000	$5,000
Limited partnerships	$1,800	$9,000
Load mutual funds	$1,000	$5,000
Options and futures	$2,000+	$10,000+

Besides the fact that you can never be sure that you're getting an unbiased recommendation from a salesperson working on commission, you're wasting unnecessary money. All good investments can be bought on a no-load (commission-free) basis. No-load mutual funds are a good example.

When you're unsure about an investment product that's being pitched to you (and even when you *are* sure), ask for a copy of the prospectus. In the first few pages, check out whether the investment includes a commission (also known as a *load*). While salespeople can hide behind obfuscating titles such as vice-president or financial consultant, a prospectus must detail whether the investment carries a commission.

Investment salespeople's conflicts of interest

Financial consultants (also known as stockbrokers), financial planners, and others who sell investment products can have enormous conflicts of interest in the strategies and specific investment products that they recommend. Commissions and other financial incentives can't help but skew the advice of even the most earnest and otherwise well-intentioned salespeople.

Numerous conflicts of interest can damage your investment portfolio. The following are the most common conflicts to watch out for:

✔ **Pushing higher-commission products.** As we discuss earlier in this chapter, commissions vary tremendously on investment products. At the worst end of the spectrum for you (and the best for a salesperson) are products like limited partnerships, commodities, options, and futures. At the best end of the spectrum for you (and therefore, the worst for a salesperson) are investments such as no-load mutual funds that are 100 percent commission-free.

What to do if you've been fleeced by a broker

You can't sue a broker just because you lose money on that person's investment recommendations. That's life in the big city. However, if you have been the victim of one of the following cardinal financial sins, you may have some legal recourse:

✔ **Misrepresentation and omission.** If you were told, for example, that a particular investment guaranteed returns of 15 percent per year and the investment ends up plunging in value by 50 percent, you were misled. Misrepresentation can also be charged if you are sold an investment with hefty commissions but were originally told that it was commission-free.

✔ **Unsuitable investments.** Retirees who need access to their capital are often advised to invest in limited partnerships (discussed in Chapter 9) for safe, high yields. The yields on most LPs end up being anything but safe. LP investors have also discovered how illiquid their investments are — some can't be liquidated for up to ten years or more.

✔ **Churning.** If your broker or financial planner is constantly trading your investments, odds are that his or her weekly commission cheque benefits at your expense.

✔ **Rogue-elephant salespeople.** When your planner or broker buys or sells without your approval or ignores your request to make a change, you may be able to collect for losses caused by these actions.

Two major types of practitioners — securities lawyers and arbitration consultants — stand ready to help you recover your lost money. You can find securities lawyers by looking under "Lawyers" in the Yellow Pages or by calling your local bar association for referrals. Arbitration consultants can be found under "Arbitrators." If you come up dry, try contacting a broker or financial planner. These sources may be able to give you names and numbers of folks they know.

Most lawyers and consultants usually ask for an upfront fee ranging from several hundred to several thousand dollars to help them cover their expenses and time.

You generally don't end up in a courtroom *The Practice*-style. You'll probably go to arbitration — an agreement you made (probably not realizing it) when you set up an account to work with the broker or planner. Arbitration is usually much quicker, cheaper, and easier for you. You can even choose to represent yourself.

✔ **Recommending active trading.** Investment salespeople sometimes advise you to trade frequently into and out of different securities. They usually base their advice on current news events or an analyst's comments on the security. Sometimes, these moves are valid; more often, they are not. In extreme cases, brokers trade on a monthly basis. By the end of the year, they've churned through your entire portfolio. Needless to say, all these transactions cost you big money in trading fees.

Diversified mutual funds (discussed in Chapter 10) make more sense for many people. You can invest in mutual funds free of sales commissions. Besides saving money on commissions, you earn better long-term returns by having an expert money manager work for you.

✔ **Pushing high-fee products.** Many of the brokerage firms that used to sell investment products only on commission are moving into fee-based investment management. This change is an improvement for investors because it reduces some of the conflicts of interest caused by commissions.

On the other hand, these brokers charge extraordinarily high fees (which are usually quoted as a percentage of assets under management) on their managed investment (wrap) accounts (see the sidebar on wrap accounts).

The value of brokerage research

One of the arguments frequently advanced by brokerage firms and the brokers who work for them is that their research is better. With their insights and recommendations, they say, you'll do better and "beat the market averages."

Wrap or managed accounts

Wrap, or *managed*, accounts are all the rage among commission-based brokerage firms. These accounts go under a variety of names but are similar in that they charge a fixed percentage of the assets under management to invest your money through money managers.

Wrap accounts are poor investments because their management expenses are extraordinarily high — often up to 3 percent per year (some even higher) of assets under management. Remember that in the long haul, stocks can return about 10 percent per year before taxes. So, if you're paying 3 percent per year to have the money managed in stocks, 30 percent of your return (before taxes) is siphoned off. And although wrap fees are tax-deductible, you'll pay tax on any returns beyond that 3 percent, so your net after-tax return may only be 4.5 to 5.5 percent. So the 3 percent wrap actually ends up depleting 40 to 50 percent of your after-tax profits!

Forbes magazine said it best in an article on wrap accounts: "Brokerage firms love wrap accounts because they're so lucrative — for them."

No-load (commission-free) mutual funds offer investors access to the nation's best investment managers for a fraction of the cost of wrap accounts. You can invest in dozens of top-performing funds for an annual expense of 2 percent per year or less (see Chapter 10).

So how do brokerage firms trick investors into paying so much more for access to investment managers? Marketing. Slick, seductive, deceptive, misleading pitches that include some outright lies.

You may be told that you're getting access to investment managers who don't normally take money from small-fry investors like you. Not a single study shows that the performance of money managers has anything to do with the minimum account they handle. Besides, no-load mutual funds hire many of the same managers who work at other money management firms.

You also may be told that you'll earn a higher rate of return, so the extra cost is worth it. You could have earned 18 to 25 percent per year, they say, had you invested with the "Star of Yesterday" investment management company. The key word here is "had." History is history. Many of yesterday's winners become tomorrow's losers or mediocre performers.

Don't believe them. A number of studies clearly demonstrate that most research is barely worth the cost of your morning paper (sometimes not even that)!

Brokerage firm analysts are often overly optimistic when it comes to predicting corporate profits. If analysts were simply inaccurate or bad estimators, you would expect that they would sometimes underestimate and other times overestimate companies' earnings. The discrepancy identifies yet another conflict of interest among many of the brokerage firms.

Brokerage firm analysts are loath to write a negative report about a company because the firms these analysts work for also solicit companies to issue new stock to the public. What better way to show your potential for selling shares at a high price to the public than by showing how much you believe in certain companies and writing glowing reports about their future prospects?

Brokerage analysts have great difficulty being objective. Investment banking (the business of helping companies sell new securities) cannot objectively be done by companies supposedly evaluating and rating the same securities for the investing public.

Experts Who Predict the Future

A common mistake that some investors make is believing that they can increase their investment returns when they follow the prognostications of certain gurus. Many of us may want to believe that some experts can divine the future of the investment world. Believing in gurus makes it easier to accept the risk that you know you're taking to make your money grow. The sage predictions in an investment newsletter or by an "expert" who is repeatedly quoted in financial publications make you feel protected. It's sort of like Linus and his security blanket.

Investment newsletter subscribers and guru followers would generally be better off instead buying a warm blanket — it has a lot more value and costs a whole lot less! No one can predict the future. If they could, they would be so busy investing their own money and getting rich that they wouldn't have the time and desire to share their secrets with you.

Investment newsletters

Many investment newsletters purport to time the markets, telling you exactly the right time to get into and out of certain stocks or mutual funds (or the financial markets in general). Such an approach is doomed to failure in the long run. By failure, we mean that this approach is not going to beat the tried-and-true strategy of buy and hold.

Before you ever consider subscribing to any investment newsletter, you should examine its track record. The newsletter's marketing materials typically hype the supposed returns that the publication's recommendations have produced. Sadly, newsletters seem to be able to make lots of bogus claims without suffering the timely wrath of securities regulators.

Mark Hulbert tracks the performance of the recommendations made by newsletter writers. Hulbert's organization looks at the cold, hard facts of actual returns and shows how your portfolio would have done if you had followed the recommendations of given newsletters.

If you had been so omniscient as to know in advance which five newsletters would give the best advice during the past 15 years (see Table 8-6), after adjusting for the level of risk that each had taken, you would have done worse in four of the five cases than the overall rate of return of the Wilshire 5000 index, the broadest measure of the overall performance of small, medium, and large companies' U.S. stocks.

Table 8-6	The "Best" Newsletters
Newsletter	*Risk-Adjusted Performance Ranking*
Systems & Forecast	108.4
The Chartist	89.1
No-Load Fund X	86.7
Investor's World	82.2
Value Line Investment Survey	80.2
Wilshire 5000 Index	100.0

Source: Hulbert's Financial Digest

Hulbert uses *risk-adjusted returns,* which are corrected for the differences in the amount of risk different newsletters took in their recommendations. For comparative purposes, the risk-adjusted return of the Wilshire 5000 index is set at 100. The best newsletter in Table 8-6, which has a rating of 108.4, has produced an 8.4 percent higher return than expected given the level of risk it takes. Note that four of the five "best" newsletters over the past 15 years have a rating less than 100, implying that their recommendations, given the risk entailed, performed worse than the Wilshire 5000 index.

If, by bad luck, you had been suckered into following the advice of some of the worst newsletters, your investment results would have been disastrous, especially in comparison to what you could have earned in treasury bills or the Wilshire 5000 stock index. Check out Table 8-7.

Table 8-7	The Worst Newsletters Compared to the Market
Newsletter Portfolio	**Past Five-Year Return**
Futures Hotline	–99%
Overpriced Stock Price	–96%
Elliott Wave Theorist	–95%
Short on Value	–86%
Option Adviser	–64%
Granville Market Letter	–62%

Source: Hulbert's Financial Digest

Don't use newsletters for predictive advice. If newsletter writers were that smart about the future of financial markets, they would be money managers making lots more money. The only types of investment newsletters and periodicals that you should consider subscribing to are those that offer research and information rather than simple predictions. We discuss those that fit the bill in the subsequent investment chapters.

Investment gurus

Investment gurus come and go. Some of them get their 15 minutes of fame on the basis of one or two successful predictions that someone in the press remembers (and makes famous). A classic example is a former market analyst at Shearson named Elaine Garzarelli.

Ms. Garzarelli became famous for predicting the stock market's plummet in the fall of 1987. Garzarelli's fund, Smith Barney Shearson Sector Analysis, was established just before the crash. Supposedly, Garzarelli's indicators warned her to stay out of stocks, which she did, and in doing so she saved her fund from the plunge.

Shearson, being a money-minded brokerage, quickly motivated its brokers to sell shares in Garzarelli's fund. In addition to her having avoided the crash, it didn't hurt that Shearson brokers were being rewarded with a hefty 5 percent sales commission for selling her fund. By the end of 1987, investors had poured nearly $700-million U.S. into this fund.

In 1988, Garzarelli's fund was the worst-performing fund among funds investing in growth stocks. From 1988 to 1990, Garzarelli's fund underperformed the Standard & Poor's 500 average by about 43 percent! In 1987 — the year of the crash — Garzarelli outperformed the S&P 500 by about 26 percent. So what she saved her investors by avoiding the crash she lost back — and more — in the years that followed. In fact, Garzarelli's performance was so dismal in the years following the crash that Shearson eventually fired her.

Despite her subpar long-term track record, Garzarelli is still widely quoted as a market soothsayer. She now manages money privately and is hawking investment newsletters. This marketing hype promoting her newsletter recently appeared in a mailed brochure entitled "The Garzarelli Edge":

> "The proven, scientific system that has produced compounded yearly gains of 20.2% since 1982!"

> "Elaine Garzarelli has called every major turn in the Dow since 1982."

Now, if the above were true, why did Garzarelli's investment fund perform so poorly, and why did Shearson fire her in the mid-1990s following numerous years of wrong predictions and dismal performance of her mutual fund? It's also humorous to note that the 20.2-percent return was reportedly "audited by a Big-6 accounting firm." Down in the fine print, however, it says, "Audit Pending." We bet it's still pending.

Every year, new gurus emerge. All it seems to take to leap to guru status these days is one right call or one good stock pick. Recently, for example, prognosticators who recommended one of the high-flying technology stocks were nearly vaulted to instant guru status as the stocks continued climbing.

Pundits who pitched investing in Presstek and Iomega attracted fairly large followings as these stocks seemed to defy gravity and rationale valuations as they rocketed ever skyward. Like Ms. Garzarelli, however, these stocks and their promoters were brought back to reality during the late 1990s when the stocks plummeted by more than 65 percent.

And like other high-flying stocks and the pundits made famous by them, many investors weren't attracted to invest in Presstek and Iomega until nearly everybody was talking about them. By then, those stocks were peaking, and those who bought got clobbered.

Herb Greenberg, a former business writer for the *San Francisco Chronicle,* held a stock market contest that a group of 13-year-olds won. The reason: They put most of their money into Iomega while it was still heading up. Does this make these 13-year-olds investing geniuses to whom we should look for guidance on the next hot stock? Of course not. Treat other pundits who happened to guess right the same way.

Commentators and experts who publish predictive newsletters and who are interviewed in the media can't predict the future. Ignore the predictions and speculations of self-proclaimed gurus and investment soothsayers. The few people who have a slight leg up on everyone else aren't going to share their investment secrets — they're too busy investing their own money! If you have to believe in something to offset your fears, believe in good information and proven investment managers. And don't forget the value of optimism, faith, and hope — regardless of What or Whom you believe in!

Final Thoughts

We cover a lot of ground in this chapter. In the remaining chapters in this section, we detail different investment choices and accounts and how to build a champion portfolio! Before you move on, here are several other issues to keep in mind as you make important investing choices:

- ✔ **Don't invest based on sales solicitations.** Companies that advertise and solicit prospective customers aggressively using tactics such as telemarketing offer some of the worst financial products with the highest fees. Companies with great products don't have to reach their potential customers this way. Of course, all companies have to do some promotion. But the companies with the best investment offerings don't have to use the hard-sell approach and get plenty of new business through word-of-mouth recommendations of satisfied customers.

- ✔ **Don't invest in what you don't understand.** The mistake of not understanding the investments you purchase usually follows from the preceding no-no — buying into a sales pitch. When you don't understand an investment, odds are good that it won't be right for you. Slick-tongued brokers (who may call themselves *financial consultants, advisers,* or *planners*) who earn commissions based on what they sell often talk you into inappropriate investments. Before you invest in anything, you should know its track record, its true costs, and how liquid it is.

- ✔ **Minimize fees.** Avoid investments that carry high sales commissions and management expenses (usually disclosed in a prospectus). Virtually all investments today can be purchased without a salesperson. Besides paying unnecessary commissions, the bigger danger in investing through a salesperson is that you may be directed to a path that's not in your best interests. Management fees create a real drag on investment returns. Not surprisingly, higher-fee investments, on average, perform worse than alternatives with lower fees. High ongoing management fees often go toward lavish offices, glossy brochures, and skyscraper salaries or toward propping up small, inefficient operations. Do you want your hard-earned dollars to support either of these types of businesses?

✔ **Pay attention to tax consequences.** Even if you never become an investment expert, you're smart enough to know that the more money you pay in taxes, the less you have to invest and play with. Channelling investment money into retirement plans allows your money to grow without taxation, and therefore faster, over time (see Chapter 12). For investments outside retirement plans, you need to match the types of investments to your tax situation (see Chapter 13).

Chapter 9

Investment Vehicles

· ·

In This Chapter

▶ Safe and boring investments: Bank and money market accounts and bonds

▶ Investments to grow on: Stocks, real estate, and small business

▶ Oddball investments: Precious metals, annuities, collectibles, and life insurance

· ·

*I*n the investment world, you can place your money in many different types of investment vehicles. Decent investment vehicles work their way methodically around the racetrack, rarely deterred but also never at a fast rate. The best ones make their way through the course at a faster clip, only occasionally slowed by a bump or detour. The worst ones sputter in fits and starts and sometimes crash and burn in a flaming heap.

Which vehicle you choose for your trip depends on where you're going, how fast you want to get there, and what risks you're willing to take along the way. If you haven't yet read Chapter 8, please do so now. In it, we cover a number of investment concepts, such as the difference between lending and ownership investments, that will enhance your ability to choose among the common investment vehicles we discuss in this chapter.

Lending Vehicles for Slow-Trip Money

Everyone should have some money riding in stable, safe investment vehicles. For example, as we discuss in Chapter 3, money that you have earmarked for your short-term bills, both expected and unexpected, should have a seat belt on in the back seat of a Volvo. Likewise, if you're saving money for a home purchase within the next few years, you certainly don't want to risk that money on the roller coaster of the stock market.

The vehicles that follow are appropriate for money that you don't want to put at great risk.

Transaction/chequing accounts

These accounts are best used for depositing your monthly income and paying for your expenditures. When you want to have unlimited cheque-writing privileges and access to your money with an ABM (automated banking machine) card, chequing accounts at local banks are a good bet. Make sure that you shop around for accounts that don't ding you $1 here for use of a bank machine and $10 there for a low balance. Another good choice is a chequing account with President's Choice Financial, which offers no-charge chequing and automatic bill payments.

With interest rates at relatively low levels as they are now, focus on avoiding monthly service charges rather than chasing after a chequing account with a slightly higher interest rate. Some banks, for example, do not require you to maintain a minimum balance to avoid a monthly service charge when you direct-deposit your paycheques.

If you don't need access to ABM machines on every other street corner — an option usually available through larger banks — you can generally get a better chequing account deal at a credit union or an alternative financial institution such as President's Choice Financial. Because you can easily obtain cash through ABM outlets in supermarkets and other retail stores, you may not need to do business with Big City Bank that has branch offices at every intersection.

In any event, you should keep only enough money in the account to service your monthly bill-payment needs. If you consistently keep more than a few thousand dollars in a chequing account, get the excess out. You can earn more in a savings or money market account, which we describe in the next section.

Savings and money market accounts

Savings accounts are available at banks and an expanding number of other institutions entering the market such as President's Choice Financial and ING Direct; money market funds are available through mutual fund companies. The major difference is that money market funds and the high-interest accounts offered by President's Choice Financial, ING Direct, and others generally pay a much better rate of interest. The interest rate paid to you, also known as the *yield,* fluctuates over time, depending on the level of interest rates in the overall economy. (Note that some banks offer money market *accounts,* which are basically like savings accounts and should not be confused with money market mutual *funds.*) In addition, the high-interest accounts typically have no transaction fees.

Bank accounts are backed by the Canada Deposit Insurance Corp. (CDIC). We wouldn't give preference to a bank account just because your investment (principal) is insured, and because of the psychological comfort some people derive from seeing branches of their bank on every second street corner.

High-interest accounts offered by ING Direct and President's Choice Financial are also covered by CDIC insurance. Your money is just as safe as with a traditional bank, as long as you don't have more on deposit than the maximum insured by CDIC. And the lack of bricks-and-mortar outlets shouldn't bother you. In fact, not having the extra expenses of branches and tellers to serve you is a major reason why these companies can pay such high interest rates on your savings. You can reach President's Choice Financial by calling 1-888-8724-724 or on the Web at www.preschoicefinancial.com. ING Direct can be reached at 1-888-464-3232 or on the Web at www.ingdirect.ca.

For an easy way to find out the lowest-cost way to do your banking, look in the consumer information section of Industry Canada's Web site at www.strategis.gc.ca for the Financial Services Charges Calculator. This cool online tool lets you compare what it will cost you to bank with various financial institutions. What's terrific about it is it gives you a precise total cost for the type of banking you do. You enter the number of different transactions you do a month — ABM withdrawals, debit card payments, deposits, automatic bill payments, and so forth. You then tell the calculator which financial institution(s) you are looking at, and it quickly calculates what your monthly fees would add up to.

While money market funds are not covered by CDIC insurance, money market funds are regulated, and dozens of money market funds invest billions of dollars of individuals' and institutions' money. We haven't heard of the industry causing an individual to lose even a penny of principal. The risk difference versus a bank account is nil. General-purpose money market funds invest in safe, short-term bank guaranteed investment certificates (GICs), Government of Canada treasury bills, provincial treasury bills, and corporate commercial paper (short-term debt), which is issued by the largest and most credit-worthy companies. Money market fund investments generally must have an average maturity of less than 180 days. In the unlikely event that an investment in a money market fund's portfolio goes sour, the mutual fund company that stands behind the money market fund would almost certainly cover the loss.

If the lack of insurance on money market funds still spooks you, here's a way to get the best of both worlds: Select a money market fund that invests exclusively in Canadian government securities, which are virtually risk-free because they are backed by the full strength and credit of the federal government. These types of accounts typically pay less interest, usually a quarter-percent less.

Bonds

When you invest in a bond, you effectively lend your money to an organization. When a bond is issued, it includes a specified maturity date at which time the principal will be repaid. Bonds are also issued at a particular interest rate or what's known as a "coupon rate." That rate is fixed on most bonds. So, for example, if you buy a five-year, 7 percent bond issued by Bombardier, you're lending your money to Bombardier for five years at an interest rate of 7 percent per year. Bond interest is usually paid in two equal semi-annual instalments.

The value of a bond generally fluctuates with changes in interest rates. For example, if you're holding a bond issued at 8 percent and rates increase to 10 percent on comparable, newly issued bonds, your bond decreases in value. (Why would anyone want to buy your bond at the price you paid if it yields just 8 percent and she can get 10 percent elsewhere?)

Bonds differ from one another in the following major ways:

- ✔ The type of institution to which you are lending your money — provincial government, federal government, mortgage holder, or corporation (corporate bonds).

- ✔ The credit quality of the borrower to whom you lend your money (in other words, the probability that the borrower will pay you the interest and return your principal as agreed).

- ✔ The length of maturity of the bond. Bonds generally mature within 30 years. Short-term bonds mature within a few years, intermediate bonds within 7 to 10 years, and long-term bonds within 30 years. Longer-term bonds generally pay higher yields but their value fluctuates more with changes in interest rates.

The overused GIC

Another type of bond is a guaranteed investment certificate (GIC), which is issued by a bank. With a GIC, as with a real bond, you agree to lend your money to an organization (in this case, a bank) for a predetermined number of months or years. Generally, the longer you agree to lock up your money, the higher the interest rate you receive.

With GICs, you typically pay a penalty for early withdrawal. If you want your money back before the end of the GIC's term, you'll get whacked with the loss of a number of months' worth of interest. Some GICs don't let you cash out early, period. Others may offer you the option of getting your money back before the GIC's term runs out, but these usually come with a lower rate of interest. GICs also don't tend to pay very competitive interest rates. You can usually beat the interest rate on shorter-term GICs (those that mature within a year or so) with the best money market mutual funds and high interest rate savings accounts, which offer complete liquidity without any penalty.

Bonds are rated by major credit-rating agencies for their safety, usually on a scale on which AAA is the highest possible rating. For example, high-grade corporate bonds (AAA or AA) are considered the safest (that is, most likely to pay you back). Next in safety are general bonds (A or BBB), which are still safe but just a little less so. Junk bonds (rated BB or lower), popularized by Michael Milken, are actually not all that junky; they're just lower in quality and have a slight (1 or 2 percent) probability of default.

Some bonds are *callable,* which means that the lender can decide to pay you back earlier than the previously agreed-upon date. This event usually occurs when interest rates fall and the lender wants to issue new, lower-interest-rate bonds to replace the higher-rate bonds outstanding. To compensate you for early repayment, the lender typically gives you a small premium or bonus over what the bond is really worth.

Ownership Vehicles to Build Wealth

The three best legal ways to build wealth are to invest in stocks, real estate, and small business.

Stocks

Stocks are the most common ownership investment vehicle and represent shares of ownership in a company. When companies go "public," they issue shares of stock that people like you and us can purchase on the major stock exchanges, such as the Toronto Stock Exchange, the New York Stock Exchange, Nasdaq or the over-the-counter market.

As the economy grows and companies grow with it and earn greater profits, stock prices generally follow suit. Stock prices don't move in lockstep with earnings, but over the years the relationship is pretty close. For example, the *price–earnings ratio* — which measures the level of stock prices relative to (or divided by) company earnings — of U.S. stocks averaged approximately 15 during the 20th century (although it's tended to be higher during periods of low inflation). A price–earnings ratio of 15 simply means that a share in a company is selling at about 15 times that company's earnings per share.

Companies that issue stock (called *publicly held* companies) include automobile manufacturers, computer software producers, fast food restaurants, hotels, magazine and newspaper publishers, supermarkets, wineries, zipper manufacturers, and everything in between! By contrast, some companies are "privately held," which means they have elected to have their stock owned by senior management and a small number of affluent outside investors. Privately held companies' stocks do not trade on a stock exchange; that means that folks like us can't buy stock in such firms.

U.S. and international stocks

Not only can you invest in company stocks that trade on the Canadian stock exchanges, but you can also invest in stocks in the United States and overseas. Aside from folks with international business connections, why would the average citizen want to do so?

Several reasons. First, many investing opportunities exist outside of Canada. If you look at the total value of all stocks outstanding worldwide, the value of Canadian stocks is less than 3 percent.

Another reason for investing in international stocks is that when you confine your investing to Canadian securities you miss a world of opportunities, not only because of business growth available in other countries but also because you get the opportunity to diversify your portfolio further. International securities markets don't move in tandem with Canadian markets. During various Canadian stock market drops, some international stock markets dropped less while others actually rose in value.

Some people hesitate to invest in overseas securities for silly reasons. In some cases, people read idiotic columns like one we came across in a big-city paper. It was entitled "Plenty of Pitfalls in Foreign Investing: Timing is all in earning a decent return." The piece went on to say, "But as with sex, commuting and baseball, timing is everything in the stock market." Smart stock market investors know better than to try to time their investments. The piece also ominously warned, "Foreign stock markets have been known to evaporate overnight." We wish we could say the same for the jobs of some bone-headed financial journalists!

Others are concerned that overseas investing hurts the Canadian economy and contributes to a loss of Canadian jobs. We have some counter-arguments. First, if you don't profit from the growth of other economies, someone else will. If there is money to be made, Canadians may as well be there to participate. Profits from a foreign company are distributed to all shareholders, no matter where they live.

Also, you must recognize that you already live in a global economy — making a distinction between Canadian and non-Canadian companies is no longer appropriate. Many companies that are headquartered in Canada also have overseas operations. Some Canadian firms derive a large portion of their revenue from their international divisions. Conversely, many firms based overseas also have operations here. Increasing numbers of companies are worldwide operations. You don't get the full benefit of international investing through buying just large multinational companies headquartered in Canada. The overseas diversification advantage is obtained by investing in companies that trade on foreign exchanges.

Companies differ in what industry or line of business they're in and they also vary in size. In the financial press, you often hear companies referred to by their *market capitalization,* which is the value of their outstanding stock (the number of total shares multiplied by the market price per share). When describing the sizes of companies, Bay Street and Wall Street have done away with such practical adjectives as "big" and "small" and replaced them with babbling expressions like "large-cap" and "small-cap" (where *cap* stands for *capitalization*). Such is the language of financial geekiness.

As with raising children or going mountain climbing, investing in the stock market involves occasional setbacks and difficult moments, but the overall journey should be worth the effort. For example, over the past two centuries the U.S. stock market has produced an annual average rate of return of about 10 percent. However, the market, as measured by the Dow Jones Industrial Average, fell more than 20 percent during 16 different periods in the 20th century. On average, these periods of decline lasted less than two years. So if you can withstand a temporary setback over a few years, the stock market is a proven place to invest for long-term growth.

You can invest in stocks by making your own selection of individual stocks or by letting a mutual fund manager (discussed in Chapter 10) do it for you.

The relative advantages of mutual funds

Efficiently managed mutual funds offer investors of both modest and substantial means low-cost access to high-quality money managers. Mutual funds span the spectrum of risk and potential returns from non-fluctuating money market funds (which are similar to savings accounts) to bond funds (which generally pay higher yields than money market funds but fluctuate with changes in interest rates) to stock funds (which offer the greatest potential for appreciation but also the greatest short-term volatility).

Mutual funds make better sense than individual securities for most investors. To illustrate, imagine the following scenario. You just bought your first home. It's an older, lived-in property with barf-brown carpets that have accumulated 20-plus years of food spills and pet accidents. You want to tear out the yucky old carpet and install hardwood floors.

Imagine that you can either redo your flooring work yourself or pay a contractor just $300 to do it for you. You would hire the contractor if you could hire him this cheaply. The only type of person who would choose to go it alone is someone who really enjoys this type of work. You're not going to be able to do a faster, better job than a full-time contractor if you do a decent job searching for a good one.

The same thinking process should go into your decision making when you consider how to invest in stocks and bonds. Investing in individual securities should be done only by those who really enjoy doing it. Mutual funds, if properly selected, are a low-cost, quality way to hire professional money managers.

In the long haul, you're likely not going to beat full-time professional managers who are investing in the securities of the same type and risk level that you are. As with hiring a contractor, you need to do your homework to find a good money manager. Even if you think that you can do as well as the best, remember that most "superstar" money managers have only beaten the market averages by a few percent per year. (See Chapter 10, which is devoted to mutual funds.)

Isn't the stock market just legalized gambling?

A student in a personal finance class Eric used to teach at the University of California at Berkeley brought in a copy of a *New York Times* article entitled "Gaming on Wall Street." In the piece, the writer said, "Increasingly, the stock market itself has become just another commodity — as its recent volatility has shown."

After having read this, the student put her comment/question to Eric in writing: "Unless you're a superstar in your field, have stock options in a high tech company, or inherited wealth, it's increasingly difficult for a working person to provide for the future merely with hard work and savings. One is forced to invest in a stock market that is acting more like a commodity and has little to do with economic rules or real value. It is more and more like gambling. I resent turning over my hard-earned money to something that resembles a casino, but there's really no other game in town. Your thoughts?"

If you've entertained similar concerns, here's what we suggest. First, consider choosing better reading material. The writer of this piece had not bothered to do his homework. If he had, he would know that, in the years before this piece was published, by historical standards the U.S. stock market was actually less volatile than normal. He also implied that the increasing stock prices were inflated and unjustified by the economy. In fact, corporate profits have been booming in recent years, and that inevitably drives stock prices higher.

Second, although the stock market can sometimes be temperamental, in the long run the market is driven by the performance of our economy. That's not gambling — that's investing.

Third, as we discuss later in this chapter, the stock market is hardly the only game in town. To build wealth, in addition to North American stock markets, you can invest in stocks overseas as well as in real estate, small business, or your own career.

A capitalistic economy isn't always fair. But it rarely rewards pessimists, spectators, and those unwilling to take some risks.

Investing in individual stocks

Our experience is that more than a few otherwise smart, fun-loving people choose to invest in individual securities because they think that they're smarter or luckier than the rest. We don't know you personally, but it's safe to say that, in the long run, your investment choices are likely not going to outperform those of a full-time investment professional.

We've noticed a distinct difference between the sexes on this issue. Perhaps because of differences in how people are raised, testosterone levels, or whatever, men tend to have more of a problem swallowing their egos and admitting that they're better off not going with individual securities. Maybe men's desires to be stock pickers are genetically linked to their not wanting to ask for directions!

Investing in individual stocks should be avoided by most folk. Success is difficult to attain; the drawbacks and pitfalls are numerous:

✔ **Significant research time and cost are required.** You should know a lot about the company you're investing in when you are considering the purchase of an individual security. Relevant questions to ask about the company are What products does it sell? What are its prospects for future growth and profitability? and How much debt does the company have? You need to do your homework not only before you make your initial investment but also on an ongoing basis as long as you hold the investment.

Don't fool yourself or let others with a vested interest fool you into believing that picking and following individual companies and their stocks is simple, requires little time, and is far more profitable than investing in mutual funds.

✔ **Your emotions will probably get in your way.** Analyzing financial statements and corporate strategy and competitive position requires great intellect and insight. However, those skills aren't nearly enough. Will you have the stomach to hold on after what you thought was a sure-win stock plunges 50 percent while the overall stock market holds steady or even climbs? Will you have the courage to dump such a stock if your new research suggests that the plummet is the beginning of the end rather than just a big bump in the road? When your money is on the line your emotions often kick in, which will undermine your ability to make sound long-term decisions. Few people have the psychological constitution to outfox the financial markets.

✔ **You're less likely to diversify.** Unless you have tens of thousands of dollars to invest in different stocks, you probably can't cost-effectively afford to develop a diversified portfolio. For example, when you're investing in stocks, you should hold companies in different industries, different companies within an industry, and so on. Not diversifying adds to your risk unnecessarily.

✔ **You'll face accounting and bookkeeping hassles.** When you invest in individual securities outside retirement plans, every time you sell a specific security you must record that transaction as part of preparing your tax return. Even if you pay someone else to complete your tax return, you still have the hassle of keeping track of statements and receipts.

Of course, you can find some people (with a vested interest) who will try to convince you that picking your own stocks and managing your own portfolio of stocks is easy and more profitable than investing in, say, a mutual fund. In our experience, such stock-picking cheerleaders usually fall into at least one of the following categories:

✔ **Newsletter writers.** Whether in print or on an Internet site, you can find plenty of pundits who pitch the notion that professional money managers are just overpaid buffoons and that you can handily trounce the pros with little investment of your time by simply putting your money into the pundits' stock picks. Of course, what these self-anointed gurus are really selling is either an ongoing print newsletter (which can run upwards of several hundred dollars per year) or your required daily visitation of their advertising-stuffed Internet sites. How else will you be able to keep up with their announced buy and sell recommendations? These supposed experts want you to be dependent upon continually following their advice. Of course, you may be wondering, "Hey, if these pundits were such geniuses at picking the best stocks, why aren't they making piles of money just investing rather than selling their supposed brilliant insights on the cheap?" Go to the head of the class and don't waste your time and money following such pundits' picks! (We discuss investment newsletters in Chapter 8 and Internet sites in Chapter 20.)

✔ **Book authors.** Go into any bookstore with a decent size investing section and you'll find plenty of books claiming that they can teach you a stock picking system to beat the system. Never mind the fact that the author has no independently audited track record demonstrating his success!

✔ **Stockbrokers.** Although a true broker will sell you whatever he thinks you'll buy in order to produce commissions, some brokers will steer you toward individual stocks for several reasons that benefit the broker and not you. First, as we discuss in Chapter 8, the high-commission brokerage firms can make handsome profits for themselves by getting you to buy stocks. Second, brokers can use changes in the company's situation to encourage you to then sell and buy different stocks, generating even more commissions. Lastly, as with newsletter writers, this whole process creates your dependency upon the broker, leaving *you* broker!

Researching individual stocks can be more than a full-time job, and if you choose to take this path remember that you'll be competing against the professionals who do so on a full-time basis. Tony has spoken at length with dozens of individual investors for his column in *The Globe and Mail* called "Me and My Money." Invariably, those who choose to invest in individual stocks share two characteristics. First, they spend a lot of time and energy in choosing and following the companies they invest in. Second, they don't do it purely for the financial returns. For some, it's an interesting hobby. For others, it's an intellectual challenge to match wits with the markets, or a way to stay informed about the world of business. If you do decide to pick your own stocks, be sure that the strategy you use is suited to the time you have to spend and your personality.

If you derive sheer ecstasy from picking and following your own stocks or want an independent opinion of some stocks you happen to own now, a good source of independent research for Canadian companies is the Canadian Shareowners Association. A membership costs $89 a year, and gets you a subscription to *Canadian Shareowner*, a bi-monthly magazine that offers updates on many stocks as well as in-depth assessments of two companies in each issue. The association also sells a reference book providing historical financial information on some 700 Canadian companies. This book is updated annually, and costs $79. You can subscribe and order publications by calling 416-595-9600 or on the Internet at www.shareowner.ca. Probably the best research reports available for U.S. stocks are from *Value Line Investment Survey*. This superb publication provides concise, user-friendly, single-page summaries of thousands of stocks. Libraries with good business sections usually carry this publication. You can order a 10-week trial by calling Value Line at 800-833-0046. We would also recommend that you limit your individual stock picking to no more than 20 percent of your overall investments.

Real estate

Over the generations, real estate owners and investors have enjoyed rates of return comparable to those produced by the stock market, thus making real estate another time-tested method for building wealth. However, real estate is not a gravy train or a simple way to get wealthy. Like stocks, real estate goes through good and bad performance periods. Most people who make money investing in real estate do so because they invest over many years.

The best place to start investing in real estate is to buy your own home. The *equity* (the difference between the market value of the home and the loan owed on it) in your home that builds over the years can become a significant part of your net worth. Among other things, this equity can be tapped to help finance other important money and personal goals such as retirement, university, and starting or buying a business.

Over your adult life, owning a home should be less expensive than renting a comparable home. The reason: As a renter, your housing costs are fully exposed to inflation (unless you're the beneficiary of a rent-controlled apartment). As a homeowner, the bulk of your housing costs — your monthly mortgage — is not exposed to inflation, except for the change in interest rates each time you renew your mortgage. And when you sell the home you live in, all the profits go directly to you without being taxed in most cases.

See Chapter 15 to learn the best ways to buy and finance real estate.

Dividend reinvestment plans for individual stock purchases

Increasing numbers of corporations allow existing shareholders to reinvest their dividends in more shares of stock without paying brokerage commissions. In some cases, companies allow you to make additional cash purchases of more shares of stock, also commission-free.

In order to qualify, you must first generally buy some shares of stock through a broker (although some companies allow the initial purchases to be made directly from them). Ideally, you should purchase these initial shares through a discount broker to keep your commission burden as low as possible. Some investment associations — including the Canadian Shareowners Association — also have plans that allow you to buy one or just a few shares to get started.

We are not enamoured of these plans because investing this way is generally available and cost-effective only for investments held outside your RRSP. Doing so increases your tax bill, especially with stocks that pay dividends.

Also, you typically need to complete a lot of paperwork to invest in a number of different companies' stock. Life is too short to bother with these plans for this reason alone.

Finally, even with those companies that do sell stock directly without charging an explicit commission as a brokerage firm would, you'll pay plenty of other fees. Many plans charge an upfront enrolment fee as well as fees for reinvesting dividends as well as another fee when you want to sell.

Real estate: Not your ordinary investment

Besides providing solid rates of return, real estate differs from most other investments in several other respects. Here's what makes real estate unique as an investment.

- ✓ **Usability.** You can't live in a stock, bond, or mutual fund (although we suppose you could glue together a substantial fortress with all the paper these companies fill your mailbox with each year). Real estate is the only investment that you can use (live in or rent out) to produce income.

- ✓ **Land is in limited supply.** Last time we checked, the percentage of the Earth occupied by land wasn't increasing. And because humans like to reproduce, the demand for land and housing continues to grow. Consider the areas that have the most expensive real estate prices in the world — Hong Kong, Tokyo, Hawaii, San Francisco, and Manhattan. In these densely populated areas, there is virtually no new land upon which to build.

- ✓ **Zoning shapes potential value.** Local government regulates the zoning of property, and zoning determines what a property can be used for. In some communities these days, local zoning boards are against big growth. This bodes well for future real estate values. Also know that, in some cases, a particular property may not have been developed to its full potential. If you can see how to develop the property, you can reap large profits.

✔ **Leverage.** Real estate is also different from other investments because to buy it you can borrow a lot of money — up to 80 to 90 percent or more of the value of the property. This is known as exercising *leverage*: With only a small investment of 10 to 25 percent down, you are able to purchase and own a much larger investment. When the value of your real estate goes up, you make money on your investment and on all the money that you borrowed. (In case you're curious, you can leverage non-retirement-plan stock and bond investments through margin borrowing. However, you will have to make a much larger "down payment" — about double to triple compared with buying real estate.)

For example, suppose that you plunk down $50,000 to purchase a property for $200,000. If the property appreciates to $250,000, on paper you've made a profit of $50,000 on your investment of just $50,000. In other words, you've made a 100 percent return on your investment. But leverage cuts both ways. If your $200,000 property decreases in value to $150,000, even though it's only dropped 25 percent in value, you've actually lost (on paper) 100 percent of your original $50,000 investment.

✔ **Hidden values.** In an *efficient market,* the price of an investment accurately reflects its true worth. Some investment markets are more efficient than others because of the large number of transactions and easily accessible information. Real estate markets can be *in*efficient at times. Information is not always easy to come by, and you may find an ultramotivated or uninformed seller. If you are willing to do some homework, you may be able to purchase a property below its fair market value, perhaps by as much as 10 to 20 percent.

Just as with any other investment, real estate has its drawbacks. For starters, it generally takes time and significant cost to buy or sell a property. Also, holding a property typically costs a good deal of ongoing money. When you're renting property, you will discover firsthand the occasional headaches of being a landlord. And, especially in the early years of rental property ownership, the property's expenses may exceed the rental income, producing a net cash drain.

The best real estate investment options

Although it is in some ways unique, real estate is like other types of investments in that prices are driven by supply and demand. You can invest in homes or small apartment buildings and rent them out. In the long run, investment-property buyers hope that their rents and the value of their properties will increase faster than their expenses.

When selecting real estate for investment purposes, remember that local economic growth is the fuel for housing demand. In addition to a vibrant and diverse job base, limited supplies of both existing housing and land on which to build are things to look for. When you identify potential properties in which you might invest, run the numbers to understand the cash demands of owning the property and the likely profitability. See Chapter 15 for help determining the costs of real estate ownership.

Real estate versus stocks

Real estate and stocks have historically produced comparable returns. Deciding between the two depends less on the performance of the markets than it does on you and your situation. Consider the following major issues when deciding which investment may be better for you.

The first and most important question to ask yourself is whether you're cut out to handle the responsibilities that come with being a landlord. Real estate is a time-intensive investment. Investing in stocks can be time-intensive as well, but it doesn't have to be if you use professionally managed mutual funds.

An often-overlooked drawback to investing in real estate is that you earn no tax benefits while you're accumulating your down payment. Retirement plans such as RRSPs (discussed in Chapter 11) give you an immediate tax deduction as you contribute money to them. If you haven't exhausted your contributions to these plans, consider doing so before chasing after investment real estate.

Also ask yourself which investments you know more about. Some folks feel uncomfortable with stocks and mutual funds because they don't understand them. If you have a better handle on what makes real estate tick, you have a good reason to consider investing in it.

Finally, what will make you happy? Some people enjoy the challenge that comes with managing and improving rental property. It's a bit like running a small business. If you're good at it and have some good fortune, you can make money and derive endless hours of enjoyment.

Although few will admit it, some real estate investors get an ego rush from a tangible display of their wealth. Sufferers of this "edifice complex" can't obtain similar pleasure from a stock portfolio that is detailed on a piece of paper (although others have been known to boast of their stock-picking prowess).

When you want to invest directly in real estate, residential housing — such as single-family homes or small multi-unit buildings — is a straightforward and attractive investment for most people. Buying properties close to home offers the advantage of allowing you to more easily monitor and manage what's going on. The downside is that you'll be less diversified — more of your investments will be dependent upon your local economy.

If you don't want to be a landlord — one of the biggest drawbacks of investment real estate — consider investing in real estate through *real estate investment trusts* (REITs). REITs are diversified real estate investment companies that purchase and manage rental real estate for investors. A typical REIT invests in different types of property, such as shopping centres, apartments, and other rental buildings. You can invest in REITs either by purchasing them directly on the major stock exchanges or by investing in a real estate mutual fund (see Chapter 10) that invests in numerous REITs.

The worst real estate investments

Not all real estate investments are good; some are not even real investments. The bad ones are characterized by burdensome costs and problematic economic fundamentals:

- **Limited partnerships.** Limited partnerships (LPs) sold through brokers and financial consultants should be avoided. LPs are inferior investment vehicles. They are so burdened with high sales commissions and ongoing management fees that deplete your investment that you can do better elsewhere. The investment salesperson who sells you such an investment stands to earn a commission of up to 10 percent or more — so only 90 cents of each dollar gets invested. Each year, LPs typically siphon off another several percent for management and other expenses. Most partnerships have little or no incentive to control costs. In fact, they have a conflict of interest to charge more to enrich the managing partners.

  Unlike a mutual fund, you can't vote with your dollars. If the partnership is poorly run and expensive, you're stuck. LPs are *illiquid.* You can't get your money out until the partnership is liquidated, typically seven to ten years after you buy in.

  Brokers who sell LPs often tell you that while your investment is growing at 20 percent or more per year, you get handsome dividends of 8 percent or so per year. Many of the yields on LPs have turned out to be bogus. In some cases, partnerships propped up their yields by paying back investors' principals (without telling them, of course). As for returns — well, most LP investors of a decade ago are lucky to have half their original investment left. The only thing limited about a limited partnership is its ability to make you money.

- **Time shares.** Time shares are another nearly certain money loser. With a time share, what you buy is a week or two per year of ownership, or usage, of a particular unit, usually a condominium in a resort location. If you pay $8,000 for a week (in addition to ongoing maintenance fees), you're paying the equivalent of more than $400,000 for the whole unit, but a comparable unit nearby may sell for only $150,000. All the extra mark-up pays the salespeople's commissions, administrative expenses, and profits for the time share development company.

  People usually get lured into buying a time share when they're enjoying a vacation someplace. They're easy prey for salespeople who want to sell them a souvenir of the trip. The cheese in the mousetrap is an offer of something free (for example, a free night's stay in a unit) for going through the sales presentation.

  If you can't live without a time share, consider buying a used one. Many previous buyers, who almost always have lost a good hunk of money, are trying to dump their shares (which should tell you something). You may be able to buy a time share at a fair price. But why commit yourself to taking a vacation in the same location and building at the same time each year? Many time shares let you trade your weeks for other times and other places; however, doing so is a hassle, you will be charged an extra fee, and your choices are usually limited to time slots that other people don't want — that's why they're trading them!

✔ **Second homes.** A sometimes romantic notion and extended part of the dreams of many Canadians is the weekend getaway — a cottage or cabin you can escape to on weekends and during summer and perhaps over the Christmas holidays. When it's not in use, you may be able to rent it out and earn some income to help defray the expense of keeping it up.

When you can realistically afford the additional costs of a second, or vacation, home, we're not going to tell you how to spend your extra cash. But please don't make the all-too-common mistake of viewing a cottage as an investment. The way most people use them, they're not. Most owners of second homes seldom rent out their property — they typically do so 10 percent or less of the time. As a result, second homes are usually money drains.

Sometimes people convince themselves that by renting their cottage out and otherwise running it as a business they can lower the costs through supposed tax benefits. Even when you qualify for some or all of them, tax benefits only partially reduce the cost of owning a property. We've seen more than a few cases in which the second home is such a cash drain that it prevents its owners from contributing to and taking advantage of tax-deductible retirement savings plans.

If you don't rent out a second-home property most of the time, ask yourself whether you can afford such a luxury. Can you accomplish your other financial goals — saving for retirement, paying for the home in which you live, and so on — with this added expense? Keeping a second home is more of a consumption than an investment decision. Few people can afford more than one home.

Investing in small business

With what type of investment have more people built great wealth? If you said the stock market or real estate, you're wrong. The answer is small business. You can invest in small business by starting one yourself (and thus finding yourself the best boss you've probably ever had), buying an existing business, or investing in someone else's small business.

Launching your own enterprise

When you have self-discipline and a product or service you can sell, starting your own business can be both profitable and fulfilling. Consider first what skills and expertise you possess that you can use in your business. You don't need a "eureka"-type idea or an Eli Whitney–type invention to justify going into small business. Millions of people operate successful businesses such as dry cleaners, restaurants, tax preparation firms, and so on that are hardly unique.

Start exploring your idea first by developing a written business plan. Such a plan should detail what your product or service will be, how you will market it, who your customers and competitors are, and what the economics of the business are, including the start-up costs.

Of all your small-business options, starting your own business involves the greatest amount of work. Although you can do this work on a part-time basis in the beginning, most people end up in their business full-time — it's your new job, career, or whatever you want to call it.

We've both run our own businesses for most of our working years and wouldn't trade that experience for the corporate life. That's not to say that running our own businesses doesn't have drawbacks and down moments. But we've seen many people of varied backgrounds, interests, and skills succeed and be happy with running their own businesses.

In the eyes of most people, starting their own business is the riskiest of all small-business investment options. But if you're going into a business that uses your skills and expertise, the risk is not nearly as great as you may think. Many businesses can be started with little cash by leveraging your existing skills and expertise. You can build a valuable company and job if you have the time to devote to building "sweat equity." As long as you check out the competition and offer a valued service at a reasonable cost, the principal risk with your business is that you won't do a good job marketing what you have to offer. If you can market your skills, you're home free.

As long as you're thinking about the risks of starting a business, consider the risks of staying in a job you don't enjoy or that isn't challenging or fulfilling you. If you never take the plunge, you may regret that you didn't pursue your dreams.

Buying someone else's business

If you don't have a specific product or service you want to sell but are skilled at managing and improving the operations of a company, buying a small business might be for you. Finding and buying a good small business takes much time and patience, so be willing to devote at least several months to the search. You will probably also need to enlist the help of financial and legal advisers to help inspect the company, look over its financial statements, and hammer out a contract.

Although you don't have to go through the riskier start-up period if you take this route, you will likely need more capital to buy a going enterprise. You also need to be able to deal with stickier personnel and management issues. The history of the organization and the way things work will predate your ownership of the business. If you don't like making hard decisions, firing people who don't fit with your plans, and coercing people into changing the way they did things before you arrived on the scene, buying an existing business likely isn't for you.

Some people perceive buying an existing business as safer than starting one. Buying someone else's business can actually be riskier. You're likely to shell out far more money upfront, in the form of a down payment to buy the business. If you don't have the ability to run the business and it does poorly, you have a lot more to lose financially. Another risk is that the business is for sale for a reason — it's not very profitable, it's in decline, or it's generally a pain in the neck to operate.

Good businesses don't come cheaply. If the business is a success, the current owner has removed the start-up risk from the business, so the price of the business should be at a premium to reflect this lack of risk. When you have the capital to buy an established business and you have the skills to run it, consider going this route.

Investing in someone else's small business

Do you like the idea of profiting from successful small businesses but don't want the day-to-day headaches of being responsible for managing the enterprise? Investing in someone else's small business may be for you. Although this route may seem easier, fewer people are actually cut out to be investors in other people's businesses. The reason: Finding and analyzing opportunities isn't easy.

Are you astute at evaluating corporate financial statements and business strategies? Investing in a small, privately held company has much in common with investing in a publicly traded firm (as is the case when you buy stock). One difference is that private firms aren't required to produce comprehensive, audited financial statements that adhere to certain accounting principles the way that public companies are. Thus, you have a greater risk of not having sufficient or accurate information when evaluating a small private firm.

Another difference is that it's harder to unearth private small-business investing opportunities. The best private companies seeking investors don't generally advertise but instead find prospective investors through networking with people such as business advisers. Increase your chances of finding private companies to invest in by speaking with tax, legal, and financial advisers who work with small businesses. You can also find interesting investing opportunities through your own contacts or experience within a given industry.

You should consider investing in someone else's business only if you can afford to lose all of what you're investing — you can lose your entire investment when investing in a small, privately held company. Also, you should have sufficient assets so that what you are investing in small, privately held companies is only a small portion (20 percent or less) of your total financial assets.

Investment Odds and Ends

In Chapter 8, we tell you that the investment world offers you only two flavours: lending investments and ownership investments. Well, we sort of oversimplified.

The investments that we discuss in this section sometimes belong on their own planet. Here are the basics on these other common, but odd, investments.

Precious metals

Gold and silver have been used by many civilizations as currency or as a medium of exchange. One advantage of precious metals as a currency is that they can't be debased by the government. With a paper-based currency, such as Canadian dollars, the government can print more to pay off debts. This process can lead to the devaluation of a currency and inflation. It takes a whole lot more work to make more gold. Just ask Rumpelstiltskin.

Holdings of gold and silver can provide a so-called *hedge* against inflation. In North America in the late 1970s and early 1980s, inflation rose dramatically. This largely unexpected rise in inflation depressed stocks and bonds. Gold and silver, however, rose tremendously in value — in fact, more than 500 percent (even after adjusting for inflation) from 1972 to 1980 (refer to Figure 8-3 in Chapter 8). Such periods are unusual. Over many decades, precious metals tend to be lousy investments. Their rate of return tends to keep up with the rate of inflation but not surpass it.

When you want to invest in precious metals as an inflation hedge, your best option is to do so through mutual funds (see Chapter 10). Don't purchase precious metals futures. They are not investments; they are short-term gambles on which way gold or silver prices might head over a short period of time. You should also stay away from firms and shops that sell coins and *bullion* (not the soup, but bars of gold or silver). Even if you can find a legitimate firm (not an easy task), the cost of storing and insuring gold and silver is quite costly. You won't get good value for your money. We hate to tell you, but the Gold Rush is over.

Collectibles

Collectibles is a catchall category for antiques, art, autographs, baseball cards, clocks, coins, comic books, diamonds, dolls, gems, photographs, rare books, rugs, stamps, vintage wine, and writing utensils — in other words, any material object that through some kind of human manipulation has become more valuable to certain humans.

Notwithstanding the few people who discover on *The Antiques Road Show* that they own an antique of significant value, as an investment vehicle collectibles are generally lousy. Dealer mark-ups are enormous, maintenance and protection costs are draining, research is time-consuming, and people's tastes are quite fickle. All this for returns that, after you factor in the huge mark-ups, rarely keep up with inflation.

Buy collectibles for your love of the object, not for financial gain. Treat collecting as a hobby, not as an investment. When buying a collectible, try to avoid the big mark-ups by cutting out the middlemen. Buy directly from the artist or producer if you can.

Life insurance with a cash value

Life insurance should not be used as an investment, especially if you haven't exhausted your contributions to retirement plans. Life insurance that combines life insurance protection with an account that has a cash value is usually known as *universal, whole,* or *variable life.* Agents love to sell it for the high commissions.

The only common reason to consider buying cash-value life insurance is if you want the proceeds to help pay some or all of the taxes due on your death. This may help you ensure that some of your assets can be passed on intact to your heirs, rather than them having to be sold to help pay your final tax bill. In this case, be sure to name your estate as the beneficiary on your policy. This will ensure the insurance money is used for your tax bill. You need to look at your potential estate and the anticipated tax bill to decide if this is a benefit of value to your heirs. (See Chapter 17 for more on life insurance and why term life insurance is best for the vast majority of people.)

Chapter 10

Mutual Funds: Investments for All of Us

*M*utual funds are managed by investment companies that pool your money with that of thousands of other like-minded individuals and invest it in stocks, bonds, and other securities. Think of it as a big investment club without the meetings! When you invest through a typical mutual fund, a few million to a billion dollars or more is invested along with your money.

Mutual Fund Benefits

Mutual funds rank right up there with microwave ovens, videocassette recorders, sticky notes, and plastic wrap as the best inventions of modern times. To understand their success is to grasp how and why funds can work for you. Read on to discover their benefits:

✔ **Professional management.** Mutual funds are managed by a portfolio manager and research team whose full-time jobs are to screen the universe of investments for those that best meet the stated objectives of the fund. These professionals call and visit companies, analyze companies' financial statements, and speak with companies' suppliers and customers. In short, the team does more due diligence and research than you could ever hope to do in your free time.

Fund managers are typically graduates of the top business and finance schools in the country, where they learn the principles of portfolio management and securities valuation and selection. (Despite their time in the groves of academe, most of them do a pretty good job of investing money.) The best fund managers typically have five or more years of experience in analyzing and selecting investments, and many measure their experience in decades rather than years.

✔ **Low cost.** The most efficiently managed stock mutual funds cost less than 2 percent per year in fees (bonds and money market funds cost even less). Because mutual funds typically buy or sell tens of thousands of shares of a security at a time, the commissions they pay are generally far less than what you pay to buy or sell a few hundred shares on your own. In addition, when you buy a *no-load fund,* you avoid paying sales commissions (known as *loads*) on your transactions. We say more about these types of funds later in this chapter.

✔ **Diversification.** Mutual fund investing enables you to achieve a level of diversification that is difficult without several hundred thousand dollars and a lot of time to invest. To go it alone, you should invest money in at least 8 to 12 different securities in different industries to ensure that your portfolio can withstand a downturn in one or more of the investments. Proper diversification allows a mutual fund to receive the highest possible return at the lowest possible risk given its objectives. We're not suggesting that mutual funds are able to escape share price declines during major market downturns. For example, over the past two decades, when the Canadian stock market has suffered occasional corrections ranging from 10 percent to 44 percent in value, mutual funds that invested in Canadian stocks certainly declined by similar magnitudes. However, the most unlucky investors during these episodes were individuals who had all of their money riding on only a few stocks. Some shares plunged in price by as much as 80 to 90 percent.

✔ **You don't need big bucks.** Most mutual funds have low minimum-investment requirements, especially for RRSP-account investors. And when you invest in a mutual fund, you get the same attention given to the rich and famous: full-time, professional money management. Even if you have a lot of money to invest, you should also consider mutual funds. Join the increasing numbers of companies and institutions (who have the biggest bucks of all) who are turning to the low-cost, high-quality money-management services that a mutual fund provides.

✔ **Audited performance records and expenses.** In their prospectuses, all mutual funds are required to disclose historical data on returns, operating expenses, and other fees. The securities regulators in each province oversee these disclosures for accuracy.

TECHNICAL STUFF

The rise of the mutual fund industry

Just as computers have replaced typewriters because they allow for more efficient word processing, mutual funds are replacing less-efficient institutions that manage money. That's not to say that banks and commission-based brokerage firms are going to disappear — but you'll probably see fewer of them in the coming years.

As for safety, mutual funds have a virtually zero risk of bankruptcy. Unlike banks and insurance companies, which have failed and will continue to fail, mutual funds have never failed and probably won't in the future. The situation in which the demand for money back (*liabilities*) exceeds the value of a fund's investments (*assets*) cannot occur with a mutual fund.

Of course, the value of a fund fluctuates with the value of the securities in which it is invested. But this variation doesn't lead to the failure or bankruptcy of a mutual fund company.

In contrast, hundreds of banks and dozens of insurance companies have failed in North America in recent decades. Banks and insurers can fail because their liabilities can exceed their assets. When a bank makes too many loans that go sour at the same time that depositors want their money back, the bank fails. Likewise, if an insurance company makes several poor investments or underestimates the number of claims that will be made by insurance policy holders, it, too, can fail.

And you don't have to worry about fund companies stealing your money. The specific securities in which a mutual fund is invested are held at a *custodian* — a separate organization independent of the mutual fund company. The use of a custodian ensures that the fund management company can't embezzle your funds and use assets from a better-performing fund to subsidize a poor performer.

✔ **Flexibility in risk level.** Among the different mutual funds, you can choose a level of risk that you're comfortable with and that meets your personal and financial goals. If you want your money to grow over a long period of time, you may want to select funds that invest more heavily in stocks. If you need current income and don't want investments that fluctuate in value as widely as stocks, you may choose more conservative bond funds. If you want to be sure that your invested principal does not drop in value because you may need your money in the short term, you can select a money market fund.

✔ **Freedom from salespeople.** Some stockbrokers (also known as *financial consultants*) and commission-based financial planners make more money by encouraging trading activity and by selling you investments that provide them with high commissions — limited partnerships and mutual funds with high load fees, for example. No-load (commission-free) mutual fund companies do not push products. Their toll-free telephone lines are staffed with knowledgeable people who earn salaries, not commissions. Their recommendations don't carry inherent conflicts of interest.

Fund Types

One of the major misconceptions about mutual funds is that they are all invested in stocks. They're not. Table 10-1 shows how the money currently invested in mutual funds breaks down:

Table 10-1	Breakdown of Money Currently Invested in Mutual Funds		
Fund Type	*Percentage of Total*	*Fund Type*	*Percentage of Total*
Mortgage	1%	Money market	10%
Dividend	5%	Balanced	16%
U.S. stocks	8%	Canadian stocks	24%
Bond and income	8%	Foreign stocks	28%

As you can see, significant mutual fund money is *not* invested in stocks. When you hear folks talk about the "riskiness" of mutual funds, even in the media, you'll know that they're overlooking this fact: All mutual funds are not created equal. Some funds, such as money market funds, carry virtually *no* risk that your investment will decline in value.

Throughout this discussion, remember that when mutual fund companies package and market their funds, the names they give their funds aren't always completely accurate or comprehensive. For example, a stock fund may not be *totally* invested in stocks. Twenty percent of it may be invested in bonds. Don't assume that a fund invests exclusively in Canadian companies, either — it may invest in international firms as well.

Note: If you haven't yet read Chapters 8 and 9, which provide an overview of investment concepts and vehicles, doing so will enhance your understanding of the rest of this chapter.

Money market funds

Money market funds are the safest type of mutual funds for those concerned about losing their invested dollars. Money market funds are like bank savings accounts in that the value of your original investment does not fluctuate. As with money you'd put into back savings accounts, money market funds are suitable for money that you can't afford to see dwindle in value.

Money market funds have several advantages over traditional bank savings accounts. First is that they have higher yields. They also can be used inside RRSPs and other registered savings plans. Finally, they make it easy to move money in and out of other mutual funds. For example, if you are rushing to make your RRSP contribution before the mid-winter deadline and don't have the time to research where your new money should be invested, park it in a money market fund. You'll earn a good rate of interest, and if you later decide it's better invested in another type of fund, it typically just takes a phone call to move your money over.

Bond funds

Bonds are IOUs. When you buy a newly issued bond you lend your money, typically to a corporation or government agency. A bond mutual fund is nothing more than a large group (pack, herd, gaggle, whatever) of bonds.

Bond funds typically invest in bonds of similar *maturity* (the number of years that elapse before the borrower must pay back the money you lend). The names of most bond funds include a word or two to provide clues about the average length of maturity of their bonds. For example, a short-term bond fund concentrates its investments in bonds maturing in the next 2 to 3 years. An intermediate-term fund generally holds bonds that come due within 7 to 10 years. The bonds in a long-term fund usually mature in 20 years or so.

In contrast to an individual bond that you buy and hold until it matures, a bond fund is always replacing bonds in its portfolio to maintain its average maturity objective. Therefore, if you know that you absolutely, positively must have a certain principal amount back on a particular date, individual bonds may be more appropriate than a bond fund.

Bond funds are useful when you want to live off interest income or when you don't want to put all your money in riskier investments such as stocks and real estate (perhaps because you plan to use the money soon). Shorter-term bond funds are typically less volatile than longer-term bond funds.

Hybrid funds

Hybrid funds invest in a mixture of different types of securities. Most commonly, they invest in bonds and stocks. These funds are usually less risky and volatile than funds investing exclusively in stocks. In an economic downturn, bonds usually hold up in value better than stocks do. However, during good economic times when the stock market is booming, the bond portions of these funds tend to drag down their performance a bit.

Hybrid mutual funds are typically known as balanced or asset allocation funds. *Balanced funds* generally try to maintain a fairly constant percentage of investment in stocks and bonds. *Asset allocation funds* tend to adjust the mix of different investments according to the portfolio manager's expectations of the market. Of course, there are exceptions — some balanced funds make major shifts in their allocations whereas some asset allocation funds maintain a relatively fixed mix. You should note that most funds that shift money around instead of staying put in good investments rarely beat the market averages over a number of years.

Hybrid funds are a way to make fund investing simple. They give you instant diversification across a variety of investing options. They also make it easier for stock-skittish investors to invest in stocks while avoiding the high volatility of pure stock funds.

Stock funds

Stock mutual funds, as their name implies, invest in stocks. These funds are often referred to as *equity* funds. Equity — not to be confused with equity in real estate — is another word for stocks. Stock mutual funds are usually categorized by the type of stocks they invest in.

Stock types are first defined by the size of a company (small, medium, and large). The total market value (capitalization) of a company's outstanding stock determines its size. Small- and mid-sized Canadian company stocks, for example, are usually defined as companies with total market capitalization of less than $500 million.

Stocks are further categorized as growth or value. *Growth stocks* are companies that are experiencing rapidly expanding revenues and profits, and typically have high stock prices relative to their current earnings or asset (book) values. These companies tend to reinvest most of their earnings back into their infrastructure to fuel future expansion. Thus, growth stocks pay low dividends.

At the other end of the spectrum are *value stocks.* Value stock investors look for good buys. They want to invest in stocks that are cheaply priced in relation to the assets and profits of the company.

These categories are combined in various ways to describe how a mutual fund invests its money. One fund may focus on large-company growth stocks; another fund may limit itself to small-company value stocks. Funds are further qualified by the geographical focus of their investments: Canada, the United States, international, worldwide, and so on (see the following section).

Funds of funds

Increasing numbers of fund providers are responding to overwhelmed investors by offering a simplified way to construct a portfolio: a mutual fund that diversifies across numerous other mutual funds. When a fund of funds is done right, it helps focus fund investors on the important big picture issue of asset allocation — how much of your investment money you put into bonds versus stocks.

Although the best of such funds of funds appear to deliver a high-quality, diversified portfolio of funds in one fell swoop, funds of funds are not all created equal and are not all worthy of your investment dollars.

The newer funds of funds being developed by the larger fund companies are investor-friendly. Look for funds of funds that add no extra fees for packaging together the individual funds.

Other funds of funds, which layer on high fees, merit a much more skeptical look. Some funds of funds charge annual operating expenses of 1 to 2 percent or more on top of the fees of the underlying mutual funds that they invest in. When you add it all up, investing in mutual funds through these funds can siphon off a whopping 3 to 4 percent annually of your investment balances.

Remember that stocks' historical annual returns average just 10 percent. So paying 3 to 4 percent in fees gives away about 30 to 40 percent of your expected returns. Not surprisingly, in terms of performance, the high-fee funds of funds have badly lagged behind the stock market indexes.

Canadian, U.S., international, and global funds

Most funds focus their investments in Canada unless they have words like *U.S., international, global, worldwide,* or *world* in their names. But even funds without one of these terms attached often invest money internationally.

The only way to know for sure where a fund is currently invested (or where the fund may invest in the future) is to ask. You can start by calling the toll-free number of the mutual fund company that you're interested in. A fund's annual report also details where the fund is investing.

The term *international* typically means that a fund can invest anywhere in the world except Canada. The term *worldwide* or *global* generally implies that a fund can invest anywhere in the world, including Canada. We generally recommend avoiding worldwide or global funds for two reasons. First, thoroughly following the financial markets and companies in so many parts of the world is difficult for a fund manager. Following financial markets and companies is hard enough to do solely in Canada or in a specific international market. Second, most of these funds charge higher operating expenses, which puts a drag on returns.

Exceptions to this rule are the funds of funds that we discuss in the sidebar, "Funds of funds." With these funds, multiple managers are at work.

Index funds

Index funds are funds that can be (and are, in many cases) managed by a computer. An index fund's assets are invested to replicate an existing market index such as the TSE 300, an index of 300 large Canadian company stocks.

Over long periods (ten years or more), index funds typically outperform about three-quarters of their peers! How is that possible? How can a computer making mindless, predictable decisions beat an intelligent, creative, MBA-endowed portfolio manager with a crack team of research analysts scouring the market for the best securities? The answer is, largely, cost. The computer does not demand a high salary or need a big corner office. And index funds don't need a team of research analysts.

Most active fund managers cannot overcome the handicap of high operating expenses that pull down their funds' rates of return. As we discuss later in this chapter, operating expenses include all the fees and profit that a mutual fund extracts from a fund's returns before the returns are paid to you. For example, the average large-cap Canadian stock fund has an operating expense ratio of 2.25 percent per year. So a Canadian stock index fund with an expense ratio of just 0.9 percent per year has an advantage of 1.35 percent per year.

Another not-so-inconsequential advantage of index funds is that you can't underperform the market. Some funds do just that due to the burden of high fees and poor management. If you were unfortunate enough to have been involved in the following loser mutual funds in the past ten years, you fared a lot worse per year in your rate of return than if you had invested in a boring old index fund (Green Line Canadian Index Fund over the same time period provided an average annual rate of return of 12.7 percent). (See Table 10-2.)

Sometimes index funds do get beaten by actively managed funds, particularly when the stock markets in general are falling. Actively managed funds may have some of their assets sitting in cash, which would hold its value when stock prices are dropping, while index funds usually have all their capital invested.

Index funds can also at times be more volatile than conservatively managed broad-based funds. This can occur when a few companies account for a substantial part of an index's movement. For instance, in the late nineties and in 2000, Nortel accounted for around 30 percent of the TSE 300 index's movement. Large-cap conservative Canadian equity funds, meanwhile, typically had much less of their capital in Nortel, and thus didn't see their returns bounce around as much as the index when Nortel's stock price went through some huge swings.

Table 10-2	Mutual Funds (Diversified) That Will Fetch a Stick
Fund	*Average Annual Rate of Return (10 years)*
Cambridge Growth	−7.3%
Industrial Equity	2.0%
Trans-Canada Value	5.4%

For money invested outside retirement plans, index funds have an added advantage: Fewer taxable distributions (discussed later in this chapter) are made to shareholders because less trading of securities is conducted and a more stable portfolio is maintained.

Yes, index funds may seem downright boring. When you invest in them, you give up the opportunity to brag to others about your shrewd investments that beat the market averages. On the other hand, you have no chance of doing much worse than the market, which more than a few mutual fund managers do.

Index funds make sense for a portion of your investments because it's very difficult for portfolio managers to beat the market.

Specialty (sector) funds

Specialty funds don't fit neatly into the previously discussed categories. These funds are often known as *sector* funds because they tend to invest in securities in specific industries.

In most cases, you should avoid investing in specialty or sector funds. Investing in stocks of a single industry defeats a major purpose of investing in mutual funds — diversification. Another good reason to avoid sector funds is that they tend to carry much higher expenses than other mutual funds.

Socially responsible funds

Increasing numbers of mutual funds that are popping up are labelling themselves *socially responsible*. This term means different things to different people. In most cases, though, it implies that the fund avoids investing in companies — tobacco manufacturers, for example — whose products or services harm people or the world at large. Because cigarettes and other tobacco products kill hundreds of thousands of people and add billions of dollars to health-care costs, most socially responsible funds shun tobacco companies.

Socially responsible investing presents a couple of problems. For example, your definition of social responsibility may not match the definition of the investment manager who's running a fund. Another problem is that even if you can agree on what's socially irresponsible (such as selling tobacco products), funds aren't always as clean as you would think or hope. Although a fund may avoid tobacco manufacturers, it may well invest in retailers that sell tobacco products.

If you want to consider a socially responsible fund, call the investment company and ask it to send you a recent annual report that lists the specific investments that the fund owns. Also consider giving directly to charities and get a tax deduction as well.

Specialty funds that invest in real estate or precious metals may make sense for a small portion (10 percent or less) of your investment portfolio. These types of funds can help diversify your portfolio because they can do better during times of higher inflation. Be careful with technology funds, which were hot during the late 1990s and early 2000. Many of these stocks are selling at premium valuations. When you invest in diversified stock funds, you get plenty of exposure to the technology sector.

Selecting the Best Mutual Funds

When you go camping in the wilderness, you can do a number of things to maximize your chances for happiness and success. You can take maps to keep you on course, food to keep you from getting hungry, proper clothing to stay dry and warm, and some first-aid gear to treat minor injuries. But regardless of how much advance preparation you do, you may have a problematic experience. You may take the wrong trail, trip on a rock and break your ankle, or lose your food to a tenacious bear that comes romping through camp one night.

And so it is with mutual funds. Although most mutual fund investors are rewarded for their efforts, there are no guarantees. You can, however, follow some simple, common sense guidelines that will keep you on the trail and increase your odds of investment success and happiness. The issues in this section are the main ones you should consider.

Cost

The charges you pay to buy or sell a fund, as well as the ongoing fund operating expenses, can have a big impact on the rate of return you earn on your investments. Many novice investors pay too much attention to a mutual fund's prior performance (in the case of stock funds) or to the fund's current yield (in the case of bond funds). Doing so is dangerous because a fund can inflate its return or yield in many (risky) ways. And what worked yesterday may flop tomorrow.

A study conducted by the Investment Company Institute in the United States confirmed what we've long observed among fund buyers. Only 43 percent of recent fund buyers who were surveyed bothered to examine the fees and expenses of the fund they ended up buying. The majority of fund buyers — 57 percent, to be exact — don't know what the funds are charging them to manage their money!

Fund costs are an important factor in the return that you earn from a mutual fund. Fees are deducted from your investment. All other things being equal, high fees and other charges depress your returns. What are a fund's fees, you ask? Good question — read on to find the answers.

Loads

Loads are upfront commissions paid to brokers who sell mutual funds. Loads typically range from 2 percent to as high as 6 or 7 percent of your investment. Sales loads have two problems:

> ✔ **First, sales loads are a needless cost that drags down your investment returns.** Because commissions are paid to the salesperson and not to the fund manager, the manager of a load fund does not work any harder and is not any more qualified than a manager of a no-load fund. Common sense suggests and studies confirm that many load funds perform *worse,* on average, than no-loads when the load is factored in.
>
> And don't think that spotting a load fund is easy. Just as some jewellers flog fake diamonds on late-night TV commercials, increasing numbers of brokers and financial planners sell bogus funds that they *call* no-loads, but these funds are *not* no-loads — they just hide the sales commission.
>
> "Stay in this fund for five to seven years," the broker will tell you, "and you don't have to pay the back-end sales charge that would normally apply upon sale of the investment." Although this claim may be true, it is also true that the fund is probably charging you very high ongoing operating expenses (often 1 percent more per year than true no-load funds) that the fund uses to pay the salesperson a hefty commission. So one way or another, the broker gets his pound of flesh (that is, his commission) from your investment dollars.

✔ **The second problem with sales loads is the power of self-interest.**
Although this issue is rarely discussed, it is even more problematic than
the issue of extra sales costs. Brokers who work for a commission are
interested in selling you commission-based investment products; therefore,
their best interests often conflict with your best interests.

Although you may be mired in high-interest debt or underfunding your
company retirement plan, some salespeople almost never advise you to
pay off your credit cards or put more money into your employer's pension
plan. To get you to buy, they may tend to exaggerate the potential benefits
and obscure the risks and drawbacks of what they sell. They don't take
the time to educate investors. We've seen too many people purchase
investment products through brokers without understanding what they're
buying, how much risk they are taking, and how these investments will
affect their overall financial lives.

The only way to be sure that a fund is truly no-load is to look at the prospectus
for the fund. Only there, in black and white and without marketing hype, must
the truth be told about sales charges and other fund fees. (An astonishing
73 percent of fund buyers surveyed by the Investment Company Institute
didn't know whether the fund they bought charged a sales load!) When you
want investing advice, hire a financial adviser on a fee-for-service basis (see
Chapter 19), which should cost you less and minimize potential conflicts of
interest.

The most common type of commission is a back-end load. Under this
arrangement, you don't pay anything to your adviser when you purchase
units of a fund. However, the adviser gets an upfront sales fee — generally 5
percent — from the fund company. There are two problems with back-end
load. First, they sometimes carry a higher annual management expense fee
than other versions of the same fund. Second, if you want to turn around and
sell the fund, you will pay a commission. This typically starts off at around 5
or 6 percent, and then falls anywhere from a half to a full percent a year for
each year you leave your money in the fund.

The problem with back-end loads is they hand-cuff you to a fund that may no
longer meet your needs, or may have evolved into an investment that is no
longer appropriate for you. If you want to move your money out of the fund
simply because you need the cash or perhaps the manager that attracted you
to it leaves to work elsewhere, you are penalized if you sell your fund units.

If you want to buy a load fund — and there are plenty of good choices
available — remember that the load is the maximum, not the required, sales
commission allowed. If you have enough business to offer them, some planners
and brokers will even sell you load funds at minimal cost, or even with no sales
charge at all, because they receive ongoing commissions called *trailer fees* as
long as you keep your money in a fund. If you do opt to pay commissions, be
sure you're getting high-quality, ongoing advice and expertise — after all,
you're already paying for it!

Operating expenses

All mutual funds charge ongoing fees. The fees pay for the operational costs of running a fund — employees' salaries, marketing, servicing the toll-free phone lines, printing and mailing published materials, computers for tracking investments and account balances, accounting fees, and so on. Despite being labelled "expenses," whatever profit a fund company extracts for running a fund is added to the tab as well.

A fund's operating expenses are quoted as an annual percentage of your investment and are essentially invisible to you. That's because they're deducted before you're paid any return. The expenses are charged on a daily basis, so you don't need to worry about trying to get out of a fund before these fees are deducted.

You can find a fund's operating expenses in the fund's prospectus. Look in the expenses section and find a line that says something like "Total Fund Operating Expenses." You can also call the fund's toll-free number and ask a representative.

Within a given sector of mutual funds (for example, money market, short-term bonds, or international stock), funds with low annual operating fees can more easily produce higher total returns for you. Although expenses matter on all funds, some types of funds are more sensitive to high expenses than others. Expenses are critical on money market mutual funds and greatly important on bond funds. Fund managers already have a hard time beating the averages in these markets; with higher expenses added on, it's nearly impossible.

With stock funds, expenses are a less important (but still significant) factor in a fund's performance. Don't forget that over time, stocks have averaged returns of about 10 percent per year. So if one stock fund charges 1 percent more in operating expenses than another fund, you're already giving up an extra 10 percent of your expected returns.

Some people argue that stock funds that charge high expenses may be justified in doing so if they generate higher rates of return. Evidence doesn't show that they do generate higher returns. In fact, funds with higher operating expenses tend to produce *lower* rates of return. This trend makes sense because operating expenses are deducted from the returns that a fund generates.

Consider sticking with funds that maintain low total operating expenses and don't charge loads (commissions). Both types of fees come out of your pocket and reduce your rate of return.

You have no reason to pay a lot for the best funds, as Table 10-3 shows. (In Chapters 12 and 13, we provide some specific fund recommendations as well as sample portfolios for investors in different situations.)

Table 10-3	Mutual Fund Operating Expense Ratios	
Fund Type	*Expense Ratio Range*	*Who Has Good Ones*
Money market funds	0.35% to 0.85%	Altamira, Elliot & Page, Industrial, Perigree, Scudder, Strategic Value
Bond funds	0.49% to 1.6%	Altamira, Bissett, C.I., Green Line, PH&N, Sceptre, Scotia, Trimark
Canadian stock	1.10% to 2%	Altamira, Bissett, C.I., Green Line, Mawer, PH&N, Sceptre, Scotia, Scudder Maxxum, Trimark
International stock	1.35% to 2.51%	AIC, BPI, Fidelity, Templeton, Trimark
Index	0.31% to 0.9%	Altamira, Bank of Montreal, CIBC, Green Line, Scotia
Specialty	1.95% to 2.85%	Altamira, AIM, Bank of Montreal, C.I., Fidelity, First Trust, Green Line, Templeton, Universal

Historical performance

A fund's *performance,* or historical rate of return, is another factor to weigh when selecting a mutual fund. As all mutual funds are required to tell you, past performance is no guarantee of future results. Analysis of historical mutual fund performance proves that some of yesterday's stars turn into tomorrow's skid-row bums.

Many former high-return funds achieved their results by taking on high risk. Funds that assume higher risk should produce higher rates of return. But high-risk funds usually decline in price faster during major market declines. Thus, in order for a fund to be considered a *best* fund, it must consistently deliver a favourable rate of return given the degree of risk it has taken.

When assessing an individual fund, compare its performance and volatility over an extended period of time (five or ten years if possible) to a *relevant* market index. For example, compare funds that focus on investing in large Canadian companies to the TSE 300 Index. Compare funds that invest in large U.S. companies to the Standard & Poor's 500 Index, and funds that invest in U.S. stocks of all sizes to the Wilshire 5000 Index. Indexes also exist for bonds, foreign stock markets, and almost any other type of security you can imagine.

Fund manager and fund family reputation

Much is made of who manages a specific mutual fund. As Peter Lynch, retired and famous former manager of the Fidelity Magellan fund, said, "The financial press made us Wall Street types into celebrities, a notoriety that was largely undeserved. Stock stars were treated as rock stars. . . ."

Although the individual fund manager is important, no fund manager is an island. The resources and capabilities of the parent company are equally important. Different companies have different capabilities and levels of expertise in relation to different types of funds. When you're considering a particular fund — for example, the Barnum & Barney High-Flying Foreign Stock fund — examine the performance history and fees not only of that fund but also of similar foreign stock funds at the Barnum & Barney company. If Barnum's other foreign stock funds have done poorly or Barnum & Barney offers no other such funds because it's focused on its circus business, those are strikes against its High-Flying fund. Also be aware that "star" fund managers also tend to be associated with higher-expense funds to pay their rock-star salaries.

Tax-friendliness

Investors often overlook tax implications when selecting mutual funds for nonretirement accounts. Numerous mutual funds effectively reduce their shareholders' returns because of their tendency to produce more taxable distributions — that is, capital gains and dividends — which we discuss later in this chapter.

"Ranking Mutual Funds on an After-Tax Basis," a pioneering study conducted by John B. Shoven and Joel M. Dickson at Stanford University, demonstrated that mutual fund capital gains distributions have a significant impact on an investor's after-tax rate of return. The Shoven and Dickson study found large differences between the before-tax and after-tax rates of return generated by stock mutual funds.

The following example highlights the dangers of picking a stock mutual fund for a non-retirement account simply on the basis of its reported rate of return. Suppose that over a five-year period the SkyHigh fund averaged a 15 percent annual rate of return, outpacing the WorldBeater fund, which averaged 12 percent per year. On the surface, it would seem that SkyHigh, beating its rival by 3 percent per year, is the better of the two funds.

But that's only part of the story. All mutual fund managers buy and sell stocks during the course of a year. Whenever a mutual fund manager sells securities, any gain or loss from those securities must be distributed to fund shareholders. Securities sold at a loss can offset those sold at a profit.

When a fund manager has a tendency to cash in more winners than losers, investors in the fund receive a high amount of taxable gains. Now suppose that over the past five years, the SkyHigh fund has made capital gains distributions averaging a whopping 10 percent of shareholder principal per year. The WorldBeater fund, on the other hand, has averaged just 3 percent in annual capital gains distributions. So, even though the Founder's fund says it produces higher total returns, *after* factoring in taxes, it doesn't.

Choosing mutual funds that minimize capital gains distributions helps you to defer taxes on your profits. By allowing your capital to continue compounding as it would in an RRSP or other retirement plan, you receive a higher total return. When you're a long-term investor, you benefit most from choosing mutual funds that minimize capital gains distributions. The more years that appreciation can compound without being taxed, the greater the value to you as the investor.

In addition to capital gains distributions, mutual funds also produce dividends that may be subject to income tax (refer to Chapter 7 for details).

Investors who purchase mutual funds outside tax-sheltered retirement plans should also consider the time of year they purchase shares in funds. December is the most common month in which mutual funds make capital gains distributions. When making purchases late in the year, ask if and when the fund may make a significant capital gains distribution. Consider delaying purchases in such funds until after the distribution date.

Your needs and goals

Selecting the best funds for you requires an understanding of your investment goals and risk tolerance. A good fund for your next-door neighbour is not necessarily a good fund for you. You have a unique financial profile.

If you've determined your needs and goals already, terrific! If you haven't, refer to Chapter 3. Understanding yourself is a good part of the battle. But don't shortchange yourself by not being educated about the investment you're considering. If you do not understand what you are investing in and how much risk you are taking, then you should stay out of the game.

Fund Rankings and Performance

Whether you're a novice or an experienced mutual fund investor, trying to get a handle on which funds are the best in various categories (such as international stocks or mortgage bonds) through mutual fund information and rating services can be overwhelming.

Reading prospectuses and annual reports

Mutual fund companies produce information that can help you make decisions about mutual fund investments. Every fund is required to issue a *prospectus*. This legal document is reviewed and audited by regulators. Most of what's written isn't worth the time it takes to slog through it.

The most valuable information — the fund's investment objectives, costs, and performance history — is summarized in the first few pages of the prospectus. This part you should read. Skip the rest, comprising mostly tedious legal details.

Funds also produce annual reports that discuss how the fund has been doing and provide details on the specific investments that a fund holds. If, for example, you want to know which countries an international fund invests in, you can find this information in the fund's annual report.

Beware the worst sources

With the popularity of mutual funds, more and more business, personal finance, and news magazines publish mutual fund articles and rankings. For a variety of reasons, much of this information isn't useful to folks trying to make informed decisions. In fact, making decisions based on some of these so-called mutual fund studies is downright dangerous.

One of the U.S.'s largest business magazines committed a number of major errors in its recent "Top Funds" analysis. First of all, the article awarded high returns without paying any attention to risk or volatility. Funds that took more risk and were able to generate higher rates of return were awarded higher rankings.

The most egregious error was the ranking of funds solely on the basis of rate of return over a three-year period. Three years is a short time to look at fund performance. This particular three-year period witnessed a nearly uninterrupted upward march in stock and bond prices. Imagine betting on an athlete to win the Olympic decathlon after the shot-put competition. Sure, a stocky, muscular type can shot-put farther than his competitors, but he may be huffing and puffing his way around the track in the 1,500-metre run.

Another example of the "garbage in, garbage out" phenomenon are rankings done using letters or grades just like your junior high school teacher did, except that your teacher's system was probably more sound. Sometimes funds are graded within broad categories based solely on total return, completely ignoring risk. And funds with entirely different objectives and which hold vastly different types of investments are grouped together. Also, some performance rankings that wind up in some newspapers can be for periods as short as *one year.*

Another mistake that some publications make in published mutual fund rankings is dumping a truckload of data on you. They then order the mutual funds alphabetically so that you sift through page after page of rows and columns of numbers. You have better things to do with your time.

Understanding your fund's performance

When you look at a statement for your mutual fund holdings, odds are that you're not going to understand it. It's not you — it's the statement.

The hardest part is getting a handle on how you're doing. Most people want to know, and have a hard time figuring out, how much they've made or lost on their investment.

You cannot deduce your return by comparing the share price of the fund today to the share price that you originally paid for the fund. Why not? Because mutual funds make distributions, both of dividends and capital gains, which lead to your getting more shares of the fund.

Distributions create an accounting problem because they reduce the share price of a fund. (Otherwise, you could buy into a fund just before it made a distribution and make a profit from the distribution.) Therefore, over time, following just the share price of your fund doesn't tell you how much money you've made or lost.

Imagine that the share price of your mutual fund is like a balloon with a small rock tied to the end of a string attached to it. The balloon (representing fund share price) struggles to rise, but the rock (representing fund distributions) keeps pulling down on the balloon.

The only way to figure out exactly how much you've made or lost on your investment is to compare the total value of your holdings in a fund today versus the total dollar amount you originally invested. When you've invested chunks of money at various points in time, this exercise becomes more complicated if you want to factor in the timing of your various investments.

The *total return* of a fund is the percentage change of your investment over a specified period. For example, a fund may tell you that in 1999 its total return was 15 percent. Therefore, if you had invested $10,000 in the fund on the last day of 1998, your investment would be worth $11,500 at the end of 1999. To find out a fund's total return, you can call the fund company's toll-free number or read the fund's annual report.

The following three components make up your total return on a fund:

- ✔ Interest and dividend income
- ✔ Capital gains distributions
- ✔ Share price changes

Interest and dividends

Both bonds and stocks can pay interest. A second source of income is dividends paid out by stocks a fund holds. When an interest or dividend distribution is made, you can receive it as cash (which is good if you need money to live on) or as more shares in the fund. In either case, the share price of the fund drops by an amount to offset the payout. So if you are hoping to strike it rich by buying into a bunch of funds just before they pay out, don't bother. You'll just end up paying more in income taxes.

If you hold your mutual fund outside a retirement plan, both interest and dividend distributions are taxable income. You'll have to pay tax on your gains whether you receive them as cash or use them to buy more units of the fund.

Interest is taxed at your full marginal tax rate. Dividends, however, are taxed at a much lower rate thanks to the dividend tax credit. As a result, dividend funds are a good bet if you are investing to earn income outside of a tax-sheltered plan such as an RRSP. (See Chapter 7 for more on how different types of investments are taxed.)

Capital gains

When a mutual fund manager sells a security in the fund, net gains realized from that sale (the difference from the purchase price) must be distributed to you as a *capital gain*. Typically, funds make one annual capital gains distribution in December, but distributions can be paid multiple times per year.

As with interest and dividend distributions, you can receive your capital gains distribution as cash or as more shares in the fund. In either case, the share price of the fund drops by an amount to offset the distribution.

For funds held outside retirement plans, your capital gains distribution is taxable. As with other fund income, capital gains are taxable whether or not you reinvest them in additional shares in the fund.

As we discuss in more detail in the next chapter, you may want to check with a fund to determine when capital gains are distributed if you want to avoid making an investment in a fund that is about to make a capital gains distribution. This increases your current-year tax liability for investments made outside of retirement plans.

Share price changes

You also make money with a mutual fund when the share price increases. This occurrence is just like investing in a stock or piece of real estate. If it's worth more today than when you bought it, you have made a profit (on paper, at least). In order to realize or lock in this profit, you need to sell your shares in the fund.

There you have it — the components of a mutual fund's total return are the following:

```
Dividends and interest + Capital gains distributions
      + Share price changes = Total return
```

Following and selling your funds

How closely you follow your funds is up to you, depending on what makes you happy and comfortable. We do not recommend tracking the share prices of your funds (or other investments, for that matter) on a daily basis. It is time-consuming and nerve-racking and will make you lose sight of the long term. You are more likely to panic when times get tough if you track your investments too closely. And for investments held outside of retirement plans, every time you sell an investment at a profit you get hit with taxes.

A monthly or quarterly check-in is more than frequent enough to follow your funds. Many publications carry total return numbers over varying periods so that you can determine the exact rate of return that you've been earning.

Trying to time and trade the markets to buy at lows and sell at highs rarely works. Yet an entire industry of investment newsletters, hotlines, online services, and the like have sprung up purporting to be able to tell you when to buy and sell. Don't waste your time and money on such nonsense (see Chapter 8 to read about gurus and newsletters).

You should consider selling a fund when it no longer meets the criteria mentioned in the section "Selecting the Best Mutual Funds" earlier in this chapter. If a fund has underperformed its peers for at least a two-year period or if a fund jacks up its management fees, it may be a good time to sell. But if you do your homework and buy good funds from good fund companies, you should need to do little trading.

Finding and investing in good funds isn't rocket science. Chapters 12 and 13 recommend some specific mutual funds using criteria discussed earlier in the chapter.

Chapter 11

Registered Retirement Savings Plans

*T*he phrase *Registered Retirement Savings Plan*, or RRSP, is perhaps the single best-known financial term in the country. Unfortunately, it's also often one of the most misunderstood. For example, many people think of an RRSP as an investment. In fact, it's a special holding account or holding place in which you can place most generally available Canadian investments, as well as some from outside our borders.

Putting money into an RRSP is an effective, easy, and efficient way to save for your retirement — and reduce your tax bill. However, to make the most out of RRSPs, you need to understand not only how to use them, but also what they are and how they offer numerous benefits.

What Is an RRSP?

The word *Registered* in Registered Retirement Savings Plan means you have made an agreement with the government. By "registering" your retirement savings plan with the government, you agree to put money away for your retirement and not touch it until that time. In return, the government gives you two valuable benefits.

First, money that you contribute to your RRSP is deductible from your taxable income. In other words, any income that you contribute to your savings plan is not taxed. Second, the government lets the savings in your RRSP grow tax-free. Any profits your RRSP investments earn are not taxable (until you collapse your plan and withdraw the funds).

The combined benefits of tax-deductible contributions and tax-deferred growth combine to supercharge your retirement savings. Here's a look at the powerful impact they can have on your ability to save for the future.

Tax-deferred contributions

Money that you contribute to an RRSP can be deducted from your income before your income tax is calculated for the year. For instance, say you made $50,000 and contributed $5,000 to your RRSP. If you claimed that $5,000 as a deduction on your tax return, your income tax would be calculated as if you had made only $45,000 that year.

Suppose that you're in a 42 percent tax bracket, which means that the government takes 42 cents of the last dollar you earn. If you contribute $1,000 to your RRSP, you save yourself $420 in tax. So the *real* out-of-pocket cost of a $1,000 contribution is only $580. In other words, contributing $1,000 to your RRSP really only leaves you short $580 in after-tax money you can put your hands on.

As shown in Table 11-1, the tax savings from contributing to an RRSP are substantial, regardless of your tax bracket.

Table 11-1	Short-Term Benefits of Tax-Deductible RRSP Contributions			
Where	*Investment Amount*	*Tax Rate*	*Tax Reduction*	*After-Tax Cost in Dollars*
Outside RRSP	$5,000	All	$0	$5,000
Inside RRSP	$5,000	24%	$1,200	$3,800
Inside RRSP	$5,000	33%	$1,650	$3,350
Inside RRSP	$5,000	42%	$2,100	$2,900
Inside RRSP	$5,000	47%	$2,350	$2,650

The benefits of tax-deductible contributions increase over time. Suppose that you're 35 and invest $5,000 of your salary this year outside an RRSP. Assuming that you're in a 40 percent tax bracket, Revenue Canada would first take $2,000 in tax, leaving you with $3,000. You invest that $3,000 in a mutual fund that earns a 10 percent compound return. After 30 years, you would have amassed a tidy $52,000. (This doesn't take into account the taxes you would likely have to pay each year on the distribution of capital gains, dividends, and interest, which would further reduce your average compound return outside an RRSP.)

But what if you had first contributed that money to your RRSP? Because Revenue Canada doesn't take any tax off your contributions, you can invest the full $5,000. Right away, that puts you $2,000 ahead. (In the real world, of course, you would have had the tax already taken off your income as it was earned. But you would receive a $2,000 tax rebate for your $5,000 contribution, so, at the end of the day, the real cost is only $3,000.)

If you invest that $5,000 in the same mutual fund inside an RRSP earning an average 10 percent compound return for 30 years, you're left with $87,000, or almost $35,000 more than you would have if you had put the money in a mutual fund. Table 11-2 shows just how valuable a tax-sheltered RRSP contribution can be to the long-term growth of your savings.

Table 11-2 Long-Term Payoff of Tax-Favoured RRSP Contributions

Where	Savings	Available for Investment	Value in 30 Years (with 10 percent growth)
Inside RRSP	$5,000	$5,000	$87,000
Outside RRSP	$5,000	$3,000	$52,000

As Table 11-2 demonstrates, the message is simple: The more money you invest to begin with, the more money you end up with for any given investment.

Recently, the government greatly reduced the tax rate for capital gains. Instead of having to include in your income three-quarters of your gains (for investments outside of an RRSP or other registered savings plan), you now include only 50 percent. If you are in the top marginal tax bracket of around 47 percent, that would mean your gains would effectively be taxed at just 23 percent. By contrast, when you take money out of your RRSP it is treated as if it was regular income and taxed at your full marginal tax rate.

While the changes to the capital gains tax rules do make investing in equities outside an RRSP much more tax-efficient, RRSPs still offer the best long-term returns. In Table 11-2, suppose you didn't pay any tax along the way for the $3,000 you invested outside an RRSP. (This would be unlikely because even an investment bought and held for the entire term would likely produce some taxable dividends.) The $52,000 that your original $3,000 had grown into, if taxed at 23 percent, would be worth $40,040. Even after being taxed at your full marginal tax rate of 47 percent, though, the $87,000 accumulated inside your RRSP would still be worth more than $46,000 — some $6,000 more than the unregistered investment.

Tax-deferred compound growth

If you put your money into an RRSP, any profits you earn with that money aren't taxed until you take the money out of your plan. Over time, the tax-free compounding leads to faster and faster growth of your retirement savings.

Tax-free compound growth occurs when interest and earnings on investments aren't taxed, so the full value is added to the original amount. This new, larger amount then earns further gains, which again are added to, or *compounded with*, your investments. Over time, this compounding leads to exponential growth. Just how well does compound growth work? A good rule to remember is that an investment that earns 10 percent compound growth annually will double about every seven years.

How to Maximize Your RRSP Savings

You need to follow only two basic rules to turn your RRSP into a real money-maker. First, begin contributing as early as you can in life. And second, try to maximize your RRSP's returns.

The benefits of starting an RRSP early

The real value in starting as early in life as possible is not simply the total amount of the extra contributions you manage to put in. It's that the longer you have money in an RRSP, the more time your savings have to compound.

Take someone who starts an RRSP when she is 28, making annual $2,000 contributions each year until she's 65. If she puts her money into a family of mutual funds that earns an average return of 10 percent, the total accumulation would be about $660,000.

But that same amount could essentially have been accumulated if she had begun putting $2,000 a year into an RRSP when she was 21 — and contributed for only seven years total (see Table 11-3). The younger you are, the less money it takes to ring up some big profits in your plan.

Even if you're just 25 and have only $1,000 to spare, put it in an RRSP! If you earn an average 10 percent a year, you'll have an extra $45,000 in your plan when you retire at 65. Just like the Concorde, your RRSP needs a good, long runway to really build up some steam. But when it takes off, the sky is the limit.

Table 11-3	The Money-Earning Potential of Starting an RRSP When You're Young		
$2,000 Contributions			
Age Beginning	**Age Ended**	**Total Years**	**Final Value at Age 65**
21	27	7	$664,000
28	65	37	$660,000

Note: Table 11-3 assumes a 10 percent annual rate of return.

Examples like the previous one are commonly used to sell the benefits of putting money into an RRSP from an early age. The problem is that if you *aren't* young, these examples can be unsettling. If you didn't find out about the benefits of RRSPs when you were young or didn't have money to contribute, you likely find it dispiriting to realize the tax savings and compound growth you missed out on. Whatever you do, don't let that stop you from taking action today. To rework that old cliché, today is the first day of the rest of your financial life!

Maximize your returns

Every February, many people dash around trying to get their RRSP contribution invested before the deadline. Rushed contributions, however, are usually made without considering investment options.

In this case, you're probably better off putting your money into a money market mutual fund or other cash-like investment, and then moving your money into better-performing investments when you have the time and energy to consider your options. By carefully assessing your RRSP investments, you can greatly boost the value of your plan, which translates directly into thousands of dollars more income to live on during retirement.

When a bargain isn't a bargain

Looking at the benefits of an RRSP contribution is often an excellent way to stem your appetite for a large expense that you may desperately want but not necessarily need. Say, for example, that you were able to put $6,000 every year into your RRSP and earned an average return of 9 percent. After 30 years, you would have accumulated an impressive $817,845.

But what if you put in only $4,500 annually, using the extra $1,500 to give yourself a week in the sun? Your total would still be a respectable $613,384. But look at it another way. Indulging yourself a little today will cost you over $200,000 in your retirement. Are your "sunfests" really worth having $200,000 less when you retire?

Do you find it tough to come up with anywhere near your maximum allowable contribution when the RRSP deadline comes around? Try an automatic deduction plan. You can tell your financial institution or RRSP holder to take a certain amount out of your bank account every few weeks — for example, when your paycheque comes in. You likely won't miss the money, and you'll be surprised at how much more you can put away.

Choosing appropriate investments is critical in maximizing the growth of your RRSP. And the more years you have before you have to collapse your plan, the larger the impact of boosting your returns by even just 1 or 2 percent.

Say you contribute $5,000 a year to your plan for 30 years, and you earn an average return of 8 percent. The final value of your plan would be just over $566,000.

But consider the results if you had taken a little more time in choosing your RRSP investments, and you had managed to earn 9 percent a year — just 1 percent more. In 30 years' time, your plan would be worth more than $681,000.

By improving your fund's performance by only 1 percent, you would end up with an extra $115,000! (See Table 11-4.)

Table 11-4	The Pay-Off from Investing Wisely: How a $5,000 Annual Contribution Will Grow	
Value at Growth Rate of . . .		
Years	*8%*	*9%*
5	$29,333	$29,924
10	$72,433	$75,965
30	$566,416	$681,538

The Different Types of RRSPs

You can get an RRSP just about anywhere — your local bank, trust company, brokerage house, insurance company, credit union, or mutual fund company.

Making an RRSP contribution is almost the same as making a regular investment with any of these companies. When you specify that your money is to go into an RRSP, however, you get a tax receipt that gives you a tax break on your contributions. In turn, you agree to follow the RRSP rules. While the names don't make complete sense, you'll often hear three different types of RRSP being pitched — *guaranteed, mutual funds,* and *self-directed* or *brokerage-house* RRSPs. Here's how to interpret what these different names mean.

Guaranteed RRSPs

Guaranteed plans are really just RRSPs in which you put your money into investments where your principal is protected, such as guaranteed investment certificates (GICs). When you do so, you lend your money to a bank or other financial institution in return for regular interest payments. Guaranteed plans pay fixed returns, and your money, if invested in GICs, is usually protected by the Canada Deposit Insurance Corporation's deposit protection.

Mutual fund RRSPs

The second basic type of RRSP is an investment in mutual funds. There are two benefits to mutual fund RRSPs. First, you can invest in stocks and bonds, which over the long haul will handily beat the returns from guaranteed investments. Second, if you set up an RRSP with a mutual fund company, you can diversify your savings by putting them into several different types of funds with the same company. Mutual fund companies usually charge an annual trustee fee ranging from $25 to $50 a year for RRSP accounts.

Self-directed and brokerage-house RRSPs

The third type of RRSP includes self-directed plans and RRSPs you open with brokerage houses. This type of plan allows you to invest in a wide range of securities. In addition to GICs and mutual funds, you can invest in individual stocks and bonds and a wide range of other securities.

You can set up a self-directed plan with most investment dealers and discount brokerages. These companies generally charge an annual fee of around $100. Some institutions are willing to reduce or eliminate their fees for self-directed

---

Can I have more than one plan?

You aren't limited to a specific number of RRSPs. You could, for example, open up a handful of RRSPs, each investing in different types of fixed-income securities or mutual funds, with different companies. There are drawbacks to having several plans, however. The paperwork can be burdensome, and it can become a real chore to follow your investments. If you invest with a number of different mutual fund companies, the trustee fees can start to add up. Finally, if you have some of your investments in foreign securities, it can be difficult to ensure that you haven't exceeded the maximum allowable foreign holdings (see the sidebar "International investing and your RRSP" on the next page).

---

plans. The discount brokerages run by the big banks and trust companies often waive the first-year fee for new plans. If you do have to pay a fee, make sure that you pay it out of your regular savings, not out of the funds in your plan.

Contribution Rules

As long as your age is 69 years or younger and you have received income from a job or from running a business or even net rental income — that is, as long as you've received *earned income* — you usually can contribute to an RRSP. There is no minimum age requirement. Even a child can have an RRSP, as long as he or she has earned income.

Contribution limits

The most you can contribute to your RRSP in any year is 18 percent of your earned income from the previous year, up to certain maximum amounts. In addition, if you're a member of a company pension plan or a deferred profit sharing plan, that membership further reduces the amount you can shelter in your plan.

In the spring or summer of each year, Revenue Canada sends all taxpayers a Notice of Assessment for the previous year. Your contribution limit for the current year is included on the statement. For example, if you've filed your 2000 tax return, you'll find your allowable contribution for 2001 on your assessment statement, which you should receive in the first half of 2001.

International investing and your RRSP

The government wants to keep you investing in Canada, so it limits how much of your RRSP funds can be invested in non-Canadian securities. The maximum you can have invested in non-Canadian assets — your RRSP's *foreign content limit* — is 30 percent, based on their cost, or *book value*. If you have a self-directed plan, you're responsible for ensuring that you don't exceed the limit. If you do go over the maximum, a tax of 1 percent per month is levied against any amount over the allowable limit.

One way to diversify your RRSP investments internationally without worrying about exceeding the limit is to invest in funds that maintain at least 80 percent of their investments in Canada and still put money into international securities. These funds qualify as 100 percent Canadian content and aren't taken into account when assessing how much "foreign" content you have in your RRSP. All companies will tell you which of their funds are RRSP eligible.

Many popular foreign funds are now also available in an RRSP-friendly wrapper. In essence, fund companies take a fund that would normally qualify as foreign content and, using advanced financial instruments, make the fund meet the Canadian content requirements. You get essentially the same securities the non-RRSP-friendly version of the fund holds, but the fund doesn't eat up any of your 30 percent foreign content limit. However, RRSP-friendly funds — often called *clone* funds — will usually have a higher management fee compared to the regular version of the fund.

It's important to review your allowable maximum contribution to ensure that the government has come up with the right figure. If Revenue Canada is too high and you overcontribute, you may risk having to pay a penalty. If its figure is too low, your plan will suffer because you won't have maximized your contribution.

In the next section, a simple guide (as simple as we could make it) helps you determine your allowable contribution. If you want, you can skip over this part and pick up again at the "RRSP withdrawals" section. You can then come back to review the following information when you get down to the nitty-gritty of working out your RRSP contribution.

Calculating your allowable contribution

To begin with, realize that the government puts absolute maximums on how much people, regardless of their situations, can contribute each year (see Table 11-5).

The contribution deadline

For any given tax year, you can make a contribution any time up to — and including — the 60th day in the next year. The last day you were allowed to contribute for the 1999 tax year, for example, was March 1, 2000. You could have contributed as early as January 1, 1999, of course.

The only positive thing that can be said about leaving your contribution to the last minute is

that it's probably good for an adrenaline rush. But consider this: If you plan ahead and make your contributions well in advance, you'll likely earn enough in extra interest over the years to pay for hours of heart-stopping bungee jumping and skydiving when you retire.

One other note: In the year you turn 69, you must contribute to your plan before December 31.

Table 11-5		Maximum RRSP Contributions	
Tax Year	*RRSP Limit*	*Min. Earned Income Req'd*	*From Year*
2000–2003	$13,500	$75,000	Previous year
2004	$14,500	$80,556	2003
2005	$15,500	$86,111	2004
After 2005		Indexed from 2005 limits	

If your company has a pension plan, your maximum RRSP contribution limit will be lower than those listed here (see upcoming sections).

A second cap on your contributions is that, for any year, you can contribute only up to 18 percent of your earned income from the *preceding* year. Now, you probably quite naturally believe that when it comes to your income, you've earned *all* of it, but the government has other ideas. When determining what qualifies as your "earned income," certain types of earnings are excluded.

Earned income includes only income sources such as these:

- ✔ Salary
- ✔ Bonuses and commissions
- ✔ Net business income
- ✔ Taxable alimony, maintenance, and child support payments received
- ✔ Net rental income

✔ Royalties

✔ Disability pension received under the Canada Pension Plan or Quebec Pension Plan

✔ Some types of taxable employment incomes, including disability and sick benefits

The following _reduce_ your earned income:

✔ Deductible alimony, maintenance and child support payments you make

✔ Most deductible employment-related expenses, including travel expenses and union dues

✔ Rental losses

The following types of income are _excluded_ from earned income:

✔ Pension benefits

✔ Most investment income

✔ Family allowance and child tax credit payments

✔ Employment insurance payments

✔ Adult training allowances

✔ Retiring allowances and severance pay

✔ Money from an income-averaging annuity

If you don't have a company pension plan, the most you can contribute in any given year, then, is the lowest of

✔ The annual maximum amount for that year, or

✔ 18 percent of your earned income in the previous year

(If no one in your family has a company pension plan, you can skip this section. Those with plans, please stay with the program.)

If you belong to a pension plan or deferred profit-sharing plan (DPSP), the government further scales back the amount it lets you contribute. The thinking is that because you have alternative sources of retirement income, you shouldn't get the full tax break allotted to people without pensions.

The government reduces your otherwise maximum allowable contribution by the value attributed for the contributions that both you and your employer make to your pension or deferred profit-sharing plan. This figure is called your _pension adjustment_, or _PA factor_. How that figure is arrived at depends on the type of plan you belong to.

Your pension adjustment is then subtracted from 18 percent of your earned income to arrive at your RRSP limit. Your pension adjustment is listed in Box 52 of your T4 slip, which you should receive from your employer before the end of every February. In general, the higher your pension the larger your pension adjustment and the lower your maximum allowable contribution.

If you belong to a defined-benefit pension plan

With a defined-benefit pension plan, the amount you receive when you retire is based upon your years of service and your income level. If you belong to this kind of plan, your pension adjustment (PA factor) is based on a calculation of the future value attributed to your pension of your previous year of employment. Your maximum contribution for 2001, for example, is 18 percent of your 2000 earned income to a maximum of $13,500, less your 2000 PA factor.

If you belong to a money-purchase pension plan

Your pension adjustment under this kind of pension plan is the total combined amount put into your pension by both you and your employer for the previous year. Your maximum contribution for 2001, for example, is 18 percent of your 2000 earned income to a maximum of $13,500, less all the 2000 pension contributions (PA factor).

If you belong to a deferred profit-sharing plan

If your employer contributes money to a deferred profit-sharing plan on your behalf, your pension adjustment equals the total of the contributions made (up to the maximum allowable DPSP contribution) for the previous year. For example, your 2001 maximum is 18 percent of your 2000 earned income to a maximum of $13,500, minus your 2000 PA factor.

Pensions and your contribution limits

Sometimes, pension benefits under a defined benefit pension plan are improved retroactively. If this happens, your RRSP contribution limit may be further reduced by a *past service pension adjustment* (PSPA).

On the other hand, you may find your contribution limits increased. For example, you may work for a company that has a pension plan. As a result, your RRSP contribution limits will be reduced by your pension adjustment. However, you may leave the company before you fully earn the rights to those benefits — before they *vest*. To give you back some of the RRSP contribution room that had been taken away because of the supposed pension benefits you were due to receive, you will get a *pension adjustment reversal* (PAR). A PAR increases your allowable RRSP contribution in the year you leave that particular job.

RRSP withdrawals

You are allowed to withdraw money out of your RRSP whenever you like, but the government will want to collect the taxes it had earlier foregone on your contributions.

When you withdraw money from your RRSP, the plan holder is required to withhold taxes on your withdrawals. The rates in all provinces (except Quebec) are 10 percent on amounts up to $5,000, 20 percent on the next $10,000, and 30 percent on withdrawals of over $15,000. In Quebec, the withholding rates are 25 percent of amounts up to $5,000, 33 percent on withdrawals up to $10,000, and 38 percent on withdrawals of $15,000 and higher.

(When you do your income tax return, you have to declare your withdrawals as income in the year you took the money out of your plan. For most people, that will mean an additional tax bill because the withholding rates in most cases are lower than the marginal tax rate.)

The withholding tax rates are calculated on each individual withdrawal. If you do need to get at your RRSP funds, take out separate withdrawals of no more than $5,000 each time to minimize the amount of withholding tax.

Spousal RRSPs

A spousal RRSP can help reduce your household's future tax bill if you are married or living common-law (see Chapter 7 for a definition) and you anticipate there will be a big gap between your income and your spouse's income when you both retire.

A spousal RRSP is simply a special kind of RRSP to which one spouse makes the contributions and is able to claim the tax deduction. However, the money then belongs to the other spouse. (While this change in official ownership worries some potential contributing partners, it shouldn't. In most cases the money in RRSPs is simply counted as part of your combined assets and divided equally between you and your spouse if you get separated or divorced.) As long as the money is left inside the plan for a minimum number of years, when it is withdrawn, it is counted as the spouse's income. The result is a spousal RRSP allows you to move some future income out of the hands of the person in the higher tax bracket, and into the hands of the spouse with the lower retirement income and therefore lower tax bracket.

The total contributions made by a spouse to both their own plan and a spousal RRSP can't exceed their allowable maximum individual contribution. In addition, there are rules to prevent the higher-earning spouse contributing to a spousal plan, claiming the deduction against income that is taxed at a high marginal rate, and then the lower-earning spouse removing the money from the plan and having it taxed at their lower marginal rate. If you contribute to a spousal plan, the money immediately belongs to your spouse. However, if they withdraw any of that contribution that year or during the next two calendar years, the withdrawal is treated as if you had earned it, and taxed at your marginal rate. (This rule does not apply if you and your spouse are separated or divorced.)

Collapsing (Closing) Your Plan

You must close out or *mature* your plan by the end of the year during which you turn 69. You can make a final contribution to your RRSP in your last year; however, instead of having 60 days into the next year to get your money in, the deadline for your final contribution is December 31.

Deciding just when to fold your plan and what to do with your funds are two of the most important financial decisions you'll ever make. Time your moves correctly and make some astute choices, and you'll find you have a much larger financial comfort zone than you expected. However, if you make your decisions at the last minute without doing your homework, you may find that your lack of attention costs you plenty in terms of a lower standard of living.

You're allowed to close out your RRSP earlier than the year in which you celebrate your 69th birthday, but your best strategy usually is to leave your RRSP alone for as long as you're allowed. This is almost always the case if you decide to choose a *Registered Retirement Income Fund* (RRIF). If you choose to go the *annuity* route, collapsing your plan a year or two early can make sense. If interest rates are relatively high, you can lock in a higher-than-average return.

Your Three RRSP Maturity Options

You have three basic options to choose from when your RRSP matures. You can simply cash out — take all the money right out of your RRSP and do what you will with it. If you do, Revenue Canada will treat the sum total of your plan as taxable income in that year. The resulting tax bill will lop off anywhere from one-third to half of your retirement savings, right then and there.

Far more practical is using the funds to buy an annuity by handing over your money to a financial institution (usually an insurance company), which then pays out regular sums to you for a period of time that you choose. This can be as short as ten years or as long as the rest of your life.

The third, and often best, choice is to convert your RRSP into another sort of registered plan that continues to enjoy tax-deferred compounding. The only condition of these accounts, called Registered Retirement Income Funds (or RRIFs), is that you take out a certain minimum amount every year.

You aren't limited to choosing one of these three options. You can choose to split your RRSP funds and use two or even all three of these different strategies.

To make the right decision for your individual circumstances, you have to consider a lot more than simply how much cash flow each option will bring in. Each strategy has its own specific tax burden and a different schedule on when those tax bills will come due to consider. Further, you need to decide how much control you want to have over how your funds are invested, and whether you want to have access to your funds. Finally, each option offers different levels of estate or survivorship protections.

Registered Retirement Income Funds (RRIFs)

An RRIF is similar in many ways to an RRSP. An RRIF allows your money to continue to grow tax-deferred, and you can invest your funds in most of the eligible RRSP investments, from money market funds to individual stocks. Also, as with an RRSP, you can have one, two, or a handful of different RRIFs.

The only difference between an RRIF and an RRSP is that you aren't allowed to put any money into your RRIF. Instead, you're required to take out a certain minimum amount each year.

These payments must start the year after you set up your RRIF. You can choose monthly, quarterly, semi-annual, or annual payments. What's more, you don't have to take your payments in cash. You can move any investment out of your RRIF without selling it. However, you must pay tax on the fair market value at the time of the withdrawal, just as if it had been taken out as income.

The main benefit of an RRIF is that you continue to have control over how and where your money is invested. This control gives you the best chance of earning healthier returns on your money. In particular, it allows you to invest in equities and bonds.

RRIFs also let you have a say about how much income you have. As long as you withdraw the required minimums, you can take out as little or as much as you wish in any given year. If you suddenly come into some money, you can leave your RRIF essentially untouched and keep ringing up tax-free growth. If you have a medical emergency, you can quickly get your hands on as much as you need at the time.

RRIFs are usually a good choice if you

✔ Enjoy managing your money.

✔ Have an indexed company pension plan that guarantees you a basic level of income.

✔ Don't immediately need to start drawing on your funds.

Another advantage of RRIFs is that you can convert them to an annuity at any time, whereas an annuity is for life: Once you sign up for an annuity, there's no changing your mind. Further, with an RRIF you have a lot more control over what happens to your money at your death.

Minimum RRIF withdrawals

Before 1993, you were required to have withdrawn all your money from your RRIF by the time you were 90. The rules changed in 1992 to allow you to maintain your RRIF as long as you live. If you opened an RRIF before 1993, your minimum withdrawals are determined by the pre-1993 rules until you hit 78 or, if you have a younger spouse, when he or she turns 78.

Your minimum withdrawals are a percentage of the market value of your RRIF at the end of the previous year. The requirement for each year is determined by your age on January 1 of that year (see Table 11-6).

Table 11-6	Minimum RRIF Withdrawals	
Age	*RRIF Opened before 1993*	*RRIF Opened 1993 and Later*
69	4.76%	4.76%
70	5.00%	5.00%
71	5.26%	7.38%
72	5.56%	7.48%
73	5.88%	7.59%
74	6.25%	7.71%
75	6.67%	7.85%
76	7.14%	7.99%
77	7.69%	8.15%
78	8.33%	8.33%

Age	RRIF Opened before 1993	RRIF Opened 1993 and Later
79	8.53%	8.53%
80	8.75%	8.75%
81	8.99%	8.99%
82	9.27%	9.27%
83	9.58%	9.58%
84	9.93%	9.93%
85	10.33%	10.33%
86	10.79%	10.79%
87	11.33%	11.33%
88	11.96%	11.96%
89	12.71%	12.71%
90	13.62%	13.62%
91	14.73%	14.73%
92	16.12%	16.12%
93	17.92%	17.92%
94 and up	20.00%	20.00%

Annuities

When you use your RRSP funds to buy an annuity, you transfer your RRSP funds over to a financial institution (usually an insurance company), which then pays them back to you a little bit at a time. You don't pay tax on any RRSP funds at the time you turn them into an annuity. The regular payments from the annuity, though, are taxable and treated by Revenue Canada as "pension" income. If you have no other pension income, up to $1,000 of the annuity payments will qualify for the Pension Income Tax Credit.

The biggest decision when buying an annuity is the length of time you want your payments to run for. One option is to pick a specific number of years, such as 5, 10, or 20. At the end of the specific time, your payments end and your annuity is fully depleted. Another choice is a *life annuity,* which provides you with payments for the rest of your life, while a *joint-life annuity* continues payments as long as you or your spouse is still alive.

Unlocking locked-in RRSPs and retirement accounts

If you leave a company in which you were a member of a pension plan, you may have earned the right to your pension benefits. However, you may not be allowed to gain access to those benefits due to the pension regulations (*locking-in* legislation). In this case, your pension benefits may be transferred to a special type of RRSP called a *locked-in RRSP* or *locked-in retirement account* (*LIRA*). Withdrawals from the locked-in account are usually subject to the same rules as the pension plan. For example, you may only be able to actually take control of the money within ten years of the retirement age specified in the pension plan.

Even then, you are still limited to what you can do. One choice is to use the money to purchase an annuity. A second option is to convert the funds into a special Registered Retirement Income Fund (RRIF) called a *Life Income Fund*, or *LIF*. Like an RRIF, you have to withdraw a set minimum as a percentage of the funds in your LIF every year. However, unlike an RRIF on which there are no maximums, a LIF has a ceiling on how much you can withdraw each year as well. Another rule that makes a LIF more restricted than an RRIF is that when you turn 80, you have to take the money inside your LIF and buy a life annuity. Some provinces have recognized that this is an unneeded rule, and have introduced *locked-in retirement income funds*, or *LRIFs*. These work much like LIFs. The big difference is that with an LRIF, there is no requirement to purchase an annuity at age 80.

If you select a life annuity, the size of your payments depends on your age and sex. Men tend to die at an earlier age than women do, so life annuity payments for males are generally higher because the funds have to last for fewer years. And obviously, the younger you are, the smaller your payments will be because (we hope) your payments will have to stretch far into the future.

You can also add a couple of wrinkles to your annuity. If you choose a life annuity, even if you die the very next week the insurance company gets to keep all the money. But if you choose a *guaranteed annuity,* you ensure that if you die before a certain number of years have passed the payments will continue and will go to your beneficiaries. You can also choose to have your payments increase gradually from year to year. Such *indexed annuities* help your income keep up with inflation.

Just how much your funds will pay you, how long you want them to continue, and the options you want are all put through complex calculations by the technical climbers of the accounting world, actuaries. Once you decide on your options, your payments can be calculated by using the statistics of how long you're likely to live and the likelihood of your dying at various ages. (Don't ask to see these numbers, because you probably don't want to know.) After you select your options, they can never be changed; they will remain in place until the annuity contract ends with your death or, if you chose the spousal survivor option, when your spouse dies.

That means that such options as indexing and guarantees all come at a price. Because these features mean that the insurance company will in all likelihood have to pay out more money, your regular payments will be lower than if you choose to go with a basic, stripped-down *defined-term annuity*.

Annuities are usually best if you

- ✔ Have small retirement savings that absolutely need to last a number of years, especially if you're young and your family has a history of living a long time.

- ✔ Must have the peace of mind that comes with knowing just how much you have to live on.

- ✔ Don't want to have to make ongoing decisions about how to invest your money.

On the flip side of these advantages are several drawbacks, including these:

- ✔ You lose all control of your savings.

- ✔ Your rate of return is fixed when you buy your plan and will likely be lower than what you could earn investing in good mutual funds. If the investment world suddenly becomes littered with far more profitable options, you'll just have to lump it.

- ✔ If you don't accept lower payments in return for an indexed annuity, you may be faced with having less buying power over the years if inflation takes off.

- ✔ If you don't take out a guarantee, or you die after the guarantee period expires, your family or other beneficiaries won't get anything on your death.

The largest drawback to annuities is that you lose all input in how your money is invested and in how much it earns for you. You also have to accept lower initial payments if you want your annuity to increase with the cost of living.

Chapter 12

Investing Money Inside Retirement Plans

*T*his chapter explains how to make decisions about investing money you currently hold inside RRSPs or other retirement plans, or money you plan to contribute to a retirement plan.

Compared to the often overwhelming world of investing outside retirement accounts, investing inside tax-sheltered retirement plans is far less complicated. There are two reasons for this:

✔ **The range of possible retirement plan investments is more limited.** Direct investments, such as real estate and investments in small, privately owned companies, are not generally available or accessible in most retirement plans.

✔ **When investing in a retirement plan, your returns aren't taxed as you earn them.** Money inside retirement plans compounds and grows without taxation. You pay taxes on these funds only when you withdraw money from the plan (direct transfers to a retirement plan at another investment firm aren't withdrawals, so they aren't taxed). So when you choose an investment for your retirement plan, don't rack your brain over dividends and capital gains; save all that worry for your money in non-retirement accounts.

Inappropriate Retirement Plan Investments

Some investments for retirement plans are simply inappropriate. This section discusses investments that you should *not* make in retirement accounts.

Annuities

Annuities have no place inside retirement plans. Annuities allow your investment dollars to compound without taxation. In comparison to other investments that don't allow such tax deferral, annuities carry much higher annual operating expenses, which depress your returns.

Purchasing an annuity inside an RRSP or other registered retirement plan is like wearing a belt and suspenders together. Either you have a peculiar sense of style, or you spend too much time worrying about your pants falling down. In our experience, many people who mistakenly invest in annuities inside retirement plans have been misled into it by investment salespeople.

Annuities pay hefty commissions, sometimes as high as 10 percent or more of the amount invested. In some cases, we think, the salespeople aren't being conniving and unethical — they just don't know any better. The insurance companies behind these products, in their enthusiasm to pump up salespeople to peddle them, conveniently skip over the details about when investing in annuities is appropriate and when it isn't.

Limited partnerships

Limited partnerships, which are sold through investment salespeople, are treacherous, high-commission, high-cost, and hence low-return investments. Part of their supposed allure, however, is the tax benefits that they generate. But when you buy and hold a limited partnership in a retirement plan, you lose the ability to take advantage of many of the tax deductions. The illiquidity of LPs may also mean that you can't make required retirement plan withdrawals when needed. These are just some of the many reasons to avoid investing in limited partnerships.

Allocating Your Money in Retirement Plans

With good reason, people are concerned about placing their retirement plan money in investments that can decline in value. You may feel that you're gambling with dollars intended for the security of your golden years.

But to attain that security, most working folks need to make their money work hard in order for it to grow fast enough. That involves taking some risk; you have no way around it. Luckily, if you have 15 to 20 years or more before you need to draw on the bulk of your retirement plan assets, time is on your side. If some of your investments drop a bit over a year or two, what's the big deal as long as the value of your investments has time to recover? The more years until you are going to retire, the greater your ability to take risk.

If you haven't yet done so, read the section on asset allocation in Chapter 8. That section helps you decide how to divide your money among different investment options based upon your time frame and risk tolerance.

Prioritizing retirement contributions

If you have access to more than one type of retirement account, prioritize which accounts to use first by what they give you in return. Your first contributions should be to employer-based plans that match your contributions. After that, contribute to any other employer plan or your RRSP, as long as your contributions are tax-deductible.

Setting up an RRSP

No-load (commission-free) mutual fund and discount brokerage firms are your best bet for setting up an RRSP. (We make specific recommendations for investments to use inside your plan later in this chapter.)

Investments and account types are different issues. People sometimes get confused when discussing the investments they make in retirement plans, especially people who have RRSPs at banks. They don't realize that you can have your RRSP at a variety of financial institutions (for example, a mutual fund company or brokerage firm). At each financial institution, you can choose among the firm's investment options for putting your RRSP money to work.

Allocating money when your employer selects the investment options

In many company-sponsored plans, you are limited to the predetermined investment options your employer offers. Plans differ in the specific options they offer, but they usually offer similar basic choices. In what follows, we discuss a plan's typical investment options, in order of increasing risk and, hence, likely return. Then, we give examples of how to allocate your money across the different types of common employer retirement plan options.

Money market/savings accounts

For regular contributions coming out of your paycheque, the money market or savings account option makes little sense. Some people who are skittish about the stock and bond markets are attracted to money market and savings accounts because those accounts cannot drop in value. However, the returns are low . . . so low that you are at great risk that your investment will not stay ahead of, or even keep up with, inflation and taxes.

For those of you who may be tempted to use a money market fund as a parking place until the time that you think stocks and bonds are cheap, don't. In the long run, you won't be doing yourself any favours if you do so. As we discuss in Chapter 8, timing your investments to attempt to catch the lows and avoid investing at the peaks is impossible. If you can figure out how to do that, you're wasting your time in whatever occupation you're now employed. You could make a fortune as a professional money manager.

You may need to keep money in the money market investment option if you use the borrowing feature that some retirement plans allow. Check with your employee benefits department for more details. You might also use a money market after you retire to hold money you expect to withdraw and spend within the next year or so.

Bond mutual funds

Bond mutual funds (which we describe in Chapter 10) invest in a mixture of typically high-quality bonds. Bonds pay a higher rate of interest or dividends than money market funds. Depending on whether your plan's option is a short-term, intermediate-term, or long-term fund (maybe you have more than one type), the bond fund's current yield is probably a percent or two higher than the money market fund's yield.

Bond funds carry higher yields than money market funds, but they also carry greater risk because their value can fall if interest rates increase. However, bonds tend to be more stable in value than stocks.

Aggressive, younger investors should keep a minimum amount of money in bond funds. Older folks who want to invest more conservatively can place more money in bonds (see the asset allocation discussion in Chapter 8).

Guaranteed investment certificates (GICs)

GICs are backed by a bank, trust company, or insurance company, and offer you a fixed rate of return projected anywhere from a few months to five years forward. The return is always positive and certain — thus you don't have the uncertainty that you would normally face with bond or stock investments.

The attraction of these investments is that your account value doesn't fluctuate (at least, not that you can see). The financial institution normally invests your money mostly in bonds and maybe a bit in stocks. The difference between what these investments generate and what you get paid in interest is profit to the GIC seller. The yield is usually comparable to that of a bond fund.

For people who would hit the eject button the moment that a bond fund slides a bit in value, GICs are soothing to the nerves. And they're certainly higher yielding than a money market or savings account.

Like bonds, however, GICs don't give you the opportunity for long-term growth of your money. Over the long haul, you should earn a better return in a mixture of bond and stock investments. In GICs, you pay for the peace of mind of a guaranteed return in the form of lower long-term returns.

Balanced mutual funds

Balanced mutual funds invest in a mixture primarily of stocks and bonds. This one-stop-shopping concept makes investing easier and smoothes out fluctuations in the value of your investments — funds investing exclusively in stocks or in bonds make for a rougher ride. These funds are solid options and, in fact, can be used for a good portion of your retirement plan contributions. Refer to Chapter 10 to learn more about balanced funds.

Stock mutual funds

Stock mutual funds invest in stocks, which usually provide greater long-term growth potential but also wider fluctuations in value from year to year. Some companies offer a number of different stock funds, including funds that invest in the United States and overseas. You should have a healthy helping of stock funds. We explain the different types of stock funds and give details on how to evaluate a stock fund in Chapter 10.

Stock in the company you work for

Some companies offer employees the option of investing in the company's stock. We generally advocate avoiding this option for the simple reason that your future income and other employee benefits are already riding on the success of the company. If the company hits the skids, you may lose your job and your benefits. You certainly don't want the value of your retirement account to depend on the same factors.

If your employer does not offer you any retirement plan investing options other than putting money in company stock, complain. Start with your benefits department.

If you think that your company has its act together and the stock is a good buy, investing a portion of your retirement plan is fine — but no more than 25 percent. Now, if your company is on the verge of hitting it big and the stock is soon to soar, you'll of course be kicking yourself for not putting more of your money into the company's stock. But when you place a big bet on your company's stock, be prepared to suffer the consequences if the stock tanks. Don't forget that lots of smart investors track companies' prospects, so odds are that the current value of your company's stock is fair.

Some employers offer employees the ability to buy company stock at a discount, sometimes as much as 15 percent, compared to its current market value. Others will even match your contribution according to a formula, up to certain limits. If you can buy stock in your employer's company this way, so much the better. When you sell the stock as your employer's plan allows, usually after a specified holding period, you should be able to lock in a decent profit.

Some asset allocation examples

Table 12-1 shows a couple of examples of how people in different employer plans might choose to allocate their investments among the plan's investment options, using the methodology that we outline in Chapter 8 for allocating money.

Table 12-1	Allocating Registered Savings Plan Investments		
Risk	**25-Year-Old, Aggressive**	**45-Year-Old, Moderate Risk**	**60-Year-Old, Moderate Risk**
Bond Fund	10%	35%	50%
Blue-Chip/Larger Company Stock Fund(s)	40%	25%	25%
Aggressive/Smaller Company Stock Fund(s)	15%	15%	5%
International Stock Fund(s)	35%	25%	20%

Investing beyond our borders

Just as you should diversify the portion of your RRSP (and other non-sheltered investment accounts) allocated to stocks amongst many different stocks, you should also diversify amongst different countries. When the Canadian market is sliding backwards, some foreign stocks may be ringing up handsome returns. Similarly, when overseas stocks are struggling, it may be time for the Canadian market to shine. While some smaller markets such as Latin America are highly volatile, investing in major industrial regions such as Europe, Australia, some of the Far East, and of course the U.S. can make your returns less volatile.

How much and what kind of foreign exposure should you have? Say you want to have a balanced portfolio with 55 percent in stocks. If you wanted to stick with the foreign content limit of 30 percent, you might consider putting 25 percent in Canadian equities, 20 percent in U.S. equities, and 10 in international equities. An even simpler approach would be to put 30 percent of your RRSP into a few conservative international mutual funds. You may also want to invest a portion of the money you have allocated for fixed-income securities in international or global bond funds.

Making allocation decisions is not a science. Use the formulas in Chapter 8 as a guideline.

Allocating money in plans that you design

With RRSPs, particularly self-directed plans, you get to select the investment options as well as the allocation of money among them.

In the sections that follow, we give some specific recipes that you may find useful for investing. To set up your RRSP at one of these firms, simply pick up your telephone and dial the company's toll-free number and ask them to mail you an account application. When you call you can also request that they mail you background on specific mutual funds you may be interested in.

The following sections discuss some sample portfolios to consider, one designed for someone keeping her RRSP invested in Altamira funds, the other for an investor with Fidelity. There are many other strong fund groups out there to work with, but we've chosen these two to give you an idea of how to spread your investments over a company's different fund offerings.

A self-directed plan lets you choose from a wide range of funds offered by many different companies. (If you're considering a mutual fund RRSP, we advise setting up a no-load plan.)

Note: In the sections that follow, we recommend a conservative and an aggressive portfolio. These terms are used in a relative sense. Because some of the recommended funds don't maintain fixed percentages of their different types of investments, the actual percentage of stocks and bonds that you end up with may vary slightly from the targeted percentages. Don't sweat it.

Where you have more than one fund choice, you can pick one or split the suggested percentage between them. If you don't have enough money today to divide it up as we suggest, you can achieve the desired split over time as you add more money to your retirement accounts.

Don't forget that you can greatly expand your universe of good mutual fund choices by dealing with a brokerage that charges you a modest commission or no commission at all on load funds.

The RRSP foreign content rules

For several years, you have only been allowed to have a maximum of 20 percent of your RRSP in foreign investments. This is calculated on the purchase cost, or book value or your portfolio. However, for 2000 the limit was raised to 25 percent and starting January 1, 2001 the foreign content limit rose to 30 percent.

As we discuss earlier in this chapter, it's wise to have a good degree of foreign securities in your RRSP and other investment portfolios. In addition to maximizing your foreign exposure to 30 percent, there are other ways to build in a higher level of foreign investment in your RRSP. First, you can purchase mutual funds that maximize their own allowable foreign content. A mutual fund can have up to 20 percent of its capital invested outside of Canada and still qualify as 100 percent Canadian content. In other words, it doesn't use up any of your foreign content allowance. Also, you can boost your foreign content limit by $3 for every $1 you invest in qualifying Canadian small businesses. For the year 2001, the maximum foreign content you could boost your foreign content limit to this way was 50 percent.

In addition, there are many versions of funds that invest largely – or solely – outside of Canada but which qualify as 100 percent Canadian content. Some other funds mirror the performance of foreign indexes such as the Dow Jones Industrial Average. Other funds are actively managed and buy and sell individual foreign securities. These funds qualify as Canadian content due to the way that they are structured. The required portion of the fund is invested here at home in conservative interest-bearing securities. The remaining money is used to buy sophisticated securities such as futures and options contract. The net result is the fund will offer up a return close to that of the index it's mirroring, or the regular non-RRSP-friendly version of the same fund. However, in most cases the returns of a foreign fund set up to qualify as Canadian content will trail the regular version of such funds. The so-called clone funds have a higher management expense ratio due to the extra cost and work involved in setting the funds up to fully fall into the Canadian content category.

Altamira

The following two Altamira (800-263-4769) recommendations are for a conservative mix and an aggressive mix, respectively.

A conservative portfolio with 50 percent stocks, 50 percent bonds

Altamira Equity — 15 percent

Altamira Bond — 30 percent

Altamira Balanced — 40 percent

Altamira Global Value — 15 percent

An aggressive portfolio with 80 percent stocks, 20 percent bonds

Altamira Capital Growth — 20 percent

Altamira Equity — 30 percent

Altamira Global Small Company — 5 percent

Altamira Global Value — 25 percent

Altamira Bond — 20 percent

Fidelity

The following two Fidelity (800-263-4077) recommendations are for a conservative mix and an aggressive mix, respectively.

A conservative portfolio with 50 percent stocks, 50 percent bonds

Fidelity Canadian Large Cap — 15 percent

Canadian Bond — 30 percent

Fidelity Canadian Balanced — 40 percent

Fidelity International Portfolio — 15 percent

An aggressive portfolio with 80 percent stocks, 20 percent bonds

Fidelity Canadian Large Cap — 40 percent

Fidelity Canadian Growth Company — 10 percent

Fidelity International Portfolio — 30 percent

Fidelity Bond — 20 percent

Self-directed or discount brokerage choices

As we discuss in Chapter 8, a discount brokerage account can allow you centralized, one-stop shopping and holding of mutual funds from a variety of the leading fund companies. Most funds are available without transaction fees. However, there may be a charge for switching funds or selling within a certain period.

Among brokerage firms or brokerage divisions of mutual fund companies, for breadth of fund offerings and competitive pricing we like TD Waterhouse (800-465-5463; www.tdwaterhouse.ca), BMO InvestorLine (800-387-7800; www.bmoinvestorline.com), Charles Schwab Canada (888-597-9999; www.schwabcanada.com), E*Trade Canada (888-872-3388; www.canada.etrade.com), and Royal Bank Action Direct (800-769-2583; www.actiondirect.com).

A conservative portfolio with 50 percent stocks, 50 percent bonds

Ivy Canadian and/or Royal Canadian Equity and/or Trimark Canadian — 15 percent

AGF International Value and/or AIM Trimark — 30 percent

Mawer Balanced Retirement Savings — 10 percent

Altamira Bond and/or Phillips, Hager & North Bond — 35 percent

Green Line Global RRSP Bond or Dynamic Global — 10 percent (International Bond funds that qualify as Canadian content)

An aggressive portfolio with 80 percent stocks, 20 percent bonds

Fidelity Growth Company and/or Bissett Small Cap — 10 percent

AIC Diversified Canada and/or AGF Canadian Growth Equity — 15 percent

Phillips, Hager & North Canadian Equity and/or Royal Canadian Equity — 15 percent

BPI American Equity RSP and/or Trimark U.S. Companies RSP — 20 percent

AGF International Value and/or BPI Global Equity Value — 20 percent

Phillips, Hager & North Bond and/or TD Canadian Bond — 20 percent

Transferring Retirement Plans

With the exception of plans maintained by your employer that limit your investment options, you can move your money held in RRSPs and RRIFs to almost any major investment firm or mutual fund company you please. Moving the money is pretty simple. If you can dial a toll-free number, fill out a couple

Should I use one investment firm or more than one?

The firms listed in this chapter offer a large enough variety of investment options, managed by different fund managers, that you can feel comfortable concentrating your money at one firm. The advantages of a focused approach are that you need to learn the nuances and choices of just one firm rather than several, and that you have fewer administrative hassles.

If you like the idea of spreading your money around, you may want to invest through a number of different firms. If you open a discount brokerage account (refer to Chapter 10), you can have your cake and eat it, too. You can diversify across different mutual fund companies through one brokerage firm. However, you'll generally pay small transaction fees on some of your purchases and sales of funds.

of short forms, and send them back in a postage-paid envelope, you can transfer an account. The investment firm to which you are transferring your account does the rest.

Transferring plans you control

Here's a step-by-step list of what you need to do to transfer a retirement savings plan to another investment firm. Even if you're working with a financial adviser, you should be aware of this process (called a *direct trustee-to-trustee transfer*) to ensure that no hanky-panky takes place on the adviser's part:

1. **Decide where you want to move the account**. We recommend several investment companies in this chapter, along with some sample portfolios within those firms.

2. **Obtain an account application and asset transfer form**. Call the toll-free number of the firm you are transferring the money to and ask for an *account application and asset transfer form* for the type of account you are transferring. You can also visit Web sites, but for this type of request we think most people find it easier to speak with a live person.

   Important note: Ask for the form for the same type of account you currently have at the company from which you are transferring the money. You can determine the account type by looking at a recent account statement — the account type should appear near the top of the form or in the section with your name and address. If you can't figure it out on a cryptic statement, call the firm where the account is currently held and ask a representative to tell you what kind of account you have.

Never, ever sign over assets such as cheques and security certificates to a financial adviser, no matter how trustworthy and honest he or she may seem. The adviser could abscond with them quicker than you can say "Bonnie and Clyde." Transfers should not be completed this way. Besides, you'll find it easier to handle the transfer the way we describe in this section.

3. **Complete and mail the account application and asset transfer form.**
   Completing these for your new investment firm opens your new account and authorizes the transfer.

You shouldn't take possession of the money in your retirement plan yourself to get it over to the new firm. The tax authorities impose huge penalties if you do a transfer incorrectly. Let the company to which you're transferring the money do the transfer for you. If you have questions or problems, the firm(s) to which you are transferring your account have armies of capable employees waiting to help you. Remember, these firms know that you are transferring your money to them, so they should roll out the red carpet.

4. **Figure out which securities you want to transfer and which need to be liquidated.** Transferring existing investments in your account to a new investment firm can sometimes be a little sticky. If you're moving cash (money market funds) or securities that trade on any of the major stock exchanges, transferring is not a problem.

If you own publicly traded securities, transferring them *as is* (known as "in kind") to your new investment firm is better, especially if the firm offers discount brokerage services. You can then sell your securities through that firm more cheaply.

If you own mutual funds unique to the institution you're leaving, check with your new firm to see if it can accept them. If not, you need to contact the firm that currently holds them to sell them.

GICs are tricky to transfer. Ideally, you should send in the transfer forms several weeks or so before the GICs mature — few people do this. If the GIC matures soon, call the bank and instruct it that when the GIC matures, you would like the funds to be invested in a savings or money market account that you can access without penalty when your transfer request lands in the bank's mailbox.

5. **(Optional) Let the firm from which you're transferring the money know that you are doing so.** If the place you're transferring from doesn't assign a specific person to your account, definitely skip this step. When you're moving your investments from a brokerage firm where you've dealt with a particular broker, the decision is more difficult.

Most people feel obligated to let their representative know that they are moving their money. In my experience, calling the person with the "bad news" is usually a mistake. Brokers or others who have a direct financial stake in your decision to move your money will try to sell you on staying. Some may try to make you feel guilty for leaving, and some may even try to bully you.

Writing a letter may seem like the coward's way out, but writing usually makes leaving your broker easier for both of you. You can polish what you have to say, and you don't put the broker on the defensive. Or (although we don't want to encourage lying) not telling the *whole* truth may be better. Excuses, such as you have a family member in the investment business who will manage your money for free, may help you to avoid an uncomfortable confrontation.

Then again, telling an investment firm that its charges are too high or that it misrepresented and sold you a bunch of lousy investments may help the firm to improve in the future. Don't fret too much — do what's best for you and what you're comfortable with. Brokers are not your friends. Even though the broker may know your kids' names, your favourite hobbies, and your birthday, you have a *business* relationship.

Transferring your existing assets typically takes a month to complete. Should the transfer not be completed within one month, get in touch with your new investment firm to determine what the problem is. If your old company is not cooperating, call a manager there to help get the ball rolling.

The unfortunate reality is that an investment firm will cheerfully set up a new account to accept your money on a moment's notice, but it will drag its feet, sometimes for months, when the time comes to relinquish your money. To light a fire under the behinds of the folks at the investment firm, tell a manager at the old firm that you're sending letters to your province's securities regulator if it doesn't complete your transfer within the next week.

Moving money from an employer's plan

When you leave a job, particularly if you are retiring or being laid off after many years of service, money-hungry brokers and financial planners probably will be on you like a pack of bears on a tree leaking sweet honey. Tread carefully and slowly if you seek financial help — be sure to read Chapter 19 to avoid the pitfalls in hiring such assistance.

When you leave a job, you are confronted with a slightly different transfer challenge: If you've earned the right to some or all of your pension benefits (called *vesting*), you have the option of transferring them into a locked-in retirement account (LIRA). In some provinces, these are called locked-in RRSPs. Check with your employer's benefits department or a tax adviser for details.

As long as your employer allows it, you may be able to leave your money in your old employer's plan. Evaluate the quality of the investment choices using the information we provide in this part of the book.

If you want to transfer your pension funds, simply inform your employer where you want your money to be sent. Prior to doing so, you should establish an appropriate account with the investment firm you intend to use. Then tell your employer's benefits department what investment firm you would like your retirement money transferred to. You can give your employer the Revenue Canada forms and lock-in agreements (if required) that have been signed by the investment firm's retirement account trustee. These forms will detail the investment firm's mailing address and your account number.

Chapter 13

Investing Money Outside Retirement Plans

. . . .

In This Chapter

▶ Taking advantage of frequently overlooked investment options

▶ Factoring taxes into your investment decisions

▶ Where to invest your emergency reserve

▶ Recommended short-, intermediate-, and long-term investments

. . . .

*I*n this chapter, we discuss investment options for money held *outside* RRSPs or other retirement plans and include specific mutual fund recommendations. Chapter 12 reviews investments for money *inside* RRSPs and other retirement plans. This distinction may seem somewhat odd — it's not one made in most financial books and articles — but we have our reasons.

Thinking of the two pots of money differently is useful.

> ✔ **Investments held outside an RRSP (or your company pension plan) are subject to taxation.** You have a whole range of different investment options to consider when taxes come into play.

> ✔ **Money held outside RRSPs or other registered plans is also more likely to be used sooner than funds held inside tax-deferred plans.** Why? Because you generally have to pay far more in income taxes to access money inside rather than outside retirement plans.

> ✔ **Funds inside RRSPs and other registered savings plans have their own nuances.** For example, when you invest through your employer's retirement plan, your investment options are usually limited to a handful of choices. And special rules govern the transfer of your retirement plan balances.

Getting Started

Suppose you've got some money sitting around in a bank savings account or money market mutual fund. Your money is earning several percent in interest, but you want to invest it more profitably. Never forget two things about investing this type of money:

- ✔ **Earning a few percent is better than losing 20 to 50 percent or more.** Just talk to most people who've bought a lousy investment! So be patient — educate yourself *before* you invest.

- ✔ **To earn a higher rate of return, you must be willing to take more risk.** (This is true unless you jump into a higher-yielding money market fund, discussed later in this chapter.) Earning a better rate of return means considering investments that can fluctuate in value — and, of course, the value can drop as much as it can rise.

You approach the vast sea of investment options and start stringing up your rod to go fishing. You hear stories of people catching big ones — cashing in big on stocks or real estate that they bought years ago. Even if you don't have delusions of grandeur, you'd at least like your money to grow faster than the cost of living.

But before you cast your investment line, consider the following frequently overlooked ways to put your money to work and earn higher returns without as much risk. These options may not be as exciting as hunting the big fish out there, but they should easily improve your financial health.

Pay off high-interest debt

Many folks have credit card or other consumer debt that costs more than 10 percent per year in interest. Paying off this debt with savings is like putting your money in an investment with a guaranteed return equal to the rate you are paying on the debt.

For example, if you have credit card debt outstanding at 14 percent interest, paying off that loan is the same as putting your money to work in an investment with a sure 14 percent annual return. Remember that the interest on consumer debt is not tax-deductible, so you actually need to earn *more* than 14 percent investing your money elsewhere in order to net 14 percent after paying taxes. Refer to Chapter 5 for more details if you're still not convinced.

Paying off some or all of your mortgage may make sense, too. This financial move isn't as clear because the interest rate is lower than on consumer debt. (See Chapter 15 for more details on this decision.)

Contribute to retirement plans

When you have a chunk of money, make sure that you take advantage of the terrific tax benefits offered by a portfolio or other retirement savings plan. (RRSPs are discussed in Chapter 11.) If you work for a company that offers to match your contributions to a retirement savings plan, try to fund your plan at the highest level you can manage.

If you need to save money outside retirement plans for short-term purposes (for example, to buy a car or a home), then by all means save money outside retirement plans. But remember that investing money outside retirement plans does not provide you with tax deductions and requires greater thought and consideration because your investments can produce taxable distributions.

Taxes on Your Investments

When you invest money outside of an RRSP, *distributions* — such as interest, dividends, and capital gains — are all exposed to taxation. Too many folks (and too many of their financial advisers) ignore the tax impact of their investment strategies. You need to pay attention to the tax implications of your investment decisions *before* you invest your money.

Consider a moderate-income person in the combined 42 percent tax bracket (federal plus provincial taxes) who keeps extra cash in a taxable bank savings or money market account paying 4 percent interest. If she pays 42 percent of her interest earnings in taxes, she ends up keeping just 2.3 percent. If she wasn't using that money as an emergency fund, she might consider putting it into a dividend-producing investment, such as a dividend mutual fund. The effective tax rate on dividend income for someone in the 42 percent tax bracket is about 25 percent — 17 percent less than the rate at which straight interest is taxed.

In the sections that follow, we give specific advice about investing your money while keeping an eye on taxes.

Savings/Emergency Reserve Investments

In Chapter 3, we explain the importance of keeping sufficient money in an emergency reserve account. From such an account, you need two things:

- **Accessibility.** When you need to get your hands on the money for an emergency, you want to be able to do so quickly and without penalty.

- **Highest possible return.** You want to get the highest rate of return possible without risking your principal.

Bank, trust company, and credit union accounts

When you have a few thousand dollars or less, your best and easiest path is to keep these excess savings in a local bank or credit union. Look first to the institution where you keep your chequing account.

Keeping this stash of money in your chequing account, rather than in a separate savings account, makes financial sense if the extra money helps you avoid monthly service charges because your balance occasionally dips below the minimum. Compare the service charges on your chequing account with the interest earnings from a savings account.

For example, suppose that you're keeping $2,000 in a savings account to earn 4 percent interest, versus earning no interest on your chequing account money. Over the course of a year, you earn $80 interest on that savings account. If you incur a $9 per month service charge on your chequing account, that's $108 per year. So, keeping your extra $2,000 in a chequing account may be better if that keeps you above a minimum balance and erases that monthly service charge. (However, if you're more likely to spend the extra money if it's in your chequing account, keeping it in a separate savings account where you won't be tempted to spend it might be better.)

Money market mutual funds

Money market funds, a type of mutual fund (see Chapter 10), are just like bank savings accounts — but better, in most cases. The best money market funds pay higher yields than bank savings accounts and offer you cheque-writing privileges.

The yield on a money market is an important consideration. The operating expenses deducted before payment of dividends is the single biggest determinant of yield. All other things being equal (which they usually are with different money market funds), lower operating expenses translate into higher yields for you.

Another factor that may be important in your choice of a money market fund is what other types of fund investing you can do at the fund company where you establish a money market fund. Doing most or all of your fund shopping, money-market and otherwise, at one good fund company can reduce the clutter in your investing life; chasing after a slightly higher yield offered by another company is sometimes not worth the extra paperwork and administrative hassle. On the other hand, there's no reason why you can't invest in funds at multiple firms (as long as you don't mind the extra paperwork), using each for its relative strengths.

Most mutual fund companies don't have many local branch offices, so you'll probably open and maintain your money market mutual fund through the fund's toll-free phone line and the mail. Distance has its advantages. Because you can conduct business by mail, Internet, and phone, you don't need to go schlepping into a local branch office to make deposits and withdrawals.

Don't fret about a deposit being lost in the mail. It rarely happens, and no one can legally cash a cheque made payable to you anyway. Just be sure to endorse the cheque with the notation "for deposit only" under your signature.

(For that matter, driving or walking to your local bank isn't 100 percent safe. Imagine all the things that could happen to you or your money en route to the bank. You could slip on a banana peel, drop your deposit down a sewer grate, or get mugged, kidnapped, or run over by a bakery truck.)

If you buy money market funds from your trust company or bank, moving money in and out of the fund is as simple as making a deposit or withdrawal from your chequing account. However, if you sell units in a money market fund, you typically will have to wait until the next business day before the money is available to you.

Never, ever pay a commission to buy or sell a money market fund. Be sure to ask if there are any "loads," as some are actually sold with a deferred sales charge (DSC), meaning you'll get hit with a commission when you move your money out of the fund.

In Table 13-1, we recommend some quality money market mutual funds.

Table 13-1	Recommended Money Market Funds	
Fund	**Operating Expense (MER)**	**Minimum to Open Account**
Altamira Short Term Canadian	0.61%	$5,000
Bissett Money Market	0.53%	$10,000
Dynamic Money Market	0.80%	$1,000
Elliott & Page Money Market	0.38%	$500
Industrial Cash Management	0.54%	$500
Mawer Canadian Money Market	0.81%	$5,000
McLean Budden Money	0.60%	$10,000
NN Life Money Market	0.75%	$2,500
Perigree T-Plus Canadian	0.48%	$2,500
Phillips, Hager & North	0.48%	$25,000

Minimum required investment

As part of the information you'll find with a fund, there is usually a mention of a minimum required investment. It's important to understand what this means. Some better fund families have higher minimum requirements than average, but you may find that you are still able to invest in these funds.

The minimum required investment is sometimes lower than the quoted figure if you are investing inside a registered account such as an RRSP or RRIF. Also, if you agree to invest regularly with a fund company — for instance, setting up a pre-authorized chequing plan that automatically moves a set amount of money out of your bank account and into the fund every two weeks or month — you may be able to invest in many plans by starting off with as little as $50 or even $25 payments.

It's important to also realize the minimum requirement is generally per person. In other words, it's the total amount of money required to start investing with that particular fund company. You may be able to split it up among a handful of their funds. You may also be able to spread it around between different types of accounts with that company. Once you have invested that required minimum, your subsequent required minimum investment with the company or in a particular fund is almost always much lower.

Canadian treasury bill (T-bill) money market funds are appropriate if you prefer a fund that invests solely in government-issued debt, which has the safety of government backing. Note that some of these funds are permitted to invest in other money market securities. Call the specific fund to ensure it is 100 percent in T-bills before you invest, if the additional security is important for you.

Table 13-2 lists a few T-bill money market funds that we recommend.

Table 13-2	Recommended T-Bill Money Market Funds	
Fund	*Operating Expense (MER)*	*Minimum to Open Account*
Altamira T-Bill	0.40%	$5,000
Dynamic Infinity T-Bill	1.00%	$1,000
Royal Canadian T-Bill	1.00%	$1,000
Scotia T-Bill	1.00%	$2,000
TD Canadian T-Bill	0.92%	$2,000 ($100 inside RRSP)
Templeton Treasury Bill	0.75%	$2,500

High-interest savings accounts

Another good choice for your savings or emergency funds is a high-interest savings account. This relatively new type of account is a good and often superior alternative to money market funds.

In many cases, high-interest savings accounts offer similar returns to what you would earn in a money market account. In addition, you can often set them up in conjunction with a chequing account. You can also arrange to have your paycheque deposited directly.

Unlike money market funds, there is no minimum deposit required — you also don't have to worry about getting dinged with commissions, charges, or fees for withdrawing your money within a certain time frame of making a deposit. Another big plus is that, unlike a money market fund, you can get at your money at any time of day, as long as your money has been in the account the required number of days. Most of these accounts allow you to access your cash simply by using a bank card at an ABM.

There are two reasons why high-interest accounts can pay such a high rate of return. The first is that they don't have to support a chain of bricks-and-mortar outlets like the large banks do. Much of your communication and transactions with the company that holds your high-interest-rate account will be by mail, phone, and over the Internet. Second, the companies that offer high-interest accounts use them as a way to win over new customers, and then sell you on other products that they may offer. These can include GICs, chequing accounts, and even mortgages. However, you are under no obligation to buy any other products if they don't suit your needs and aren't competitive with your other options.

Dealing with a company that doesn't have any actual branches in your neighbourhood or town may be somewhat unnerving. However, your money is generally just as safe as if it were in a traditional savings account. Just be sure to check that, like the two companies mentioned below, the institution is a member of the CDIC, an insurance program that protects your savings up to $60,000. We recommend a few high-interest savings accounts below.

ING Direct

ING Direct is part of the Amsterdam-based ING Group. In 2000, ING's Investment Savings Account was paying around 5 percent — just about what one-year GICs were offering, and far beyond what you would have earned in a regular savings account.

There is no minimum balance required, and there are no fees. The only restriction you'll face is that you have to wait five days after making a deposit before you can withdraw those funds. Interest is earned daily on your balances, and compounded monthly. You also get a bank card with your account. While it can be used to withdraw money at any ABM, there is a transaction fee each time you use the card. However, ING is quickly installing its own machines in Canadian Tire stores, and you can use those machines at no charge.

President's Choice Financial

Loblaw Companies Limited took its well-known President's Choice brand of food products, hooked up with Canadian Imperial Bank of Commerce, and developed the President's Choice Financial line of financial products, which now includes banking accounts, mortgages, and GICs.

Like ING, President's Choice started off with banking accounts, but has taken a slightly different approach. The President's Choice Financial Interest First savings account is a stripped-down affair that doesn't include a bank card or ABM access to your funds. Instead, access is provided through an accompanying chequing account that comes with a bank card. You use the chequing account to deposit and withdraw funds, and move money from the chequing account into the savings account to earn the best return. To move money from one account to another, you simply give your instructions to the company over the phone, by mail, or using the Internet.

The savings account interest rate is usually comparable to ING's — in late 2000, for instance, it was 5 percent. The chequing account has tiered interest rates. If your balance is only a few hundred dollars, you'll make next to nothing. However, the rates rise along with your balance. If you have more than $10,000 in your chequing account, for instance, there's no need to use the savings account at all because the chequing account will generally pay essentially the same rate.

You can use the bank card without getting nicked for fees at any CIBC bank machine. You can also use the card at any other ABM, but you'll have to pay the Interac transaction fee. A President's Choice Financial chequing account can also be used to pay bills, which you can arrange to have done automatically.

Investing Money for the Longer Term

Important note: This section (together with its recommended investments) assumes that you have a sufficient emergency reserve stashed away and are already taking advantage of tax-deductible RRSP contributions. Refer to Chapter 3 for more on these goals.

Which investments you should consider depends on your comfort level with risk. But your choice of investments should also be suited to how much time you have until you plan to use the money. We're not talking about investments that you won't be able to sell on short notice if need be (most of them you can). Investing money in a more volatile investment is riskier if you need to liquidate it in the short term.

For example, suppose that you're saving money for a down payment on a house and are about one year away from having enough to make your foray into the real estate market. If you had put this "home" money into the stock market near the beginning of one of the stock market's 20- to 50-percent corrections, a year later you'd have been a mighty unhappy camper. You could have seen a substantial portion of your money vanish in short order and your home dreams put on hold.

Most of the following recommended investments are different types of no-load (commission-free) mutual funds. Mutual funds can be sold on any business day, usually with a simple phone call. Funds come with all different levels of risk, so you can choose funds that match your time frame and desire to take risk. (Chapter 10 discusses all the basics of mutual funds.)

The different investment options in the remainder of this chapter are organized by time frame. All the recommended investment funds that follow assume that you have at least a several-year time frame. The following are summaries of the different time frames:

- **Short-term investments.** These investments are suitable for a period of a few years — perhaps you're saving money toward a home or some other major purchase in the near future. When investing for the short term, look for liquidity and stability — features that rule out real estate on one hand and stocks on the other. Recommended investments include shorter-term bond funds, which are higher-yielding alternatives to money market funds. If interest rates increase, these funds drop slightly in value — a couple of percent or so (unless rates rise tremendously). We also discuss guaranteed investment certificates later in this chapter.

- **Intermediate-term investments.** These investments are appropriate for more than a few but less than ten years. Investments that fit the bill are intermediate-term bonds and well-diversified hybrid funds (which include some stocks as well as bonds).

- **Long-term investments.** If you have a decade or more, then you can consider potentially higher-return (and therefore riskier) investments. Stocks, real estate, and other growth-oriented investments can earn the most money if you're comfortable with the risk involved.

Asset allocation

Asset allocation is the process of figuring out what portion of your wealth you should invest in different types of investments. You frequently (and most appropriately) practise asset allocation with retirement plans. Ideally, more of your saving and investing should be conducted through tax-sheltered retirement plans. That's generally the best way to lower your long-term tax burden (see Chapter 11 for details).

If you have sufficient assets that you plan to invest outside retirement plans, for that portion of your investments that you intend to hold for the long term (ten or more years) see the asset allocation section in Chapter 8.

Bond funds

Bond funds pay taxable distributions (mostly interest) that generally are taxed at your full marginal tax rate. Just like interest earned from a savings account, you have to pay tax on any interest generated by bond funds each year, whether the interest is distributed to you or reinvested in your fund. As a result, you're far better off holding bond funds inside your RRSP where the interest isn't taxed and the full amount of your earnings can be reinvested.

Table 13-3 lists some bond funds we recommend.

Table 13-3	Bond Funds		
Fund	**Investments**	**Operating Expenses (MER)**	**Minimum to Open Account**
Short- to Mid-term			
Altamira Short-Term Government Bond	Government, mortgage-backed securities	1.48%	$1,000
CIBC Canadian Short-Term Bond Index	Government	0.90%	$500
Fidelity Canadian Short-Term Bond	Government, corporate, mortgage-backed securities	1.34%	$500
Phillips, Hager & North Short-Term Bond and Mortgage	Government and mortgage-backed securities	0.68%	$25,000

Fund	Investments	Operating Expenses (MER)	Minimum to Open Account
Scotia Canadian Short-Term Income	Government, corporate	1.32%	$500
Scudder Canadian Short Term Bond	Mostly government, some corporate	0.85%	$1,000/$500 inside RRSP
Talvest Income	Government, mortgage-backed securities, some corporate	1.69%	$500
TD Short-Term Monthly Income	Mostly corporate	1.02%	$2,000/$100 inside RRSP
Trimark Government Income	Government, mortgage-backed securities	1.31	$500
Longer Term			
Altamira Bond	Mostly government	1.47%	$1,000
Beutel Goodman Income	Government, corporate	0.72%	$2,500
McLean Budden Fixed Income	Mostly government	0.70%	$10,000
Phillips, Hager & North Bond	Government, corporate	0.58%	$25,000
Sceptre Bond	Government, corporate	0.95%	$5,000
TD Canadian Bond	Government, corporate	1.01%	$2,000/$100 inside RRSP
Trimark Canadian Bond	Government, corporate	1.30%	$500

Guaranteed investment certificates (GICs)

For many decades, *guaranteed investment certificates* (GICs) have been the investment of choice for folks with some extra cash that is not needed in the near term. The attraction is that you get a higher rate of return on a GIC than on a bank savings account. And unlike bond funds, your principal does not fluctuate in value.

Inflation-indexed bonds

Like a handful of other nations, the government of Canada now offers *inflation-indexed* government bonds. Because a portion of these bonds' return is pegged to the rate of inflation, they offer investors a safer type of bond investment option.

To understand the relative advantages of an inflation-indexed bond, take a brief look at the relationship between inflation and a normal bond. When an investor purchases a normal bond, he is committing himself to a fixed yield over a set period of time — for example, a bond that matures in ten years and pays 7 percent interest. However, changes in the cost of living (inflation) are not fixed and are difficult to predict.

Suppose an investor had put $10,000 into a regular bond in the 1970s. During the life of his bond, he would have unhappily watched escalating inflation. During the time he held the bond and by the time his bond matured, he would have witnessed the erosion of the purchasing power of his $700 of annual interest and $10,000 of returned principal.

Enter the inflation-indexed bond. Say you have $10,000 to invest and you buy a ten-year, inflation-indexed bond that pays you a *real rate of return* (this is the return above and beyond the rate of inflation) of, say, 3 percent. This portion of your return is paid out in interest. The other portion of your return is from the inflation adjustment to the principal you invested. The inflation portion of the return gets put back into principal. So if inflation were running at about 3 percent, as it has in recent years, your $10,000 of principal would be indexed upwards after one year to $10,300. In the second year of holding this bond, the 3 percent real return of interest would be paid on the increased ($10,300) principal base.

If inflation skyrocketed and was running at, say, 10 percent rather than 3 percent per year, your principal balance would grow 10 percent per year, and you'd still get your 3 percent real rate of return on top of that. Thus, an inflation-indexed bond investor would not see the purchasing power of his invested principal or annual interest earnings eroded by unexpected inflation.

Inflation-indexed bonds can be a good investment for conservative, inflation-worried bond investors, as well as taxpayers who want to hold the government accountable for increases in inflation. The downside: Inflation-indexed bonds can yield slightly lower returns, since they are less risky compared to regular bonds.

Compared to bonds, however, GICs have a couple of drawbacks.

✔ First, in a GIC your money is not usually accessible unless you cough up a fairly big penalty — typically six months' interest. With a no-load (commission-free) bond fund, if you need some or all of your money next week, month, or year, you can access it without penalty.

✔ A second and less-often-noted drawback is that a good deal of your earnings on them usually end up in Revenue Canada's hands. The interest earned on a GIC is taxed at your full marginal tax rate, the same rate as your salary (unless you hold the GIC in your RRSP).

In the long run, you should earn more and have better access to your money in bond funds than in GICs. If you're in the lowest tax bracket (24–25 percent), and you have a bad day whenever your bond fund takes a dip in value, then consider GICs. Just make sure that you shop around to get the best interest rate.

Dividend funds

Dividend funds, which come with terrific tax savings built in, are often a good choice if you want regular income from an investment outside your RRSP. These funds invest primarily in the preferred shares of Canadian companies, as well as in common shares that usually pay regular dividends.

 The income you receive from the fund will benefit from the dividend tax credit, which means that you pay a lower tax rate on dividend income than on regular interest income.

 The only drawback to dividend income funds is that they have a higher risk than other fixed-income funds that invest in bonds or mortgages. Also, some funds broaden their investments to include common stocks that have lower yields in the hope of using capital gains to boost their performance. The main purpose of an income fund, though, is strong after-tax returns, so be sure to find a fund that almost exclusively invests in preferred shares or common stocks with regular, strong dividends. Table 13-4 lists recommended dividend funds.

Table 13-4	Recommended Dividend Funds		
Company	*Fund*	*Operating Expense (MER)*	*Minimum to Open Account*
AGF	Canadian Dividend	1.80%	$1,000/$100 inside RRSP
Altamira	Dividend	1.80%	$1,000
Bissett	Dividend Income	1.44%	$10,000
BMO	Dividend	1.78%	$500
Phillips, Hager & North	Dividend Income	1.14%	$5,000
Royal	Dividend	1.88%	$1,000
Scotia	Canadian Dividend	1.14%	$500

Don't buy GICs for the CDIC insurance

Much is made, particularly by bankers, of the CDIC insurance that comes with bank and trust company GICs. The lack of this insurance on high-quality dividend income mutual funds shouldn't be a big concern for you, though. Dividend income funds invest almost exclusively in safe preferred shares and blue-chip common stocks. The companies behind these shares only infrequently suspend dividends; even if a fund held a stock that did stop paying a dividend, that stock would probably be only a small fraction of the value of the fund, so it would have little impact.

Besides, the CDIC itself is no Rock of Gibraltar. Banks have failed and will continue to fail. Yes, you are insured if you have $60,000 or less in a bank or trust company, but if the institution crashes, you may have to wait a long time and settle for less interest than you thought you were getting. You are not immune from harm, CDIC or no CDIC.

If the insurance promised by CDIC backing allows you to sleep better, you can invest in treasury bills, which are government-backed bonds.

Stock funds

Listed in Table 13-5 are stock funds, which are appropriate if you don't want current income. Note that all the funds in Table 13-5 are intended as long-term investments. That's because funds that avoid bonds and dividend-producing stocks focus on growth stocks.

Note that *all* the funds in Table 13-5 are intended as long-term investments.

Table 13-5	Recommended Stock Funds		
Company	*Fund*	*Operating Expense (MER)*	*Minimum to Open Account*
Small- to Medium-Cap Canadian Funds			
Bissett	Small Cap	2.00%	$10,000
BMO	Special Equity	2.36%	$500
CIBC	Canadian Small Companies	2.40%	$500
Fidelity	Canadian Growth Company	2.55%	$500
Scotia	Canadian Small Cap	2.37%	$500
Talvest	Millenium Next Generation	2.50%	$500

Company	Fund	Operating Expense (MER)	Minimum to Open Account
Large-Cap Canadian Funds			
AGF	Canadian Growth Equity	2.82%	$1,000/$100 inside RRSP
AIC	Diversified Canada	2.26%	$250
AIM	Trimark Canadian	1.64%	$500
Bissett	Canadian Equity	1.28%	$10,000
Acuity	Clean Environment Equity	2.51%	$500
Mackenzie	Ivy Canadian	2.46%	$500
Phillips, Hager & North	Canadian Equity	1.15%	$25,000
Royal	Canadian Equity	2.08%	$1,000
Spectrum	Canadian Equity	2.38%	$500
U.S. Funds			
AIM	American Blue Chip Growth	3.05%	$500
TD	U.S. Index	0.66%	$2,000/$100 inside RRSP
TD	U.S. Index –e (Only available on-line)	0.11%	$1,000/$100 inside RRSP
C.I.	BPI American Equity	2.49%	$500
Phillips, Hager & North	U.S. Equity	1.13%	$10,000
Royal	U.S. Equity	2.22%	$1,000
Scudder Maxxum	Janus American Equity	2.90%	$500
Spectrum	American Equity	2.38%	$500
International/Global Funds			
AGF	International Value	2.66%	$1,000/$100 inside RRSP
AIC	World Equity	2.37%	$250

(continued)

Table 13-5 *(continued)*

Company	Fund	Operating Expense (MER)	Minimum to Open Account
AIM	Trimark	1.63%	$500
C.I.	Global	2.40%	$500
CIBC	International Small Co.	2.50%	$500
Fidelity	International Portfolio	2.51%	$500
Mawer	World Investment	1.65%	$5,000
Templeton	Growth	2.00%	$500

Real estate

Real estate can be a financially and psychologically rewarding investment. It can also be a money pit and a real headache if you buy the wrong property or get a tenant from hell. (We discuss real estate as an investment in Chapter 9 and explain the nuts and bolts of buying real estate in Chapter 15.)

Small-business investments

Investing in your own business or someone else's established small business can be a high-risk but potentially high-return investment. The best options are those you understand well. Refer to Chapter 9 for more information about small-business investments.

Chapter 14

Investing for Educational Expenses

In This Chapter

▶ The right and wrong ways to save for university and college

▶ Calculating how much to save

▶ How to pay for university or college when the time comes

▶ How the financial aid system works

▶ Good and bad investments for educational costs

*I*f you're like most parents or potential future parents, just turning to this chapter makes you anxious. Such trepidation is understandable. Much of what you read about educational expenses, particularly university and college expenses, says that if costs keep rising at the current rate you'll have to spend several tens of thousands of dollars to give your youngster a quality education.

Quality education for your child need not, and probably won't, cost you as much as those gargantuan projections suggest. Whether you've already started saving or are about to begin a regular education investment plan, your emotions may lead you astray. The hype about educational costs may scare you into taking a path that is less financially beneficial than others that are available.

Neglecting RRSPs: A Big Mistake

You want what's best for your children. As a parent, that's a given. Not only do you want to be able to provide good learning opportunities for them when they are young, but you also want to give them choices. When little Homer and Gwendolyn fill out their university applications, you don't want to have to say that you can't afford to send them to their dream school.

We know that you're going to think that our advice sounds selfish. But you have to provide for your own financial security before saving for your child. Let us explain.

If you're a frequent flyer, think back to your most recent trip by airplane. Remember what the flight attendants instructed you to do in an emergency? In the event of a loss of air pressure that necessitates the use of oxygen masks, put your own oxygen mask on *first*. Only then should you help your children with their oxygen masks.

Consider for a moment why airlines recommend this approach. Although your instinct may be to ensure that your children are safe before taking care of yourself, by taking care of yourself first, you're stronger and better able to help your children.

Similarly, in regard to your personal finances, you need to take care of yourself first. You should save and invest through an RRSP or other retirement savings plans that give you significant tax benefits.

Take care of your long-term financial needs first (for example, by saving through an RRSP). By doing so, you strengthen your financial health, which better enables you in the long run to help your kids with their educational expenses. (See Chapters 7 and 11 to learn how to reduce your taxes and save for retirement.)

How Will You Pay Educational Expenses?

If you concentrate today on contributing to your RRSP or company pension plan and paying down your mortgage, you'll have a number of options when your kids graduate from high school. If you've paid down some — or all — of your mortgage, you can borrow against the paid-up value of your home (your *home equity*), usually at or near the lowest interest rate available (the *prime rate*).

You'll also already have some strong momentum and compounding going on if you've been building up your retirement savings. You've also established a savings habit. When your kids get close to university age, you can divert your RRSP or other retirement plan contributions to help pay their education costs. When they graduate, you can easily resume your RRSP contributions.

You can even take advantage of the allowable RRSP contributions you missed out on because you're allowed to carry forward unused contributions indefinitely. (Revenue Canada tracks this for you. You'll find a summary on the income tax return assessment notice you receive every year.) This will leave you in much better financial shape than if you had forgone contributions to your RRSP or company retirement savings plan when you were younger in order to start an educational savings program.

Further, when your kids are ready to go to university you'll likely be in your peak earning years, so some extra funds will probably be available.

What will university or college cost?

University and college can cost a lot. The total costs vary substantially from school to school. The average annual cost (including tuition, fees, books, supplies, room, board, and transportation) is running around $9,000 per year. Higher-level professional degrees cost even more. Ouch!

Is all this expense worth it? Although many critics of higher education claim that the cost of a post-secondary education should not be rising faster than inflation and that costs can, and should, be contained, denying the value of going to university or college is hard. Investing in education is usually worth the effort and the cost.

The definition of an investment is an outlay of money for an expected profit. Unlike a car that depreciates in value each year that you drive it, an investment in education yields monetary, social, and intellectual profit. A car is more tangible in the short term, but an investment in education (even if it means borrowing money) gives you more bang for the buck in the long run.

Universities and colleges are now finding themselves subject to the same types of competition that for-profit companies confront. As a result, schools are having to clamp down on rising costs. As with any other product or service purchase, it pays to shop around. You can find good values — schools that offer competitive pricing *and* provide a quality education.

Setting realistic savings goals

If you have money left over *after* taking advantage of retirement plans, by all means try to save for your children.

Be realistic about what you can afford for university expenses given your other financial goals, especially saving for retirement (refer to Chapter 8). Being able to pay the full cost of a post-secondary education or anything approaching the full cost is a luxury of the affluent. If you aren't a high-income earner, consider trying to save enough to pay a third or at most half of the cost. You can easily make up the balance through loans, your child's employment before and during university, and the like.

Fill out Table 14-1 to help you get a handle on how much you should be saving.

Note: Don't worry about correcting for inflation. This worksheet takes care of that through the assumptions made on the returns of your investments as well as the amount that you save over time. This way of doing the calculations works because you assume that the money you're saving will grow at the rate of education inflation.

If your child has expensive taste in schools, you may want to tack on 20 to 30 percent to the following average figures:

- ✔ Average cost of a four-year university education today: $35,000 to $40,000.

- ✔ Average cost of a four-year private U.S. college education today: $90,000 U.S.

Table 14-1	How Much to Save for University
Figure Out This	*Write It Here*
1. Cost of school you think your child will attend.	$_____
2. Percent of costs you'd like to pay (for example, 20% or 40%)	× _____%
3. Line 1 times line 2 is amount you'll pay (in today's dollars).	= $_____
4. Number of months until your child reaches university age.	÷ $_____ months
5. *Amount to save per month (today's dollars). Line 3 answer divided by line 4 answer.	= $_____/month

The amount you need to save (calculated in line 5) needs to be increased once per year by the increase in university inflation — 5 or 6 percent should do.

How to Save for Educational Expenses

If you have sufficient funds to take care of your other needs, such as contributing to an RRSP, terrific! You can also start for your children's post-secondary education. But just as important as the investments you choose is the way in which you organize your savings efforts.

You can set up an effective savings plan for post-secondary education expenses two basic ways. The first option is a Registered Education Savings Plan (RESP). RESPs have recently become much more attractive, thanks to increased contribution limits and a government plan to subsidize your contributions.

The second is to use an *in-trust account.* Under this arrangement, you put money into a special account and invest it on your child's behalf. Which approach is best depends on your financial situation as well as your assessment of just how likely it is that your children will attend university or college.

RESPs

Until recently, Registered Education Savings Plans were, at best, a reasonable way to save for your child's education. However, if your child didn't end up going to university or college you had to forfeit every penny of earnings on the money you had put away. But recent changes to the RESP rules have turned them into an attractive and profitable way to build up an education fund.

You can put up to $4,000 for each child into an RESP each year, up to a total lifetime maximum of $42,000 per child. You're allowed to contribute money for up to 21 years, but the plan must be closed down within 25 years of being set up. Money that you contribute to an RESP isn't tax deductible, but any gains inside the plan aren't taxed. When your child is ready to go to school, money from the plan can be taken out tax-free and used for a variety of education-related expenses.

Before the regulations were updated, the biggest drawback to RESPs was that if your child didn't go to a post-secondary institution, you forfeited the earnings. They either had to go to another child, to an educational institution, or, in the case of pooled or "scholarship" RESPs, to other children in the program.

New rules, though, now allow you to transfer up to $50,000 of earnings from an RESP to your RRSP or a spousal RRSP, as long as you have the contribution room available. Any earnings that can't be transferred in this way can still be moved out of the RESP, but they're taxed at your marginal tax rate plus an additional 20 percent penalty. You can take out your original contributions — your principal — without any penalties or restrictions.

The big kicker that has made RESPs truly worthwhile, though, is the new RESP grant, called the *Canada Education Savings Grant,* or CESG. The government will contribute to your RESP an additional 20 percent of any contribution you make for a child, up to a maximum grant of $400 per year. The grant is available in every year the child is 17 or under on December 31. If you don't contribute enough in any year to get the full $400 grant, you can earn the unused portion in later years. The total lifetime maximum you can receive under this program is $7,200.

How scholarship RESPs work — and often don't pay!

Scholarship RESPs are offered by a number of organizations, including the Canadian Scholarship Trust, University Scholarship Trust, and Children's Education Trust of Canada.

The traditional offerings were *pooled funds*. Your contributions were pooled with those of other considerate parents and grandparents and invested in safe but low-earning investments, such as T-bills, Canada Savings Bonds, and mortgages. These types of RESPs have three major strikes against them.

First, because they invest in guaranteed investments, their rate of return is much lower than your money could earn in a broadly based conservative international equity mutual fund. To ride out the ups and downs of the equity markets, you should generally be able to leave your money invested for seven to ten years. If you start an RESP savings program when your child is born, you have more than enough time — two to three times, in fact — to be able to benefit from the long-term higher returns offered by stocks (unless, of course, you have a little genius on your hands who will toddle off to university before he's old enough to babysit).

The second drawback is highlighted by the word *scholarship,* which these plans usually feature in big, bright letters in their marketing materials. Don't let this fool you. A true scholarship is something your child earns on his or her own by earning high grades, by excelling at a particular subject, or by developing an interest or expertise in a particular area. The only justification for calling the payout from these plans a scholarship is that some children in the plans receive more than the combined value of their families' contributions and the earnings on that money. The reason is that with traditional "pooled" plans if your child doesn't go to a qualifying educational institution you forfeit all the earnings on your money. You get back only your original contributions. The interest is distributed among the other children in the plan who do go on to university or college.

Finally, these pooled plans typically have lots of costs and fees that can really add up. Those can include a sales charge, often disguised by the cute name "enrolment fee," as well as deposit charges, trustee and administration fees, and so on.

Now that the RESP rules have changed to allow you to get back the earnings on your contributions (either by transferring them to your RRSP or by paying a hefty tax), the scholarship-type fund providers have come up with a new offering. In addition to their traditional "pooled" funds, most offer individual accounts, where your contributions earn interest for your child alone. If your child doesn't use the money to go to school, then you can claim the earnings. Although this makes them somewhat more attractive, you still have to deal with the many administrative charges, and your contributions are still typically invested in guaranteed investments, limiting the growth of your savings.

There are two basic types of RESPs. The first are so-called "scholarship" plans. Because these plans are limited to investing in mostly guaranteed investments, the rate of return on your plan is mediocre. Read the sidebar "How scholarship RESPs work — And often don't pay!" to see how you can end up actually losing all the gains earned on your contributions.

A much better choice is self-directed or mutual fund RESPs. You can open these with most brokerage and mutual fund firms, often at no charge. A self-directed or mutual fund RESP allows you to choose from a wide range of investments. If you start an RESP when your children are still in diapers, these plans are a much better choice because they allow you to benefit from the larger earnings potential of equities and equity mutual funds.

In-trust accounts

Also known as informal trusts, *in-trust accounts* allow you to save money for your child's future and have a portion of your earnings compound tax-free. These accounts also go by the name *ITF* (which stands for "in trust for") *account.* The account is "in trust" because minors can't enter into financial contracts. There are no restrictions on contributions to an in-trust account. You can put in as much or as little you wish at any time.

Once money is inside an informal trust, it belongs to the child. All profits on investments inside the trust are taxed. The person who contributes the money pays taxes on the dividends and income, but the child is responsible for paying taxes on any capital gains. Because most children have insufficient income to actually have to pay any tax, that portion of the account can compound tax-free. Because of this, the best investments for an in-trust account, especially if there are many years left before the child will need the money, are equity mutual funds where most of the profits are in the form of capital gains.

If you set up an in-trust account and contribute only Child Tax Benefit payments, the above tax rules don't apply. All the gains, whether they're in the form of capital gains, interest, or dividends, are taxed to the child.

The big drawback to informal trusts is that when the child turns 18, the money and all the profits legally become hers to spend as she wishes. There are no rules about what the money must be spent on, so your child could use it for purposes other than an education, such as starting his or her own small business. Although you can hope that little Johnny or Jenny will spend the money wisely, there's nothing you can do if, on the day of his 18th birthday, Johnny empties his account and buys a convertible.

Using your RRSP for education expenses

Under the federal government's Lifelong Learning Plan, you can tap your RRSP to help finance a post-secondary education or full-time training for either yourself or your spouse. You can withdraw up to $10,000 a year from your RRSP for four years. The maximum amount you can withdraw over that time is capped at $20,000.

Much like the RRSP Home Buyer's Plan (which we discuss in Chapter 15), there are several drawbacks to using your RRSP to fund an education. While the withdrawals are not taxed, you have to repay the money to your RRSP in equal instalments over ten years. The first payment has to be made within 60 days after the end of the fifth year after your first withdrawal.

Any repayments not made are included in the taxable income of the person who made the withdrawal. In addition, you will likely find it difficult to repay what you've taken out for education expenses as well as continue your regular contributions. In that case, you will have to be able to get by on less if you have been factoring your tax rebate from a regular RRSP contribution into your cash flow, since your repayments don't earn you a deduction. Further, borrowing money from your plan, as well as delaying new contributions while you repay those funds, will significantly reduce the long-term growth of your retirement savings.

Certain steps are involved in setting up an in-trust account. You must clearly lay out when you open the account the role of everybody involved. The person who puts money into the account is known as the "settlor" or contributor. The law requires that a different person have the responsibility of overseeing how the money is invested (the trustee) on behalf of the child (the beneficiary). When you set up an account, ensure that you use the proper phrasing: your name (if you are the trustee) followed by "in trust for" and then your child's name.

Loans, Grants, and Scholarships

Now you may be wondering how you'll come up with the money to pay for educational expenses even if you stash money into retirement plans *and* manage to put some away into an RESP. We don't have just one correct solution, because how you'll help pay for your child's university or college costs depends on your own unique situation. However, in many cases even if you have some available cash that can be directed to pay the school bills as they come in you will probably have to borrow some money.

Government student loans program

Run by the federal government, the *Canada Student Loan Program* (*CSLP*) provides loans to university and college students through the banking system. The provinces administer the loans through their own separate student aid offices. Each province also has its own loan scheme that's rolled in with the CSLP.

Students generally make only one combined application to receive loans from both programs, although interest and conditions on the federal loan and the provincial loan differ slightly. To qualify, students must be citizens or permanent residents of Canada, attend an institution recognized by the program, and meet the criteria for being either part-time or full-time students. Students must also live in a province that participates in the Canada Student Loans Program (the only two that don't are Quebec and the Northwest Territories — these two regions run their own distinct loans programs to which the federal government contributes).

Regardless of where they're going to go to school, your kids must apply to the province in which they live. Applications can be obtained from any university or college or by calling your provincial student loans program. Find the number in the blue pages of your telephone book. You can also find out more online by searching for the Student Information Guide or Student Loans Program at www.hrdc-drhc.gc.ca.

Part of the assessment of your application involves examining your entire family's income. The assessment is based entirely on cash flow — assets don't come into the picture at all. As a result, it doesn't pay to neglect contributing to your RRSP or company retirement savings plan, or paying down your mortgage.

The loan programs demand that parents assist in paying the education costs of any dependent children. Even if parents absolutely refuse to assist their children, their ability to pay will still be taken into account when the application is assessed. In order not to be classified as a dependant, a child must have graduated from high school at least four years earlier or have been in the workforce for at least 24 months.

If the loan is approved, your children should go to the financial aid office when they enrol at their university or college. They'll be given some loan documents, which they can then take to the bank of their choice. (The loans are administered through the big banks, but they're guaranteed by the provincial and federal governments.) A number of credit unions and *caisses populaires* are also approved student loan providers. The maximum amount available varies depending on which province the student lives in.

The federal and provincial governments pay the interest on the debt until the student either graduates or withdraws. At that point, the federal government stops paying its share of the interest, and the student is responsible for the debt. Some of the provinces, however, will continue to pay the debt costs on their part of the loan for an additional six months.

The interest rate on the two components is calculated differently. The rate on the federal part of the loan is fixed once a year at a percent or so above the best rates offered by financial institutions (the prime rate). The provinces tend to use a floating rate. For example, a province might charge prime plus 1 percent on its loans, with the rate rising and falling along the going prime rate.

Even though the federal government stops paying the interest on its portion of the combined loan at graduation, students aren't required to start repaying the federal or provincial component of their loan until six months after graduation. Generally, this due date falls on November 1. At that time, students must negotiate a schedule with their bank. While students are largely free to choose whatever repayment time frame they like, both the federal and provincial loans must be completely paid off within 114 months (ten years minus six months). After the student signs agreements for the two separate loans, most institutions will consolidate the debts and work out a single payment schedule.

Once upon a time, many students saw these loans as giveaways because the government didn't seem all that interested in collecting from people who walked away from their obligations. Those days are long gone. Both Ottawa and the provinces have become aggressive in tracking down delinquents and getting their money back. The federal government can even take what it's owed out of the tax refunds of those who are behind on their payments. Worse yet, many past-due student loans are now routinely handed over to collection agencies, and the students end up with a nick on their credit rating.

Bankruptcy is also now much less of a reasonable option if a student's post-school debt becomes unbearable. In addition to the negative impact it will have on the student's credit rating, the rules surrounding student bankruptcy have been tightened. In the past, a student loan would not be discharged in a bankruptcy if the student filed for bankruptcy within two years of being in school. However, changes to the bankruptcy rules in 1998 mean that a student would now have to have been out of school for a minimum of ten years before filing for bankruptcy to have their student loans discharged.

Some tips: Loans, grants, and scholarships

A number of grant programs are available through schools and the government as well as through independent sources. Employers, banks, credit unions, and community groups also offer grants and scholarships.

Many scholarships and grants don't require any extra work on your part — simply apply for financial aid through universities and colleges. Other programs need seeking out — check directories and databases at your local library, your child's school counselling department, and college financial aid offices. Also try local organizations, churches, employers, and so on. You have a better chance of getting scholarship money through these avenues.

Post-secondary scholarship search services are generally a waste of money; in some cases, they're scams. Some of these services charge up to $100 just to tell you about scholarships that either you're already being considered for or that you aren't even eligible for.

Your child can work and save money during high school and university. In fact, if your child qualifies for financial aid he or she may be expected to contribute a certain amount to education costs from savings and from employment during the school year or summer breaks. Besides giving your child a stake in his or her own future, this training encourages sound personal financial management down the road.

Students who support a spouse or child or who have a disability can also often obtain nonrepayable grants. Disabled students can get up to $5,000 a year in grants from the Canada Student Loan program, as well as grants from their province, depending on where they live.

The borrowing versus saving debate

More than a few investment firms and financial planners argue that, in the long run, saving for your children's university expenses is far cheaper than borrowing for them. This claim isn't always true. If you have finite funds and contribute to an RRSP instead of saving for your child's education, and then separately borrow the money needed for college costs later, you can come out ahead.

These organizations and planners have a conflict of interest in that they can't sell you investments if you channel your savings into your employer's retirement plan. They have every reason to scare you into action (and into their hands).

Good and Bad Investments for Educational Funds

Financial companies pour millions of dollars into advertising for investment and insurance products that they claim are the best ways to make your money grow for your little gremlins — we mean children. Don't get sucked in by the ads.

What makes for good and bad investments in general applies to investments for educational expenses, too. Stick with basic, proven, lower-cost investments (Chapter 9 explains what generally to look for and beware of). This section focuses on considerations specific to university and college funding.

Good investments: No-load mutual funds

As we discuss in Chapter 10, the professional management and efficiency of the best no-load mutual funds makes them a tough investment to beat. Chapters 12 and 13 provide recommendations for investing money in funds both inside and outside tax-sheltered retirement plans.

The important issue is to gear the investments to the time frame involved until your children need to use the money. The closer your child gets to attending university and using the money saved, the more conservatively the money should be invested.

Bad investments

Life insurance policies that have cash values are some of the most oversold investments to fund university costs. The usual pitch is this: Because you need life insurance to protect your family, why not buy a policy that you can borrow against to pay for university?

The reason you shouldn't is that you're better off contributing to retirement plans. These investments give you an immediate tax deduction that saving through life insurance does not. Because life insurance that comes with a cash value is more expensive, parents are more likely to make a second mistake — not buying enough coverage. If you need and want life insurance, you're better off buying lower-cost term life insurance (see Chapter 17).

Another poor investment for university or college expenses is one that fails to keep you ahead of inflation, such as savings or money market accounts. You need your money to grow to afford educational costs down the road.

Prepaid tuition plans should generally be avoided. A few schools have developed plans to allow you to pay costs at a specific school (calculated for the age of your child). The allure of these plans is that by paying today, you eliminate the worry of not being able to afford rising costs in the future.

This logic doesn't work for several reasons. First, odds are quite high that you don't have the money today to pay in advance. If you have that kind of extra dough around, you're better off using it for other purposes (and you're unlikely to worry about rising costs anyway). You can invest your own money — that's what the school's going to do with it anyway.

Besides, how do you know which university or college your child will want to attend and how long it might take Junior to get through? Coercing your child into the school you've already paid for is a sure ticket to long-term problems in your relationship with your teenager.

Overlooked investments

Too often, we see parents knocking themselves out to make more money so that they can afford a bigger home, costlier cars, and vacations and to send their kids to more expensive (and therefore supposedly better) private high schools, universities, and colleges. Sometimes families want to send younger children to costly elementary schools, too. Families stretch themselves with outrageous mortgages or complicated living arrangements to get into neighbourhoods with top-rated public schools or to send their kids to expensive private elementary schools that they can barely afford.

The best school in the world for your child is you and your home. The reason many people we know, including ourselves, were able to attend some of the top educational institutions in this country is that concerned parents worked hard, not just at their jobs, but at spending time with the kids while they were growing up. Rather than working to make more money (with the best of intentions to buy educational games or trips or to send the kids to better schools), in our humble opinion, some parents could do more for their kids by focusing more time on the child.

We see parents scratching their heads about their child's lack of academic interest and achievement — they blame the school or TV or society at large. These factors may contribute to the problem, but education begins in the home. Schools can't do it alone.

Living within your means not only allows you to save more of your income, but also it can free more of your time to raise and educate your children. Don't underestimate the value of spending more time with your kids and giving them your attention.

Chapter 15

Real Estate

. . . .

In This Chapter

▶ To buy or not to buy

▶ Determining how much to spend and what to buy

▶ Understanding mortgages

▶ Finding a great property

▶ How to work with real estate agents

▶ Putting a deal together

▶ Issues after you buy

. . . .

*B*uying a home or investing in real estate can be a financially and psycho-logically rewarding experience. On the other hand, owning real estate can be a real pain in the butt. Purchasing and maintaining property can be time-consuming, emotionally draining, and financially painful.

Perhaps you are looking to escape your rented apartment and buy your first home. Or maybe you're interested in cornering the local real estate market and making millions in investment property. In either case, you can learn many lessons from real estate buyers who have travelled before you.

Note: Although this chapter focuses primarily on real estate in which you would live — otherwise known by those in the trade as *owner-occupied property* — much of what is in the chapter is relevant to real estate investors. For additional information on buying investment real estate — property that you rent out to others — see Chapter 9.

To Buy or Continue Renting?

You may be tired of moving from rental to rental. Perhaps your landlord doesn't adequately keep up the place, or you have to ask permission to hang a picture on the wall. You may desire the financial security and rewards that seem to come with home ownership. Or maybe you just want a place to call your own.

The advantages of renting

Renting has its advantages. Some financially successful renters who we've seen include people who pay low rent, either because they've made housing sacrifices or they live in a rent-controlled building. If you're consistently able to save 10 percent or more of your earnings, you're probably well on your way to achieving your future financial goals.

As a renter, you can also enjoy your free time not worrying about or being responsible for fixing up the property — that's your landlord's respon-

sibility. You also have more financial and psychological flexibility as a renter. If you want to move, you can generally do so a lot easier as a renter than as a homeowner.

Another problem that you won't have in renting over the long haul is having a lot of your money tied up in your home. Some people enter their retirement years with a substantial portion of their wealth in their homes. As a renter, you have all your money in financial assets that you can probably tap into more easily.

Any one of these reasons is a good enough reason to *want* to buy a home. But you should take stock of your life and your financial health *before* you know whether you can or should buy a home and how much you can really afford to spend. It's time to ask yourself some bigger questions.

What's your timeline?

From a financial standpoint, you really shouldn't buy a place unless you can anticipate being there for at least three years and preferably five or more. Buying and selling a property entails a lot of expenses, including the cost of getting a mortgage (which can include appraisal fees, brokerage fees, and insurance), inspection expenses, moving costs, lawyer's fees, and real estate agents' commissions. To cover these transaction costs plus the additional costs of ownership, a property needs to appreciate about 10 percent.

If you may need or want to move in a couple of years, counting on that kind of appreciation is risky. If you're lucky and happen to buy before a sharp upturn in housing prices, you may get it. If you're not, you will probably lose money on the deal.

Some people are willing to invest in real estate even when they don't expect to live in it for long and would consider turning their home into a rental. Doing so can work well financially in the long haul, but don't underestimate the responsibilities that come with being a landlord. Also, most people need to sell their first home in order to tap all the cash that they have in it to buy the next one.

Can you afford to buy?

Although buying and owning your own home can be a wise financial move in the long run, it is a major purchase that can and probably will send shock waves through the rest of your personal finances. You will probably take out a mortgage — really just a loan secured by the property you're buying — where the payments are spread out or *amortized* over 25 years to finance your purchase. The home you buy will need maintenance over the years. Owning a home is a bit like running a marathon: Just as you have to be in good physical shape to successfully run a marathon, you should be in good financial health when you buy a home. For as long as you own the home, you will be paying for something or other all the time.

Don't let your home control your financial future. We have seen too many people fall in love with a home and make a rash decision without taking a hard look at the financial ramifications. Take stock of your overall financial health, especially where you stand in terms of retirement planning, *before* you buy property or agree to a particular mortgage.

Lenders look primarily at annual income when determining how much a potential home buyer can borrow; they pay no attention to a borrower's overall financial situation. Whether you have no money already tucked away into retirement savings or have several children to clothe, feed, and send to university, you qualify for the same size loan as other people with the same income (assuming equal outstanding debts).

So don't trust the lender when he tells you what you can afford according to some formulas that the bank uses to determine what kind of a credit risk you are. Only you can figure out how much you can afford, because only you know what your other financial goals are and how important they are to you.

Here are some important financial questions no lender will ask you or care about but that you should ask yourself before buying a home:

- ✔ Are you saving enough monthly to reach your retirement goals?

- ✔ How much do you spend (and want to continue spending) on fun things such as travel and entertainment?

- ✔ How willing are you to budget your expenses in order to meet your monthly mortgage payments and other housing expenses?

- ✔ How much of your children's expected university educational expenses do you want to be able to pay for?

The other chapters in this book can help you answer these important questions. Chapter 3 in particular will help you think through saving for important financial goals.

Many new homeowners run into financial trouble because they don't know their spending needs and priorities and don't know how to budget for them. Some of these owners have trouble curtailing their spending despite the large amount of debt they just incurred; in fact, some spend even more because all sorts of furniture and remodelling expenditures can be made for their home. Many people prop up their spending habits with credit. For this reason, a surprisingly large percentage — some studies say about half — who borrow additional money against their home equity use the funds to pay consumer debts.

How much will lenders allow you to borrow?

All mortgage lenders want to know your ability and the likelihood of your repaying the money you borrow. So you have to pass a few tests that calculate the maximum amount the lender is willing to lend you. For a home in which you will reside, lenders total up your monthly housing expenses. They define your housing costs as:

```
Mortgage payment + Property taxes + Insurance
```

Lenders typically loan you up to about 30 to 32 percent of your monthly gross (before taxes) income for the housing expense. This is called the *gross debt-service ratio*. If you're self-employed, it's a little more complicated. Lenders will often want to see your financial statements and your income tax returns from the last several years, and many decide on a case-by-case basis.

Lenders also consider your other debts when deciding how much to lend you. A lot of other debt diminishes the funds available to pay your housing expenses. To your monthly housing expense, lenders add the amount you need to pay down your other consumer debt (auto loans, credit cards, and so on). The monthly total costs of these debt payments plus your housing costs typically cannot exceed 40 percent. This is known as your *total debt-service ratio*.

An old guideline says that you can borrow up to three times (or two and one-half times) your annual income when buying a home. But this is a really rough estimate. The maximum that a mortgage lender loans you depends on interest rates. If rates fall (as they have during much of the past decade), the monthly payment on a mortgage of a given size also drops.

Table 15-1 gives you a ballpark idea of the maximum that you're probably eligible to borrow. Multiply your gross annual income by the number in the second column to determine the maximum size mortgage you can get. For example, if you're getting a mortgage with a rate around 7 percent and your annual income is $50,000, multiply 3.5 × $50,000 to get $175,000, the approximate maximum mortgage allowed. Lower interest rates make buying real estate much more affordable.

Table 15-1 What's the Approximate Maximum You Can Borrow?	
When Mortgage Rates Are	*Multiply Your Gross Annual Income* by This Figure to Determine the Maximum You May Be Able to Borrow*
4%	4.6
5%	4.2
6%	3.8
7%	3.5
8%	3.2
9%	2.9
10%	2.7
11%	2.5

*If you're self-employed, this is your net income (after expenses but before taxes).

What's the cost of owning versus renting?

An important financial consideration for many renters is the cost of owning a home. Some people assume that owning costs more. In fact, owning a place doesn't have to cost a truckload of money. It may even cost less than renting.

On the surface, buying a place seems a lot more expensive than renting. You're probably comparing your monthly rent (anywhere from a couple hundred dollars to more than $1,000, depending on where you live) to the purchase price of a property, which is usually a much larger number — $100,000, $250,000, or more. When you consider a home purchase, you're forced to think about your housing expenses in one huge chunk rather than in small monthly instalments like a rent cheque.

Tallying up the costs of owning a place can be a useful and not-too-complicated exercise. To make fair the comparison between ownership and rental costs, you need to figure what it would cost on a *monthly basis* to buy a place you desire versus what it would cost to rent a *comparable* place. The worksheet in Table 15-2 enables you to do such a comparison. *Note:* In the interest of reducing the number of variables, all this "figuring" assumes a fixed-rate mortgage. (We discuss mortgages later in this chapter.)

Also, we have ignored what economists call the *opportunity cost of owning.* In other words, when you buy, the money that you put into your home can't be invested elsewhere, and the forgone investment return on that money, say some economists, should be considered a cost of owning a home. We choose to ignore this for two reasons. First, and most importantly, we don't agree with this line of thinking. When you buy a home, you *are* investing your money — in real estate — which, as we discuss in Chapter 9, historically has offered solid long-term returns. Second, we have you ignore opportunity cost because it greatly complicates the analysis.

Table 15-2	Monthly Expenses: Renting Versus Owning
Figure Out This	*Write It Here ($ per month)*
1. Monthly mortgage payment (see "Mortgage")	$_____
2. Plus monthly property taxes (see "Property taxes")	+ $_____
3. Equals total monthly mortgage plus property taxes	= $_____
4. Plus insurance ($30 to $150/mo., depending on property value)	+ $_____
5. Plus maintenance (1% of property cost divided by 12 months)	+ $_____
6. Equals total costs of owning (add lines 3, 4, and 5)	= $_____

Now, compare Line 6 in Table 15-2 with the monthly rent on a comparable place to see which comes out (roughly) ahead, owning or renting.

Mortgage

To determine the monthly payment on your mortgage, simply multiply the relevant number ("Multiplier") from Table 15-3 by the size of your mortgage expressed in (divided by) thousands of dollars. For example, if you are taking out a $100,000 mortgage at 8 percent amortized over 25 years, then multiply 100 by 7.63 for a $763 monthly payment.

Table 15-3	Your Monthly Mortgage Payment "Multiplier"	
Interest Rate	*15-Year Amortization*	*25-Year Amortization*
5.0%	7.88	5.82
5.5%	8.14	6.10
6.0%	8.40	6.40
6.5%	8.66	6.70
7.0%	8.93	7.00
7.5%	9.21	7.32

Interest Rate	15-Year Amortization	25-Year Amortization
8.0%	9.49	7.63
8.5%	9.77	7.96
9.0%	10.05	8.27
9.5%	10.34	8.61
10.0%	10.62	8.94
10.5%	10.92	9.29
11.0%	11.21	9.62
11.5%	11.51	9.97
12.0%	11.81	10.32

Property taxes

Ask a real estate person, mortgage lender, or your local assessors' office what your annual property tax bill would be for a house of similar value to the one you are considering buying. Divide this amount by 12 to arrive at your monthly property-tax bill.

Consider the long-term cost of renting

When you crunch the numbers to see what owning rather than renting a comparable place may cost you on a monthly basis, you may discover that owning isn't as expensive as you thought. Or you may find that owning costs somewhat more than renting. This discovery may tempt you to think that, financially speaking, renting is cheaper than owning.

Be careful not to jump to conclusions. Remember that you're looking at the cost of owning versus renting *today*. What about 5, 10, or 30 years from now? As an owner, your biggest monthly expense — the mortgage payment — doesn't rise steadily, it only fluctuates. If interest rates are higher or lower when your mortgage term expires and you renew your loan, your payments will rise — or fall — accordingly. Your property taxes, homeowner's insurance, and maintenance expenses, which are generally far less than your mortgage payment, are the items that increase with the cost of living.

When you rent, however, your entire monthly rent is subject to the vagaries of inflation. The exception to this rule is when you live in a rent-controlled unit, where the annual increase allowed in your rent is capped. Rent control does not eliminate price hikes; it just limits them.

Suppose that you are comparing the costs of owning a home that costs $200,000 to renting that home for $1,200 a month. Table 15-4 compares the cost of owning the home to your rental costs over 25 years. This assumes that you take out a mortgage loan equal to 75 percent of the cost of the property at a fixed rate of 7.5 percent, meaning your mortgage payments would be $1,097 (rounded up to $1,100) and that the rate of inflation of your homeowner's insurance, property taxes, maintenance (which for the ownership example starts off totalling $450 a month), and rent is 4 percent per year.

Table 15-4	Cost of Owning versus Renting over 25 Years	
Year	*Ownership Cost per Month*	*Rental Cost per Month*
1	$1,550	$1,200
5	$1,626	$1,404
10	$1,740	$1,708
20	$2,048	$2,528
25	$2,253	$3,076

As you can see in Table 15-4, it costs a little more in the first few years to own the home than to rent it. In the long run, however, owning becomes less expensive. This is because more of your rental expenses increase with inflation. And don't forget that you're building equity in your property as a homeowner, and that equity will be quite substantial by the time that you have your mortgage paid off.

If you've been paying attention, you may be thinking that if inflation doesn't rise 4 percent per year, renting could end up being cheaper. This is not necessarily so. Suppose there's no inflation. Your rent shouldn't escalate, but home ownership expenses (property taxes, maintenance, and insurance) shouldn't, either. And with no inflation, you can probably refinance your mortgage at a rate lower than 7.5 percent. If you do the math, you'll see that owning should still cost less in the long run with lower inflation, but the advantage compared to renting is less than during periods of higher inflation.

Financing Your Home

Once you've looked at your financial health, figured out your timeline, and compared renting to owning costs, you're partway to owning your own home. Unless you're independently wealthy, now you need to confront acquiring a hunk of debt to buy a home. A mortgage loan from a bank or other source makes up the difference between the cash you intend to put into the purchase and the agreed-upon selling price of a piece of real estate. Without a mortgage, most people can't buy the home they want.

The monthly mortgage payments, which consist of interest and principal to repay your loan balance, are huge expenses. Did you know that you may end up paying more for the *interest* on your mortgage than you will for your humble abode itself?

Assume that your new pad costs $200,000. To buy it, you borrow $150,000 and contribute $50,000 from your savings for the down payment. If you borrow that $150,000 with a 25-year fixed-rate mortgage at 7.5 percent, you end up paying more than almost $180,000 *in interest* over the life of your loan. (Although you'll pay back some of these interest dollars many years from now when the dollar will likely, thanks to inflation, be worth less than it is today, you're still going to spend a truckload of dollars in interest.)

So taking the time to educate yourself about how to get the best possible deal on a mortgage and ancillary fees is a very wise financial move. More importantly, you won't be able to buy your dream home unless you can finance its purchase.

Understanding the different types of mortgages

Like many other financial products, zillions of different mortgages are available to choose from. The differences can be important or trivial, expensive or cost-free. First, the big differences.

There are four main features you'll have to understand when selecting your mortgage. The first is the number of years you choose to spread your home loan out over. Called the *amortization,* this is the period used to calculate your monthly payments. The second is the period or *term* — typically anywhere from six months to five years or more — that your mortgage agreement runs for. The third factor you'll need to consider is whether you want the interest rate on your loan to fluctuate with the general level of interest rates or remain fixed. Finally, you can choose a mortgage that allows you to pay off some or all of your mortgage at any point during your term.

Ideally, you should weigh the pros and cons of each mortgage type and decide what's best for your situation *before* you go out to purchase a piece of real estate or refinance a loan. In the real world, most people ignore this advice. The excitement of purchasing a home tends to cloud one's judgment. Our experience has been that few people look at their entire financial picture before making major real estate decisions. You may end up with a mortgage that could someday seriously overshadow your delight in your little English herb garden out back.

Consider the issues that we discuss in this section before you decide which kind of mortgage is right for you.

Short-term and long-term mortgages

When you take out a consumer loan to buy, for example, a car, you have to decide how long you will take to pay the money back. Say you choose four years. Over that time, you'll have to pay back the full amount you originally borrowed, plus interest. After the four years is up, you'll have paid your lender all the money you borrowed, and all the interest on the borrowed funds.

Mortgages are essentially home loans, but they differ in one significant way. When your mortgage payments are calculated, you can choose the number of years over which you want to stretch out the repayment of the principal, with your interest costs being calculated over that period and included in your regular payments. This is a distinct and separate issue from the *term*. The term is the length of time you want the loan agreement with that particular lender to run. When the term expires, your loan is over. You can choose to sign up for another loan for whatever term you like, either with the same lender or a different financial institution. You can even pay off some or all of your mortgage at that point if you have the money available.

You can choose a term of anywhere from six months or a year to five years. Some lenders also offer seven- and ten-year terms. Generally, the longer the term you choose, the higher your interest rate.

Selecting a long term (four to five years or longer) guarantees your payments for that entire period, often an important consideration for those who are on tightly controlled budgets. But you do pay a premium for this insurance.

A short term, such as a six-month or one-year agreement, means that you have to renew much more frequently, putting you at the mercy of current interest rates. If rates have moved up by the time your term ends and you have to renew, your monthly payments will also be higher. On the other hand, if rates fall you profit from the drop.

Choosing between a short-term and a long-term mortgage

When choosing your term, you are making a trade-off. If you choose a short term, you risk having rates rise between now and your next renewal date. If you go long and rates don't rise, you pay more than you need to.

Going long

This approach is often a good choice if you are in the early years of home ownership. Once you're locked in, you know exactly how much your mortgage will cost for years to come. You don't have to make any new decisions about your home loan for a long time. And your heart won't jump every time interest rates do. But this peace of mind comes at a price.

Five-year rates, for example, typically range anywhere from 1 percent to more than 3 percent higher than six-month rates. You pay a kind of insurance premium to protect yourself against the possibility of higher rates in the future. Ask yourself if the cost is worth it. Often, you'll find that both the financial and security risks of going short are not as great as you think.

Longer terms are worth considering if you're just starting out, or you find your finances stretched to the limit. If an unexpected jump in rates would push your payments beyond what you can comfortably handle, then lock in at a rate you know you can afford for several years.

When shouldn't almost anybody choose a long-term mortgage? When rates are at historical all-time highs. Remember, the reason for going long is to lock in a rate that protects you from renewing at an even higher rate. Otherwise, everyone would select a short term. Sure, it's hard to know if rates have peaked. But by staying short, you can quickly capture the gains when rates fall back down again.

Staying short

You'll have to take your chances at the mortgage rate roulette wheel more often if you choose a short term. If you can handle the uncertainty — both psychologically and financially — you'll be rewarded by rates that are consistently lower than long-term rates. Making decisions more often also allows you to fine-tune your strategy and gives you more opportunity to reduce your principal.

Be warned, however, that interest rates fluctuate. If they jump quickly, they can just as easily fall back to where they started or even lower. The moral of the story is don't base your decisions on short-term movements. Make sure that you have enough of a financial cushion to afford the higher payments that you'll have to make if rates have risen by the time your renewal date rolls around.

Assessing your best choice

Your decision depends on your ability to live with risk. Staying short means more uncertainty, but you're almost certain to have lower mortgage costs unless rates keep marching up without coming back down. Choose long and you may sleep better, but you pay a premium for those worry-free nights.

If you're still unsure about which route to follow, don't worry. It's something that everybody goes through. Next time you're at a party, just start asking people about the choices they've made with their mortgages. You're bound to hear all sorts of tales about thousands of dollars lost or saved.

Open and closed mortgages

When you choose a *closed* mortgage, you're stuck with the terms of the deal until your loan agreement ends, or matures. You can refinance only if your lender lets you, and often that can involve paying stiff penalties. The upside of a closed mortgage is that, because the lender knows it can depend on your regular payments, your rates are lower.

Growing competition, however, has forced lenders to build in ways for you to pay off significant portions of your loan even within a closed mortgage. For example, the right to pay off 10 percent of your initial principal amount on each anniversary of your agreement is common.

In contrast to a closed mortgage, an *open* mortgage allows you to pay off part or all of the loan at any time without penalty. That can be a valuable option if you expect to come into a substantial sum of money or if you know you'll sell your home shortly. By completely paying off an open mortgage, you effectively terminate your contract with the lender. An open loan gives you flexibility to adapt your loan to changes in your financial picture or the economic situation. You have to pay more for this feature, usually 1 to 2 percent.

If falling rates are too tough to resist, but you want something less risky than a variable rate (which we describe in the next section), consider a fixed open mortgage. Your rate is guaranteed, but if rates fall to an even more attractive level you can lock in at that point without any penalty. If you want to play the interest game, this allows you to keep your options open while still protecting you should rates go up instead of down. It's usually not worth paying the premium that lenders charge for open mortgages, though, and you have other options.

Today's numerous prepayment options allow you to pay down significant sums during the life of your mortgage. In addition, more and more homeowners opt for shorter and shorter terms. Simply rolling over six-month terms, for example, is often a very sound strategy. At the end of each term, you're free to pick whatever term you like, from whatever lender you want, if you meet the lender's basic requirements. You also have the option of paying off any amount of your principal that you choose.

Otherwise, however, if you're trying to take advantage of low or falling rates, there is now a much better alternative available, called a six-month convertible. We talk more about convertible mortgages later in this chapter.

Fixed- and variable-rate mortgages

If you choose a *fixed-rate mortgage,* your payments don't change during your mortgage term. You lock in an interest rate that's fixed for the entire length of your term. With a fixed-rate mortgage, there's nothing complicated to track, and there's no uncertainty. If you like getting your daily newspaper delivered at the same time every day, you're gonna like fixed-rate mortgages.

In contrast to a fixed-rate mortgage, a *variable-rate mortgage* (sometimes referred to as an *adjustable mortgage*) carries an interest rate that (no surprise here!) varies. Usually tied to the lender's prime rate, it moves, jumps, rises, falls, and otherwise can't sit still, just like a fidgeting child.

The return for putting up with this volatility is that the rate is usually the lowest available at any point in time. Variable rates generally are set at, or slightly above, the lender's prime rate, and they rise and fall accordingly.

Some lenders offer protection from soaring rates by putting an absolute ceiling on how high your rate can go. You pay a slightly higher rate for a capped variable, usually around 1 percent above that of a regular variable.

If rates are on their way up, you're better off locking in to a fixed-rate mortgage before the rates go any higher. And if rates are going down, you should select a variable rate and go along for the ride. So some people ask, "Shouldn't the likelihood of interest rates going up or down determine whether I take a fixed-rate or variable-rate mortgage?"

Good question. The problem is that there really is no accurate way to predict which way rates are going. Even the pros on Bay Street can't make these predictions with any consistent accuracy, as we discuss in Part III.

But if you feel that rates are likely to fall and you prefer the variable option, you should understand the risks involved. A rise in interest rates can mean that at some point your monthly payment won't even cover the interest cost of your loan. If this happens, the outstanding interest is added to your balance. Once that figure hits about 105 to 110 percent of the original loan amount, you can expect to hear from your lender. You'll either have to make a lump-sum payment against your principal or lock in to a fixed term.

If you decide that a variable-rate mortgage is the way to go, you also have to pass some extra tests. Due to their volatility, variable-rate mortgages often have lower lending limits. Many lenders won't let you borrow more than 70 percent of your property's appraised value. In some cases, you must also select an amortization period of 20 years or less.

Variables are variable in another way: No other type of mortgage differs so much from lender to lender. Every aspect, from the terms available to whether you can pay the loan off early, varies widely depending on the institution. It's important to ask specific questions about any variable mortgage — and make sure that the answers are there on paper — before signing on the dotted line.

There's a relatively unpromoted player on the mortgage scene that can save you from having to decide whether the potential savings from lower rates is worth all this worry. It's called a *convertible mortgage,* and it's one of the best-kept secrets in the mortgage game. A convertible loan offers many of the benefits of a variable-rate mortgage, with very little downside. For more information, see the sidebar on "Convertible mortgages" below.

Understanding other lender fees

In addition to charging you points and the ongoing interest rate, lenders tack on all sorts of other upfront fees in processing your loan. You should know the total of all lender fees so that you can determine how much completing your home purchase will cost you and can compare different mortgages.

Convertible mortgages

Although convertible mortgages vary from lender to lender, the basic principle remains the same. You get six months or a year of security, usually at the same rate as a fixed mortgage for the same term — usually the lowest rate going. At any point during that time, you can "convert" your mortgage to a different term; you can also choose between an open or closed loan.

The benefit of convertibles is that they allow borrowers to avoid paying a premium for longer-term fixed rates. At the same time, you're protected against rapidly rising rates because you can lock in at any time, rather than having to wait until your term expires or paying a hefty penalty. If rates should suddenly rise, you can simply lock in a longer-term rate. Meanwhile, you also save yourself the extra premium for an open mortgage.

If rates are falling, you can lock in the lower rates at any point. It often pays to simply ride out the term and, if rates are still falling at that point, to just sign up for another six-month convertible.

The important point with a convertible loan is to check the fine print for specific conditions. One institution, for example, allows you to convert only to a five-year term. Even if you let the six months elapse, you're automatically signed up. In essence, this is really a 5½ year mortgage, with the possibility of lower rates for a maximum of the first six months.

Most lenders allow you to convert at any time to any term you wish. The only across-the-board restriction is that you can't convert during the term to another six-month convertible. The other drawback to convertibles is that if you want to renew partway through the six months, you can't change lenders. That means losing some bargaining power, which can cost you a quarter or a half percentage point.

Lenders can nickel and dime you with a number of fees other than points. Actually, you pay more than nickels and dimes — $300 here and $50 there adds up in a hurry! Here are the main culprits:

- ✔ **Application and processing fees.** Some lenders charge several hundred dollars to complete your paperwork and process it through their under-writing (loan evaluation) department. The justification for this fee is that if your loan is rejected or you decide not to take it the lender needs to cover the costs. Most lenders return this fee to you upon closing when you go with their loan (after you're approved).

- ✔ **Credit report.** Some lenders charge a modest fee to pay for the cost of obtaining a copy of your credit report. This report tells the lender whether you've been naughty or nice to other lenders in the past. If you have problems on your credit report, clean them up before you apply (see our discussion of this issue later in this chapter).

- ✔ **Appraisal.** The property for which you are borrowing money needs to be valued. If you default on your mortgage, a lender doesn't want to get stuck with a property worth less than you owe. The appraisal cost is typically several hundred dollars for most residential properties.

Get a written itemization of charges from all lenders you are seriously considering so that you have no surprises when you close on your loan and so that you can more readily compare different lenders' mortgages. And to minimize your chances of throwing money away on a loan for which you might not qualify, ask the lender whether you for some reason might not be approved. Be sure to disclose any problems on your credit report or problems with the property that you are aware of.

How to buy with less money down

When you buy a home, ideally you should make a down payment of at least 25 percent of the purchase price of the property. Why? Because you'll generally be able to qualify for the most favourable terms on a mortgage with such a down payment, and you'll also be able to avoid the added cost of mortgage insurance. To protect against their losing money in the event you default on your loan, lenders usually require manager insurance, which on a typical mortgage costs several hundred dollars per year.

Many people don't have the equivalent of 25 percent or more of the purchase price in savings to buy a home without private mortgage insurance. Here are a number of solutions for coming up with that 25 percent faster or buying with less money down and solving the down-payment blues:

- ✔ **Go on a spending diet.** One sure way to come up with a down payment is to raise your savings rate by slashing your spending. Take a tour through Chapter 6 to learn strategies for doing so.

✔ **Consider lower-priced properties.** Some buyers want their first home to be a palace. Smaller properties and ones that need some work can help to keep down the purchase price and, therefore, the required down payment.

✔ **Find partners.** You can usually get more home for your money when you buy a building in partnership with one, two, or a few people. Make sure that you write up a legal contract to specify what will happen if a partner wants out.

✔ **Seek reduced-down-payment financing.** Some property owners or developers may be willing to finance your purchase with as little as 5 to 10 percent down. You can't be as picky about properties because not as many are available under these terms — many need work or haven't yet sold for other reasons.

✔ **Take out a second mortgage.** Take out a traditional mortgage for the first 75 percent and then arrange a second mortgage on the remainder. You'll likely have to arrange this through a mortgage broker for a fee. You'll usually have to pay 2 to 3 percent more than the rate on your first mortgage.

✔ **Obtain a high-ratio mortgage.** If you have a down payment of at least 10 percent of the purchase price, you can obtain a high-ratio mortgage from most lenders. However, you're required to buy special mortgage insurance. If your application is approved, your lender will organize this for you. The insurance is provided by the Canada Mortgage and Housing Corporation (CMHC), which is run by the federal government. The insurance is there to protect your lender — not you — in case you fail to meet your payments.

Your down payment determines your insurance rate, which can run as high as 2.5 percent. You pay the premium only once — when you take out your mortgage. You're required to insure the entire loan, not just the difference between your down payment and the 25 percent required for a conventional loan. On a $100,000 mortgage, that could mean paying up to $2,500 in insurance. If you don't have the money, you can ask your lender to add the insurance premium to your loan. Of course, that means you'll likely end up paying twice or three times that amount back over the life of the mortgage once all the interest costs are added in.

✔ **Use the CMHC first-time home buyers program.** This special program lets you put down as little as 5 percent. The total amount of your loan is restricted to certain levels, depending on where in the country you live. You can select any term you want, just as for a regular mortgage. However, you must meet a debt-service test: Your cash flow has to be sufficient to meet the payments on a three-year term. You also have to buy mortgage insurance, which can be as high as 2.5 percent of your loan.

> ✔ **Get assistance from family.** If your parents, grandparents, or other relatives have money dozing away in a savings or GIC account, they may be willing to lend (or even give) you the down payment. You can pay them a higher rate of interest than they have been earning (but still lower than what you would pay to borrow from a bank) and thus be able to buy a home — a win/win situation.

The RRSP Home Buyers' Plan

You can borrow up to $20,000 from your RRSP to buy a house without paying any extra taxes or penalties under the federal government's Home Buyers' Plan.

For hopeful home buyers, the plan can be useful, but it is by no means perfect. The plan has a number of strict conditions and some potentially big costs, too. It's vital that you understand all the specifics, despite their positively desert-like aridity. Knowing what you're getting into now can save you a lot of financial worries down the road.

One important restriction is that neither you nor your spouse is allowed to make a contribution to your RRSP in the year that you withdraw funds under the plan. The government doesn't want people to put money into their plan, get the tax break, and then draw on the same funds to use as part of a down payment. If you've been making regular contributions to your RRSP, and you've been building the tax refund into your budget, you need to prepare for this loss in cash flow.

Repayment rules

There are strict rules governing how quickly you have to repay the money you've borrowed from your RRSP. You must repay the money into your RRSP within 16 years. The minimum you have to repay each year starting with the second year after you make your withdrawal is the equivalent of $\frac{1}{15}$ of the amount borrowed.

Keep in mind those payments aren't considered RRSP contributions, and you don't get any tax write-offs for them. And if you miss a payment or part of a payment, the government treats that money as if you had withdrawn it directly from your RRSP. The sum is included as part of your income for that year, and you have to pay tax on it. Ouch!

If you're currently finding it tough to put money into your RRSP, it will be twice as hard if you use your retirement funds for a down payment. Before you can even think of making a fresh contribution, you have to replace the required portion of the borrowed funds for that year. If that leaves you unable to make a direct RRSP contribution for that year, you miss out on a big tax break and a large tax refund. You also forgo the tax-free compound growth you could have earned from that new contribution.

Loss of potential growth in your RRSP

By taking money out, you lose all the potential growth from those funds as long as that money isn't in your plan. The younger you are, the higher the cost is to you. Unfortunately, the only way to understand the dangers this option poses for your RRSP is to do battle with a few numbers.

Suppose that you're 30 and that you borrow $18,000 from your plan to buy a home. You have to repay $1,200 a year, or $100 a month, for the next 15 years. The alternative would have been to borrow the money, say, as a second mortgage. If you borrowed the money at 10 percent and spread the loan over 15 years, the monthly payments would be $193.50. So the extra cost of borrowing the money from a bank or trust company instead of your RRSP is $93.50 a month.

But you have to balance that off against the gains possible by leaving that $18,000 in your RRSP. Earning an average of 10 percent a year, in 40 years that money would grow to more than $800,000. By comparison, if it were left in for 35 years, it would be worth just over $500,000.

This is an extreme example, but it amply demonstrates the true cost of borrowing "free" from your RRSP. The actual cost depends on how old you are and how quickly you're able to repay the borrowings. In general, if you're over 40 the price may not be too steep. In addition, if you use the plan to buy a home and it appreciates steadily, the growth on the value of your house will offset some of the forgone growth in your RRSP. You may be able to get the best of both worlds by borrowing from your RRSP and repaying the loan quickly, say in the first three or four years after you have settled into your new home.

In general, you're probably better off borrowing the money, even if that means taking out a second mortgage or a high-ratio mortgage. Just make sure that you can afford the higher interest rate charges or the mortgage insurance premium.

Should you consider faster mortgage payoff?

The appeal of paying off your mortgage sooner is enticing. So if you can afford the higher payments on your mortgage, you'd be silly not to make them, right? Not so fast. You're really asking whether you should pay off your mortgage slowly or more quickly. And the answer isn't simple — it depends.

You need to think through this decision despite the fact that entire books have been written extolling the virtues of owning your home without mortgage debt as soon as possible. Those books come complete with endless rows and columns of numbers so that you can look up how much you save through a faster payback.

If you have the time and inclination (and a good financial calculator), you can calculate how much interest you can save or avoid through a faster payback. We have a friendly word of advice about spending hours crunching numbers: *don't.* You can make this decision by considering some qualitative issues.

Consider alternative uses for savings

First, think about *alternative uses* for the extra money you'd be throwing into the mortgage paydown. What's best for you depends on your overall financial situation and what else you can do with the money. If you would end up blowing the extra money at the racetrack or on an expensive car, pay down the mortgage. That's a no-brainer.

But suppose that you take the extra $100 or $200 per month that you were planning to add to your mortgage payment and contribute it to an RRSP instead. That step may make financial sense. Why? Because contributions to RRSPs (discussed in Chapter 11) are tax-deductible.

When you add an extra $200 to your mortgage payment to pay off your mortgage faster, you get no tax benefits. Zero, *nada,* zippo! When you dump that $200 into an RRSP, you get to subtract that $200 from the income on which you pay taxes. If you're paying 40 percent in federal and provincial income taxes, you shave $80 (that's $200 multiplied by 40 percent) off your tax bill.

In fact, choosing between putting more money into your RRSP or paying down your mortgage involves a lot of serious number-crunching, and the results depend on your mortgage rate, how many years you have left before your mortgage is paid off, as well as the return you'll earn in your RRSP. Because of all these variables — some of which are hard to nail down — a good compromise is to maximize your RRSP contributions and to take the tax refund that the contributions earn you and put it down against your mortgage.

Cut your costs at renewal time

No matter how long your mortgage is amortized for, your actual contract with your lender expires at the end of each term. When you renew, you're really entering into an entirely new agreement. This gives you complete flexibility to change any or all of the terms of your mortgage, from payment levels and the amortization period to the frequency of instalments. You can even change lenders if you wish.

A few months before your renewal date, shop around for guaranteed rate offers from a handful of lenders. Sixty- and sometimes ninety-day guarantees are common. Getting your renewal rate guaranteed in advance protects you from sudden increases in rates before your renewal. You can also use the guarantee to negotiate better rates from your current mortgage company. If it won't match the competition, you're free to transfer your mortgage to another financial institution.

Finding the best lender

As with other financial purchases, you can save a lot of money by shopping around. It doesn't matter whether you do so on your own or hire someone to help you. Just do it!

On a 25-year, $150,000 mortgage, for example, getting a mortgage that costs 0.5 percent less per year saves you about $14,000 in interest over the life of the loan (given current interest rate levels). That's enough to buy a decent car! On second thought, save it!

Doing it yourself

You can find many mortgage lenders in most areas. Although having a large number to choose from is good for competition, it also makes shopping a chore.

Large banks whose names you recognize from their advertising may not offer the best rates. Make sure that you check out some of the smaller lending institutions in your area as well.

Real estate agents can also refer you to lenders with whom they've done business. Those lenders don't necessarily offer the most competitive rates — the agent simply might have done business with them in the past.

Look also in the real estate section of one of the larger Sunday newspapers in your area for charts of selected lender interest rates. These tables are by no means comprehensive or reflective of the best rates available. In fact, many of them are sent to newspapers for free by firms that distribute mortgage information to mortgage brokers. Use them as a starting point by calling the lenders who list the best rates.

Hiring a mortgage broker

Insurance agents peddle insurance, real estate agents sell real estate, and mortgage brokers deal in mortgages. They buy mortgages at wholesale from lenders and then mark them up to retail to you. The difference, or *spread,* is their income. The terms of the loan obtained through a broker are generally the same as you would obtain from the lender directly.

A mortgage broker gets paid a percentage of the loan amount — typically 0.5 to 1 or 2 percent. This commission is negotiable, especially on larger loans that are more lucrative. Ask a mortgage broker what his cut is. Many people don't, so some brokers may act taken aback when you inquire. Remember, it's your money!

The chief advantage of using a mortgage broker is that the broker can shop among various lenders to get you a good deal. If you're too busy or aren't interested in shopping around for a good deal on a mortgage, a competent mortgage broker can probably save you money. A broker can also help you through the tedious process of filling out all those horrible documents lenders demand before giving you a loan. And if you have credit problems or an unusual property, a broker may be able to match you with a hard-to-find lender willing to offer you a mortgage.

In evaluating a mortgage broker, be on guard for those who are lazy and don't continually shop the market looking for the best mortgage lenders. Some brokers place their business with the same lenders all the time, and those lenders don't necessarily offer the best rates. Also watch out for those who are salespeople who earn big commissions pushing certain loan programs that are not in your best interests. They aren't interested in taking the time to understand your needs and discuss your options. Check a broker's references.

Even if you plan to shop on your own, talking to a mortgage broker may be worthwhile. At the very least, you can compare what you find with what brokers say they can get for you. Just be careful. Some brokers tell you what you want to hear and then aren't able to deliver when the time comes.

When a loan broker quotes you a really good deal, make sure to ask who the lender is. (Most brokers refuse to reveal this information until you pay the few hundred dollars to cover the appraisal and credit report.) You can check with the actual lender to verify the interest rate the broker quotes you and make sure that you're eligible for the loan.

Increasing your approval chances

A lender can take several weeks to complete your property appraisal and evaluation of your loan package. When you're under contract to buy a property, having your loan denied after waiting several weeks could mean that you lose the property as well as the money you spent applying for the loan and having the property inspected. Some property sellers may be willing to give you an extension, but others won't.

Here's how to increase your chances of having your mortgage approved:

✔ **Get your finances in shape before you shop.** You're not going to have a good handle on what you can afford to spend on a home until you whip your personal finances into shape. Do so before you begin to make offers on properties. This chapter and book can help you. If you have consumer debt, get rid of it — the more credit card, auto loan, and other consumer debt you rack up, the less mortgage you qualify for. In addition to the high interest rate on consumer debt and the fact that it encourages you to live beyond your means, you now have a third reason to get rid of it. Hang on to the dream of a home and plug away at paying off consumer debts.

✔ **Clear up credit report problems.** Late payments, missed payments, or debts that you never bothered to pay can come back to haunt you. If you think there are problems on your credit report, get a copy before you apply for your mortgage. The major credit bureaus are Equifax (800-465-7166), and Trans Union (905-575-4420).

Mistakes crop up on credit reports. The only way to fix them, unfortunately, is to get on the phone with the credit bureaus and start squawking. When specific creditors have reported erroneous information, call them, too. If the customer service representatives you talk with are no help, dash off a nice letter to the president of each company. For bona fide problems documented on your credit report, try explaining them to your lender. Should the lender be unsympathetic, try calling other lenders. Tell them your credit problems upfront and see whether you can find one willing to give you a loan. Mortgage brokers (discussed earlier) can also help you shop for lenders in these cases.

✔ **Get preapproved or prequalified.** *Prequalified* means that you've spoken with a lender about your financial situation and they've calculated the maximum they will lend you based upon what you've told them. *Preapproval* is more in-depth and includes a lender's actual review of your financial statements. Although neither is binding upon a lender to actually make you a mortgage loan, preapproval means more, especially in qualifying you financially in the eyes of a seller. Just be sure not to waste your time and money getting preapproved if you're not really ready to get serious about buying.

✔ **Be upfront about problems.** The best defence against loan rejection is to avoid it in the first place. You can sometimes head off potential rejection by disclosing to your lender anything that may cause a problem before you apply for the loan. That way, you have more time to correct problems and find alternative solutions.

✔ **Work around low/unstable income.** When you're self-employed or have been changing jobs, your recent economic history may be as unstable as a communist country trying out capitalism. One way around this problem is to make a larger down payment. If you put down 30 to 35 percent or more, you may be able to get a no-income-verification loan. You may try getting a co-signer, such as a parent, another relative, or even a rich friend. As long as they aren't borrowed up to their eyeballs, they can help you qualify for a larger loan than you can get on your own. Be sure that all parties understand the terms of the agreement, including who is responsible for monthly payments!

Finding the Right Property and Location

Shopping for a home can be fun. You get to peek inside other people's refrigerators and drawers. But for most people, finding the right house at the right price can take a lot of time. It can also entail a lot of compromise when you're buying with partners or a spouse (or children, if you choose to share the decision-making with them).

A good agent (or several in different areas) can help with the legwork. Here are the main things to consider.

Condo, townhouse, co-op, or detached home?

Some people's image of a home is a single-family dwelling — a stand-alone house with a lawn and white picket fence. In some areas, however, particularly in higher-cost neighbourhoods, non-single-family housing is more common. *Condominiums* (you own the unit and a share of everything else), *townhouses* (attached or row houses), and *co-operatives* (you own a share of the entire building) are higher-density housing units.

The allure of non-single-family housing is that it is generally less expensive. In some cases, as an owner, you don't have to worry about some of the general maintenance because the owner's association (which you pay for, directly or indirectly) takes care of it.

If you don't have the time, energy, or desire to keep up a property, shared housing can make sense. Shared housing may also provide you with better security than a stand-alone home, and you generally get more living space for your dollar.

As investments, however, single-family homes generally do better in the long run. Shared housing is easier to build and hence easier to overbuild; on the other hand, single-family houses are harder to put up because more land is required. But most people, when they can afford it, still prefer a stand-alone home.

That said, you should remember that a rising tide raises all boats. In a good real estate market, all types of housing appreciate, although single-family homes tend to do better. Shared-housing values tend to increase best in densely populated urban areas with little available land for new building.

If you can afford a smaller single-family home instead of a larger shared-housing unit, buy the single-family home. Be especially wary of buying shared housing in suburban areas with lots of developable land.

Cast a broad net

Before you start your search, you may have an idea about the type of property and location that you are interested in or think you can afford. You may think, for example, that you can afford only a condominium in the neighbourhood you want. But if you take the time to check out other communities, you may be surprised to find one that meets most of your needs and has affordable single-family homes. You'd never know that, though, if you narrowed your search too quickly.

Even if you've lived in an area for a while and think that you know it well, look at different types of properties in a number of different areas before you start to narrow your search. Be open-minded and be sure to know which of your many criteria for a home you *really* care about. You may have to be flexible on some of your preferences.

Find out actual sale prices

Don't look at just a few homes listed at a particular price and get depressed because they're all dogs or you can't afford what you really want. Before you decide to renew your apartment lease, remember that properties often sell for less than the price at which they are listed.

Find out what the places you look at end up selling for. Doing so gives you a better sense of what you can really afford as well as what places are really worth. Ask the agent or owner who sold the property what the sales price was or contact the town's assessors' office about how to obtain property sales price information.

Research the neighbourhood and area

Even (and especially) if you fall in love with a house at first sight, go back to the neighbourhood at different times of day and on different days of the week. Travel to and from your prospective new home during commute hours to see how long your commute will really be. Knock on a few doors and meet your potential neighbours. You may discover, for example, that a flock of chickens lives in the backyard next door or that the street and basement flood every other winter.

What are the schools like? Go visit them. Don't rely on statistics about test scores. Talk to parents and teachers — what's really going on at the school? Even if you don't have kids, the quality of the local school has direct bearing on the value of your property. Is crime a problem? Call the local police department. Will future development be allowed? If so, what type? Talk to the planning department. What will your property taxes be? Is the property located in an area susceptible to major risks, such as floods, mud slides, fires, or earthquakes? Consider these issues even if they are not important to you, because they can affect the resale value of your property.

Once you buy a home, you're stuck with it. Make sure that you know what you're getting yourself into *before* you buy.

Working with Real Estate Agents

When you buy (or sell) a home, you'll probably work with a real estate agent. Real estate agents, like many people who call themselves "financial consultants," earn their living on commission. As such, their incentives are different from yours and can be at odds with what's best for you.

Unlike commission-based financial consultants, who are really salespeople with loftier-sounding titles, real estate agents do not hide the fact that they get a cut of the deal. Property buyers and sellers usually understand the real estate commission system. We credit the real estate profession for calling its practitioners "agents" and not coming up with some silly title such as "housing consultants."

A top-notch real estate agent can be of significant help in your purchase or sale of property. On the other hand, a mediocre, incompetent, or greedy agent can be a real liability. Real estate agents don't have as bad a reputation as used-car salespeople, but it's not great, either. The following quotations capture some fundamental problems among real estate agents:

> ". . . *Commissions are overpriced, quality of service bears no relation to commission levels, agents face serious conflicts of interest, most buyers are inadequately represented by agents, and agents dominate most state regulatory bodies. The residential real estate industry functions as a cartel that overcharges home buyers and sellers over $10 billion a year.*"
>
> — Consumer Federation of America
> (a non-profit consumer advocacy group)

> "*For the most part agents look out for themselves. The problem . . . is the commission. The only way you're going to get someone to really look out for your interests is to pay him an hourly fee. If he gets a commission, his overwhelming motivation is to see that the deal closes with a minimum of effort on his part.*"
>
> — John T. Reed, Residential Property Acquisition Handbook

Real estate agents' top conflicts of interest

Real estate agents, because they work on commission, face numerous conflicts of interest. Some agents may not even recognize the conflicts in what they're doing. This section discusses what to watch out for in recognizing agents' most common conflicts of interest.

Buy now, sell now

"You must buy now! Prices and interest rates are low, but they could rise any day."

"The market could worsen before it gets better — you'd better sell now."

Because agents work on commission, it costs them when they spend time with you and you don't buy or sell. They want you to complete a deal, and they want that deal as soon as possible — otherwise, they don't get paid.

Don't expect an agent to give you objective advice about what you should do given your overall financial situation. Examine your overall financial situation *before* you decide to begin working with an agent.

Spend more (and take an adjustable mortgage)

Because real estate agents get a percentage of the sales price of a property, they have a built-in incentive to encourage you to spend more. Adjustable-rate mortgages (discussed earlier in this chapter) allow you to spend more because the interest rate starts at a lower level than that of a fixed-rate mortgage. Thus real estate agents are far more likely to encourage you to take an adjustable. But adjustables are a lot riskier — you must understand these drawbacks before signing up for one.

Buy my company's listings

Agents often receive a higher commission selling listings belonging to other agents in their office. Beware.

Especially problematic are cases in which the same agent represents both the property seller and the property buyer in the transaction. Agents holding open houses for sale may try to sell to an unrepresented buyer whom they meet at the open house. There's no way one person can represent the best interests of both sides.

I don't waste my time working with small fries like you

Because agents work on commission and get paid a percentage of the sales price of the property, many are not interested in working with you if you can't or simply don't want to spend a lot. Some agents may reluctantly take you on

Buyer's brokers

Increasing numbers of agents are marketing themselves as *buyer's brokers*. Supposedly, they represent your interests as a property buyer exclusively.

Legally speaking, buyer's brokers may sign a contract saying that they represent your — and only your — interests. Before this enlightened era, all agents contractually worked for the property seller.

The title *buyer's broker* is one of those things that sounds better than it really is. Agents representing you as buyer's brokers still get paid only when you buy. And they still get paid on commission as a percentage of the purchase price. So they still have an incentive to sell you a piece of real estate, and the more expensive it is, the more commission they make.

as a customer but then give you little attention and time. Before you hire an agent, check references to make sure that he has worked well with buyers like you.

Buy in my area

Real estate agents typically work a specific territory. As a result, they usually can't objectively tell you the pros and cons of the surrounding region. Most won't admit that you may better meet your needs by looking in another town (or some other part of town) where they don't normally work. Before you settle on an agent (or an area), spend time on your own learning the pros and cons of different territories. If you do want to look seriously in more than one area, find an agent in each who specializes in that area.

Get your loan from my favourite lender

If you don't get approved for a mortgage loan, your entire real estate deal will unravel. So it's a good thing that real estate agents want you to get approval for a loan. But it may cause them to refer you to a more expensive lender who has the virtue of high approval rates. Be sure to shop around — you can probably get a loan and get it more cheaply.

Also, beware of agents who may refer you to mortgage lenders and mortgage brokers who pay agents referral fees. Such payments clearly bias a real estate agent's "advice."

Use this inspector — He's easy

Home inspectors are supposed to be objective third parties who are hired by prospective buyers to evaluate the condition of a property. The inspector's job is to uncover problems that your novice eye can't see. We've heard of tougher (nitpicky) inspectors referred to as "deal killers" by disgruntled real estate agents. Some inspectors get more referrals from agents because they aren't tough. But you'll be the one who's sorry if your newly acquired home has undiscovered problems due to an inadequate inspection.

I'm helping the seller cover up problems

Some agents, under pressure to get a house listing for sale, agree to be accomplices and not disclose known defects or problems with the property. In most cases, it seems, the seller may not explicitly ask an agent to help cover up a problem, but the agent may look the other way or not tell the whole truth. Never buy a home without having a home inspector look it over from top to bottom.

They scratch my back and I scratch theirs

Some agents refer you to lenders and inspectors that have referred business to them. A referral, of course, should first and foremost be based on the competence of the person to whom you're being referred. Too often in referrals, this criterion is minor or, in some cases, nonexistent. Some agents also solicit and receive referral fees (or bribes) from mortgage lenders, inspectors, and contractors to whom they refer business.

Qualities to look for in real estate agents

Whether you're hiring an agent to work with you as a buyer or seller, you want someone who is competent and with whom you can get along. Working with an agent costs you a lot of money — make sure that you get your money's worth.

Interview several agents. Check references. Ask agents for the names and phone numbers of at least three clients with whom they've worked in the past six months in the geographical area in which you are looking. You should look for these traits in any agent you work with:

✔ **Full-time employment.** Some agents work in real estate as a second or even third job. Information in this field changes constantly. The best agents work at it full time to stay on top of the market.

✔ **Experience.** Hiring someone with experience doesn't necessarily mean looking for an agent who's been kicking around for decades. Many of the best agents come into the field from other occupations, such as business or teaching. Some sales, marketing, negotiation, and communication skills can certainly be learned in other fields, but experience in this field does count.

- **Honesty and integrity.** You're trusting your agent with a lot. If the agent doesn't level with you about what a neighbourhood or particular property is really like, you suffer the consequences.

- **Interpersonal skills.** An agent has to be able to get along not only with you but also with a whole host of other people involved in a typical real estate deal: other agents, property sellers, inspectors, mortgage lenders, and so on. An agent doesn't have to be Mr. or Ms. Congeniality, but he or she should be able to put your interests first without upsetting others.

- **Negotiation skills.** Putting a real estate deal together involves negotiation. Is your agent going to exhaust all avenues to get you the best deal possible? Be sure to ask the agent's references how well the agent negotiated for them.

- **High-quality standards.** Sloppy work can lead to big legal or logistical problems down the road. If an agent neglects to recommend an inspection, for example, you may be stuck with undiscovered problems after the deal is done.

Agents sometimes market themselves as *top producers,* which means that they sell a relatively larger volume of real estate. This title doesn't count for much for you, the buyer. It may be a red flag for an agent that focuses on completing as many deals as possible. When you're buying a home, you need an agent who has the following additional traits:

- **Patience.** When you're buying a home, the last thing you need or want is an agent who tries to push you into making a deal. You need an agent who is patient and willing to allow you the necessary time to get educated and make the best decision for yourself.

- **Local market and community knowledge.** When you're looking to buy a home in an area in which you're not currently living, an informed agent can have a big impact on your decision.

- **Financing knowledge.** As a buyer, especially a first-time buyer or someone with credit problems, you should look for an agent who can refer you to lenders who can handle your type of situation, which can save you a lot of legwork.

Buying and selling real estate require somewhat different skills. Few agents can do both equally well. No law or rule says that you must use the same agent when you sell a property as when you buy. Don't feel obliged to sell through the agent who worked with you as a buyer just because he sends you holiday cards every year asking how the garden is growing. Remember, he works on commission.

Putting Your Deal Together

Once you've done your homework on your personal finances, understood how to choose a mortgage, and researched neighbourhoods and home prices, you'll hopefully soon close in on your goal. Eventually you'll find a home you'd like to buy. Before you make that first offer, though, you need to understand the importance of negotiations, inspections, and other elements of a real estate deal.

Negotiating 101

When you work with an agent, the agent usually handles the negotiation process. But you need to have a plan and strategy in mind — otherwise, you might overpay for your home. Here are some recommendations for getting a good deal:

- **Never fall in love with a property.** If you have money to burn and you can't imagine life without the home you've just discovered, then pay what you will. Otherwise, always remind yourself that other good properties are out there. Having an actual backup property in mind never hurts.

- **Learn about the property and owner before you make your offer.** How long has the property been on the market? What are its flaws? Why is the owner selling? For example, if the seller is moving because she got a job in another town where she's about to close on a home purchase, she may be eager to get her money out and may be willing to reduce the price. The more you understand about the property that you want to buy and the seller's motivations the better able you will be to draft an offer that meets both parties' needs.

Games real estate agents play to get a deal done

The thirst for a commission brings out the worst in some agents. They'll tell you fibs to motivate you to buy on the seller's terms. One common one is to say that other offers are coming in on the property you're interested in. Or they'll say that the seller already turned down an offer for *x* dollars because he is holding out for a higher offer.

Another tactic is the car dealer trick — blaming the office manager for not allowing them to reduce their commission. The bottom line is that if it's not in writing, be skeptical. Be sure to spend the time needed to find a good agent and to understand an agent's potential conflicts of interest (see the section on agents earlier in the chapter).

✔ **Get comparable sales data to support your price.** Too often, home buyers and their agents pick a number out of the air when making an offer. But if the offer has no substance behind it, the seller will hardly be persuaded to lower his asking price. Pointing to recent and comparable home sales to justify your offer price strengthens your case.

✔ **Remember that price is only one of several negotiable items.** Sometimes sellers get fixated on selling their homes for a certain amount. Perhaps they want to get at least what they paid for it themselves several years ago. You may be able to get a seller to pay for certain repairs or improvements or to offer you an attractive loan without all the extra loan fees that a bank would charge. Likewise, the real estate agent's commission is negotiable, too.

Inspect, inspect, inspect

When you buy a home, you're probably making one of the biggest (if not *the* biggest) purchases of your life. Unless you've built homes and done contracting work yourself, you probably have no idea what you're getting yourself into when it comes to furnaces and termites.

Spend the money and time to hire inspectors and other experts to evaluate the major systems and potential problem areas of the home. Areas that you want to check include

✔ Overall condition of the property

✔ Electrical, heating, and plumbing systems

✔ Foundation

✔ Roof

✔ Pest control and dry rot

✔ Seismic/slide/flood risk

Inspection fees often pay for themselves. When problems are uncovered that you weren't aware of, the inspection reports give you the information you need to go back and ask the property seller to fix the problems or reduce the purchase price of the property to compensate you for correcting the deficiencies yourself.

As with other professionals whose services you retain, interview a few inspection companies. Ask which systems they inspect and how detailed a report they will prepare for you (ask for a sample copy). Ask them for names and phone numbers of three people who used their service within the past six months.

Never accept a seller's inspection report as your only source of information. When a seller hires an inspector, he may hire someone who won't be as diligent and critical of the property. What if the inspector is buddies with the seller or agent selling the property? By all means, review the seller's inspection reports if they are available, but get your own as well.

And here's one more inspection for you to do: The day before you close on the purchase of your home, do a brief walk-through of the property to make sure that everything is still in good order and that all the fixtures, appliances, curtains, and other items that were to be left as per the contract are still there. Sometimes, sellers (and their movers) "forget" what's to be left or try to test your powers of observation.

After You Buy

After you buy a home, over the months and years ahead you'll make a number of important decisions regarding your castle (or shoe box). This section discusses key issues and what you need to know to make the best decision for each.

Refinancing early

Three reasons motivate people to refinance early. One is obvious: to save money because interest rates have dropped. Refinancing can also be a way of raising capital for some other purpose. A final reason is to get out of one type of loan and into another. The following sections should help you decide whether refinancing makes sense for you.

Refinancing options

Lower rates look very appealing when you look at how much more money would stay in your bank account every month by cutting your mortgage payments. That's hard cash you could put toward other purposes or use to pay down your principal.

If you have an open mortgage, of course, you can renew whenever current rates are more attractive. Find a new term you're comfortable with and sit back and count your savings. Better yet, keep your payments at the previous level and use the drop in rates to take years off your mortgage. And remember: When you refinance, you terminate your deal with your current lender. You're free to shop around your mortgage to other lenders. Or you could get a few offers to use as leverage to get your current lender to chop a quarter or even half a percent off its published rates.

Most mortgages, however, are closed. And although your lender may be willing to allow you to refinance early, it will want to be compensated for some — or all — of its losses. After all, if you want to refinance to reduce your rate from 11 percent to 8 percent, the banks aren't exactly going to leap at the chance to make 3 percent less on your loan, now are they?

The first step is to get your mortgage agreement out and read the fine print. Growing competition means that some lenders have made it easier for you to get out of your current loan. But this is a marketing edge they don't particularly want to tout unless they have to. After all, if you don't read your agreement and simply assume that you're stuck paying higher rates than you may need to, you don't really expect banks and trust companies to bring that to your attention — do you?

The three months' interest penalty

Your mortgage agreement may allow you to refinance your loan by paying the equivalent of three months' interest on your outstanding balance. This refinancing rule applies to all CMHC-insured loans. In addition to high-ratio mortgages, loans financed by mortgage-backed securities must be insured with CMHC; it can be worth your while to check with your lender to see if this rule applies to you. Further, by law any mortgage with a term longer than five years also becomes open on the fifth anniversary, with the same three-month penalty applying.

Although they don't widely promote the fact, several of the big banks now also allow you to refinance under the same terms at any point after the third anniversary of your present agreement. But remember, it's unlikely that your lenders will alert you to the money you could be saving.

Whether the three-month penalty is worth paying is different in every case. It depends on the difference between your existing rate and what current rates are as well as on how much remains in your principal. Your best bet is to ask your lender to work the numbers out for you. The lender may not be that happy about doing so, but you should get the answers you need.

The interest-rate differential (IRD) penalty

The most common penalty is something called the *interest-rate differential* (IRD). The IRD is the value today of the income the lender gives up by allowing you to refinance.

Say you're paying 10 percent and have two years left in your term. Your lender calculates how much it can make by taking the balance of your loan and lending it out elsewhere. Then it will ask you to make up the difference so that it can break even on the deal. The problem is that paying the IRD leaves you breaking even as well. The money you save with lower rates will be wiped out by the compensation you'll have to pay.

Another potential problem is that nobody can say with certainty where interest rates are headed. You lose out if rates fall and are lower at the end of your present term. If that happens, you've gone through an awful lot of tedious paperwork only to be locked in at a higher term than you would be paying if you had simply sat tight.

Mortgage life insurance

Shortly after you buy a home or close on a mortgage, you'll start getting mail from all kinds of organizations who keep track of publicly available information about mortgages. Most of these organizations want to sell you something, and they don't tend to beat around the bush.

"What will your dependants do if you meet with an untimely demise and they are left with a gargantuan mortgage?" they ask. Fair enough. In fact, this is a good financial-planning question. If your family is dependent upon your income, can they survive financially if you and your income disappear from life as we know it?

Don't waste your money on mortgage life insurance. You may need life insurance to provide for your family and help meet large obligations such as mortgage payments or educational expenses for children. But mortgage life insurance is grossly overpriced. (Read the life insurance section in Chapter 17 for advice about term life insurance.) You should consider mortgage life insurance only if you have a health problem and the mortgage life insurer does not require a physical examination. Be sure to compare it with term life options.

Is getting a reverse mortgage a good idea?

Increasing numbers of homeowners are finding, particularly in their later years of retirement, that they lack cash. Their largest asset is usually the home in which they live. Unlike other investments, such as bank accounts, bonds, or stocks, a home does not provide any income to the owner unless he or she decides to rent out a room or two.

A *reverse mortgage* allows a homeowner who's low on cash to tap into home equity. For an elderly homeowner, this can be a difficult thing to do psychologically. Most people work hard to feed a mortgage month after month, year after year, until finally it is all paid off. What a feat and what a relief after all those years!

Taking out a reverse mortgage reverses this process. Each month, you get a cheque from the reverse mortgage lender that you can spend on food, clothing, travel, or whatever suits your fancy. The money you receive each month is really a loan from the bank against the value of your home, which makes the monthly cheque free from taxation. Other advantages of a reverse mortgage are that it allows you to stay in your home and use its equity to supplement your monthly income.

The main drawback is that a reverse mortgage can deplete the estate that you may want to pass on to your heirs or use for some other purpose. Also, some loans require repayment within a certain number of years. The fees and the effective interest rate you are charged to borrow the money can be quite high.

Because some loans require the lender to make monthly payments to you as long as you live in the home, lenders assume that you will live long so that they don't lose money in making these loans. If you end up keeping the loan for only a few years because you move, for example, the cost of the loan is extremely high.

You may be able to create a reverse mortgage within your own family network. This technique can work if you have family members who are financially able to provide you with monthly income in exchange for ownership of the home when you pass away.

There are also other alternatives to tapping home equity. One is to simply sell your home and buy a less expensive property or rent a place. Any profit you make when you sell the home you live in is tax-free.

Selling your house

The day will someday come when you will want to sell your house. If you're going to sell, make sure that you can afford to buy the next home you desire. Be especially careful if you're a trade-up buyer — that is, you're going to buy an even more expensive home. All of the affordability issues discussed at the beginning of this chapter apply. Also consider the following issues.

Selling through an agent

Selling and buying a home demand agents with different strengths. When you're selling a property, you want an agent who can get the job done efficiently and for as high a price as possible. As a seller, you should seek agents who have marketing and sales expertise and are willing to put in the time and money necessary to sell your house. Don't necessarily be impressed by an agent who works for a large company. What matters more is what the agent is going to do to market your property.

When you list your house for sale, the contract that you sign with the listing agent includes specification of the commission to be paid if the agent is successful in selling your house. In most areas of the country, agents usually ask for a 6 percent commission. In an area that has lower-cost housing, they may ask for 7 percent.

Regardless of the commission an agent says is "typical," "standard," or "what my manager requires," *always* remember that commissions are negotiable. Because the commission is a percentage, you have a much greater ability to get a lower commission on a higher-priced house. If an agent makes 6 percent selling both a $200,000 house and a $100,000 house, the agent makes twice as much on the $200,000 house. Yet selling the higher-priced house does not take twice as much work. (Selling a $400,000 house certainly doesn't take four times the effort of selling a $100,000 house.)

If you live in an area with higher-priced homes (above $250,000), you have no reason to pay more than a 5 percent commission. For expensive properties ($500,000 and up), a 4 percent commission is reasonable. You may find, however, that your ability to negotiate a lower commission is greatest when an offer is on the table. Because you don't want to give other agents (working with buyers) a reason not to sell your house, have your listing agent cut his take rather than reducing the commission that you advertise that you're willing to pay to an agent who brings you a buyer.

In terms of the length of the listing sales agreement you make with an agent, three months is reasonable. When you give an agent too long a listing (6 to 12 months), the agent may simply toss your listing into the multiple listing book and expend little effort to get your property sold. Practically speaking, you can fire your agent whenever you want, regardless of the length of the listing agreement. But a shorter listing may be more motivating for your agent.

Selling without a real estate agent

The temptation to sell without an agent is usually to save the commission that an agent deducts from your house's sale price. If you have the time, energy, and marketing experience, you can sell your house and possibly save some money.

The major problem with attempting to sell your house on your own is that you can't generally list it in the *multiple listing service* (MLS), which only real estate agents can list properties in. Some people have said, and we concur, that the MLS functions as an effective near monopoly over the selling of houses. And if you're not listed in the MLS, many potential buyers will never know that your house is for sale. Agents working with buyers don't generally look for or show their clients properties that are for sale by owner.

Besides saving you time, a good agent can help ensure that you're not sued for failing to disclose known defects of your property. If you decide to sell your house yourself, make sure that you have access to a legal adviser who can review the contracts.

Should you keep your home until prices go up?

Many homeowners are tempted to hold on to their properties when they need to move if the property is worth less than when they bought it or if the real estate market is soft. It's probably not worth the hassle of renting out your property or the financial gamble of holding on to it. If you need to move, you're better off in most cases selling your house.

You may reason that in a few years the real estate storm clouds will clear and you can sell your property at a much higher price. Here are three risks associated with this way of thinking:

- ✔ You can't know what's going to happen to property prices in the next few years. They might rebound, but they could stay the same or drop even further. A property generally needs to appreciate at least a few percent per year just to make up for all the costs of holding and maintaining it.

- ✔ If you haven't been a landlord, don't underestimate the hassle and headaches associated with this job.

- ✔ Once you convert your home into a rental property, you need to pay tax on your profit when you sell it if it does appreciate. This tax wipes out much of the advantage of having held onto the property until prices recovered. (If you want to be a long-term rental property owner, you may be able to do a *tax-free exchange* into another rental property once you sell.)

A good reason to hold on to a home that has plunged in value is that you would realize little cash from selling *and* lack other money to come up with the down payment to purchase your next property.

Should you keep your home as investment property if you move?

It's worth considering converting your home into rental property if you need or want to move. Don't consider doing so unless it really is a long-term proposition (ten or more years). As discussed in the preceding section, selling rental property has tax consequences.

One advantage to keeping your current home as an investment property after you move is that you already own it. Locating and buying investment property takes time and money. You also know what you have with your current home. If you go out and purchase a property to rent, you're starting from scratch.

If your property is in good condition, consider what damage renters might do — few renters will take care of your home the way that you will. Also consider whether you're cut out to be a landlord. For more information, read the section in Chapter 9 that discusses real estate as an investment.

Part IV
Protecting What You've Got

The 5th Wave — By Rich Tennant

"I'm sorry, Mr. Binkman, but if you look closely, your policy with us is for otter insurance, not auto insurance. By the way, your otter wasn't hurt in the accident, was he?"

In this part . . .

We show you how to obtain the right kind of insurance to shield you from the brunt of unexpected major expenses and protect your assets and future earnings. Just because insurance is boring doesn't mean you can ignore it! We reveal which types of insurance you do and do not need, what to include and what not to include in your policies, and how much of which things you should insure. Plus, you finally face other creepy but important stuff such as wills, probate, and estate planning.

Chapter 16

Insurance Basics

• •

In This Chapter

▶ How the insurance industry works

▶ Our three laws of buying insurance

▶ How to get the insurance coverage you need at the best price

▶ What to do if you are denied coverage

▶ How to get your claim money

• •

*U*nless you work in the industry (by choice), insurance is, for most people, a dreadfully boring topic. Most people associate insurance with disease, death, and disaster and would rather do just about anything other than review or spend money on insurance. But because you don't want to deal with money hassles when you are coping with catastrophes — illness, disability, death, fires, floods, earthquakes — you must take care of insurance well before you need it.

Insurance is probably the least understood and least monitored area of personal finance. Studies by the U.S. non-profit National Insurance Consumer Organization show that more than nine in ten people purchase and carry the wrong types and amounts of insurance coverage. Our own experience speaking with people about the insurance coverage they have or should have confirms this statistic. Most people are overwhelmed by all the jargon in sales and policy statements. As a result, people get insurance from the wrong companies, pay more than is necessary for their policies, or get insured through companies with poor reputations for servicing customers with claims on their policies.

Insurance: A Big, Inefficient Business

Consider these tantalizing tidbits about the insurance industry: Some 340 insurance companies employ more than 200,000 people. In addition to agents employed directly by the insurance companies, there are an additional 40,000 brokers who sell policies.

In *The Invisible Bankers*, an insightful book on the insurance industry, author Andrew Tobias makes the observation that to accomplish their goals, insurance companies in the U.S. need 20 times more employees than the IRS (the U.S. tax department) and 3 times more employees than the U.S. Postal Service!

Unlike mutual funds, which are often available directly from the companies that issue them, virtually all insurance is sold through insurance agents and brokers who work on commission. Because of the commission structure, shopping around for the best deal and figuring out — and buying — policies and features that are in your best interests are difficult tasks. Equally problematic is the fact that insurers exert tremendous control and influence, through lobbying and representation on insurance regulatory boards, over governments — the entities that are supposed to oversee them.

Why all these details about the insurance industry? Because understanding the industry will help you comprehend the weird stuff you see on policies, the high costs of many policies, and the inefficiency of many insurers. And, we hope, you will also become informed enough to make your voice heard when you speak to insurers and government regulators about ways to improve insurance for consumers.

Eric and Tony's Three Laws of Buying Insurance

We know your patience and interest in learning about insurance may be limited, so we've boiled it down to three fairly simple but powerful concepts that can easily save you thousands of dollars over the rest of your insurance-buying years. And while you're saving money, you can still get the coverage you need to avoid a financial catastrophe.

Law 1: Insure for the big, not the small, stuff

Imagine, for a moment, that you're offered a chance to buy insurance that reimburses you for the cost of a magazine subscription in the event the magazine folds and you don't get all the issues you paid for. Because a magazine subscription doesn't cost much, we don't think you would buy that insurance.

What if you could buy insurance that pays for the cost of a restaurant meal if you get food poisoning? Even if you're splurging at a fancy restaurant, you don't have a lot of money at stake, so you'd probably decline that coverage as well.

The point of insurance is to protect against losses that would be financially catastrophic to you, not to smooth out the bumps of everyday life. The examples above are silly, but some people buy equally silly policies without knowing it, as we illustrate in this section.

Avoid small-potato policies

A good insurance policy can seem expensive. A policy that doesn't cost much, on the other hand, can fool you into thinking that you're getting something for next to nothing. Policies that cost little also cover little — they are priced low because they aren't covering large potential losses.

The following are examples of common, small-potato insurance policies that are generally a waste of your hard-earned dollars. As you read through this list, you may find examples of policies that you yourself have bought and that you feel paid for themselves. We can hear you saying, "But I collected on that policy you're telling me not to buy!" Sure, getting the satisfaction (the revenge?) of being "reimbursed" for the hassle of something being lost or going wrong is always nice. But consider all such policies that you have bought or could buy over the course of your life. You're not going to come out ahead in the aggregate — if you did, insurance companies would lose money! These policies aren't worth the cost relative to the small potential benefit. On average, insurance companies pay out just 60 cents in benefits on every dollar collected. Many of the following policies pay you back even less — around 20 cents in benefits (claims) for every insurance-premium dollar spent.

Extended warranty and repair plans

Isn't it ironic that right after the salesperson persuades you to buy a television, computer, or car — in part by saying how reliable the goods are — he tries to convince you to spend more money to insure against the failure of the item? If the stuff is so good, why do you need insurance?

Product manufacturers' warranties typically cover any problems that occur in the first three months to a year. After that, should you need to pay for a repair out of your own pocket, it won't be a financial catastrophe. Extended warranty and repair plans are expensive and unnecessary insurance policies.

Home warranty plans

If your real estate agent or the seller of the home wants to pay the cost of a home warranty plan for you, turning down the offer would be ungracious (as grandma would say, you shouldn't look a gift horse in the mouth). But don't buy this type of plan for yourself. In addition to requiring some sort of fee (around $30 to $50) if you need a contractor to come out and look at a problem, home warranty plans often limit how much they'll pay for problems.

Your money is much better spent on hiring a competent inspector to uncover problems and fix them *before* you buy the home. Everyone buying a house should expect to spend money on repairs and maintenance. Buying insurance that covers you only for smaller repairs and maintenance is a waste of money.

Dental insurance

If your employer pays for dental insurance, take advantage of it. But you shouldn't pay for this coverage on your own. Dental insurance generally covers a couple of teeth cleanings each year and limits payment for more expensive work.

Credit life and credit disability policies

Many direct-mail firms try to sell policies that pay a small benefit in case you die with an outstanding loan (a credit life policy) or that pay a small monthly income in the event of a disability (a credit disability policy). Credit card companies usually sell these policies. Some companies sell insurance to pay off your credit card bill in the event of your death or disability.

The cost of such insurance seems low, but that's because the potential benefits are small. In fact, given what little insurance you're buying, these policies are extraordinarily expensive. When you need life or disability insurance, purchase it. But get enough coverage and buy it in a separate, cost-effective policy (see Chapter 17 for more details).

One exception to the above rule is if you are in poor health and you can buy these insurance policies without a medical evaluation. In that case, these policies may be the only ones you have access to. This is another reason that these policies are expensive. If you're in good health, you are paying for the people with poor health who can enrol without a medical examination and who undoubtedly make more claims.

Daily hospitalization insurance

Hospitalization insurance policies that pay a certain amount per day, such as $100, are often sold to older people. These policies prey on people's fears of running up big hospital bills. Health care beyond that covered by your province's health insurance is expensive — there's no doubt about that.

If you need extra coverage, what you really need is a comprehensive (major medical) health insurance policy. One day in the hospital can lead to several thousand dollars in charges, so that a $100-per-day policy might pay for less than an hour of your 24-hour day! These policies don't offer coverage for the big-ticket expenses. If you don't have a comprehensive extended health insurance policy, read about them in Chapter 17.

Insuring packages in the mail

You buy a $40 gift for a friend, and when you go to the post office to ship it, the friendly postal clerk asks if you want to insure it. For a couple of bucks, you think, why not? Canada Post may have had a bad reputation for many reasons — and that reputation has improved substantially in recent years — but it rarely loses or damages things. Go spend your money on another gift instead!

Contact lens insurance

The things that people in this country come up with to waste money on just astound us. Contact lens insurance really does exist! The money goes to replace your contacts if you lose or tear them. Lenses are cheap. Don't waste your money on this kind of insurance.

Little-stuff riders

Many policies that are worth buying, such as auto and disability insurance, have all sorts of add-on riders. These are extra bells and whistles that insurance agents and companies like to sell because of the high profit margin (for *them*). On auto insurance policies, for example, you can buy a rider for a few bucks per year that pays you each time your car needs to be towed. Having your vehicle towed isn't going to bankrupt you, so it isn't worth insuring against.

Likewise, small insurance policies that are sold as add-ons to bigger insurance policies are usually unnecessary and overpriced. For example, you can buy some disability insurance policies with a small amount of life insurance added on. If you need life insurance, purchasing a sufficient amount in a separate policy is less costly.

Take the highest deductible you can afford

Most insurance policies have *deductibles* — the maximum amount you must pay in the event of a loss before your insurance coverage kicks in. On many policies, such as auto and homeowner's/renter's coverage, most folks opt for a $100 to $250 deductible.

Here are two benefits to taking a higher deductible:

- ✔ **You save premium dollars.** Year in and year out, you can enjoy the lower cost of an insurance policy with a high deductible. You may be able to shave 15 to 20 percent off the cost of your policy. Suppose, for example, that you can reduce the cost of your policy by $150 per year by raising your deductible from $250 to $1,000. That $750 worth of coverage is costing you $150 per year. Thus, you would need to have a claim of $1,000 or more every five years — highly unlikely — to come out ahead. If you are that accident-prone — guess what? — the insurance company will crank up your premiums.

- ✔ **You don't have the hassles of filing small claims.** If you have a $300 loss on a policy with a $100 deductible, you need to file a claim to get your $200 (the amount you're covered for after your deductible). Filing an insurance claim can take hours of time and can be an aggravating experience. In some cases, you may even have your claim denied after jumping through all the necessary hoops.

When you have low deductibles, you may file more claims (although this doesn't necessarily mean that you'll get more money). After filing more claims, you may be rewarded with higher premiums — in addition to the headache of preparing those blasted forms! Filing too many claims may even cause cancellation of your coverage!

Buy insurance to cover financial catastrophes

You should insure against what could be a huge financial loss for you or your dependants. The price of insurance isn't cheap, but it is relatively small in comparison to the potential total loss.

The beauty of insurance is that it spreads risks over many thousands and sometimes millions of other people. Should your home burn to the ground, paying the rebuilding cost out of your own pocket probably would be a financial catastrophe. If you have insurance, the premiums paid in by you and all the other homeowners collectively can easily pay the bills.

Think for a moment about what your most valuable assets are. (No, they're not your dry wit and your charming personality.) Also consider potential large expenses.

- ✔ During your working years, your most valuable asset is probably your future earnings. If you were disabled and unable to work, what would you live on? That's why long-term disability insurance exists. If you have a family that is financially dependent on your earnings, how would your family manage financially if you died? Life insurance can fill the financial void left by your death.

- ✔ If you're a business owner, what would happen if you were sued for $1,000,000 for negligence in some work that you messed up? Liability insurance can bail you out.

- ✔ In this age of soaring medical costs, you can easily rack up significant bills in short order. That's why you may need extended medical health insurance coverage that covers you for expenses your provincial plan doesn't. (See Chapter 17 for more on health insurance.)

Psychologically, buying insurance coverage for the little things that are more likely to occur is tempting. You don't want to feel like you're wasting your insurance dollars. You want to get some of your money back, darn it! You are more likely to get into a fender bender with your car or have a package lost in the mail than you are to lose your home to fire or suffer a long-term disability. But if the fender bender costs $500 (which you end up paying out of your pocket because you took our advice to take a high deductible), it isn't going to be a financial disaster.

On the other hand, should you lose your ability to earn an income because of a disability or are sued for $1,000,000 but are not insured against such catastrophes, you will not only be extremely unhappy but you will also face financial ruin. "Yes, but what are the odds," we hear people rationalize, "that I'll suffer a long-term disability or that I'll be sued for $1,000,000?" We agree that the odds are quite low, but the risk is there. The problem is that you just don't know what bad luck will befall you or when.

And don't make the mistake of thinking that you can figure the odds any better than the insurance companies can. The insurance companies predict the probability of your making a claim, large or small, with a great deal of accuracy. That's why they employ armies of number-crunching actuaries to calculate the odds of bad things happening and the frequency of current policyholders making particular types of claims. The companies price their policies accordingly.

So, buying or not buying insurance based on your perception of the likelihood of needing the coverage is foolish. Insurance companies aren't stupid; in fact, they are ruthlessly smart! When insurance companies price policies, they look at a number of factors to determine the likelihood of your filing a claim. Take the example of auto insurance. If you're a single male, age 20, living the fast life in a large city, driving a macho, turbo-sports car, and having two speeding tickets in the past year, you're gonna pay a whole lot more than a couple in their 40s, living in a rural area, driving a four-door sedan, and having a clean driving record.

Law II: Buy broad coverage

Another major mistake people make when buying insurance is purchasing coverage that is too narrow. Such policies often seem like cheap ways to put their greatest fears to rest. For example, instead of buying life insurance, some folks buy flight insurance at an airport self-service kiosk. They seem to worry more about their mortality when getting on an airplane than they do when getting into a car. If they die on the flight, their beneficiaries collect. But should they die the next day in an auto accident or get some horrible disease — which is statistically far more likely than going down in a jumbo jet — the beneficiaries don't collect anything from flight insurance.

The medical equivalent of flight insurance is cancer insurance. Older people, fearful of having their life savings depleted by a long battle with this dread disease, are easy prey for unscrupulous insurance salespeople pitching this narrow insurance. If you get cancer, cancer insurance pays the bills. But what if you get heart disease, diabetes, AIDS, or some other disease? Cancer insurance won't pay these costs.

Our misperceptions of risks

How high do you think your risks of expiring prematurely are if you're exposed to toxic wastes or pesticides or if you live in a dangerous area that has a high murder rate? Well, actually, these risks are quite small when compared to the risks you're subjecting yourself to when you get behind the wheel of a car or light up yet another cigarette.

ABC reporter John Stossel was kind enough to share the results of a study done for him by physicist Bernard Cohen who compared different risks. Cohen's study showed that our riskiest behaviours are smoking and driving. Smoking whacks an average of seven years off a person's life, whereas driving a car results in a bit more than half a year of life lost on average. Toxic waste shaves an average of one week off your life span.

Knowing what's risky and what isn't is part of what you need to know. Unfortunately, you can't buy a formal insurance policy to protect yourself against all of life's great dangers and risks. But that does not mean that you must face these dangers as a helpless victim. Simple changes in behaviour can help you fight the odds.

Personal health habits are a good example. If you're overweight, eat fatty, high-cholesterol foods, drink excessively, and don't exercise, you're asking for trouble, especially during post-middle age. Engage in these habits, and you're dramatically increasing your risk of heart disease and cancer.

So does this mean that we should all eat bean sprouts, stay out of cars, never light up, and cease being concerned about toxic waste? No. But you should understand the consequences of your behaviours before you engage in them and minimize big risks accordingly.

If you're reading this chapter, you obviously want to find out about insurance. Our point is this: You can buy all the types of traditional insurance that we recommend in this book and still not be well-protected for the simple reason that you're overlooking uninsurable risks. But just because you can't buy formal insurance to protect against some risks doesn't mean that you can't drastically reduce your exposure to such risks by modifying your behaviour.

Our fears in life are natural and inescapable; they are also often arbitrary and irrational. Although we may not have control over the emotions that our fears invoke, we must often ignore those emotions in order to make rational insurance decisions. In other words, getting shaky in the knees and sweaty in the palms when boarding an airplane is okay, but letting your fear of flying cause you to make poor insurance decisions is not okay, especially when those decisions affect the lives of your loved ones.

You can't possibly predict what's going to happen to you. You want to get the broadest possible coverage that you can. Buy life insurance, not flight insurance. Buy major medical coverage, not cancer insurance.

Law III: Shop around and consider buying direct

Whether you're looking at auto, home, life, disability, or other types of coverage, some companies may charge double or triple the rates that other companies charge for the same coverage. The companies charging the higher rates may not be better about paying claims, however. You may even end up with the worst of both possible worlds — high prices *and* lousy service.

Most insurance is sold through agents and brokers who earn commissions based on what they sell. This, of course, tends to bias what they recommend that you buy. A study done by Cummins and Weisbart and cited in Andrew Tobias's book *Invisible Bankers* confirms this bias: ". . . 48% of the time, an agent's decision on where to place a customer's business was based on which insurer paid the highest commission."

Not surprisingly, policies that pay agents the biggest commissions also tend to be more costly. In fact, insurance companies compete for the attention of agents by offering bigger commissions than other insurers. If you browse through magazines and other publications targeted to insurance agents, you'll often see ads in which the largest text is the commission percentage offered to agents who sell the advertiser's products.

Besides the attraction of policies that pay higher commissions, agents also get hooked, financially speaking, to companies whose policies they sell frequently. Once an agent has sold a certain amount of a company's insurance policies, he is rewarded with higher commission percentages on any future sales. Just as airlines bribe frequent flyers with mileage bonuses, insurers bribe agents with fatter commissions for their loyalty.

Shopping around is a challenge not only because most insurance is sold by agents working on commission but also because insurers set their rates in mysterious ways. Every company has a different way of analyzing how much of a risk you are; one company may offer low rates to your brother-in-law but not to you and vice versa.

Despite the obstacles, several strategies exist for obtaining low-cost, high-quality policies. The following tips offer smart ways to shop for insurance. (Chapters 17 and 18 recommend how and where to get the best deals on specific types of policies.)

Employer and other group plans

When you buy insurance as part of a larger group, you generally get a lower price because of the purchasing power of the group. Most health and disability policies that you can access through your employer are less costly than equivalent policies that you can buy on your own.

The financial health of your insurers

In addition to the price of a policy and the insurer's reputation and track record for paying claims, an insurer's financial health is an important consideration when you choose a company. If you faithfully pay your premium dollars year after year, you'll be upset if the insurer goes bankrupt right before you have a major claim.

Insurance companies can fail just like any other companies. A number of organizations evaluate and rate, with some sort of letter grade, the financial viability and stability of insurance companies. The major rating agencies include A. M. Best Canada, Dominion Bond Rating Service, Canadian Bond Rating Service, Moody's, and Weiss Research.

The rating agencies' letter-grade system works just the way it does in high school: A is better than B or C. Each company uses a different scale. Some companies have as their highest rating AAA, and then AA, A, BBB, BB, and so on. Others use A, A–, B+, B, B–, and so on. Just as some teachers grade more easily, some firms have a reputation for giving out a greater number of high grades. Others, such as Weiss Research, are tough graders. Unlike in school, however, you want the tough critics when researching where to put your money and future security.

Just as it is a good idea to get more than one medical opinion, two or three financial ratings can give you a better sense of the safety of an insurance company. Stick with companies that are in the top two — or, at worst, three — levels on the different rating scales.

You can obtain current rating information about insurance companies, free of charge, by asking your agent for a listing of the current ratings. Ask the insurer itself if you are interested in a policy sold without the involvement of an agent.

Although the financial health of an insurance company is important, it's not as big a deal as some insurers (usually those with the highest ratings) and agents make it out to be. Just as financially unhealthy banks are taken over and merged into viable ones, sickly insurers usually follow a similar path under the direction of insurance regulators.

In most insurance company failures, claims still get paid. The people who usually lose out are those who had money invested in life insurance or annuities with the failed insurer. Even then, you'll typically get back 80 or 90 cents on the dollar of your account value with the insurer, but you may have to wait years to get it.

Likewise, many occupations have professional associations through which you may be able to obtain lower-cost policies. Not all associations offer better deals on insurance, so make sure to compare what they offer (policy features and costs) with other options available to you.

One exception to the rule that group policies offer better value than individual policies is with life insurance. Group life insurance plans usually aren't cheaper than the best life insurance policies that you can buy individually. However, group policies may have the attraction of convenience (ease of enrolment and avoidance of lengthy sales pitches from life insurance salespeople). Group life insurance policies that allow your enrolment without a medical evaluation will probably be more expensive because such plans attract more people with health problems who couldn't get coverage on their own. If you're in good health, you should definitely shop around for life insurance (see Chapter 17 to find out how).

Insurance agents who want to sell you an individual policy can come up with 101 reasons why buying from them is preferable to buying through your employer or some other group. In most cases, agents' arguments for buying an individual policy from them include a lot of self-serving marketing hype. In some cases, agents tell outright lies (which are hard to detect if you're not insurance-savvy).

One valid issue agents will raise is that, if you leave your job, you'll lose your group coverage. Sometimes that may be true. For example, if you know that you'll be leaving your job to become self-employed, securing an individual disability policy before you leave your job makes sense. However, your employer's health insurer may allow you to convert your health insurance policy into an individual one when you leave.

In the chapters that follow, we explain what you need in the policies that you are looking for so that you can determine whether a group plan meets your needs. In most cases, group plans, especially through an employer, offer good benefits. So as long as the group policy is cheaper than a comparable individual policy, you'll save money buying through the group plan.

The straight scoop on commissions and how insurance is sold

The commission paid to an insurance agent is never disclosed through any of the documents or materials that you receive in the process of buying insurance. This information ought to be disclosed by insurers and agents, just as sales charges on mutual funds are disclosed through a prospectus.

The only way you can know what the commission is on a policy and how it compares with other policies is to ask the agent. Nothing is wrong or impolite about asking. It's your money, after all, that pays the commission. You need to know whether a particular policy is being pitched harder because of its higher commission.

Commissions are typically paid as a percentage of the first year's premium on the insurance policy. (Many policies pay smaller commissions on subsequent years' premiums.) On life and disability insurance policies, for example, a 50 percent commission on the first year's premium is not unusual. On life insurance policies that have a cash value, commissions of 80 to 100 percent of your first year's premium are possible. Commissions on health insurance are lower, but generally not as low as commissions on auto and homeowner's insurance.

Insurance without sales commissions

Your best bet for getting a good insurance value is to buy policies from the increasing number of companies that are selling their policies directly to the public without the insurance agent and the agent's commission. Just as you can purchase no-load mutual funds directly from an investment company without paying any sales commission (refer to Chapter 10), you also can buy no-load insurance. Be sure to read Chapters 17 and 18 for more specifics on how to buy insurance directly from insurance companies.

Dealing with Insurance Problems

When you seek out insurance or have insurance policies, sooner or later you're bound to hit a roadblock. Although insurance problems can be among the more frustrating in life, in the sections ahead we explain how to successfully deal with the more common obstacles.

Help! I've been denied coverage!

Just as you can be turned down when you apply for a loan, you can also be turned down when applying for insurance. For medical, life, or disability insurance, a company may reject you if you have an existing medical problem (a pre-existing condition) and are therefore more likely to file a claim. When it comes to insuring assets such as a home, you may have difficulty getting coverage if the property is deemed to be in a high-risk area.

Here are some strategies to employ if you are denied coverage:

- **Ask the insurer why you were denied.** Perhaps the company made a mistake or misinterpreted some information that you provided in your application. Should you be denied coverage because of a medical condition, see what information the company has on you and whether the information is accurate.

- **Request a copy of your medical information file.** Many people don't know that just as you have a credit report file that details your use (and misuse) of credit, you also have a medical information report. You can request a current copy of your medical information file by writing to the Medical Information Bureau at 330 University Avenue, Suite 501, Toronto, Ontario, M5G 1R7. You can also call them at 416-597-0590. If a mistake is on your report, you have the right to request that it be fixed. However, the burden is on you to prove that the information in your file is incorrect. This can be a major hassle — you may even need to contact physicians that you've seen in the past because their medical records could be the source of the incorrect information.

✔ **Shop other companies.** Just because one company denies you coverage doesn't mean that all insurance companies will. Some insurers better understand certain medical conditions and are more comfortable accepting applicants with those conditions. Most insurers, however, charge a person with a blemished medical history a higher rate than a person with a perfect health record, but some companies penalize you less than others. An agent who sells policies from multiple insurers, called an *independent agent,* can be helpful because he or she can shop among a number of different companies.

✔ **Learn about provincial high-risk pools.** Check with your provincial insurance regulator (see the government blue pages section of your local phone directory) if you're turned down for health or property insurance. Some provinces and provincial industry associations provide insurance for those who can't get it from insurance companies. This high-risk pool coverage is usually bare bones, but it beats going without any coverage.

✔ **Check for coverage availability before you buy.** If you're considering buying a home, for example, and you can't get coverage, the insurance companies are trying to tell you something. What they are effectively saying is, "We think that property is so high-risk, we're not willing to insure it even if you pay a high premium."

Help! My insurer is hassling me about paying a claim

In the event that you suffer a loss and file an insurance claim, you may hold the happy belief that your insurance company will cheerfully and expeditiously pay your claims. Given all the money that you've shelled out for coverage and all the hoops you jumped through to be approved for coverage in the first place, that's a reasonable expectation.

Insurance companies may refuse to pay you what you think you are owed for many reasons, however. In some cases, they may actually be right — your claim may not be covered under the terms of the policy. At a minimum, the insurer wants documentation and proof of your loss. Other people who have come before you have been known to cheat, so insurers won't simply take your word, no matter how honest and ethical you are.

In other cases, though, you're right, and the insurance company is just jerking you around. Some companies view paying claims as an adversarial situation and take a "negotiate tough" stance. Thinking that all insurance companies are going to pay you a fair and reasonable amount unless you make your voice heard is a mistake.

The tips that we discuss in this section help you to ensure that you get paid everything your policy entitles you to.

Document your assets and case

When you're insuring assets, such as your home and its contents, having a record of what you own helps your case. A videotape is the most efficient record, but a handwritten list detailing your possessions works, too. Just remember to keep this record away from your home — if your home burns to the ground, you'll lose your documentation, too!

If you are robbed or are the victim of an accident, get the names, addresses, and phone numbers of witnesses. Take pictures of property damage and solicit estimates for the cost of repairing or replacing what's lost or damaged. File police reports if appropriate, if for no other reason than to bolster your documentation for the insurance claim.

The best offence is a good defence. If you've kept records of valuables and can document their cost, you should be in better shape.

Prepare your case

Filing a claim should be viewed the same way as preparing for a court trial or a tax audit. Any information that you provide verbally or in writing can and will be used against you to deny your claim. First, you should understand whether the policy you bought covers your claim (this is why getting the broadest coverage possible helps). Unfortunately, the only way to find this out is by getting out the policy and reading it. Policies are hard to read because they use legal language in non-user-friendly ways.

A possible alternative is to call the claims department and, *without* providing your name, ask a representative whether a particular loss (such as the one that you just suffered) is covered under its policy. You have no need to lie to the company, but you have no need to tell the representative who you are and that you're about to file a claim, either. Your call is informational so that you can understand what your policy covers. Some companies are not willing to provide detailed information, however, unless a specific case is cited.

After you initiate the claims process, keep records of all conversations and all copies of documents that you have given to the insurer's claims department. If you have problems down the road, this "evidence" may bail you out.

For property damage, you should get at least a couple of reputable contractors' estimates. Demonstrate to the insurance company that you're trying to shop for a low price, but don't agree to use a low-cost contractor without knowing that he or she can do quality work.

Remember, your claim is a negotiation

To get what you're owed on an insurance claim, you must approach most claims' filings for what they are — a negotiation that is often not cooperative. And the bigger the claim, the more your insurer will play the part of adversary.

A number of years ago, when Eric filed a homeowner's insurance claim after a winter storm significantly damaged his backyard fence, he was greeted on a weekday by a perky, smiley adjuster. Once the adjuster entered his yard and started to peruse the damage, her demeanour changed dramatically, and she quickly adopted a combative, hard-bargainer-type attitude.

While standing on his back porch a good distance away from the fences in his yard that had been blown over by wind and crushed by two large trees, the adjuster said that the insurer preferred to repair damaged fences rather than replace them. "With your deductible of $1,000, I doubt this will be worth filing a claim for," she said.

The fence that had blown over, she reasoned, could have new posts set in concrete. As Eric had already begun to clean up some of the damage for safety reasons, he presented to her some pictures of what the yard looked like right after the storm; she refused to take them. She took some measurements and said she'd have her settlement cheque to him in a couple of days. The settlement she faxed was for $1,119, nowhere near what it would cost Eric to fix the damage that was done.

Be persistent

When you take an insurance company's first offer and don't fight for what you're due, you could be leaving a lot of money on the table. To make Eric's long fence-repair story somewhat shorter, after *five* rounds of haggling with the adjusters, supervisors, and, finally, managers, he was awarded payment to replace the fences and clean up most of the damage. Although all the contractors he had contacted recommended that the work be done this way, the insurance adjuster discredited their recommendations by saying, "Contractors try to jack up the price and recommended work once they know an insurer is involved."

His final total settlement came to $4,888, more than $3,700 higher than the insurer's first offer. Interestingly, his insurer backed off its preference for repairing the fence when the contractor's estimates for doing that work exceeded the cost of a new fence.

Eric was understandably disappointed with the behaviour of his insurance company. Having faithfully paid his premiums for years and having never filed a claim, he expected they would be cooperative and not combative. Whoops! We know from conversations with others that Eric's homeowner's insurance company is not unusual in its adversarial strategy, especially with larger claims. And to think that his insurer has one of the "better" track records for paying claims!

Enlist support

If you do your homework and you're not making progress with the insurer's adjuster, ask to speak with supervisors and managers. That's what Eric had to do to get the additional $3,700 that was needed to get things back to where they were before the storm.

The agent who sold you the policy may be helpful in preparing and filing the claim. A good agent can help increase your chances of getting paid and getting paid sooner. When you're having difficulty with a claim for a policy obtained through your employer or other group, speak with the benefits department or a person responsible for interacting with the insurer. These folks have a lot of clout because of the potential threat to the agent and/or insurer of losing the entire account.

For policies that you buy on your own, if you're having problems getting a fair settlement from the insurer try contacting your province's insurance regulator. You can find the phone number in the government blue pages of your phone book, through an agent, or possibly in your insurance policy.

Another option is to hire a public adjuster who, for a percentage of payment (typically 5 to 10 percent), can negotiate with insurers on your behalf.

When all else fails and you have a major claim at stake, try contacting a lawyer who specializes in insurance matters. You can find these specialists in the Yellow Pages of your phone directory under "lawyers." Expect to pay around $150 or more per hour. Consider looking for a lawyer who is willing to negotiate on your behalf, help draft letters, and so on, on an hourly basis without filing a lawsuit. Your province's department of insurance, the local bar association, or other legal, accounting, or financial practitioners also may be able to refer you to someone.

The possible headache in filing a claim is another reason to take the highest insurance deductibles you're comfortable with. Remember that insurance is to protect against large, not small, losses. With a high deductible and a small loss, you'll save yourself some haggling.

Chapter 17

Insurance on You

● ●

In This Chapter
▶ Life insurance
▶ Disability insurance
▶ Travel medical insurance
▶ Overlooked personal insurance

● ●

*M*ultiply your typical annual income by the number of remaining years you plan to work — you come up with a pretty big number, don't you? That dollar amount equals probably your most valuable asset — your ability to earn an income — and you probably need to protect it. You need to buy some insurance on you.

This chapter explains the ins and outs of buying insurance that protects your income: life insurance, in case of death, and disability insurance, in case of an accident or illness that prevents you from working. We tell you what coverage you should have, where to look for it, and what to avoid.

In addition to protecting your income, you also need to insure against financially catastrophic expenses. We are not talking about December's credit card bill; you're on your own with that one. We are talking about the type of bills that are racked up from a major surgery, a six-week stay in the hospital, and the need for expensive prescription drugs and follow-up treatment. Medical expenses today can make even the most indulgent shopping mall spending spree look dirt-cheap. To protect yourself from potentially astronomical medical bills, you also should evaluate whether you need to purchase health insurance beyond what your province provides.

Life Insurance

You generally need life insurance only when other people depend on your income.

Don't waste your money on life insurance for children

You've surely heard of Gerber baby food. Well, the folks at Gerber knew that their brand name had clout with parents, so they sat around racking their brains about what else they could pitch to parents.

So Gerber established a life insurance company that now has billions of dollars of life insurance in force. The only problem is that the company specializes in selling life insurance policies on individuals who don't need it: children.

Gerber's "Grow-Up" policy provides $5,000 of life insurance for children. The marketing materials say, "Life insurance for the child you love . . . $1 a week at most ages. . . ."

Sounds like such a deal, but it's really a rip-off that contradicts the entire logic of life insurance. Unless your kid was the star of the *Home Alone* movies, you are not financially dependent on any of your children; your children are dependent on you! As any parent knows, kids cost a good deal of money — kids don't earn money!

And if a person does need life insurance coverage, of what use is a piddling $5,000 worth of coverage? And a buck a week is hardly a deal — for that cost, a young adult could buy about ten times as much coverage ($50,000)!

Insurance agents love to prey on the emotional bond between parents and children. In a written sales pitch, one agent said, ". . . as long as the policies remain in-force, your signature(s) will always be there as a reminder of your very thoughtful financial gift."

Agents also love to sell cash-value life insurance on kids because such policies pay the agent a hefty commission (25 percent of all cash-value policies in the U.S. are sold on children). Part of the supposed allure is that the huge premiums that you pump into such policies partly go into a savings account for the child's future. As you see later in this chapter, cash-value life insurance is a costly life insurance and investment choice. If you want to secure your children's financial future, follow the advice in this book and pass this information on to your children. Don't waste money on life insurance on your kids — they don't need it.

That means that a lot of people don't need life insurance to protect their incomes: single people, working couples who could maintain an acceptable lifestyle if one of the incomes was gone, independently wealthy people who don't need to work, and retired people who are living off of their retirement nest egg.

But if others are either fully or partly dependent on your paycheque (usually a spouse and/or children) you should buy life insurance, especially if you have major financial commitments such as a mortgage or years of child-rearing ahead. Also consider life insurance if an extended family member is currently or likely to be dependent on your future income.

How much do you need?

When you need life insurance, deciding how much to buy is as much a subjective thing as it is a quantitative decision. We've seen some worksheets that are incredibly long and tedious (some are worse than your tax returns). There's no need to get fancy. If you're like us, your eyes start to glaze over if you have to complete 20-plus lines of calculations. Figuring out how much life insurance you need doesn't have to be that complicated.

The main purpose of life insurance is to provide a lump-sum payment that replaces the deceased person's income. The question you need to ask yourself is how many years of income you want to replace. Table 17-1 provides a simple way to calculate how much life insurance you should consider purchasing. To replace a certain number of years of income, simply multiply the appropriate number in the table by your annual after-tax income.

Table 17-1	Life Insurance Need Calculation
Years of Income to Replace	*Multiply Annual After-Tax Income* By*
5	4.5
10	8.5
20	15
30	20

*You can roughly determine your annual after-tax income by getting out last year's tax return. Subtract the federal, provincial, and other payroll deductions you paid from your gross employment income.

Another way to determine the amount of life insurance to buy is to think about how much you will need to pay for major debts or expenditures, such as your mortgage, other loans, and university for your children. For example, if you'd like your spouse to have enough of a life insurance death benefit to be able to pay off half of your mortgage and pay for half of your children's university education, then simply add half of your mortgage amount to half of their estimated university costs (refer to Chapter 14 for approximate numbers) and buy that amount of life insurance.

The Canada Pension Plan or Quebec Pension Plan, if you're covered, can provide *survivors'* benefits to your spouse and children. Contact the government's Income Security Programs information service at 800-277-9914 (or visit the Human Resources Development Canada — HRDC — Web site at http://www.hrdc.gc.ca/isp/common/home.shtml) to obtain an estimate of your benefits.

"Other" life insurance

Contemplating the possibility of your untimely demise is surely depressing. You'll likely feel some peace of mind in purchasing a life insurance policy to provide for your dependants.

However, let's take things a step further. Suppose you (or your spouse) do pass away. Do you think simply buying a life insurance policy will be sufficient "help" for the loved ones you leave behind? Probably not. Surely your contribution to your household involves far more than being a breadwinner.

For starters, you should make sure that all of your important financial documents — investment account statements, insurance policies, employee benefits materials, small-business accounting records, and so on — are kept in one place (such as a file drawer) that your loved ones know about.

Do you have a will? See Chapter 18 for more details on wills and other estate-planning documents.

You might also consider providing a list of key contacts — such as whom you recommend calling (or what you recommend reading) in the event of legal, financial, or tax quandaries.

So, in addition to trying to provide financially for your dependants, you should also take some time to reflect upon what else you can do to help point them in the right direction on matters you've historically handled. In most couples, it's natural for one spouse to take more responsibility, say, for money management. That's fine; just make sure to talk about what's being done so that in the event the responsible spouse dies, the remaining person knows how to jump into the driver's seat.

If you have kids, and even if you don't, how about giving thought to philosophical leave-behinds for your loved ones? It could be something like a short note telling them how much they meant to you and what you'd like them to remember about you.

HDRC can tell you how much your survivors will receive per month in the event of your death. You should factor this benefit into the amount of life insurance that you calculate in Table 17-1. For example, suppose that your annual after-tax income is $30,000 and the Canada Pension Plan should provide $6,000 annually. Therefore, for the purposes of Table 17-1, you should determine the amount of life insurance needed to replace $24,000 annually ($30,000 – $6,000), not $30,000.

Term versus cash-value life insurance

We're going to tell you how you can save hours of time and thousands of dollars. Ready? *Buy term life insurance.* (The only exception is if you have a high net worth — a couple million bucks or more — in which case you may want to consider other options. See the estate-planning section in Chapter 18.) If you've already figured out how much life insurance to purchase and this is all the advice you need to go ahead, skip the rest of this section and jump to the "Buying term insurance" section that follows.

The following information is for the rest of you who want the details behind our recommendation for term insurance. Or maybe you've heard (and have already fallen prey to) the sales pitches from life insurance agents, most of whom love selling cash-value life insurance because of its huge commissions.

We'll start with some background. Despite the variety of names that life insurance marketing departments have cooked up for policies, life insurance comes in two basic flavours:

- **Term insurance.** This is pure life insurance: You pay an annual premium for which you receive a predetermined amount of life insurance protection. If the insured person passes away, the beneficiaries collect; otherwise, the premium is gone. In this way, term life insurance is similar to auto or homeowner's insurance.

- **Cash-value insurance.** All other life insurance policies (whole, universal, variable, and so on) combine life insurance with a supposed savings feature. Your premiums not only pay for life insurance, but some of your dollars are also credited to an account that grows in value over time, assuming you keep paying your premiums. On the surface, this sounds potentially attractive. People don't like to feel that all their premium dollars are getting tossed away.

  But there's a big catch. For the same amount of coverage (for example, for $100,000 of life insurance benefits), cash-value policies cost you anywhere from four to ten times more than comparable term policies.

Insurance salespeople know the buttons to push to get you interested in buying the wrong kind of life insurance. Here are typical arguments that they make for purchasing cash-value polices, followed by our perspective.

"It's all paid up after x years. You don't want to be paying life insurance premiums for the rest of your life, do you?"

Agents pitching cash-value life insurance show you all sorts of projections that imply that after the first ten or so years of paying your premiums, you won't need to pay more premiums to keep the life insurance in force. The only reason that you may be able to stop paying premiums is that you've poured so much extra money into the policy in the early years of payment. Remember that cash-value life insurance costs four to ten times as much as term.

Imagine that you're currently paying $500 a year for auto insurance and an insurance company comes along and offers you a policy for $4,000 per year. The representative tells you that after ten years you can stop paying and still keep your same coverage. We're sure that you wouldn't fall for this sales tactic, but many people do when they buy cash-value life insurance.

You also need to be wary of the projections because they often include unrealistic and lofty assumptions about the investment return that your cash balance can earn. When you stop paying into a cash-value policy, the cost of each year's life insurance is deducted from the remaining cash value. If the rate of return on the cash balance is not sufficient to pay the insurance cost, the cash balance begins sliding, and eventually you will receive notices saying that your policy needs more funding to keep the life insurance in force.

"You won't be able to afford term insurance when you're older."

As you get older, the cost of term insurance increases because the probability of your dying rises. But life insurance is not something you need all your life! It's typically bought in a person's younger years when financial commitments and obligations outweigh financial assets. Twenty or 30 years later, the reverse should be true.

When you retire years from now, you probably won't need life insurance to protect your employment income because there won't be any to protect! You might have needed life insurance when you were raising a family and/or had a substantial mortgage you were responsible for, but by the time you retire, the kids should be out on their own (you hope!) and the mortgage should be paid down.

In the meantime, term insurance saves you a tremendous amount of money. For most people, it takes 20 to 30 years for the premiums they are paying on a term insurance policy to finally catch up to (equal) the premiums they've been paying all along on a comparable amount of cash-value life insurance purchased today.

"You can borrow against the cash value at a low rate of interest."

Such a deal! It's your money in the policy, remember? If you deposited money in a savings or money market account, how would you like to pay for the privilege of borrowing your own money back? Borrowing on your cash-value policy is potentially dangerous: You increase the chances of the policy exploding on you — leaving you with nothing to show for your premiums.

"Your cash value grows tax-deferred."

Ah, a glimmer of truth at last. The fact that the cash-value portion of your policy grows without taxation until you withdraw it is true. But if you want tax-deferral of your investment balances, you should first take advantage of your RRSP. An RRSP gives you an immediate tax deduction for your current contributions in addition to growth without taxation until withdrawal. Money paid into a cash-value life insurance policy gives you *no* upfront tax deductions.

Life insurance tends to be a mediocre investment. The insurance company generally quotes you an interest rate for the first year only. After that, most companies pay you what they want. If you don't like the future interest rates, you can be penalized for quitting the policy. Would you ever invest your money in a bank account that quoted an interest rate for the first year only and then penalized you for moving your money within the next seven to ten years?

"It's forced savings."

Many agents argue that a cash-value plan is better than nothing — at least it's forcing you to save. This is silly reasoning because so many people drop cash-value life insurance policies after just a few years of paying into them.

You can accomplish "forced savings" without using life insurance. An RRSP can be set up for automatic monthly transfers. You can also set up monthly electronic transfers from your bank chequing account to contribute to mutual funds held inside an RRSP (see Chapter 10).

Summary

Insurance salespeople aggressively push cash-value policies because of the high commissions that insurance companies pay them. Commissions on cash-value life insurance range from 50 to 100 percent of your first year's premium. An insurance salesperson, therefore, can make *four to ten times more money* (yes, you read that right) selling you a cash-value policy than he can selling you term insurance.

You are ultimately paying the high commissions that are built into these policies when you purchase cash-value life insurance. As you can see in a policy's cash-value table, you won't get back any of the money that you dump in the policy if you quit the policy in the first two to three years. The insurance company can't afford to give you any of your money back in those first few years because so much of it has been paid to the selling agent as commission. That's why these policies explicitly penalize you for withdrawing your cash balance within the first seven to ten years.

Because of the high cost of cash-value policies relative to the cost of term, you are more likely to buy less life insurance coverage than you need — that's the sad part of the insurance industry's pushing of this stuff. *The vast majority of life insurance buyers need more protection than they can afford to buy with cash-value coverage.*

Cash-value life insurance makes sense for a small percentage of people such as a small-business owner who owns a business worth more than one to two million dollars and who would not want his heirs to be forced to sell the business to pay taxes in the event of his death. Cash-value life insurance may also make sense as a way to have your savings grow tax-free. However, you should first ensure that you are maximizing your allowable RRSP contributions, and have taken care of any non-deductible debt.

Purchase low-cost term insurance and do your investing separately. Life insurance is rarely a permanent need; over time, you can gradually reduce the amount of term insurance that you carry as you accumulate more assets.

Buying term insurance

Term insurance policies have several features to choose from. So that you can make an informed decision about purchasing term insurance, we cover the important elements in this section.

How often your premium adjusts

As you get older, the risk of dying increases, so the cost of your insurance goes up. Term insurance can be purchased so that your premium adjusts (increases) annually or every 5, 10, 15, or 20 years. The less frequently your premium adjusts, the higher the initial premium and its incremental increases will be.

The advantage of a premium that locks in for, say, 15 years is that you have the security of knowing how much you'll be paying each year for the next 15 years. You also don't need to go through medical evaluations as frequently to qualify for the lowest rate possible.

The disadvantage of a policy with a long-term rate lock is that you'll be paying more in the earlier years than you would on a policy that adjusts more frequently. In addition, you may want to change the amount of insurance you carry as your circumstances change, so you would be throwing money away if you dump a policy with a long-term premium guarantee before its rate is set to change.

Policies that adjust the premium every five to ten years offer a happy medium between price and predictability.

Guaranteed renewability

This feature guarantees that the policy cannot be cancelled because of poor health. Guaranteed renewability is standard practice on better policies. Do not buy a life insurance policy without this feature unless you expect that your life insurance needs will disappear when the policy is up for renewal.

Guaranteed renewal rates

When assessing the costs of different policies, what really matters is the overall amount you'll pay for your coverage for all the years that you'll require life insurance. Be sure that the premiums you'll pay each time you renew are guaranteed and laid out term-by-term in your policy. To evaluate different policies, have the agent do a *present value comparison* of the total amount you'll pay in premiums over the period you estimate you'll require life insurance. This figure represents what a policy would cost if you had to pay for all your years of coverage in a single payment today.

Where to buy term insurance

A number of sound ways to obtain high-quality, low-cost term insurance are available. If you choose to buy through a local agent — because you know her or because you'd prefer to buy from someone close to home — you should still invest a few minutes of your time to get quotes from one or two of the following sources to get a sense of what's available in the insurance market. Gaining familiarity with the market can prevent an agent from selling you an overpriced, high-commission policy.

Here are some sources for low-cost term insurance (be sure to also ask any groups, professional associations, or business organizations you belong to about low-cost term insurance offerings):

- ✔ **Blue Cross** (1-800-873-2583 or `www.bluecross.ca`)
- ✔ **Canadian Automobile Association** (800-387-0649 or `www.caa.ca`)
- ✔ **RBC Insurance** (800-769-2526 or `www.rbcinsurance.ca`)
- ✔ **TD Insurance** (800-338-0218 or `www.tdbank.ca/tdinsurance`)
- ✔ **Zenith Insurance** (800-531-8080 or `www.zenithinsurance.ca`)

To get a sense of what your premiums will be with various companies, try the online quotation service at `www.termforsale.net`.

How to get rid of cash-value life insurance

If you were snookered into buying a cash-value life insurance policy and want to part ways with it, do so. *But don't cancel the coverage until you first secure new term coverage.* When you need life insurance, you don't want to leave open a period when you're not covered (Murphy's Law says *that's* when disaster will strike).

Ending a cash-value life insurance policy has tax consequences. For most of these policies, you must pay tax on the amount you receive that is in excess of the premiums you paid over the life of the policy. If you want to withdraw the cash balance of your life insurance policy, consider checking with the insurer or a tax adviser to clarify what the tax consequences may be.

If you're considering cash-value life insurance

Don't expect to get objective information on this important decision from most people who sell cash-value life insurance. Beware of insurance salespeople masquerading under the guise of self-anointed titles, such as estate planning specialists or financial planners.

As we discuss earlier in the chapter, purchasing cash-value life insurance may make sense if you expect your death may trigger tax problems for your estate and heirs. However, cash-value life insurance is just one of numerous ways to reduce taxes due when you die. Read the section in Chapter 18 on estate planning.

One type of cash-value life insurance — *universal life* — separates out the insurance and investment components of your policy. Depending on the insurance company, you may be able to choose from a range of investments, including those that mirror the performance of various stock market indexes. However, universal insurance as an investment generally is attractive only if you have maximized your RRSP contributions and you anticipate being able to continue doing that for most of your working life. The reason is that you get an immediate tax break on your RRSP contributions, something universal life insurance doesn't offer. And in order to benefit from the tax-free growth universal policies offer on the investment portion of your plan, you must be able to stick with the premiums. Another strike against universal policies is the high commissions and other fees. Finally, if you want to get at the money that is built up in the investment part of your plan while you are still alive, you'll have to pay tax on any withdrawals, just like you do on withdrawals from an RRSP or RRIF. You may be able to get around this by borrowing against the value of your policy. The loan is used to supplement your retirement income. The interest cost is added to your loan, which gets paid off using the proceeds from your policy when you die.

Disability Insurance

As with life insurance, the purpose of disability insurance is to protect your income. The only difference is that you're protecting the income for yourself (and perhaps also your dependants). If you're completely disabled, you still have living expenses, but you probably can't earn employment income.

We're talking here about long-term disabilities. If you throw out your back while reliving your athletic glory days with your aging adult body and wind up in bed for a couple of weeks, that won't be as much of a disaster to your finances as it is to your ego! What would be a financial disaster, however, is if you're disabled in such a way that you can't work for several years.

Most large employers offer disability insurance to their employees. Many employees of smaller companies and all self-employed people are left to fend for themselves and don't have disability coverage. Being without disability insurance is a risky proposition, especially if, like most working people, you need your employment income to live on.

If you're married and your spouse earns a large enough income that you can make do without yours, then you may consider skipping disability coverage. The same is true if you've already accumulated enough money for your future years (you're financially independent). Keep in mind, though, that your expenses may go up if you are disabled and require specialized care.

For most people, dismissing the need for disability coverage is easy. The odds of suffering a long-term disability seem so remote — and they are. But if you meet up with bad luck, disability coverage can relieve you (and possibly your family) of a major financial burden.

Most disabilities are caused by medical problems, such as arthritis, heart conditions, hypertension, and back/spine or hip/leg impairments. Some of these ailments are caused by advancing age, but more than a third of disabilities are suffered by people under age 45. The vast majority of these medical problems cannot be predicted in advance, particularly those caused by random accidents.

If you think that you have good disability coverage through government programs, you'd better think again:

- ✔ **Government benefits.** In general, you must have paid into the Canada Pension Plan or Quebec Pension Plan in order to receive CPP/QPP disability benefits. If you were disabled after December 31, 1997, you are normally required to have paid into the plan for at least four of the last six years. To qualify, you must also not be able to work regularly at any job, and your disability must be either long-term or likely to lead to your death. Further, CPP/QPP disability payments are quite low because they are intended to provide only for basic, subsistence-level living expenses. In 2000, for example, the maximum CPP disability payment was $917.43 a month.

- ✔ **Worker's compensation.** Worker's compensation, if you have such coverage through your employer, pays you if you're injured on the job but does not pay any benefits if you get disabled away from your job. You need coverage that pays regardless of where and how you are disabled.

How much disability insurance do you need?

You need enough disability coverage to provide you with sufficient income to live on until other financial resources are available. If you don't have much saved in the way of financial assets and you would want to continue with the lifestyle supported by your current income, get enough disability coverage to replace your entire take-home (after-tax) monthly pay.

The benefits you purchase on a disability policy are quoted as dollars per month that you receive if disabled. So if your job provides you with a $2,000-per-month income after payment of taxes, then seek a policy that provides a $2,000-per-month benefit.

If you pay for your disability insurance, the benefits are tax-free (but hopefully you won't ever have to collect them). Should your employer pick up the tab, your benefits are taxable, so you need a higher amount of benefits.

In addition to the monthly coverage amount, you also need to select the duration of time you want a policy to pay you benefits. You need a policy that pays benefits until an age at which you become financially self-sufficient. For most people, that's age 65 or so. You may want to obtain disability coverage that pays you until a later age if you anticipate needing your employment income past your mid-60s.

On the other hand, if you've crunched some numbers (refer to Chapter 3) and see that you expect to be financially independent by age 55, you can get a policy that pays benefits up to that age — it'll cost you less than one that pays benefits to you until age 65. If you're within five years of being financially independent or able to retire, five-year disability policies are available, too. You might also consider such short-term policies because you're sure that someone (for example, a family member) can support you financially over the long term.

Other features you need in disability insurance

Disability insurance policies have many confusing features. Here's what to look for — and look *out* for — when purchasing disability insurance:

- ✔ **Definition of disability.** An *own-occupation* disability policy provides benefit payments if you cannot perform the work you normally do. Some policies pay you only if you're unable to perform a job for which you are *reasonably trained*. Other policies revert to this definition after a few years of being own-occupation.

  Own-occupation policies are the most expensive because there's a greater chance that the insurer will have to pay you. The extra cost may not be worth it for you unless you're in a high-income or specialized occupation, and you'd have to take a big pay cut to do something else (and you wouldn't be happy about a reduced income and the required lifestyle changes).

✔ **Non-cancellable and guaranteed renewable.** These features guarantee that your policy cannot be cancelled because of poor health conditions. With policies requiring periodic physical exams, you can lose your coverage just when you're most likely to need it.

✔ **Waiting period.** This is the "deductible" on disability insurance — the lag time between the onset of your disability and the time you begin collecting benefits. As with other types of insurance, you should take the highest deductible (longest waiting period) that your financial circumstances allow. The waiting period significantly reduces the cost of the insurance and eliminates the hassle of filing a claim for a short-term disability. The minimum waiting period on most policies is 30 days, and the maximum can be up to one to two years. Try a waiting period of three to six months if you have sufficient emergency reserves.

✔ **Residual benefits.** This option pays you a partial benefit if you have a disability that prevents you from working full time.

✔ **Cost-of-living adjustments (COLAs).** This feature automatically increases your benefit payment by a set percentage or in accordance with changes in inflation. The advantage of a COLA is that it retains the purchasing power of your benefits. A modest COLA, such as 4 percent, is worth having.

✔ **Future insurability.** A clause that many agents encourage you to buy, future insurability allows you, regardless of health, to buy additional coverage. For most people, paying for the privilege of buying more coverage later is not worth it if the income that you earn today fairly reflects your likely long-term earnings (except for cost-of-living increases). Disability insurance is sold only as a proportion of your income. People who may benefit from the future insurability option are those whose income is artificially low now and who not only are confident of its rising significantly in the future but also need to protect it. (For example, you just got out of medical school and are earning a low salary while being enslaved as a resident.)

✔ **Insurer's financial stability.** As we discuss in Chapter 16, you should choose insurers that will be here tomorrow to pay your claim. But don't get too hung up on the safety of the company; benefits are paid even if the insurer fails because the province or another insurer almost always bails the insurer out. Many policies are also protected up to certain limits by CompCorp, an industry-run compensation scheme.

Where to buy disability insurance

The best place to buy disability insurance is through your employer or professional association. Unless these groups have done a lousy job shopping for coverage, group plans offer better value than you can purchase on your own. Just make sure that the plan that's offered meets the specifications discussed in the preceding section.

Don't trust an insurance agent to be enthusiastic (or even honest) about the quality of a disability policy your employer or other group is offering. Agents have a huge conflict of interest when they criticize these options because your group insurance cuts them out of the picture.

If you don't have access to a group policy, then check with your agent or a company you already do business with. Tread carefully when purchasing disability insurance through an agent. Some agents try to load down a policy with all sorts of extra bells and whistles to pump up the premium and their own commission.

If you buy disability insurance through an agent, use a process called *list billing*. With list billing, you sign up with several others for coverage at the same time and are invoiced together for your coverage. It can knock up to 15 percent off an insurer's standard prices. Ask your insurance agent how this works.

Travel Medical Insurance

An emergency ward or doctor's waiting room likely isn't on your list of must-sees when you head out of the country. But you simply can't predict whether a visit to a medical facility will end up being part of your itinerary when you leave our home and native land.

If you head out of Canada on vacation, for business, or just a day-shopping trip across the border, you need to ensure you are properly insured against unexpected medical expenses. Without sufficient *travel medical coverage*, an accident or illness that strikes while you are out of Canada could in turn damage your financial health.

Other "insurance" to protect your income

Life insurance and disability insurance replace your income if you die or suffer a disability. But you could also see your income reduced or completely eliminated if you lose your job. Although no formal insurance exists to protect you against the forces that can cause this to happen, you can do some things to reduce your exposure to such risk.

Make sure that you have an emergency reserve of money that you can tap into if you lose your job. (Chapter 3 offers specific guidelines for deciding how much money is right for you.)

Another form of "insurance" is to continually attend to your skills and professional development. Not only does upgrading your education and skills ensure that you are employable if you have to hit the streets to look for a new job, but it may also help you keep your old one and earn a higher income.

As long as you belong to your province's health care plan, you already have some coverage outside of Canada. However, each provincial plan covers you only up to certain levels, with maximums established for various procedures and other medical costs. The amounts that provincial plans will pay have been shrinking, though, and what your provincial health plan pays might be only a fraction of the final bill.

Don't blindly assume that you're adequately covered if you have a premium credit card that trumpets medical coverage. The eligibility requirements can be highly confusing, and the rules are regularly changed. With some premium cards, for instance, you're only covered for a certain number of days for each trip you make. You may be covered for trips up to 21 days in length, for instance, so if you're injured on the 22nd day, your card company won't pay any of the medical expenses.

If you are travelling on company business, it's wise to check with your benefits department before you leave. While most corporations provide medical insurance for employees who are travelling on business, the policies can be complicated and can leave you exposed. For instance, you may be covered during the week while you're on company business, but not if you choose to stay over for the weekend to enjoy a little skiing at a nearby resort. Should you break your leg on the slopes, you may find you're responsible for any bills because company policy doesn't cover injuries sustained on personal time.

Where to buy travel medical insurance

Be sure to take a look at your family's overall need. Many providers now offer plans that will cover your family. If you travel a lot, check into annual plans, which cover you up to a maximum number of days outside the country over 12 months.

Here are some sources for low-cost travel medical insurance:

- ✔ **Belair Direct** (800-268-8551 or www.belairdirect.com)
- ✔ **Canadian Automobile Association** (800-387-0649 or www.caa.ca)
- ✔ **Ingle Health** (800-268-8551 or www.ingle-health.com)
- ✔ **RBC Insurance** (800-769-2526 or www.rbcinsurance.ca)
- ✔ **TD Insurance** (800-338-0218 or www.tdbank.ca/tdinsurance)

The Most Overlooked Form of Insurance

You buy disability insurance to replace your income in the event of a long-term disability, life insurance to provide money to those dependent on your income in the event of your death, and perhaps extended health insurance to cover extra medical expenses. Many people buy all the right kinds of personal insurance, spending a small fortune over the course of their lives in the process. Yet they overlook the obvious, virtually free protection: taking care of themselves.

If you work all day at a desk and use many of life's modern conveniences, you could end up being the Great Canadian Couch Potato. Odds are that you've heard of most of these forms of "life insurance," but if you're still on the couch, the advice apparently didn't sink in.

So, for you sofa spuds, here are seven healthful tips:

- ✔ Don't smoke.
- ✔ Drink alcohol in moderation, if you drink at all.
- ✔ Get plenty of rest.
- ✔ Exercise regularly.
- ✔ Eat healthfully (refer to Chapter 6 for diet tips that improve your health and save you money).
- ✔ Get regular health care checkups to detect medical, dental, and vision problems.
- ✔ Take time to smell the roses.

Chapter 18

Insuring Your Assets

· ·

In This Chapter

▶ Homeowner's/renter's insurance

▶ Automobile insurance

▶ Planning your estate

· ·

*I*n Chapter 17, we discuss the importance of protecting your future income from the possibilities of disability, death, or large, unexpected medical expenses. But you also need to insure major assets that you have acquired in the past: your home, your car, and your personal property.

You need to protect some of these assets for two reasons:

✔ **Your assets are valuable.** If you were to suffer a loss, replacing the assets with money out of your own pocket could be a financial catastrophe.

✔ **A lawsuit could drain your finances.** This reason is less well-known. If someone were injured or killed in your home or because of your car, a lawsuit could be even more financially devastating than an outright loss of the asset.

Homeowner's/Renter's Insurance

When you buy a home, most lenders require that you purchase homeowner's insurance. But even if they don't you are wise to do so, because your home and the personal property within it are worth a great deal and would cost a bundle to replace.

As a renter, damage to the building in which you live is not your financial concern, but you still have personal property that you may want to insure. And there's also the possibility, albeit remote, that you could be sued by someone who is injured in your rental.

When shopping for a homeowner's or renter's policy, you should consider the important features that we cover in this section.

Dwelling coverage: The cost to rebuild

How much would you have to spend to *rebuild* your home if you lost it completely in a fire, an attack of locusts, or whatever? The cost to rebuild should be based on the size (square footage) of your home. Neither the purchase price nor the size of your mortgage has anything to do with how much *dwelling coverage* you need.

If you're a renter, rejoice that you don't need this coverage. If you're a condominium owner, find out whether the coverage that the condo association has bought for the entire building is sufficient.

Be sure that your homeowner's policy includes a *guaranteed replacement cost* provision. This useful feature ensures that the insurance company will rebuild the home even if the cost of construction is more than the policy coverage. If the insurance company underestimates your dwelling coverage, then *it* has to make up the difference.

Unfortunately, insurers define guaranteed replacement cost differently. Some companies pay for the full replacement cost of the home, no matter how much it ends up costing. Other insurers set limits. For example, some insurers may pay up to only 25 percent more than the dwelling coverage on your policy. Ask your insurer how it defines guaranteed replacement cost.

If you have an older property that has many costly-to-replace features that do not meet building codes, consider buying a rider that pays for code upgrades. This covers the cost of rebuilding your home to comply with building codes that are more stringent today than when your home was built. Ask your insurance company what your basic policy covers and what it doesn't cover. Some companies include a certain amount (for example, 10 percent of your dwelling coverage) for code upgrades in the base policy.

Personal property coverage

On a homeowner's policy, the amount of personal property coverage is typically derived from the amount of dwelling coverage you carry. Generally, you get personal property coverage of 50 to 75 percent of the dwelling coverage. This is usually more than enough.

We are not fans of riders that you can buy to cover jewellery, computers, furs, and other somewhat costly items that may not be fully covered by typical homeowner's policies. Ask yourself if your out-of-pocket expense from the loss of such items would constitute a financial catastrophe. Unless you have tens of thousands of dollars' worth of jewellery or computer equipment, for example, skip such riders.

Some policies come with *replacement-cost guarantees,* which pay you for the cost to replace an item. This payment can be considerably more than what a used item was worth before it was damaged or stolen. When this feature is not part of the standard policy sold by your insurer, you may want to purchase it as a rider, if available.

As a renter or condominium owner, you need to choose a dollar amount of the personal property that you want covered. Tally it up instead of guessing — the total cost of replacing all your personal property may surprise you.

Make a list — or even better, take pictures or make a video — of your belongings with an estimate of what they're worth. Keep this list updated; you'll need it if you have to file a claim. Keeping receipts for major purchases may also help your case. No matter how you document your belongings, don't forget to keep the documentation somewhere besides your home — otherwise, it could be destroyed along with the rest of your house in a fire or other disaster.

Liability insurance

Liability insurance protects you financially against lawsuits arising from bad things that happen to others on your property, including wounds inflicted by the family pit bull or terrible tabby (of course, you should keep Bruno restrained during guests' visits, even those from your in-laws). At a minimum, get enough insurance to cover your financial assets. Buying extra coverage is inexpensive and well worth the cost. With the number and size of liability lawsuits in Canada rising, $1 million in coverage is certainly not excessive.

The probability of being sued is low, but if you are sued and lose you could owe big bucks. If you have substantial assets to protect, you might consider an umbrella or excess liability policy (which we discuss later in this chapter).

Liability protection is one of the side benefits of purchasing a renter's policy — you protect your personal property as well as insure against lawsuits. (But don't be reckless with your banana peels if you get liability insurance!)

Flood and earthquake insurance

As we recommend in Chapter 16, purchase the broadest possible coverage when buying any type of insurance. The problem with homeowner's insurance is that it is not comprehensive enough — it doesn't typically cover losses due to earthquakes and floods. You must buy such disaster coverage piecemeal.

If an earthquake or flood struck your area and your home was destroyed, without proper coverage you would be out tens, if not hundreds, of thousands of dollars. Yet, many people don't carry these important coverages, often due to misconceptions:

- ✔ **"Not in my neighbourhood."** Many people mistakenly believe that earthquakes, for example, occur only in California and Japan. We wish this were true for those of you who live in the true North, strong and free, but it's not. Vancouver is built on a major fault line, and known (though not very active) fault lines lie in eastern Canada, including the Ottawa-Hull region. The cost of earthquake coverage is based on insurance companies' assessment of the risk of your area and property type, so you shouldn't decide whether to buy insurance based on how small you think the risk is. The risk is already built into the price.

  Floods can also be a very real and potentially financially devastating hazard, as those who lived in southern Manitoba when the Red River overflowed its banks in 1997 found out. Floods have also caused extensive and costly damage in many other parts of the country, including Quebec, Ontario, and Alberta. Like earthquakes, floods are not a covered risk in standard homeowner's policies, so you need to purchase a flood-insurance rider. Check with your current homeowner's insurer or with those recommended in this chapter.

- ✔ **"The government will bail me out."** The vast majority of government financial assistance is through low-interest loans. Loans, unfortunately, need to be repaid, and the money comes out of your pocket. Even if you do receive government money with no strings attached, it may be a long time in coming and likely won't come anywhere near to covering all of your losses.

- ✔ **"In a major disaster, insurers would go bankrupt anyway."** This is highly unlikely given the reserves that insurers are required to keep and the fact that the insurance companies *reinsure* — that is, they buy insurance to back up the policies they write.

The only homeowners at risk who might consider not buying earthquake or flood coverage are people who have little equity in their property and who are willing to walk away from the property and the mortgage in the event of a major quake or flood. Keep in mind that doing so damages your credit report because you will have essentially defaulted on your loan.

You may be able to pay for much of the cost of earthquake or flood insurance by raising the deductibles on the main part of your homeowner's/renter's insurance and other insurance policies, such as those for autos. You can more easily afford the smaller claims, not the big ones. If you think flood or earthquake insurance is too costly, compare those costs with the costs you will incur to completely replace your home and personal property. Buy this insurance if you live in an area that has a chance of being affected by these catastrophes.

To help keep the cost of earthquake insurance down, consider taking a 10 percent deductible. Most insurers offer deductibles of 5 or 10 percent of the cost to rebuild your home. Ten percent of the rebuilding cost is a good chunk of money. But what you want to insure against is losing the other 90 percent.

Deductibles

As we discuss in Chapter 16, the point of insurance is to protect against catastrophic losses, not the little losses. By taking the highest deductibles you're comfortable with, you'll save on insurance premiums year after year, and you won't have to go through the hassle of filing small claims.

Special discounts

You may qualify for special discounts. Companies and agents that sell home-owner's and renter's insurance don't always check to see if you're eligible for discounts. After all, the more you spend on policy premiums, the more money they make! If your property has a security system, if you are older, or if you have other policies with the same insurer, you may qualify for a lower rate. Don't forget to ask.

Where to buy homeowner's or renter's insurance

Each insurance company prices its homeowner's and renter's policies based on its own criteria. So the lowest-cost company for your friend's property might not be so for yours. You have to shop around at several companies to find the best rates. The following is a list of companies that historically offer lower-cost policies for most people and that have decent track records with customer satisfaction and payment of claims:

- ✔ **Belair Direct** (800-268-8551 or `www.belairdirect.com`)
- ✔ **Certas Direct Insurance** (formerly CIBC Insurance) (888-275-2422 or `www.certasinsurance.com`)
- ✔ **Direct Protect** (800-810-4990 or `www.directprotect.com`)
- ✔ **e-Insurers** (800-565-5386 or `www.e-insurers.com`)
- ✔ **RBC Insurance** (800-769-2526 or `www.rbcinsurance.ca`)
- ✔ **TD Insurance** (800-338-0218 or `www.tdbank.ca/tdinsurance`)
- ✔ **Zenith Insurance** (800-531-8080 or `www.zenithinsurance.ca`)

Don't worry that some of these companies require you to call an 800 number for a price quote. This doesn't mean they are unreachable. This process saves you money because these insurers don't have to pay commissions to local agents hawking their policies. These companies have local claims representatives to help you when and if you do have a claim.

A number of the previously named companies sell other types of insurance (for example, life insurance). But don't assume that if they offer the best value in home (or auto) insurance, their other offerings are as competitively priced.

You may have access to more specific information for your province. Some provincial insurance departments conduct surveys of insurers' prices and tabulate complaints received. Look up your province's department of insurance phone number in the government blue pages of your local phone directory, or visit the Canadian Council of Insurance Regulators Web site at www.ccir.org to find links to each province's department that oversees insurance companies.

The Financial Service Commission of Ontario publishes an annual consumer claims satisfaction survey. You'll find it online at www.fsco.gov.on.ca. Go to the section called "Consumer Brochures," and click on the "claimsin" icon.

Auto Insurance

Over the course of your life, you'll probably spend tens of thousands of dollars on auto insurance. Much of the money that people spend on auto insurance is not spent where it is most needed. In other cases, it is simply wasted. You should look for the following important features when searching for an auto insurance policy.

Third-party liability insurance

As with homeowner's liability insurance, auto liability insurance provides insurance against lawsuits. Especially in a car, accidents happen. Third-party liability insurance protects you against two events. The *bodily injury liability* component covers you if your vehicle injures someone else. *Property damage liability insurance* covers you against damage caused by your vehicle to someone else's property.

If you are just beginning to accumulate assets, do not mistakenly assume that you do not need liability protection — it's a provincial requirement.

Typically your premiums for the two coverages are broken out, but there is one single combined figure for your total liability coverage. The provincial requirements are quite low — $50,000 to $200,000, depending on where you live. Make sure that you have at least enough to cover your assets. (Coverage of double to five times your assets is preferable.) Don't forget that your future earnings, which are an "asset," can be garnished in a lawsuit. You may want to consider a total of $1 million, or even $1.5 to $2 million. The cost will still make up only a small portion of your total annual premiums.

Uninsured or underinsured motorist liability

When you are in an accident with another motorist and he doesn't carry his own liability protection or doesn't carry enough, *uninsured or underinsured motorist liability coverage* allows you to collect for lost wages, medical expenses, and pain and suffering incurred in the accident.

Should you already have comprehensive health and long-term disability insurance, then uninsured or underinsured motorist liability coverage is largely redundant. However, this coverage is mandatory.

To provide a death benefit to those financially dependent on you in the event of a fatal auto accident, buy term life insurance (see Chapter 17).

Coping with teen drivers

If you have a teenage driver in your household, in addition to worrying a lot more, you are going to be spending a lot more on auto insurance. Try to keep your teenager out of your car as long as possible. It's the best advice we can offer.

If you allow your teenager to drive, you can take a number of steps to avoid spending all of your take-home pay on auto insurance bills:

✔ Make sure that your teen does well in school. Some insurers offer discounts if your child is a high academic achiever and has successfully completed an extra-curricular driver's education class.

✔ Get price quotes from several insurers to see how adding your teen driver to your policy affects the cost.

✔ Have your teenager share in the costs of using the car. If you pay all the insurance, gas, oil changing, and maintenance bills, your teenager won't value the privilege of using your "free" car.

Of course, letting teens drive shouldn't just be about keeping your insurance bills to a minimum. Auto accidents are the No. 1 cause of death for teens. So, before you let your teen drive, be sure to educate him about the big risks of driving and the importance of not riding in a car driven by someone who is intoxicated. Also be sure that your teens drive in safe cars.

Deductibles

To keep your auto insurance premiums down and to eliminate the need to file small claims, take the highest deductibles you are comfortable with (most people should consider $500 to $1,000). On an auto policy, two deductibles exist: *collision* and *comprehensive.* Collision applies to claims arising from collisions (note that some policies allow you to bypass collision coverage when you rent a car if you have collision coverage on your own policy. Don't assume your coverage will apply to a rental car, though. Be sure to first read through your policy or ask the person who sold you your policy). Comprehensive applies to other claims for damages not caused by collision (for example, a window broken by vandals).

As your car ages and is worth less, you can eventually eliminate your comprehensive and collision coverages altogether. The point at which you do this is up to you. Remember that the purpose of insurance is to compensate you for losses that are financially catastrophic to you. For some people, this amount may be as high as $5,000 or more — others would choose $1,000 as their threshold point. Insurers won't pay more than the book value of your car, regardless of what it costs to repair or replace it.

Special discounts

You may be eligible for special discounts on auto insurance. Don't forget to tell your agent or insurer if your car has a security alarm, air bags, or antilock brakes. If you're older or have other policies or cars insured with the same insurer, you may also qualify for discounts. And make sure that you're given appropriate "good driver" discounts if you've been accident- and ticket-free in recent years.

And here's another idea: *Before* you buy your next car, call insurers and ask for insurance quotes for the different models that you're considering. The cost of insuring a car should factor into your decision as to which car you buy because the insurance costs will be a major portion of your car's ongoing operating expenses.

Little-stuff coverage to skip

Auto insurers have dreamed up all sorts of riders, such as towing and rental car reimbursement. On the surface, these riders appear to be inexpensive. But the riders are expensive given the little that you'd collect from a claim plus the hassle of filing.

Overlooked auto insurance: Safe driving

A pipe bomb explodes in a crowded park and kills a person. An airplane crashes and several dozen people die.

Such tragic events are well-covered by our media, but the number of deaths that make the front pages of our newspapers pales in comparison to the approximately 3,500 people who die on Canada's roads every year.

We're not suggesting that our national media should start reporting every automobile fatality. Even 24 hours of daily *Newsworld* coverage probably could not keep up with all the accidents on our roads. But the real story with auto fatalities lies not in the who, what, and where of specific accidents but in the why. When we ask that question, we see how many of them are preventable.

No matter what kind of car you drive, you can and should drive safely. Stay within the speed limits and don't drive while intoxicated or tired, or in adverse weather conditions. Wear your seat belt — a U.S. Department of Transportation study found that 60 percent of auto passengers killed were not wearing their seat belts. And don't try to talk on your cell phone and write notes on a pad of paper attached to your dashboard while balancing your coffee cup between your legs!

You can also greatly reduce your risk of dying in an accident by driving a safe car. You don't need to spend buckets of money to get a car with airbags, reinforced sides, front- and rear-impact resistance, and good visibility. The *Consumer Reports* annual auto buying guide and Phil Edmonston's annual *Lemon-Aid* car guides all contain lots of good information on individual car model safety.

Riders that waive the deductible under certain circumstances make no sense, either. The point of the deductible is to reduce your policy cost and the hassle of filing small claims.

Accident benefits coverage replaces some of your income that is lost due to an accident, and pays for some other medical and rehabilitation expenses. If you are killed, this coverage also will pay some funeral expenses as well as payments to your survivors. If you and your passengers are covered by a provincial health plan and have disability insurance, this coverage isn't really necessary, especially if you also are covered by an extended health benefit plan. However, a minimum level of this coverage is required in almost all provinces.

Roadside assistance, towing, and rental car reimbursement coverage will pay only small dollar amounts and aren't worth buying. In fact, if you belong to an automobile club, you may already have some of these coverages.

Where to buy auto insurance

You can use the same list presented earlier in this chapter for homeowner's insurers to obtain quotes for auto insurance.

Umbrella Insurance

Umbrella or *excess liability* insurance is additional liability insurance that is added on top of the liability protection on your home and car(s). If you had $1,000,000 liability insurance on both your property and auto insurance, you could buy a 2.5-million-dollar umbrella liability policy for around $200 a year to add to the existing liability insurance that you have on your home and car. This is a small cost for big protection. There is a growing trend in Canada of people who are hit with lawsuits of more than one million dollars related to their cars and homes.

Umbrella or excess liability insurance is generally sold in increments of one million dollars. So how do you decide how much you need if you have a lot of assets? As we've said with other insurance coverages, you should have at least enough liability insurance to protect your assets and preferably enough to cover twice the value of those assets.

Purchasing umbrella or excess liability insurance through your existing homeowner's or auto insurance company is usually necessary.

Estate Planning

Estate planning is the process of determining what will happen to your assets after you die. Thinking about this in the context of insurance may seem a bit odd. But the time and cost of various estate-planning manoeuvres is really nothing more than buying insurance: You are ensuring that after you die, everything will be taken care of as you wish and that taxes will be minimized. Thinking about it in this way can help you to better evaluate whether certain options make sense at particular points in your life.

Investment insurance

Insurance companies do not sell policies that protect the value of your investments. But you can shield your portfolio from many of the dangers of a fickle market through diversification.

If all of your money is invested in bank accounts or bonds, you're exposed to the risks of inflation, which can erode your money's purchasing power. Conversely, if the bulk of your money is invested in one high-risk stock, your financial future could go up in smoke if that stock explodes.

Chapter 9 discusses the benefits of diversification and how to choose investments that do well under different conditions. Chapter 10 discusses why mutual funds are powerful investment vehicles that make diversification easy and cost-effective.

Depending upon your circumstances, you may eventually want to contact a lawyer who specializes in estate-planning matters. However, educating yourself first about the different options is worth your time. More than a few lawyers have their own agendas (increased fees) about what you should do, so be careful. And most of the estate-planning strategies that you're likely to benefit from do not require hiring a lawyer.

Wills, living wills, and medical powers of attorney

When you have children who are minors (dependants), a *will* is a necessity. A will names the guardian to whom you entrust your children if both you and your spouse die. Should you and your spouse both die without a will (called *intestate*), the province (courts and social service agencies) decides who will raise your children. Therefore, even if you cannot decide at this time who would raise your children, you should *at least* appoint a trusted guardian who could decide for you.

A will still makes good sense even if you don't have kids because it gives instructions on how to handle and distribute all your worldly possessions. When you die without a will, your province decides how to distribute your money and other property, according to provincial law. Therefore, your friends, more-distant relatives, and favourite charities will probably receive nothing.

Without a will, your heirs are legally powerless, and the province may appoint a public executor to supervise the distribution of your assets at a fee of around 5 percent of your estate. A bond typically must also be posted at a cost of several hundred dollars.

Living wills and a medical power of attorney are useful additions to a standard will. A *living will* tells your doctor what, if any, life-support measures you would prefer or do not want. A *medical power of attorney* grants authority to someone you trust to make decisions with a physician regarding your medical care options.

If you are struggling with a life-threatening disease or condition, you and you alone should be able to decide when to keep on battling and when to cease trying to actively defeat your illness. Write to your provincial and federal MPs and demand that living wills be given full legal standing.

The simplest and least costly way to prepare a will, a living will, and a medical power of attorney is to begin by using a high-quality, user-friendly software packages. You may then want to have a lawyer go over them for you to ensure you've covered all the bases and the documents are legally sound. Be sure to give copies of these documents to the guardians and executors named in the documents.

You don't need a lawyer to make a legal will. Most lawyers, in fact, prepare wills and living trusts using software packages! What makes a will *valid* is that it is witnessed by two people — and signed by you, of course!

Probate and living trusts

Because of our quirky legal system, even if you have a will, some or all of your assets must go through a court process known as *probate*. Probate is the legal process for administering and implementing the directions in a will.

Probate can be a lengthy, expensive hassle for your heirs — with fees ranging as high as 1.5 percent of the value of the estate, depending on your province. In addition, your assets become a matter of public record as a result of probate.

Property and assets that are owned in joint tenancy generally pass to heirs without having to go through probate. If you have designated a beneficiary, proceeds from an RRSP, RRIF, or insurance policy also do not require probate. Your family home, joint bank account, and other assets should also not be subject to probate if you register their ownership as "*joint and survivor.*" Most other assets pass through probate.

A *living trust* effectively transfers assets into a trust. You control those assets and can revoke the trust whenever you desire. The advantage of a living trust is that, upon your death, assets can pass directly to your beneficiaries without going through probate.

Living trusts are likely to be of greatest value to people who meet the following criteria:

- Age 60 and older
- Single
- Assets worth more than $1,000,000 that must pass through probate (including real estate, non–retirement plans, and small business)

As with a will, you do *not* need a lawyer to establish a legal and valid living trust. Legal fees to establish a living trust can range from $700 to $2,000 and higher. A competent lawyer who charges reasonable fees is of greatest value to people with large estates (see the next section) who do not have the time, desire, and expertise to maximize the value derived from estate planning.

Note: Living trusts keep assets out of probate but have nothing to do with minimizing capital gains taxes triggered when you die.

Estate planning to minimize taxes when you die

While Canada doesn't have estate taxes like the U.S., your death will likely result in one final tax bill, and a potentially large one! When you die, the government taxes your assets such as stocks, real estate, and so on as if you had sold them all at their fair market value at the time of your death. If those assets are worth more than their purchase price, the result will generally be a taxable capital gain.

The key exception to this rule is if you leave your assets to your spouse, including a common-law spouse. In this case, the assets simply transfer tax-free to your spouse. When they in turn die, the difference between the original purchase price and their market value at that time will be used to calculate any taxable gains. The rule also doesn't apply if you leave your assets to a spousal trust.

Assets in registered plans such as an RRSP or RRIF are treated as regular income in the year that you die. To avoid this, name your spouse as the beneficiary of any RRSPs or RRIFs. Your spouse can then transfer the assets to their own RRSP or RRIF.

Whether or not you need to do some planning to reduce the tax bill that will arise when you die depends on several issues. First and most important is how much of your assets you will use up during your life. This depends on how much your assets grow over time, as well as how rapidly you spend money. During retirement, you will (hopefully) be using your money.

We've seen too many affluent individuals worry throughout their retirement how taxes will impact their estate. If your intention is to leave your money to your children, grandchildren, or a charity, why not start giving while you're still alive so that you can enjoy the act? There are no limitations on the amount of money you can give away to adult family members other than your spouse. By giving away money, you reduce your estate and, therefore, the amount of money that may be subject to tax.

If you give assets to your spouse while you are living, you'll be subject to the attribution rules. If you give money or investments, such as stocks or bonds, the government attributes any income or loss or any capital gains (or losses) back to you. If you give your children or others assets beyond cold hard cash, there may also be a tax bill to pay. If you give away assets, Revenue Canada deems that you have sold those assets at their market value. Any difference between what you paid and the value at the time you gave them away will be deemed a taxable capital gain.

In addition to gifting, establishing in your will that a trust will be set up when you die — a *testamentary trust* — can also help reduce taxes. With a testamentary trust, you can choose to have some or all of your assets transferred to the trust when you die, with your intended heirs named as the beneficiaries.

The advantage of a testamentary trust is that it's taxed as if it were a separate individual. As a result, it can take advantage of our graduated tax rates. For example, say you had assets that would earn $25,000 a year. If you left those assets directly to an heir, that income would be added to their existing yearly income, and might get taxed at the top marginal tax bracket of around 50 percent. On the other hand, that same income — if it belonged to a trust — would be taxed at the lowest tax rate of around 24 percent. In addition to set-up fees trusts have other costs, including trustee fees, along with the need to file a tax return for the trust each year.

Buying cash-value life insurance is another estate planning tool, but one which, unfortunately, is overused. People who sell cash-value insurance — that is, insurance salespeople and others masquerading as financial planners — too often advocate life insurance as the one and only way to deal with minimizing taxes upon your death. In reality, other methods are usually superior in most cases because they don't require wasting money on life insurance.

Small-business owners whose businesses are worth $1,000,000 or more may want to consider cash-value life insurance under specialized circumstances. If you lack the necessary additional assets to pay expected taxes and you don't want your beneficiaries to be forced to sell the business, you can buy cash-value life insurance to pay expected taxes.

Part V

Where to Go for More Help

The 5th Wave   By Rich Tennant

"You may want to talk to Phil-he's one of our more aggressive financial planners."

In this part . . .

We help you sift through the morass of financial resources competing for your attention and dollars. Many people who call themselves financial planners claim to be able to make you rich, but we show you how you may end up poorer if you don't choose an adviser wisely. Finally, we discuss how to benefit from the financial coverage in print and on the air while sidestepping problematic advice in those media.

Chapter 19
Financial Planners

"*The financial planning business has two problems. One is credibility, and the other is conflict of interest.*"

— Fortune *magazine*

"*When I was a child, my father told me to pick a field where you only need to be mediocre to be great. I chose personal financial planning.*"

— financial planner Jim Schwartz, as quoted in *The Wall Street Journal*

Hiring a competent, ethical, and unbiased financial planner or adviser to help you make and implement financial decisions *can* be money well spent. But if you pick a poor adviser or someone who really isn't a financial planner but a salesperson in disguise, things could get worse instead of better. So before we talk about the different types of help to hire, let's take a little journey with Alice to give you an idea of what you're up against in the land of financial planners. (Don't give up hope, though! Later on in the chapter we offer advice on how to find objective, cost-effective financial help.)

Alice in Financial-Planner Land

This is the true story of Alice and her search for financial help. Her story illustrates many of the pitfalls in finding a good financial planner.

Alice's adventures

First, on the recommendation of her accountant, Alice called a *financial consultant,* who was a *certified financial planner* (CFP) at a well-known investment (brokerage) firm. Although Alice explained that she wanted a conservative investment, the broker sold her a mutual fund that, unbeknownst to Alice, primarily held *aggressive growth* (volatile) stocks.

After buying the fund and getting her first account statement a few days later, Alice noticed that there were several thousand dollars less in the fund than she had invested. The broker had told her he earned a 4 percent commission, but assured her that she need not concern herself with it because the fund paid him and it wouldn't affect her investment.

After a little investigation, Alice discovered that the fund had, in fact, paid the broker out of her investment — a hefty 6.5 percent commission. Thus, the broker had not only lied about where the commission dollars came from (all such commissions come from the investors' money), but he had also understated the size of his commission.

Understandably steamed, Alice called the regulating agency, and after she jumped through many hoops, the brokerage firm coughed up nearly $2,000 for the broker's fib about the commission amount.

Thinking that perhaps men and women simply don't communicate well, Alice next turned to a female financial planner on the recommendation of a friend. The planner told Alice: "Women need to stick together." Then she promptly tried to sell Alice a limited partnership that, the planner said, was *sure* to return upward of 20 to 40 percent per year.

Alice took a gander at the *prospectus* — a delightfully long document written by lawyers — and saw in black and white on page two that the partnership paid the selling broker a 10 percent sales commission (which, she now knew, would be deducted from her investment).

Because Alice is a conscientious investor, she did more research in financial books and magazines and learned that limited partnerships are also handicapped by high, ongoing management fees. Alice did not return the dozen or so follow-up calls ("to see how you are doing") from her "sister" financial planner and fortunately passed on the partnership.

Wanting to learn more before her next attempt to get help, Alice enrolled in an "adult education class" at a local college. Alice, a student eager to learn, attended all the classes but soon felt only more confused. The world of finance and investments, her teacher said, is *very, very complicated.* Unless, of course, you're a financial expert.

The teacher, a "certified financial planner," told the class that he was just such an expert. He offered a free, one-hour consultation to all his students at the end of his "course." During her free session, Alice was told that she should invest in an *annuity*. Investigation, however, revealed (you guessed it) high sales commissions and management fees.

Alice was also uncomfortable because planner number three hadn't inquired about other aspects of her situation and seemed intent only on selling her an annuity. Annuities did not make sense for her, she later learned, because she was nearly retired and in a low tax bracket.

At this point, most people probably would have bought a good financial book or put their money in a mattress or the next best place — their local bank — but Alice really wanted to talk to someone about her money issues and ideas.

After listening to a financial planner on a radio call-in program, Alice had the planner mail his background materials to her. In addition to a certified-financial-planning credential, *this* planner had a seemingly endless list of other lofty-sounding credentials, such as RIA, BSCE, LLB, and MBA.

Quite wary of sales commissions by now, Alice also liked the sound of the planner's fee: $350 for his time to help with her investment decisions and to discuss her other financial questions. Partway through their two-hour, $350 consultation, however, planner number four tried to persuade Alice that what she really needed was to hire him as an ongoing manager of her money. For just $2,000 per year for the service (commissions and management fees were extra), he would trade her in and out of investments based on his economic analyses and expert prognostications.

That seemed like a lot of money to Alice, who had $150,000 to invest, and she did not like the thought of turning over her money to someone who could move it around among various investments without her approval. Besides, she was interested in learning more about finance, and this "planner" kept telling her how complicated it is to make investing and other financial decisions. Alice therefore declined planner number four's sales pitch for managing her investments, whereupon the moody planner stormed out of her house, complaining that she had wasted his time (for which he had in hand his $350 cheque for a mere two hours!).

Lessons learned from Alice's journey

Alice's case highlights four major problems that people often encounter when hiring financial help:

✔ First, you absolutely, positively *must* do your homework before hiring any financial adviser. Just look at Alice: Despite enthusiastic recommendations from her accountant and a friend, Alice ended up with bad advice from biased advisers.

✔ Second, the financial planning and brokerage fields are minefields for consumers. The fundamental problem is the enormous conflict of interest that is created when "advisers" sell products that earn them sales commissions to people who believe they are getting unbiased advice. Selling ongoing money management services, as Alice learned from the last "adviser," creates conflicts of interest as well.

As an analogy, imagine that you have flu symptoms. Would you be comfortable seeing a physician who didn't charge for office visits but made money only by selling you drugs? Maybe you don't *need* the drugs — or at least not so many expensive ones. Maybe what you really need is Mom's chicken soup and 16 hours of sleep.

In its review of the financial planning industry, *Consumer Reports* said, "Financial planners often end up being wolves in sheep's clothing with hidden agendas to sell mutual funds, for example, or life insurance." Respected financial columnist Jane Bryant Quinn of *Newsweek* says, "Planners are supposed to pull apart your finances and suggest better ways of meeting your goals. They purport to be objective. But they can't be if they work for brokerage firms or insurance companies or if their income depends on sales commissions from the products they sell."

✔ Third, financial advisers often like to make things far more complicated than need be, and they're generally not interested in educating you. As others have observed, financial planning is hardly the only occupation guilty of this. As author George Bernard Shaw put it, "All professions are conspiracies against the laity."

The more you know and the more you realize that investing and other financial decisions needn't be complicated, the more you'll realize you don't need to spend gobs of money, or any money at all, on financial planners and advisers. If you look in the mirror, you see the person who is most qualified to be your best financial adviser and who has your best interests at heart.

✔ Fourth, don't place a whole lot of faith in credentials, especially the Certified Financial Planning (CFP) moniker, which *Forbes* magazine columnist Gretchen Morgensen called a "meaningless label," adding, "When picking a financial planner, pay a lot of attention to how the planner is compensated. Pay no attention to CFPs. . . ."

What's truly amazing about Alice's situation is that none of the so-called financial "planners" ever bothered to ask about her insurance and debt situation. As it turns out, Alice not only lacked adequate homeowner's insurance, but she also amazingly had no health insurance!

The credentialization of Canada: What credentials qualify a financial adviser?

It seems that everywhere we turn today, more and more people carry credentials after their names. We have certified lactation consultants, certified foot reflexologists, and registered dietitians.

Among salespeople, especially in the financial services industry, the use of dubious credentials and self-anointed and misleading titles is on the rise. Stockbrokers are no longer called stockbrokers — they are "financial consultants" and "financial advisers." Some life insurance agents now call themselves "estate planning specialists." Next thing you know, when you visit an auto dealer, you'll speak with a certified transportation consultant, and when you buy your next home, it will be through a certified housing consultant rather than a real estate agent. It seems that everything today is *certified* — even the once "used car" is now referred to by some dealers as "certified pre-owned"!

Speaking of "certified," tens of thousands of people have earned the Certified Financial Planning credential. This is basically a home-study course that, unlike gaining entrance into medical, law, or business school, virtually anyone can undertake. The test itself isn't difficult to pass — an astounding 74 percent of people recently enrolled in the U.S. College for Financial Planning passed the CFP test. Gaining admission to a top professional school and becoming an architect, attorney, or doctor is exponentially more difficult and demanding.

The CFP Board of Standards, which licenses the CFP credential, claims that the combination of passing a test and meeting continuing education requirements ensures that their profession is doing the best that it can. To that, we and others who regularly observe CFP incompetence and conflicts of interest, politely say "Bunk!"

✔ The CFP tests nothing of a planner's business ethics or how the planner earns income.

✔ The CFP exam covers arcane financial details, which are rarely encountered by consumer-oriented planners and could easily be contained in a handy reference book.

✔ The CFP curriculum has little practical information on the important topics of asset allocation and mutual fund selection.

✔ And the few individuals who don't pass the CFP exam on the first try are told what answers they got wrong so that they can focus their time memorizing the trivial details and pass the exam on the second try.

Boston Globe columnist Charles Jaffe took the CFP exam and concluded that ". . . financial planning is a long way from qualifying as a profession."

Unfortunately, the vast majority of people with CFPs work on commission and are employed by securities and insurance brokerage firms, so they're not really financial planners so much as salespeople with a "credential." Most of the rest sell ongoing money management services.

Meeting the CFP continuing education requirements is also a bit of a sham. CFPs can attend what amount to sales presentations by companies pitching financial products to earn continuing education credit hours. Another method is for CFPs to read financial planning journals, which have multiple choice and true–false questions in the back. The planner can take the test on his or her own time and even refer to the relevant articles to find the answers!

If you are interested in hiring financial help, be sure to read "Interviewing a Potential Financial Adviser," later in this chapter, where we detail questions you should ask a financial adviser before you hire him or her, including how to make sense of all the credential gobbledygook.

Alice also had some relatively high-interest consumer debt that none of the "planners" ever asked about, probably because paying off her debt would have diminished the funds that Alice would have available for investment. Alice could afford both the insurance and debt payoff. In short, no one had taken the time to explain to Alice the costs and risks of not getting her financial house in order.

Finally, in case you're wondering, Alice did happily invest her money in a nice portfolio of commission-free mutual funds (see Chapter 10), which have been performing just swimmingly for her over the years.

Your Financial Management Options

Everyone has three basic choices about how to approach managing money: You can do nothing, you can do it yourself, or you can hire someone to help you.

Doing nothing

The *do-nothing* approach has a large following (and you thought you were the only one!). People who fall into this category may be leading terribly exciting, interesting lives and are therefore too busy to attend to something as mundane as dealing with their personal finances. Or they may be leading terribly mundane lives but are too busy fantasizing about more appealing ways to spend their time. For both types, everything from a major UFO sighting to taking out the garbage captures the imagination more than thinking about financial management.

But the dangers of doing nothing are many. Problem areas, left to themselves, get worse. Putting off saving for retirement or ignoring your buildup of debt eventually comes back to haunt you. Not carrying adequate insurance can be devastating when an accident occurs. Fires in the west, flooding in the prairies, and even ice storms in Ontario and Quebec all show how precariously we live in paradise.

Even if the do-nothing approach has been yours all your life, you are now officially promoted out of it! You bought this book to learn more about personal finance and to make changes in your money matters, right? So take control and keep reading!

Doing it yourself

The do-it-yourselfers learn enough about financial topics to make informed decisions on their own. Doing anything yourself, of course, requires you to invest some time to learn the basic concepts and keep up with changes. For some, personal financial management becomes a challenging and absorbing interest. Others focus on what they need to do to get the job done efficiently.

It's a myth that if you self-direct your finances and make your own decisions, you will spend endless hours doing so. The harder part for most people is catching up to where they should be and correcting past mistakes. After you get things in order, which you can easily do with this book as your companion, you should not need to spend more than an hour or two every few months on your personal finances (unless a major issue, like a real estate purchase, comes up).

Some in the financial advisory business like to make things seem so complicated that they compare what they do to brain surgery! Their argument goes, "You wouldn't perform brain surgery on yourself, so why would you manage your money yourself?" Well, to this we say, personal financial management *ain't* brain surgery — not even close. You can manage on your own and, in fact, you can do better than what most advisers can do for you. Why? Because, you're not subject to conflicts of interest, and you care the most about your money.

Hiring financial help

Realizing that you need to hire someone to help you make and implement financial decisions can be a valuable insight. Spending a few hours and several hundred dollars to hire a competent professional can be money well spent, even if you have a modest income or assets. But you need to know what your money is buying.

Financial planners or advisers make money in one of three ways:

- ✔ They can earn commissions based on sales of financial products.
- ✔ They can charge a percentage of your assets that they are investing.
- ✔ They can charge by the hour.

As you can see from Alice's journey into this area at the beginning of this chapter, hiring financial assistance can be anything but a tea party. The following sections help you differentiate among the three main types of financial planners.

Commission-based "planners"

Commission-based planners may not really be planners, advisers, or counsellors at all — they may be basically salespeople. Many *stockbrokers* and *insurance brokers* of prior decades are now called *financial consultants* or *financial service representatives* in order to glamorize the profession and obscure how they are compensated. Ditto for insurance salespeople calling themselves *estate planning specialists.*

That's like a Honda dealer calling himself a *transportation consultant.* A Honda dealer is a salesperson who makes a living selling Hondas, period. He's definitely not going to tell you nice things about Ford, Chrysler, or Toyota cars — unless, of course, he happens to sell those, too. He also has no interest in educating you about money-saving public transit possibilities!

As we discuss earlier in this chapter, salespeople and brokers masquerading as planners can have an enormous self-interest when they push certain products, particularly those products that pay generous commissions. Being paid on commission can tend to skew their recommendations toward certain strategies (such as buying investment or life insurance products) and causes the salespeople to ignore or downplay other aspects of your finances. For example, they'll gladly sell you an investment rather than persuade you to pay off your high-interest debts.

If you have built up a relationship with a commission-based planner who you feel is trustworthy and who's advice takes in your larger financial circumstances, great. Just remember that they are still getting paid — they make their money through the commissions on the products they sell you. In other words, you are still paying for their services, so regularly reassess whether you are getting your money's worth.

Table 19-1 gives you an idea of the commissions that a financial planner/salesperson can earn through selling particular financial products.

Table 19-1	Financial Product Commissions
Product	*Commission*
Life insurance ($250,000, age 45):	
Term life	$150 to $600
Universal/whole life	$1,020 to $2,580
Disability insurance:	
$4,000/month benefit, age 35	$345 to $1,200
Investments ($20,000):	
Mutual funds	$200 to $1,200
Limited partnerships	$1,400 to $2,000
Annuities	$1,000 to $1,800

Percentage-of-assets-under-management advisers

A generally better choice than a commission-based planner is a financial adviser who charges a percentage of the assets that are being managed or invested. This compensation system removes the incentives to sell you products with high commissions and to initiate lots of transactions to generate more of those commissions.

Although it is an improvement over product-pushers working on commission, the fee-based system has flaws, too. First off, suppose that you're trying to decide whether to invest in stocks, bonds, or real estate. A planner who earns her living managing your money may not recommend real estate because that would deplete your investment capital. The planner also may not recommend paying down your mortgage for the same reason — she'll claim that you can earn more investing your money (with her help, of course) than it will cost you to borrow.

Fee-based planners are also sometimes interested in managing money only for those who have already accumulated a fair amount of it — which rules out most people.

Hourly based advisers

Often your best bet for professional help with your personal finances is an adviser who charges for his time. Because he doesn't sell any financial products, his objectivity is maintained. He doesn't perform money management, so he can help you make comprehensive financial decisions dealing with loans, retirement planning, and selecting good investments including real estate, mutual funds, and small business.

The primary risk in selecting an hourly based planner is incompetence. You can address this by checking references and learning enough yourself to discern between good and bad financial advice. Another risk comes from not clearly defining the work to be done and the approximate total cost before you begin. You should also review some of the other key questions outlined later in this chapter.

A drawback of an entirely different kind occurs when you don't follow through on the recommendations of your adviser. You paid for her work but didn't act on it, so you didn't capture its value. If part of the reason that you hired the planner in the first place was that you're too busy or not interested enough to make changes to your financial situation, then you should look for this support in the services you buy from the planner.

Should you just need someone as a sounding board for ideas or to recommend a specific strategy or product, you can hire an hourly based planner for one or two sessions of advice. You save money doing the legwork and implementation on your own. Just make sure that the planner is willing to give you specific enough advice that you can implement it.

Should You Hire a Financial Planner?

Most people reading this book don't need to hire a financial planner. But just because you're financially savvy, you shouldn't be too quick to write off the value of hiring help.

Good reasons for hiring a financial planner can be the same reasons for hiring someone to clean your home or do your taxes. If you're too busy or don't enjoy doing it or you're terribly uncomfortable making decisions on your own, using a planner for a second opinion makes good sense. And if you shy away from numbers and bristle at the thought of long division, a good planner can help you.

How a good financial planner can help

The following gives you a rundown of some of the important things a competent financial planner can assist you with.

- **Identifying problems and goals.** Many otherwise intelligent people have a hard time being objective about their financial problems. They may ignore their debts or have unrealistic goals and expectations given their financial situations and behaviours. And many are so busy with other aspects of their lives that they never take the time to think about what their financial goals are. A good financial planner can give you the objective look you need.

  Surprisingly, some people are in a better financial position than they thought in relation to their goals. Good counsellors really enjoy this aspect of their jobs — good news is easier and much more fun to deliver.

- **Identifying strategies to reach your financial goals.** Your mind may be a jumble of various plans, ideas, and concerns, along with a cobweb or two. A good counsellor can help you sort out your thoughts and can propose alternative strategies for you to consider in accomplishing your financial goals.

- **Setting priorities.** You could be doing dozens of things to improve your financial situation, but making a few key changes could probably have the greatest value. Equally important is to identify the changes that fit your overall situation and that won't keep you awake at night fretting about them. Good planners help you prioritize.

- **Saving research time and hassle.** Even if you know what major financial decisions are most important to you, doing the research can be time-consuming and frustrating if you don't know where to turn for good information and advice. A good planner does research to match your needs to the best available strategies and products. So much lousy information is out there on various financial topics that you can easily get lost, discouraged, sidetracked, or swindled. A good adviser can prevent you from making a bad decision based on poor or insufficient information.

✔ **Purchasing commission-free financial products.** When you hire a planner who charges for her time, you can easily save hundreds or thousands of dollars by avoiding the cost of commissions in the financial products you buy. This commission-free situation is especially valuable when it comes to purchasing investments and insurance.

✔ **Providing an objective voice for major decisions.** Deciding when to retire, how much to spend on a home purchase, and where to invest your money are big decisions. Getting swept up in the emotions of these issues can cloud your perspective and objectivity. A competent and sensitive adviser can cut through this cloud to raise issues and provide sound counsel.

✔ **Helping you to just do it.** Deciding what you need to do is not enough — you have to actually do it, too. And although you can use a planner for advice and make all the changes on your own, a good counsellor can help you follow through with your plan as well. After all, part of the reason you hired the adviser in the first place may be that you're too busy or uninterested to manage your finances.

✔ **Mediating.** If you have a spouse or partner, financial decisions can produce some real fireworks, particularly with financial decisions involving the extended family. Although a counsellor can't be a therapist, a good one can be sensitive to the different needs and concerns of each party and can try to find middle ground on the financial issues you're grappling with.

✔ **Making you money and allowing you peace of mind.** The whole point of professional financial planning is to help you make the most of your money and help you plan for and attain your financial and personal goals. In the process, the financial planner should show you how to enhance your investment returns; reduce your spending, taxes, and insurance costs; increase your savings; improve your insurance coverage for catastrophes; and achieve your financial independence goals. And last but not least: Putting your financial house in order should take some weight off your mind — like that clean, light-headed feeling after a haircut.

Why financial planners aren't for everyone

As we discuss in the next section, finding a good financial planner ain't easy. That's a good reason why you should be sure you want to hire an adviser before you venture out in search of a competent one.

Although some people can benefit from the advice of a knowledgeable and ethical financial planner, you should also consider your personality type before you decide to hire help. Our experience has been that some people (believe it or not) enjoy the research and number-crunching. If this is you or if you're not really comfortable taking advice, you'd be better off doing your own homework and creating your own plan.

Likewise, if you have a specific tax or legal matter, you're better off hiring a good professional who specializes in that field rather than a financial planner.

The Frustrations of Finding Good Financial Planners

Overwhelmed and undereducated consumers like Alice, especially those in low- and middle-income brackets, have few attractive options if they want to hire financial help. The vast majority of the people who call themselves *financial planners* and *financial consultants* sell products and work on commission, which, as Alice found in the previous section, creates enormous potential conflicts of interest. Those conflicts stem from the fact that the broker has an incentive to recommend strategies and sell products that pay generous commissions and to ignore strategies and products that pay no or low commissions.

Of the few financial advisers who are *fee-only,* some make most of their fees from money-management services. (*Fee-only* or *fee-based* means that the advisers' fees are paid by their clients, not by companies whose products they recommend.) Thus, fee-based advisers tend to focus on those who have already accumulated significant wealth. Fee-based advisers may also have conflicts of interest in that they gravitate toward strategies and recommendations that involve their ongoing management of your money and may ignore or dismiss tactics that diminish the pool of investment money that they can manage for you for an ongoing fee.

The following sections describe some of the problems associated with finding a good planner.

Regulatory problems

A pretty basic problem of oversight afflicts the financial planning field. Oversight is minimal *at best.* Except in Quebec, anyone can hang out a shingle and call him- or herself a financial planner.

Financial planners *should* have to disclose in writing, prior to working with a client, how they are compensated. This would make it easier for people to know how the planner earns a living. And it would eliminate much of the need for more formal government regulation.

Letting the Big Bad Wolf guard the Three Little Pigs

The International Association of Financial Planners (IAFP) and the Institute of Certified Financial Planners (ICFP) are the two primary U.S. trade associations (which are in the process of merging) that represent most financial planners. Unfortunately, these organizations tend to promote the status quo in the industry because they *are* the industry. Their membership and leadership are policing themselves. In fact, the associations have lobbied government to defeat laws aimed at regulation of their membership's sales practices rather than advocating what's ethical or best for the public.

Financial planners' top conflicts of interest

All professions have conflicts of interest. Some fields have more than others, and the financial planning field is one of those fields. Knowing where some of the land mines lie can certainly help. Here, then, are the most common reasons that planners may not have 20/20 vision when giving financial directions.

Selling and pushing products that pay commissions

If a financial planner isn't charging you a fee for his time, you can rest assured he is earning commissions on the products he'll try to sell you. In order to sell financial products, this planner must be licensed to deal in those products. A person who sells financial products and earns commissions from those products is often more of a salesperson than a financial planner. Financial planning involves taking an objective, holistic look at your financial puzzle to find the pieces that fit it well, something that many brokers are neither trained nor financially motivated to do.

To make it even harder for you to discern planners' agendas, you can *not* assume that planners who do charge fees for their time don't also earn commissions selling products. Sadly for people seeking financial advice, compensation *double-dipping* is becoming more common.

Selling products that provide a commission can tend to skew a planner's recommendations. Products that carry commissions mean that you have fewer of your dollars working in the investments and insurance you buy. Because a

"Financial planning" in banks

Over the past couple of decades, banks have witnessed an erosion of the money in their coffers and vaults. The reason is simple — increasing numbers of investors realized that banks are generally lousy places to build wealth. The highest yielding bank savings accounts and guaranteed investment certificates barely keep an investor ahead of inflation. If you factor in both inflation and taxes, these bank "investments" provide no real growth on your investment dollars.

Increasingly, banks have "financial representatives" and "investment specialists" sitting in their branches waiting to pounce on bank customers with big balances. In some banks, these "financial planners" are simply brokers who are out to sell investments that pay them (and the bank) hefty sales commissions.

Although you may expect your bank account balances to be confidential and off-limits to the eager eyes of investment salespeople in a bank, numerous studies have demonstrated that banks are betraying customer trust.

- First, many customers have no idea that these bank reps are earning commissions and that those commissions are being siphoned out of customers' investment dollars.

- Second, many customers are mistaken (partly due to the banks' and salespeople's poor disclosure) in believing that these investments, like bank savings accounts, are CDIC-insured and cannot lose value.

- Finally, many of the reps in banks are inexperienced and don't understand what they are selling and what is suitable for particular customers.

commission is earned only when a product is sold, such a product or service is often more attractive in the planner's eyes than any other option. For example, if the planner sells disability insurance that you could obtain at a lower cost through your employer or a group trade association (see Chapter 17), he may overlook or criticize your most attractive option (buying through your employer) and focus on *his* most attractive option — selling you a higher-cost disability policy on which he derives a commission.

Another danger of trusting the recommendation of a commission-based planner is that she may steer you toward the products that have the biggest payback for her. These products are among the *worst* for you because they siphon off even more of your money upfront to pay the commission. They also tend to be among the costliest and riskiest financial products available.

Planners who are also commission-greedy may try to *churn* your investments. They encourage you to buy and sell at the drop of a hat, attributing the need to changes in the economy or the companies you've invested in. More trading means more commissions for the broker.

Taking a narrow view

Because of the way they earn their money, some planners are biased in favour of certain strategies and products. As a result, they do not typically keep your overall financial needs in mind. For example, if you have a problem with accumulated credit card debts, some planners may never know (or care) because they're focused on selling you an investment product. Likewise, a planner who sells a lot of life insurance tends to develop recommendations that require its purchase.

Not recommending saving through your employer's retirement plan

One of your best financial options is to take advantage of saving through your employer's retirement savings plan(s) if it is one in which your employer makes contributions along with the money you put in. Although this method of saving may not be as exciting as risking your money in cattle futures, it's not as dull as watching paint dry — and, most importantly, it's like getting an untaxed bonus. Some planners may be reluctant to recommend taking full advantage of this option: It doesn't leave much money for the purchase of their commission-laden investment products.

Ignoring debts

Sometimes, your best investment is to pay off outstanding loans, whether credit card, auto, or even mortgage debts. But some financial planners don't recommend this strategy because paying down debts depletes the capital with which you could otherwise buy investments — the investments that the broker may be trying to sell you to earn a commission or the adviser would like to manage for an ongoing fee.

Not recommending real estate and small-business investments

Like paying off debts, investing in real estate and small business takes away from your interest and ability to invest elsewhere. Many planners won't help with these choices. They may even tell you tales of real-estate and small-business-investing disasters to give you cold feet.

Sure, the value of real estate can go down just like any other investment. But over the long haul, owning a home makes good financial sense for most people. With small business, the risks are higher, but so are the potential returns. Don't let a financial planner convince you that these options are foolish — in fact, if you do your homework and know what you're doing, you can make higher rates of returns investing in real estate and small business than you can in traditional securities such as stocks and bonds. See Part III to read more about your investing options.

Selling ongoing money-management services

The vast majority of financial planners/advisers who don't work on commission make their money by managing your money for an ongoing fee percentage (typically 1 to 3 percent annually of your investment). Although this removes the incentive to *churn* your account (frequently trade your investments) to run up more commissions, it's a service that you're unlikely to need.

An ongoing fee percentage still creates a potential conflict of interest; the financial planner may tend to steer you away from beneficial financial strategies that reduce the asset pool from which he derives his percentage. Financial strategies such as maximizing contributions to your employer's retirement savings plan, paying off debts like your mortgage, investing in real estate or small business, and so on may make the most sense for you but may not be recommended by an adviser who works on a percentage of assets under management basis.

The latest rage, particularly among brokerage firms, is the *wrap account* (also known as the *managed account*). Wrap accounts can cost you upward of 3 percent of your assets annually. As we explain in Part III, you can hire *professional money managers* for 2 percent per year or less.

Selling legal services

More and more planners are getting into the business of drawing up *trusts* and providing other estate planning services for their clients. Although these and other legal documents may be right for you, far lower-cost options are available if your situation is not complicated (see Chapter 18).

If you want advice on whether you need these legal documents, do a little investigating: Do some additional reading or consult an adviser who won't actually perform the work. Legal matters are complex enough that the competence of someone who doesn't specialize in it full-time should be carefully scrutinized. If you do ultimately hire someone to perform estate planning services for you, hire someone who specializes and works at it full-time. Read the section in Chapter 18 to learn more about estate planning.

Scaring you unnecessarily

Some planners put together nifty computer-generated projections showing that you will need millions of dollars by the time you retire to maintain your standard of living. Or that tuition will cost gazillions of dollars by the time your two-year-old is ready for university.

Waking up a client to the realities of his or her financial situation is an important and difficult job for a good financial planner. But some unscrupulous planners take this task to an extreme, deliberately scaring you into buying what they're selling. They paint a bleak picture and imply that you can fix your problems only if you do what they say. Don't let them scare you — read this book and get your financial life in order.

Creating dependency

Another conflict-of-interest issue: Some financial planners have a tendency to create dependency, making things seem so complicated that their clients feel as though they could never manage their finances on their own. If your adviser is reluctant to tell you how you can educate yourself about personal money management, or if she advises you that your time would be better spent learning yoga, you've probably found a *self-perpetuating consultant.*

How to Find a Good Financial Planner

Locating a good financial planner who is willing to work with the not-yet-rich-and-famous and who doesn't have conflicts of interest can be like finding a needle in a haystack. Two methods that can serve as good starting points are personal referrals and associations.

Personal referrals

One of the best ways to find a good financial planner is to get a personal referral from a satisfied customer who is someone you trust. A referral from an accountant or a lawyer whose judgment you've tested can help as well.

Word of mouth is how the best financial planners continue to build their practices. Satisfied customers are any professional's best and least costly marketers.

However, never *ever* take a recommendation from anyone as gospel. We don't care *who* is making the referral — even if it's your mother or the Pope. You must do your homework: Ask the planner the interview questions we list later in this chapter. We've seen people get into real trouble because of blindly accepting someone else's recommendation. *Remember:* The person making the recommendation is (probably) not a financial expert. He or she could be just as bewildered as you are.

You may get referred to a planner or broker who returns the favour by sending business to the tax, legal, or real estate person who referred you. Good professionals don't do tit for tat. Hire professionals who make referrals to others based on their competence and ethics.

Associations

Associations of financial planners are more than happy to refer you to planners in your area. But as we discuss earlier in this chapter, the major trade associations are composed of planners who sell products and work on commission.

A good place to start is:

> Canadian Association of Financial Planners (CAFP)
> 439 University Ave., Suite 1710
> Toronto, Ontario M5G 1Y8
> 416-593-6592 or 800-346-2237;
> www.CAFP.org

The CAFP controls the Registered Financial Planner designation (RFP), which has stricter requirements than many other "financial adviser" designations. To be an RFP, planners must meet certain educational requirements, pass a national six-hour exam, maintain liability insurance, and do at least 30 hours of professional development a year. Members agree to abide by a code of ethics, which includes telling their clients upfront how they are compensated. Also, accredited RFP practitioners must carry professional errors and omissions insurance. After all, everybody makes mistakes at times.

Write or call the CAFP and ask for the directory of its members, called *The Consumer Guide to Financial Planning*. Beyond phone numbers and addresses, you'll also find information on each planner's qualifications, areas of expertise, and, importantly, how he or she is paid.

Interviewing a Potential Financial Adviser

Don't consider hiring a financial adviser until you have read the rest of this book. If you're not educated about personal finance, how can you possibly evaluate the competence of someone you might hire to help you make important financial decisions?

We firmly believe that you are your own best financial adviser. However, we know that some people don't want to make financial decisions without getting assistance. Perhaps you're busy, or you simply can't stand making money decisions.

But recognize that when you hire a financial adviser, you have a lot at stake. Besides the cost of his services, which generally don't come cheaply, you're placing a lot of trust in the adviser's recommendations. The more you know, the better the adviser you'll end up working with and the fewer services you'll need to buy.

These ten questions get to the core of an adviser's competence and professional integrity. Get answers to these questions *before* you decide to hire a financial adviser.

BEWARE

Ways that planners of dubious distinction cultivate clients

The channel through which you hear of a planner may provide clues to a planner's integrity and way of doing business. Beware of planners you find (or that find you) through these avenues:

✔ **Cold calling.** You've just come home after a hard day. No sooner has your posterior hit the recliner to settle in for the night when the phone rings. It's Joe the financial planner, and he wants to help you achieve all your financial dreams. *Cold calling* (the salesperson calls you, without an appointment) is the most inefficient way a planner can get new clients. It's also intrusive and is typically used by aggressive salespeople who work on commission.

✔ **Adult education classes.** Here's what often happens at some adult education classes given at local universities: You pay a reasonable fee for the course. You go to class giddy at the prospect of learning how to manage your finances. And then the instructor ends up being a broker or financial planner hungry for clients. He confuses more than he conveys. He's short on specifics. But he'll be more than happy to show you the way if you contact (and hire) him outside of class.

Instructors for these courses are paid to teach. They don't need to solicit clients in class, and, in fact, it's unethical for them to do so. We should note, however, that part of the problem is that some universities take advantage of the fact that they know such "teachers" want to solicit business. So the universities set the pay at a low level, thinking, erroneously, that they'll save money. So, *never* assume that someone who is teaching a financial-planning course at a local college is ethical, competent, or looking out for your best interests. Although we may sound cynical in so saying, assume that these people are none of the above until they clearly prove otherwise.

Ethical instructors who are there to teach do not solicit clients and may actively discourage students from hiring them. Smart universities pay their instructors well and weed out the instructors who are more interested in building up their client base than teaching.

✔ **"Free" seminars.** This is a case of "you get what you pay for." Because you don't pay a fee to attend "free seminars," and the "teachers" don't get paid, either, these events can tend to be more clear-cut sales pitches. The "instructor" may share some information, but the goal of some seminar leaders is to establish himself or herself as an expert and to whet the prospects' appetites.

Note: Be especially wary of seminars targeted at selected groups, Basic financial planning is not specific to gender, ethnicity, or marital status.

Don't assume that the financial planner giving a presentation at your employer's office is the right planner for you, either. It's surprising how little investigation some corporate benefits departments conduct on the people they let in. In most cases, planners are accepted simply because they don't charge. One organization gave preference to planners who, in addition to doing free presentations, also brought in a catered lunch! Guess what — this attracted lots of the brokers who sell high-commission products.

What percentage of your income comes from fees paid by your clients versus commissions from the products that you sell?

The best answer in many cases is, "100 percent of my income comes from fees paid by clients." Anything less than 100 percent means the person you're speaking to is a salesperson who potentially has a vested interest in recommending certain strategies and product purchases.

Sadly, more than a few "financial advisers" don't tell the truth. In an undercover investigation done by *Money* magazine, nearly one-third of advisers who claimed they were fee-only turned out to be brokers who sold investment and insurance products on a commission basis. How can you ferret these people out? The simplest way is to get them to put how they are compensated down in writing.

What percentage of fees paid by your clients is for ongoing money management versus hourly financial planning?

The answer to how the adviser is paid provides a big clue as to whether the planner has an agenda to convince you to hire him to manage your money. If what you want are objective and specific financial planning recommendations, you should seek advisers who derive their income from hourly fees. Many counsellors and advisers call themselves "fee-based," which usually means they make their living managing money for a percentage.

Some advisers do not tell you the truth. Also be aware that some advisers have been known to operate two separate companies. One company claims to give advice on a fee-basis. However, the other (generally hidden) company sells products or manages money.

If you want a money manager, you can hire the best quite inexpensively through a mutual fund or, if you have substantial assets, you can hire an established money manager (refer to Chapter 10).

What is your hourly fee?

Rates, as with legal and tax advisers, vary all over the map. We've seen and heard of fees as low as $50 per hour all the way up to several hundred dollars per hour. If you shop around, you can find terrific planners who charge around $100 per hour and who work faster than a snail's pace.

Because good planners spend a reasonable portion of their time researching and running their business, don't assume they're getting rich at your expense at this rate. Running a business is costly, but you shouldn't pay hundreds of dollars per hour unless you're wealthy and want an adviser who works only with people like you. Also, be aware that a number of planners who manage money or sell products charge very high hourly rates because they don't really want to work with people on an hourly fee basis.

Do you also perform tax or legal services?

Be wary of someone who claims to be an expert beyond one area. The tax, legal, and financial fields are vast in and of themselves and are difficult for even the best and brightest adviser to cover simultaneously. One exception is the accountant who also performs some basic financial planning by the hour. Likewise, a good financial adviser should have a good grounding in tax and legal issues that relate to your personal finances. Larger firms may have specialists available in different areas.

What work and educational experience qualifies you to be a financial planner?

There's no one right answer here. Ideally, a planner should have experience in the business or financial services field. Some say to look for planners with at least five or ten years of experience. We've always wondered how planners earn a living their first five or ten years if folks won't hire them until they reach these benchmarks! A good planner should also be good with numbers, speak in plain English, and have good interpersonal skills.

Education is sort of like food. Too little leaves you hungry. Too much might leave you feeling stuffed and uncomfortable. And less of high quality is better than a lot of low quality.

As we discuss earlier in this chapter, don't place too much value in the CFP (certified financial planner) degree. Most advisers with this "credential," which can be earned by taking a self-study course at home, sell investments.

Because investing decisions are a critical part of financial planning, take note of the fact that the most common designations of educational training among professional money managers are MBA (master of business administration) and CFA (chartered financial analyst).

Have you ever sold limited partnerships? Futures? Commodities?

The correct answers here are *no, no, no, no*. If you don't know what these disasters are, refer to Chapter 9. Also, be wary of any financial adviser who once dealt in these areas but claims to have seen the light and reformed his ways.

Professionals with poor judgment may not repeat the same mistakes, but they're more likely to make some new ones at your expense. Our experience is that even advisers who have "reformed" are unlikely to be working by the hour. Most work on commission or want to manage your money for a hefty fee.

Do you carry liability insurance?

You wouldn't (or shouldn't) let contractors into your home to do work without knowing they have insurance to cover any mistakes they make, should they cause your home to look like the one in the movie *The Money Pit*. Likewise, you should insist on hiring a planner who carries protection in case she makes a major mistake for which she is liable. Make sure that she carries enough coverage given what she is helping you with.

Some counsellors may be surprised by this question or may think you're a problem customer looking for a lawsuit. On the other hand, accidents happen; that's why insurance exists. So if the planner doesn't have liability insurance, she missed one of the fundamental concepts of planning: Insure against risk. Don't you make the same mistake by hiring her.

Can you provide references of clients with needs similar to mine?

Take the time to ask other people who have used the planner what the planner did for them. Inquire what the adviser's greatest strengths and weaknesses are. You can learn a bit about the planner's track record as well as style. And because you want to have as productive a relationship as possible with your planner, the more you learn about the planner, the easier it will be for you to hit the ground running if you hire him.

Some financial advisers offer a "free" introductory consultation. If this is offered to allow you to check out the adviser and it makes you feel more comfortable about hiring that planner, fair enough. But be careful: Most "free" consultations are offered by planners who work on commission or who will try to sell you ongoing money management services. So the "free" consultation may end up being a big sales pitch for certain products or services offered through the adviser.

The fact that a planner doesn't offer a "free" consultation may be a good sign. Counsellors who work strictly by the hour and are busy can't afford to burn an hour of their time for an in-person "free" session. They also need to be careful of folks seeking "free" advice. Such advisers usually are willing to spend some time on the phone answering background questions. They should also be able to send background materials by mail and provide references.

Will you provide specific strategies and product recommendations that I can implement on my own if I choose?

This is an important question. Some advisers may indicate that you can hire them by the hour. But then they provide only generic advice without many specifics. Some planners even *double dip* — they charge an hourly fee to make you feel like you're not working with a salesperson. Then they try selling commission-based products. Also be aware that some advisers say you can choose to implement their recommendations on your own, but then recommend only financial products that carry commissions.

How is implementation handled?

Ideally, find an adviser who lets you choose whether you want to hire him to help with implementation after the recommendations have been presented to you. If you know that you will follow through on the advice and can do so without further discussions and questions, don't buy the planner's time to implement.

On the other hand, if you hired the counsellor in the first place because you lack the time, desire, and/or expertise to manage your financial life, building implementation into the planning work makes good sense. If you're the type of person who needs to tie a string around a finger to remember to do something but then forgets why the string is there, pay for the necessary hand-holding.

Chapter 20

On Air, in Print, on the Internet, and Computer Money Management

*Y*ou won't lack for options when it comes to finding radio and television news, Internet sites, newspapers, magazines, books, and software that talk about money (explicitly and implicitly) and purport to help you get rich. Tuning out poor sources and focusing upon the best is the real challenge.

Since you probably don't consider yourself a financial expert, more often than not you won't know who to believe and listen to. This chapter helps you solve that problem.

The Mass Media

For better and for worse, the mass media has had profound influences on our culture. On the good side, news is widely disseminated these days, so if a product is recalled or a dangerous virus breaks out in your area, you'll probably hear about it, perhaps more than you want to through the media — and perhaps from tuned-in family members!

The downsides are plenty, though.

Alarmists

Imagine sitting down to watch the evening news and hearing the following stock market report:

> *"On Wall Street today, stock prices dropped a bit less than one percent, extending the market's decline of the past week. The reason: There were more people wanting to sell than those wanting to buy. For the year, the U.S. market is still up 15 percent, which is well above the historical average annual return of 10 percent."*

Now, contrast that report with the following report for the same day:

> *"Stocks plunged sharply today as the Dow Jones Industrial Average plummeted more than 100 points to close at its lowest level in the past 168 hours. Dell Computer saw its shares get creamed 10 percent as the company issued a profit warning that third-quarter revenues would take a big hit due to the Taiwan earthquake. Banking stocks got hammered again, and the sector is now off more than 20 percent from its peak this past spring."*

 While the second news report goes into more detail, it is meant to be more provocative and anxiety-producing. Most of the daily stock market reports we hear in the media are like this rather than the mundane, calming first report. Many news producers, in their quest for ratings and advertising dollars, seek to be alarming.

Poor values

Daily doses of North American mass media, including all the advertising that comes with it, essentially communicate the following messages to us:

- ✔ Your worth as a person is directly related to your physical appearance (including the quality of clothing and jewellery you wear) and your material possessions — cars, homes, electronics, and other gadgets.

- ✔ The more money you make, the more "successful" you clearly are.

- ✔ The more famous you are (especially movie and sports stars), the more you're worth listening to and admiring.

- ✔ Don't bother concerning yourself with the consequences of your behaviour before engaging in it.

- ✔ Delaying gratification and making sacrifices is for boring losers.

So bad is some of the programming in the mass media that former U.S. Secretary of Education and Republican William J. Bennett teamed up with Democratic Senator Joseph Lieberman to create the Silver Sewer Award to be presented each year to a deserving media organization in recognition of its outrageous contribution to the degradation and coarsening of our culture and its unswerving dedication to the pursuit of profit above principle.

The latest Silver Sewer Award dishonoured recipient was the Fox Television Network and its CEO, Rupert Murdoch. Lieberman and Bennett said Murdoch had ". . . led one of America's largest, most successful, most powerful television networks into the gutter. He is now responsible for what is perhaps the worst — the most crude, cynical and insulting — material ever to be broadcast to the American public over network television airwaves. . . .There seems to be almost nothing that Fox will not broadcast. Its shows are filled with vulgarity, lewdness, promiscuity, violence and overall decadence."

Continually inundating yourself with poor messages absolutely can cause you to behave in a way that undermines your long-term happiness and financial success. Don't support (by watching) media that don't reflect your values and morals.

Worship of prognosticating pundits

Perhaps the only thing the media loves more than hyping short-term news events is to quote and interview experts. What's the economy going to do next quarter? What's stock XYZ going to do next month? What's the stock market going to do in the next hour? No, we're not kidding about that last one — stock market cable channel CNBC regularly interviews floor traders from the New York Stock Exchange late in the trading day to get their opinions about what the market will do in the last hour before closing!

Prognosticating pundits keep many people tuned in since their advice is constantly changing (and therefore entertaining and anxiety-producing), and gives investors hope that they can manoeuvre their investments in advance to outfox future financial market moves. Common sense suggests, though, that no one has a working crystal ball, and if they did, they certainly wouldn't share such insights gratis with the mass media. (For more on experts who purport to predict the future, see Chapter 8.)

Radio and Television

Over the years, money issues have received increased coverage through the major media of television and radio. Is that because managing your money is so much more complicated than it was a generation ago? Not really — while we have more financial products and services to choose from these days, the best of these can simplify rather than complicate your financial life. For example, while there are far more mutual funds to choose from today than in decades past, many of the better fund companies offer funds of funds to simplify the process of building a portfolio of mutual funds.

Particular topics gain more coverage in radio and television because it helps draw more advertising dollars (which follow what people are watching). When you click on the radio or television, you don't pay a fee to tune in (pay cable channels being an exception). Advertising won't necessarily prevent a medium from delivering objective, in-your-best-interests coverage of a topic, but it sure doesn't help.

Can you imagine, for example, a financial radio or television correspondent saying:

> *"We've decided to stop providing financial market updates every five minutes because we've found it causes some investors to become addicted to tracking the short-term movements in the markets and to lose sight of the bigger picture. We don't want to encourage people to make knee-jerk reactions to short-term events."*

Another problem with both of these media is soundbite-itis. Many producers and network executives believe that if you go into too much detail, viewers and listeners will change channels.

Now, as we discuss elsewhere in this chapter and book, radio and television are hardly the only media that offer some poor advice and cause investor myopia. The Internet can be even worse, for example. And, we've read plenty of lousy money books over the years.

Newspapers and Magazines

Despite the Internet and other supposed sources of competition, financial print publications have also mushroomed in recent years. Compared with radio and television, print publications generally offer lengthier discussions of topics. And, in the more financially focused publications, the editors who work on articles generally have more background in the topics they write about.

Even within the better publications, we find a wide variety of quality, so don't instantly believe what you read, even if you read a piece in a publication you like. Here's how to get the most from financial periodicals:

✔ **Read some back issues.** At your local library or perhaps through the publication's Web site, read some issues that are at least one to two years old. While reading old issues may seem silly and pointless, it can actually be enlightening. By reviewing a number of past issues at a sitting, you can begin to get a flavour for a publication's style, priorities, and philosophies. You can also generally get old content gratis.

✔ **Look for solid information and perspective.** Headlines reveal a lot about how a publication perceives its role. Publications with cover stories such as "10 hot stocks to buy now!" and "Funds that will double your money in the next three years!" are probably best avoided. Look for articles that seek to educate with accuracy, not stories that predict what will happen in the short term.

✔ **Note bylines.** Over time, as you read a given publication, you should begin to make note of the different writers. As you get to know who the better ones are, you can skip over the ones you don't care for and spend your limited free time reading the best.

✔ **Don't react.** Here's a common example of how not to use information and advice you glean from publications. You have some cash that you want to invest. You read an article about investing in real estate investment trusts and then go out the next week and buy several. Then you see a mention of some technology stock funds and invest in some of those. Eventually, your portfolio becomes a mess of investments that reflect the history of what you have read rather than an orchestrated, well-thought-out investment portfolio.

Books

One of our favourite ways to get a crash course on a given financial topic is to read a good book. As with the other types of resources discussed in this chapter, you definitely have to choose carefully — there's plenty of mediocrity and garbage out there (please see our discussion in Chapter 2 about the publishing and book business).

Good books can go into depth on a topic in a way that simply isn't possible in other resources. Books also aren't cluttered with advertising and the conflicts inherent therein.

Here's a list of some of our favourite financial titles:

✔ *A Random Walk Down Wall Street* by Burton Malkiel (Norton)

✔ *Money Logic: Financial Strategies for The Smart Investor* by Moshe A. Milevsky with Michael Posner (Stoddart)

✔ *Stocks for the Long Run* by Jeremy Siegel (McGraw Hill)

- ✔ *Winning the Education Savings Game* by Tim Cestnick (Prentice Hall)

- ✔ *Gordon Pape's Buyer's Guide to Mutual Funds* (Prentice Hall)

- ✔ *Tax Planning for You and Your Family,* produced by KPMG (Carswell)

- ✔ *Raising Your Business* by Joanne Thomas Yaccato and Paula Jubinville (Prentice Hall)

- ✔ *Built to Last: Successful Habits of Visionary Companies* by James Collins and Jerry Porras (Harper Business)

- ✔ *Make It Legal: What Every Canadian Entrepreneur Needs to Know about the Law* by Margaret Kerr and JoAnn Kurtz (John Wiley & Sons)

- ✔ And, not surprisingly, our latest book, *Investing For Canadians For Dummies*, published by CDG Books

Computers and Personal Finance

Soon, everybody is going to own a computer. And every business is soon to have an Internet site. So shouldn't you just join up with everyone else in the cyber-universe?

The short answer is *no*. We know plenty of people who don't own a computer or who use one sparingly and who do an excellent job of managing their money.

Although a computer may be able to assist you with your personal finances, it's simply one of many tools. Computers are really best at performing routine tasks faster: processing lots of bills or performing many calculations.

Computers aren't smart, and computers and all the accompanying paraphernalia, while cheaper than years ago, certainly aren't cheap. And never assume that just because you're accessing something financial through your computer, the information you're accessing is any good or that it's even information at all.

The Internet

Are you tired of hearing about the Internet? We're finding more and more people who are — and who can blame them? Sure, the Internet is changing the world, but certainly not always for the better and not always in such a big way.

Consider the way we shop. Okay, you can buy things online that in the past you couldn't. Big deal — what's the difference between calling a toll-free number and doing mail order, which many of us did for years before the Internet got commercialized, and clicking your computer mouse to buy an object you desire? Purchasing things online simply broadens the avenues through which you can spend money. We see a big downside here: Overspending is easier for some who surf the Internet a lot.

How about the way we invest? Some of the best Web sites allow you to more efficiently access information that may help you make important investing decisions. However, this doesn't mean your computer and modem allow you to compete at the same level as a professional money manager. No, the playing field ain't level. The best pros work at their craft full-time and have far more expertise and experience than the rest of us. Some non-professionals have been fooled into believing that investing online makes them better investors. Our experience has been that people who spend time online daily dealing with investments tend to trade and react more to short-term events and have a harder time keeping the bigger picture and their long-term goals and needs in focus.

If you know where to look, you can more easily access some types of information. However, there's a lot of crappola online — just as on other advertiser-dominated media like television and radio.

Tread carefully on the Web

"Go surfing!"

"Cool!"

No, you're not eavesdropping on a southern California beach conversation. To hear promoters of companies with sites on the globe's largest computer network known as the Internet, you may think that the Internet is not only a hip place to be but The Place to Be.

We're increasingly asked questions like, "How do I research investments through the Internet?" or, "How can I use the Internet to manage my personal finances?"

Our answer — "very carefully."

Like information from any medium, you have to sift out the good from the bad. If you blindly navigate the Internet and naively think that everything out there is useful "information," "research," or "objective advice," you will be in for a rude awakening.

Most personal finance sites on the Internet are free, which — guess what — means that these sites are basically advertising or are dominated and driven by advertising. If you're looking for written material by unbiased experts or journalists — well — you can find some on the Web, but there's far more biased and uninformed stuff.

Consider the source

A report on the Internet published by a leading investment-banking firm provides a list of the "coolest finance" sites. On the list is the Web site of a major bank. Because it's been a long time since we were in junior high school, we're not quite sure what cool means anymore. If cool can be used to describe a well-organized and graphically pleasing Web site, then we guess we could say that the bank's site is cool.

However, if you are looking for sound information and advice, then the bank's site is decidedly "uncool." It steers you in a financial direction that benefits, not surprisingly, the bank and not you. For example, in the real estate section, users are asked to plug in their gross monthly income and down payment, which are used to spit out the supposed amount that users can "afford" to spend on a home. No mention is given to other financial goals and concerns — such as saving for retirement — that affect one's ability to spend a particular amount of money on a home.

Consider this advice in the lending area: "Maybe you can have it now. When you don't have the cash on hand for important purchases, we can help you borrow what you need. From a new car, to that vacation you've been longing for, to new kitchen appliances, you can make these dreams real now." Click on a button on the bottom of this screen — and presto, you're on your way to racking up credit card and auto debt. Why bother practising delayed gratification, living within your means, or buying something used if getting a loan is "easy" and comes with "special privileges"?

Watch out for "sponsored" content

Another problem to watch out for on Internet sites is "sponsored" content, a euphemism for advertising under the guise of editorial content. Often buried in small print in an obscure part of the Web page or site, you'll find a disclaimer or note saying that an article is sponsored by (in other words, paid advertising by) the "author."

For example, one mutual fund site states that its "primary purpose is to provide viewers with an independent guide that contains information and articles they can't get anywhere else." The "content" of the site suggests otherwise. In the "Expert's Corner," material is reprinted from a newsletter that advocates frequent trading in and out of mutual funds to time market moves. Turns out that the "article" is "sponsored by the featured expert": In other words, it's a paid advertisement. (The track record of the newsletter's past recommendations, which isn't discussed, is poor.)

Steer clear of biased financial planning advice

We also suggest skipping much of the financial planning advice offered by financial service companies with financial products to sell, or at the least, approaching with an understanding that by definition it will be narrowly focused. Such companies cannot take the necessary objective, holistic view required to render useful advice. Investment companies, for example, may prod you into establishing university savings accounts with them without pointing out the benefits of funding your employer's retirement savings plan instead (refer to Chapter 13 for more details).

Shun short-term thinking

Many financial Internet sites provide real-time stock quotes as a hook to some site that is cluttered with advertising. Our experience working with individual investors is that the more short-term they think, the worse they do, and checking your portfolio during the trading day certainly promotes short-term-ism.

Also, beware of tips offered around the electronic water cooler — message boards. As in the real world, chatting with strangers and exchanging ideas is fine. However, if you don't know the identity and competence of message board posters or chat room participants, why would you follow their financial advice or stock tips? Getting ideas from various sources is okay, but educate yourself and do your homework before making personal financial decisions.

If you want to best manage your personal finances and learn more, remember that there's a grain of truth in the old expression, "You get what you pay for." Free information on the Internet, especially that which is provided by companies in the financial services industry, is generally self-serving. Stick with information providers who have proven themselves offline or who don't have anything to sell, except objective information and advice. Where appropriate in this chapter, we recommend useful Internet sites that meet these criteria.

Software

Software is a computer program that is either packaged in a box about as big as a hardcover book such as *War and Peace* or can be downloaded online. Most of the mass-marketed financial software packages sell for under $100. If you've ever used a word-processing program such as Word or WordPerfect, or a spreadsheet program such as Excel or Lotus 1-2-3, then you've used software.

The benefits of using financial software

Although the number of personal finance software packages and online sites is mushrooming rapidly, quality is having a hard time keeping up, especially among the free Internet sites. Most of the best financial tools for your computer fall into the software category and can help you in the following ways:

✔ Good software can guide you to better organization and management of your personal finances.

✔ Good software can help you complete mundane tasks or complex calculations more quickly and easily and provide basic advice in unfamiliar territory.

✔ Good software can make you feel in control of your life.

Mediocre and bad software, on the other hand, can make you feel stupid or, at the very least, make you want to tear your hair out. Lousy packages usually end up in the software graveyard.

Having reviewed many of the packages available, we can assure you that if you are having a hard time with some of the programs out there (even sometimes the more useful ones), you are not at fault. Too many packages assume that you already know things such as your tax rate, your mortgage options, and the difference between stock and bond mutual funds. Much of what's out there isn't user-friendly and is too technically oriented. Some of it is even flawed in its financial accuracy.

A good software package, like a good tax or financial adviser, should be your partner in helping you better manage your finances. It should simply and concisely explain financial terminology and provide a road map to help you make decisions by offering choices and recommendations so that you can "play" with alternatives before following a particular course of action.

With increasing regularity, financial software packages are being designed to do more than one task or to address more than one area of personal finances. But no package covers the whole range of issues in your financial life.

Computer Money Tasks

In the remainder of this chapter, we detail important personal financial tasks that your computer can help you accomplish. We also provide our recommendations for the best software and Web sites where appropriate to help you accomplish these chores.

Pay your bills and track your money

Every month, you write out by hand a bunch of cheques to the same organizations and people you wrote cheques to last month and the month before that. Chequebook software automates the process of paying your bills. When you have to make your monthly payment to the phone company, for example, your monthly cheque, already made payable to the phone company, pops up on-screen at your command. All you have to do is fill in the new amount that you have to pay and print your cheque on your computer's printer. (As we discuss later in this section, for a small monthly fee and often for free, you also can pay your bills electronically, completely eliminating the process of writing and mailing in cheques.)

Chequebook programs can track your cheque writing and prepare reports that detail your spending by category — so that you can get a handle on where the fat is in your budget. One drawback of using these programs to track your spending is that they only capture what is entered. So the amount and spending category of your individual credit card and cash purchases, which for most people are substantial, are omitted unless you enter such data (or have a card from a financial institution that is set up to let you download your credit card transactions via your computer's modem). For a complete discussion on how to track your spending, please see Chapter 4.

Quicken and Microsoft's Money are good programs that we've reviewed in this category. In addition to offering the printed cheques and electronic bill-payment features, each of these packages is a financial organizer. The programs allow you to list your investments and other assets and your loans and other financial liabilities.

In addition to a significant investment of your time to learn a software program, another drawback is cost — computer cheques are pricey. If you order cheques directly from the software manufacturers (order forms come with your software), expect prices of about $75 for 500 cheques. You can beat those prices by ordering from other companies.

You can avoid dealing with any paper cheques at all — written or printed — if you sign up with your financial institution to have your bills paid automatically. Most regular household bills, including hydro, heating, telephone, and often even property taxes can be paid this way. Generally you request a form from the utility or other company, and provide them with your account information and a voided cheque. Once your account is set up, you will continue to receive a paper statement. However, you don't need to make a payment — the money is automatically taken out of your bank account on the due date. Not only does this save you time and effort, it also helps protect your credit rating and save you late payment fees by ensuring your bills are paid in full and on time.

Plan for retirement

Good retirement planning software and online calculators can help you to plan for retirement by crunching the numbers for you. But they can also teach you how particular changes — such as your investment returns, rate of inflation, or your savings rate — can affect when, and in what style, you can retire. The biggest time savings aspect of retirement planning software and Internet sites is that they let you more quickly play with and see the consequences of changing the assumptions.

Tracking your investment returns often isn't worth the headache

Accurately tracking the return on your investments can be an extremely complicated, tedious, and time-consuming task — exactly the type of chore that computers were designed to relieve us of. Although you would think that a number of excellent investment tracking software packages would be on the market today, we feel that such available packages are . . . well . . . complicated, tedious, and time-consuming. At this point anyway, these programs are often not any more efficient than the old-fashioned method of pencil, paper, and a calculator.

Our big gripe with the investment tracking software programs is that most of them don't allow you to determine your investment's total return. And the programs that do require lots of your time to get to that point. Your effective or *internal rate of return* (IRR), which compares your original amounts invested to the current market value, is the best way to measure the success of your investments over time.

Most of the other packages calculate your *cost basis,* which is your original investment plus reinvested dividends and capital gains, for which you would have already paid taxes in a nonretirement account. When you sell a nonretirement account investment, you need to know the cost basis for tax purposes (refer to Chapter 7). Cost basis reports make your returns look less generous because reinvested distributions increase your original investment and seemingly reduce your returns. We know from direct experience that investors often look at the cost basis reports — which are sometimes misleadingly named "investment performance" or "investment analysis" — and assume that the reports tell them what their total investment returns are. Using software for cost basis calculations is generally not worthwhile because most investment companies provide cost basis information to you upon request or when you sell an investment.

If you want to analyze your historic returns, you need to gather all your old account statements (if you can find them) and enter every investment you made as well as all reinvestments of dividends, interest, and capital gains distributions.

For buy-and-hold mutual fund investors, investment-tracking software has limited benefit given the time required to enter your data. Mutual funds and many other published resources tell you what the funds' total return was for the past year, so you don't need to enter every dividend and capital gain distribution for yourself.

As for calculating the return of your overall portfolio with the old-fashioned method of paper and pencil mentioned above, simply weight the return of each investment by the portion of your portfolio invested in it. For example, with a simple portfolio equally divided between two investments that returned 10 percent and 20 percent respectively, your overall portfolio return would be 15 percent.

Investment tracking software can be more useful for stock traders. In our experience, stock traders don't usually track their overall returns. If they actually used one of these programs, they could at least see how all their trading depresses their returns.

Prepare your taxes

Properly used, good tax preparation software can save you time and money. The best programs "interview" you to gather the necessary information and select the appropriate forms based on your responses. Of course, you're still the one responsible for locating all the information needed to complete your return. More experienced taxpayers can bypass the interview and jump directly to the forms they know they need to complete. These programs also help flag overlooked deductions and identify other tax-reducing strategies.

Among the better tax preparation programs we've reviewed are QuickTax, CanTax, and GriffTax.

If you're mainly after tax forms, you can get them without charge in tax preparation books or through the Canada Customs and Revenue Agency (formerly Revenue Canada) Web site (www.ccra-adrc.gc.ca).

Research investments

Much of the better information in the online world is geared toward investing in individual stocks. So if you have given up on being the next Warren Buffett and instead invest in mutual funds, the online world will be of less use to you.

The advantage of going online isn't that you profit from getting news sooner or from tapping into the latest predictions of yet more gurus, but that you can access useful resources more quickly and more cheaply than you could before (that is, if your Internet connection is speedy and you know where to look). Rather than schlepping off to the library and fighting over the favourite investing reference manuals, ponying up hundreds of dollars to buy print versions for your own use, or slogging through voice mail hell when you call government agencies, you can access a variety of materials with your computer. You can also usually pay for just what you need:

- ✔ **Sedar.com.** This site provides free access to the various documents publicly traded Canadian companies and mutual funds must file with the regulators. You'll find everything from annual reports and financial statements to news releases here. The site is also loaded full of promotion-free material on mutual funds. You can find performance details here for most funds, as well as financial statements and annual reports which offer a breakdown on just which securities each fund holds.

- ✔ **Disclosure-investor.com.** This site supplies information from Securities and Exchange Commission filings and other sources on public companies. Disclosure is a useful place to start if you already have particular stocks in mind and want to learn more about the companies' businesses and financials. Disclosure holds your hand through the process of navigating and understanding the various documents. To sidestep the commercial online service's charges, you can access SEC documents directly via the SEC's Internet site (`www.sec.gov`), but be aware that navigating this site takes patience. All public corporations, as well as mutual funds, file with the agency.

✔ **Globeandmail.com.** The home site to the various sites run by the *Globe and Mail*, it gives access to many of the business and related stories published in the paper. You'll also find the articles for the *Globe*'s helpful Net Worth personal finance section, including Tony's Me and My Money column, here. On the investment selection front, both the *Globe*'s mutual fund and stock market sites offer excellent filtering features. For example, in a few clicks you can get a detailed list of low-cost, low-fee index funds that qualify as Canadian content for your RRSP.

Trade online

If you've done your investing homework, trading securities online may save you money and perhaps some time. For years, discount brokers (which we discuss in Chapter 8) had been heralded as the low-cost source for trading. Now, online brokers have set a new lower-cost standard.

A number of the newer discount brokers have built their securities brokerage business around online trading. By eliminating the overhead of branch offices, and by accepting and processing trades by computer, online brokers keep their costs and brokerage charges to a minimum. Cut-rate electronic brokerage firms are for people who want to direct their own financial affairs and don't want or need to work with a personal broker. However, some of these brokers have limited products and services. Our own experiences with reaching live people at some online brokers has been trying — we've had to wait more than ten minutes on hold before a customer service representative answered the call.

While online trading may save you on transaction costs, it can also encourage you to trade more than you should, resulting in higher total trading costs, lower investment returns, and higher income tax bills. Following investments on a daily basis encourages you to think short term. Remember that the best investments are bought and held for the long haul (see Part III for more information).

Read and search periodicals

Many business and financial publications are going online to offer investors news and financial market data. Leading business publications such as the major Canadian newspapers and business publications, and leading U.S.

magazines such as Forbes (`www.forbes.com`) and Business Week (`www.businessweek.com`) put their magazines' content on the Web, which also allows you to conduct searches for articles on specific topics that interest you. Be careful, though, as we discuss in the next chapter, to take with many grains of salt what you read and hear in the mass media. Much of the content revolves around tweaking people's anxieties and dwelling on the latest crises and fads.

Buy life insurance

If loved ones are financially dependent upon you, you probably know that you need some life insurance. But, add together the dread of life insurance salespeople and a fear of death, and you have a recipe for procrastination. While your computer can't stave off the grim reaper, it can help you find a quality, low-cost policy that can be much less costly than the most expensive options, without having to deal with high-pressure sales tactics.

The best way to shop for term life insurance online is by starting off with one of the online agency quotation services such as `www.kanetix.com`, `www.term4sale.com`, and `www.winquote.net`. At each of these sites, you fill in your date of birth, whether you smoke, how much coverage you'd like, and for how long you'd like to lock in the initial premium. A new Web page pops up with a list of low-cost quotes (based on your health) from a number of different insurance companies.

Invariably, the quotes are ranked by how cheap they are. While cost is certainly an important factor, many of these services don't do as good a job explaining what other important factors to consider when doing your comparison shopping. For example, the projected and maximum rates after the initial term has expired are sometimes not covered. Be sure to ask about these other future rates before you agree to a specific policy. You may also need to do some further research, particularly if you are in terrific health. Most online quote services only offer a few health categories, but some companies use many more when deciding rates.

If you decide to buy a policy, you can then use your quotes to ensure you're getting a good price through a broker, and a policy that doesn't cut corners on coverage and features in order to have that price. Some companies are beginning to allow consumers to fill in an online application form. And, we're sorry to say, in addition to having to deal with snail mail, you're still going to have to deal with a "medical technician" who will drop by your home to check on your health status . . . at least until some computer genius figures out a way for you to give a blood and urine sample online!

Prepare legal documents

Just as you can prepare a tax return with the advice of a software program, you can also prepare common legal documents. This type of software may save you from the often-difficult task of finding a competent and affordable attorney.

Using legal software is generally preferable to using fill-in-the-blank documents. Software has the built-in virtues of directing and limiting your choices and preventing you from making common mistakes. Quality software also incorporates the knowledge and insights of the legal eagles who developed the software. And it can save you money.

When your situation isn't unusual, legal software may work well for you. As to the legality of documents that you create with legal software, remember that a will, for example, is made legal and valid by your witnesses; the fact that a lawyer prepares the document is not what makes it legal. Wills are important documents, and you may still want to have a lawyer go over what you're prepared to ensure that it will have the effects that you intended. Another useful role that lawyers can perform is to make sure that you have covered all the possible eventualities.

Even if you plan on having a lawyer draft your will, using a will-drafting program will familiarize you with the process and terminology, as well as help you organize your thoughts. This can not only save you legal fees, but also help ensure your will truly reflects your wishes.

Part VI
The Part of Tens

"I can always tell when Philip is working on family finances. A 'cursor' appears on both sides of the computer screen."

In this part . . .

You find some fun and useful chapters that will help you with financial strategies for ten life changes and remind you of ten things more important than money. Why "tens"? Why not!

Chapter 21

Eric and Tony's Tips for Ten Life Changes

....

Some of life's changes come unexpectedly, like earthquakes. Others you can see coming when they are still far off on the horizon, like a big storm moving in off the ocean. Whether a life change is predictable or not, your ability to navigate successfully through its challenges and to adjust quickly to its new circumstances depends largely on your degree of preparedness.

Perhaps you find our comparison of life changes to earthquakes and storms to be a bit negative. After all, some of the changes we discuss in this chapter should be occasions for joy, and here we are comparing them to natural disasters. But realize that what one defines as a "disaster" has everything to do with his or her preparedness. To the person who has stored no emergency rations in his basement, the big snowstorm that has trapped him in his home could mean problems. But to the prepared person with plenty of food and water, that same storm could mean a vacation from work and a relaxing week in the midst of a winter wonderland.

Before we discuss critical financial issues for you to deal with before and during major life changes, here are some general tips that apply to all life changes:

- ✔ **Stay in financial shape.** An athlete is best able to withstand physical adversities during competition by training and eating well in advance. Likewise, the more sound your finances are to begin with, the better able you'll be to deal with life changes.

- ✔ **Changes require change.** Even if your financial house is in order, a major life change — starting a family, buying a home, starting a business, divorcing, retiring — should prompt you to review your personal financial strategies. Why? Because life changes often affect your income, spending, insurance needs, and ability to take financial risk.

- ✔ **Make changes sooner rather than later.** Being human, most of us procrastinate. But with a major life change on the horizon, procrastination can be costly. You (and your family) might overspend and accumulate high-cost debts, lack proper insurance coverage, or take other unnecessary risks. Early preparation can save you from these pitfalls.

✔ **Manage stress and your emotions.** Life changes often are accompanied by stress and other emotional upheavals. During changes, don't make knee-jerk decisions. Take the time to become fully informed and recognize and acknowledge your feelings. Educating yourself is key, and you may want to hire experts to help (refer to Chapter 19). Don't abdicate decisions and responsibilities to advisers — the advisers may not have your best interests at heart or fully appreciate your needs.

Here, then, are the major life changes that you may have to deal with at some point in your life. We wish you more of the good changes than the bad.

Starting out: your first job

If you've just graduated from university or some other program, or are otherwise entering the workforce, your increased income and reduction in educational expenses are probably a welcome relief. You would think, then, that more young adults wouldn't have financial trouble and challenges. But they do, largely because of poor financial habits picked up at home or from the world at large. Here's how to get on the path to financial success:

✔ **Don't use consumer credit.** The use and abuse of consumer credit can cause financial pain and hardship well into adult life. You'd like furniture, a new television, and lots of fun vacations, but all these things cost money. To get off on the right financial foot, young workers should shun the habit of making purchases on credit cards that they can't pay for in full when the bill arrives in the mail. The simple solution if you overspend and run up outstanding credit card balances: Don't carry a credit card. Cash and cheques worked fine for decades before credit cards arrived on the scene. If you need the convenience of making purchases with a piece of plastic instead of cash or cheques, get a debit card (see Chapter 5).

✔ **Get in the saving and investing habit.** Should you hope to someday own a home and cease full-time work, you'll need to save over many years. Ideally, your savings should be directed into an RRSP because of the tax benefits, unless you want to accumulate down-payment money for a home or small business purchase (see Chapter 3). Thinking about a home purchase or retirement is usually not in the active thought patterns of first-time job seekers. We're often asked, "At what age should a person start saving?" To us, that's similar to asking at what age you start brushing your teeth. Well, when you have teeth to brush! So we say you should start saving and investing money from your first paycheque. Try starting to save 5 percent and then eventually 10 percent of every paycheque. If you're having trouble saving money, track your spending and make cutbacks as needed (refer to Chapters 4 and 6).

✔ **Get insured.** Many people starting out are able to rationalize themselves out of buying insurance. When you're young and healthy, it's hard to imagine life otherwise. Many twentysomethings give little thought to the potential for not being able to earn an income due to long-term health problems. But because accidents and unexpected illnesses can strike at any age, forgoing coverage can be financially devastating. Buying disability coverage, which replaces income lost to a long-term disability, in a first full-time job with more limited benefits is wise. And as you begin to build your assets, consider making out a will so that your assets go where you want in the event of your death.

✔ **Continue your education.** Once you're out in the workforce, you (like many other people) may realize how little you've learned in formal schooling that can be used in the real world and, conversely, how much you need to learn (like personal financial management) that school never taught you. Read, learn, and continue to grow. Continuing education will help you to advance in your career and enjoy the world around you.

Changing jobs or careers

During your adult life, you will almost surely change jobs — perhaps as often as several times a decade. We hope that most of the time you'll be changing by your own choice. But let's face it: Job security is not what it used to be. Corporate downsizing has made victims of even the most talented workers.

Always be prepared for a job change. No matter how happy you are in your current job, knowing that your world won't fall apart if you are not working tomorrow will give you an added sense of security and encourage an openness to possibility. Whether it's a job change by choice or necessity, the following financial manoeuvres will ease the transition:

✔ **Structure your finances to afford an income dip.** Spending less than you earn always makes good financial sense, but if you're coming up to a possible job change, this is even more important, particularly if you are entering a new field or starting your own company and you expect a short-term income dip. Many people view a lifestyle of thriftiness as restrictive, but ultimately those thrifty habits can give you *more* freedom to do what you want to do. Be sure to keep an emergency reserve fund (refer to Chapter 8).

If you lose your job, batten down the hatches. Normally, when you lose your job through no choice of your own, you get little advance warning. That does not mean, however, that you can't do anything financially. Evaluating and slashing your current level of spending may be necessary. Everything should be fair game, from how much you spend on housing to how often you eat out to where you do your grocery shopping. Avoid at all costs the temptation to maintain your level of spending by accumulating consumer debt.

✔ **Evaluate the total financial picture when relocating.** At some point in your career, you may have the option of relocating. But don't call the moving company until you understand the financial consequences of such a move. You can't simply compare salaries and benefits between the two jobs. Also compare the cost of living between the two areas: That includes housing, commuting, provincial income taxes, property taxes, food, utilities, and all the other major expenditure categories that we discuss in Chapter 4.

Getting married

Ready to tie the knot with the one you love? Congratulations — we hope that you'll have a long, healthy, and happy life together. In addition to the emotional and moral commitments that you and your spouse make to one another, you'll probably be merging many of your financial decisions and resources. It would be highly unusual for you and your spouse to have identical money personalities; after all, opposites often attract. Even if you are largely in agreement about your financial goals and strategies, managing as two is different than managing as one.

✔ **Take a compatibility test.** Too many couples never discuss their goals and plans before marriage; failing to do so breaks up way too many of these marriages. Finances are just one of many issues to discuss. Others include expectations for having and raising children, dealing with in-laws, career goals, and so on. A good way to minimize your chances for heartache is to ensure that you know what you're getting yourself into. Ministers, priests, and rabbis sometimes offer premarital counselling to surface issues and differences. Don't let romance blind you to important issues vital to the long-term health of your marriage.

✔ **Consider taxes.** More than a few couples actually allow their joint tax burdens to influence when and even if they marry. The only way to know what will happen to your tax bill is to get out a tax return and plug in the relevant numbers and see what Revenue Canada will do to you after you're married. Put strategies to work to cut your household's total tax bill. Have the higher-earning spouse pay all the household expenses. This leaves the lower-earning spouse with more money for investments, which are then taxed at a lower rate. Consider setting up a spousal RRSP. (See Chapter 11 for more details.) Be sure to prepare your tax returns together to make the best use of your household's credits and deductions. (Refer to Chapter 7 for more details.)

✔ **Discuss and set joint goals.** Once you are married, you and your spouse should set aside time once a year or every few years to discuss personal and financial goals for the years ahead. If for no other reason, talking about where you want to go helps ensure that you're rowing your financial boat in the same direction.

✔ **Decide whether to keep finances separate or jointly managed.** Some couples choose to keep separate financial accounts, whereas others pool resources. Philosophically, we like the idea of pooling better. After all, marriage is a partnership and shouldn't be a "his" versus "hers" affair. In some marriages, however, spouses choose to keep some money separate, particularly for spending purposes so that they don't feel the scrutiny of a spouse with different spending preferences. Spouses who have been through divorce may choose to keep the assets they bring into the new marriage separate in order to earmark and protect their assets in the event they divorce again. As long as you're jointly accomplishing what you need to, some separation of money is okay. But for the health of your marriage, don't hide money from one another, and, if you're the higher-income spouse, don't assume power and control over your joint income. If you run your own business and hire your spouse, though, separate accounts are a must.

✔ **Coordinate and maximize employer benefits.** If one or both of you have access to a package of employee benefits through an employer, understand how best to make use of those benefits. Coordinating and using the best that each package has to offer is like giving yourselves a pay raise. For example, if you both have access to health insurance, compare which of you has better benefits. Likewise, one of you may have a better retirement savings plan — one that matches and offers superior investment options. Unless you can afford to save the maximum through both your plans, saving more in the better plan will increase your combined assets. (*Note:* If you're concerned about what happens if you save more in one of your retirement plans and then divorce, you'll sleep better knowing that in most provinces that money is considered part of your joint assets to be divided equally.)

✔ **Discuss life and disability insurance needs.** If you and your spouse can make do without each other's income, you might not need any income-protecting insurance. However, if, like many husbands and wives, both spouses depend upon each other's incomes, or if one spouse depends fully or partly on the other's income, you may each need to have long-term disability and term life insurance policies (refer to Chapter 17).

✔ **Update your wills.** When you marry, you should update your wills. If you haven't gotten around to making a will, having a will is potentially more valuable when you're married, especially if you want to leave money to others in addition to your spouse, or if you have children for whom you should name a guardian. See Chapter 18 for more on wills.

✔ **Reconsider beneficiaries on investment and life insurance.** With RRSPs and life insurance policies, you name beneficiaries to whom the money or value in those accounts will go in the event of your passing. When you marry, you will probably want to rethink beneficiaries.

Starting a small business

Many people aspire to be their own bosses, but far fewer people actually leave their jobs in order to achieve that dream. Psychologically and financially, giving up the apparent security of a job with benefits and a built-in network of co-workers is difficult for most people. Going into small business is not for everyone, but don't let inertia stand in your way. Here are some tips to help get you started and increase your chances for long-term success:

✔ **Prepare to ditch your job.** Do you spend all or nearly all that you earn while employed and haven't banked a war chest? Many people in such a situation never leave their jobs behind to pursue their entrepreneurial dreams because they feel dependent upon their paycheques. Live as Spartan a lifestyle as you can while you are employed to maximize your ability to save money; you will simultaneously be developing thrifty habits that will help you weather the reduced income and increased expenditure period that comes with most small-business start-ups. You might also consider easing into your small business by working at it part-time in the beginning, with or without cutting back on your normal job.

✔ **Develop a business plan.** If you research and think through your business idea, you'll not only reduce the likelihood of your business failing and increase its success if it thrives, but you'll also feel more comfortable taking the entrepreneurial plunge. A good business plan should be a blueprint for how you expect to build the business. It should describe in detail the business idea, the marketplace you'll be competing in, your marketing plans, and expected revenue and expenses.

✔ **Replace your insurance coverage.** Before you finally decide to leave your job, set the wheels in motion to get proper insurance coverage. With disability insurance, securing coverage before you leave your job is best so that you have income to qualify for coverage. If you have life insurance through your employer, you should secure new individual coverage as soon as you know you're going to leave your job (refer to Chapter 17 for more details).

✔ **Establish a retirement savings plan.** Once your business is making a profit, consider establishing an RRSP or other retirement savings plan. As we explain in Chapter 11, such plans allow you to shelter up to 18 percent of your income from taxation.

Buying a home

Many Canadians end up buying a home. To be a financial success, you need not own a home, but home ownership certainly offers financial rewards. Over the course of your adult life, the real estate that you own should appreciate in value. Additionally, someday you should have your mortgage paid off, which will greatly reduce your housing costs. As a renter, on the other hand, your full housing costs will increase over time with inflation.

If you're considering buying a home:

- ✔ **Get your overall finances in order.** Before you consider buying a home, you need to analyze your current budget, your ability to afford debt, and your future financial goals. Make sure that your expected housing expenses still allow you to save properly for retirement and other long- or short-term objectives. Don't buy a home based upon what lenders are willing to lend. Read and digest the relevant portions of this book to get your financial house in order before you buy.

- ✔ **Determine if now's the time.** Especially if you're a first-time home buyer, buying if you don't see yourself staying put three to five years rarely makes financial sense. Buying and selling a home gobbles up a good deal of money in transaction costs — you'll be lucky to recoup all those costs even within a five-year period. Also, if your income is likely to drop or you have other pressing goals, such as starting a business, you might wait to buy.

To learn more about buying a home, be sure to read Chapter 15.

Having children

If you thought being a responsible adult, holding down a job, paying your bills on time, and preparing for your financial future was tough, wait 'til you add kids to the equation. Most parents find that, with kids in the family, the already precious commodities of free time and money become even more precious — sometimes even extinct. The more efficiently you learn how to manage your time and money, the better able you will be to have a sane, happy, and financially successful life as a parent.

Here are some key things to recognize and to do both before and after you begin your family:

- ✔ **Set your priorities: You can't do it all and have it all.** As with many other financial decisions, starting or expanding a family requires that you financially plan ahead. Set your priorities and structure your finances and living situation accordingly. Is it more important to have a bigger home in a particular community, or would you rather have less pressure to work and spend more time with your family? Keep in mind that a less hectic work life not only gives you more free time but also often reduces your cost of living by decreasing meals out, dry-cleaning costs, daycare expenses, and so on.

- ✔ **Take a hard look at your budget.** If you've had a hard time living within your means before children, then you definitely should take an honest look at how your income and spending will change after your family grows. In addition to diaper changes and less sleep at night, children mean increased spending. At a minimum, expenditures for food and clothing will increase. But you're also likely to spend more on housing, insurance,

Budgeting for life changes

One thing is certain about life: It changes — marriage, buying a home, family expansion, starting a business, divorce, retirement, or the death of a spouse. Although some life events bring joy and others sorrow, all bring financial change. If you don't manage this change, it may end up managing and ruling you.

We've witnessed the best of savers turn into deficit financiers due to the financial upheaval and shock waves from a major life event — even those events that were anticipated. You should budget ahead for life changes.

For example, if you'd like to take the entrepreneurial plunge and leave your full-time job, you should know whether you can afford to do that and what impact changed expenses and income would have on your ability to save money. Wannabe parents, likewise, should consider how increased expenses and a likely reduction in income would affect their monthly budget.

Going through this exercise is a great way to estimate what impact a child or other significant life change will have on your financial situation. Consider the nervous expectant parents who went through this budgeting exercise because they were wondering what financial impact having a baby would have on their household finances. Their findings: Given their expected spending, the parents would go from saving 12 percent of their annual incomes to spending 5 percent more than they earned. But the lower-income spouse was also surprised to see that, by working half-time rather than full-time, the couple's net savings would actually increase thanks largely to lower taxes and lower child care and work-related expenses.

In Chapter 4, we provide suggested categories for tallying your expenses — such as housing, clothing, auto, cable TV, furniture, insurance, telephone, other utilities, education, and so on. You can adjust and create new spending and income categories to match your personal financial situation.

As you plan for your next life change, remember the limitations of quantitative analysis. It can't factor in the non-financial considerations such as how you feel about working more or less because of a life change. Crunching numbers may also mistakenly give you the illusion of control. Those expectant parents that we told you about earlier learned that they were having three new additions to their family and not just one!

daycare, and education. On top of that, if you want to play an active role in raising your children, working at a full-time job won't be possible for both parents. So while you consider the added expenses, you may also need to factor in a decrease in income.

No simple rules exist for estimating how children will affect your household's income and expenses. On the income side, figure out how much you'll want to cut back on work. On the expense side, statistics show that the average household with school-age children spends about 20 percent more than those without. A more scientific approach would be for you to go through your budget category by category and estimate how kids will change your spending (use the worksheets in Chapter 4).

✔ **Boost insurance coverages *before* getting pregnant.** Before you try to have a baby, be sure that you have adequate disability insurance, as pregnancy is considered a pre-existing condition. And most families-to-be should buy life insurance. Buying life insurance *after* the bundle of joy comes home from the hospital is a risky proposition — if Mom or Dad develops a health problem, she or he could be denied coverage. Also consider buying life insurance for a stay-at-home parent. Even though that parent is not bringing in income, if he or she were to pass away, hiring assistance could cripple the family budget.

✔ **Check maternity leave with your employer.** Many larger employers offer extra maternity leave for women and, in rare but thankfully increasing cases, for men. Some employers also top up what you receive from the Employment Insurance system. Understand the options and the financial ramifications before you consider the leave and ideally before you get pregnant.

✔ **Update your will.** If you had a will before starting a family, you'll need to do a new one. If you don't have a will, make one now. With children in the picture, you'll need to name a guardian in your will who will be responsible for raising your children should you and your spouse both pass away. Although choosing a guardian is a daunting decision, even more frightful is the thought of letting courts decide who would raise your children.

✔ **Understand child care tax benefits.** If you have children under the age of 18, you may be eligible for the Child Tax Benefit, a non-taxable benefit. In 2000, the annual benefit was set at $1,104 per child, plus an extra $76.92 for the third and subsequent children. There is an additional benefit set at $219 in 2000 for each child under seven if no child care expenses are claimed. (Alberta has different payment schedules than the rest of the country.) These benefits are decreased on a sliding scale if your household income exceeds a certain amount, which in 2000 was $30,004.

In addition, there is a National Child Benefit supplement available for low-income families. The amounts in 2000 were $976.92 for the first child, $771 for the second, and $693.96 for any additional children. This benefit also gets phased out if your family's net income exceeds a certain level, which in 2000 was $21,214.

Child care expenses can also be deducted if they were incurred in order for you or your spouse to earn an income. In a two-parent family, the deduction must usually be claimed by the lower-earning spouse. Single parents who are students, as well as households where both spouses are studying at a post-secondary institution, can also claim this deduction. In 2000, you could claim up to $7,000 in expenses for each child under the age of 7, and $4,000 for children age 7 to 16. The total you can claim is limited to two-thirds of your earned income. Some provinces also have an additional child care tax credit for lower-income families.

✔ **Don't indulge the children.** Toys, art classes, sports, field trips, and the like can rack up big bills, especially if not controlled. Some parents place few if any limits on children's programs. Most parents don't set guidelines on extracurricular activities. Some put their children's desires ahead of all other financial needs and goals. Others mindlessly follow the example of peers' families. Introspective parents have shared with us that they feel some insecurity about providing the best for their children. The parents (and kids) that seem happiest and most financially successful are those who clearly distinguish between material luxuries and family necessities.

As children get older and become indoctrinated into the world of shopping, all sorts of other purchases come into play. Consider giving your kids a weekly allowance and letting them learn how to spend and manage it. And when they're old enough, having your kids get a part-time job helps teach financial responsibility as well.

Caring for aging parents

There comes a time for many of us when we reverse roles with our parents. Instead of being the one who is cared for, you become the caregiver or the caretaker. As your parents age, they may need help with a variety of issues and living tasks. Although it's unlikely that you'll have the time or ability to perform all these functions yourself, you may well end up being the coordinator of service providers who can.

Here are some things to consider when caring for aging parents:

✔ **Get help where possible.** In most communities, a variety of non-profit organizations offer information and sometimes even counselling to families grappling with caring for elderly parents. You might best find your way to such resources through your province's health department as well as recommendations from local hospitals and doctors. You'll especially want to get assistance and information if your parents may need some sort of home care, nursing home care, or assisted living arrangement.

✔ **Get involved in their health care.** Your aging parents may already have a lot on their minds or simply may not be able to coordinate and manage all the health care providers giving them medications and advice. Try, as best as you can, to be their advocate. Speak with their doctors to understand their current medical condition and need for various medications and to help coordinate caregivers. Visit nursing homes and speak with prospective care providers.

✔ **Understand tax breaks.** If you are financially supporting your parents, you may be eligible for a number of tax credits and deductions for elder care. If you support a parent who is mentally or physically infirm, you can generally claim most related medical expenses as a tax credit. You can also claim the *equivalent-to-married* credit if you are single, widowed, divorced, or separated and supporting a parent. Also explore the caregiver credit. This is worth up to $400 if an elderly or infirm relative lives with you for whom you provide in-home care. However, you cannot claim this credit if you claim the equivalent-to-spouse credit.

✔ **Discuss getting the estate in order.** Parents don't like talking and thinking about their demise and usually feel awkward discussing it with their children. But opening a dialogue between you and your folks about such issues can be healthy in many ways. Discussing wills, living wills, living trusts, and estate planning strategies (refer to Chapter 18) can not only make you aware of your folks' situation but can also improve their plans to both their benefit and yours.

✔ **Take some time off.** Caring for an aging parent, particularly one who is having health problems, can be time-consuming and emotionally draining. If you were already juggling the responsibilities of a job, marriage, and parenthood before your parents needed help, you now may well feel completely overwhelmed. Do yourself and your parents a favour and use some vacation time to help get things in order. Although not the kind of vacation you probably envisioned, the time should reduce your stress and help you get more on top of things.

Divorcing

Sadly, half of all marriages end in divorce. In most marriages destined to split up, there are early warning signs that both parties recognize; sometimes, however, one spouse surprises the other with an unexpected request for divorce.

Whether planned or unexpected, here are some key things to consider when getting a divorce:

✔ **Question the divorce.** Some say that divorcing is too easy, and we tend to agree. Although some couples are indeed better off to part their ways, others give up too easily, thinking that the grass is greener elsewhere only to later discover that all lawns have weeds and crabgrass. Just as with a lawn that isn't watered and fertilized, relationships can wither without nurturing.

Money and disagreements over money are certainly a contributing factor to marital unhappiness. Unfortunately, in many relationships, money is wielded as power by the spouse who earns more of it. Try talking things over, perhaps with a marital counsellor; invest in making your relationship stronger, and reap the dividends for years to come.

✔ **Separate your emotions from the financial issues.** Separating your feelings from your finances is easier said than done. Feelings of revenge may be common in some divorces, but they will probably only help to ensure that the lawyers get rich at your expense as the two of you butt heads. If you really want a divorce, work at doing it efficiently and harmoniously so that you can get on with your lives.

✔ **Detail resources and priorities.** Draw up a list of all the assets and liabilities that you and your spouse have. Be sure that you get all the financial facts, including investment account records and statements. Once you know the whole picture, begin to think about what is and is not important to you financially and otherwise.

✔ **Educate yourself about personal finance and legal issues.** Divorce sometimes forces non–financially oriented spouses to get a crash course in personal finance at a difficult emotional time. We hope that this book can help educate you financially. In terms of the legal issues of divorce, visit a bookstore and pick up a good legal guide or two about divorce.

✔ **Choose advisers carefully.** Odds are that you will retain the services of one or more specialists to assist you with the myriad issues, negotiations, and concerns of your divorce. Legal, tax, and financial advisers can help, but recognize their limitations and conflicts of interest. Lawyers, unfortunately, benefit financially the more complicated things become and the more you haggle with your spouse. Don't use your divorce lawyer for financial or tax advice — your lawyer probably knows no more than you do in these areas. Also, realize that in most provinces you don't need a lawyer to get divorced. As for choosing tax and financial advisers, if you think you need that type of help, refer to Chapters 7 and 19 for how to find good advisers.

✔ **Analyze your spending.** When you go back to being single, although your "household" expenses will surely be less, you'll probably have to make do with less income. Some people find themselves financially squeezed in the early years following a divorce. In addition to helping you adjust to a new budget, analyzing your spending needs pre-divorce will help you negotiate a fairer settlement with your spouse.

✔ **Review needed changes to insurance.** If you are covered under your spouse's employer insurance plan, be sure to set the wheels in motion to get those coverages replaced (refer to Chapter 17). If you or your children will still be financially dependent upon your spouse post-divorce, be sure that the divorce agreement mandates life insurance coverage. And you should revise your will (see Chapter 18).

✔ **Revamp your retirement plan.** With changes to your income, expenses, assets, liabilities, and future needs, your retirement plan will surely need an overhaul post-divorce. Refer to Chapter 3 for a reorientation.

Receiving a windfall

Whether through inheritance, stock options, small-business success, or lottery winnings, you may receive a financial windfall at some point in your life. Like many who are totally unprepared psychologically and organizationally for their sudden good fortune, you may well find that a flood of money can create more problems than it solves. If you're saying, "I should have such problems," fair enough. Who wouldn't rather be rich than poor?

Here are a few tips to help you make your financial windfall the pleasant experience that it should be:

- **Take the time to educate yourself.** If you've never had to deal with significant wealth, there's no reason that we'd expect you to know how to handle it. Don't rush and pressure yourself to invest it as soon as possible. Leaving the money where it is or stashing it in one of the higher-yielding money market funds or high-interest savings accounts recommended in Chapter 13 is a far better short-term solution than jumping into investments that you don't understand and haven't taken the time to research.

- **Beware the sharks.** You may begin to wonder if someone has posted your net worth, address, and home telephone number in the local newspaper and on the Internet. Brokers and financial advisers may flood you with marketing materials, telephone solicitations, and lunch date requests. These folks who pursue you do so for a reason: They want to convert your money into their income either by selling you investment and other financial products or by managing your money. Stay away from the sharks, educate yourself, and take charge of your own financial moves. Decide on your own terms whom to hire and seek them out. Most of the best advisers that we know don't have the time or philosophical orientation to chase after prospective clients.

- **Recognize the emotional side of coming into a lot of money.** One of the side effects of accumulating wealth quickly is that you may have feelings of guilt or otherwise be unhappy, especially if you expected money to solve your problems. Getting a big inheritance from your folks may make you feel guilty if you didn't invest in your relationship with them and now, with their passing, you regret how you interacted with them. As another example, if you poured endless hours into a business venture that finally paid off, all that money sitting in your investment accounts may leave you with a hollow feeling if you divorced and lost friends through neglecting your relationships.

- **Pay down debts.** One of the simplest and best investments you can make if you come into wealth is to pay off your debts. Consider the entrepreneur who was frustrated because he didn't know how to invest several million dollars he had. Partly because he had worked so hard in his business to build his wealth, he was worried about losing money on investments. He had a decent-size home mortgage at 8 percent interest, which made complete sense for him to pay off. We generally borrow money to buy things that we otherwise couldn't buy in one fell swoop. When you have plenty of money, getting rid of debts is an especially good move. Just be sure to inquire about any possible penalties, such as trying to pay off a mortgage mid-term.

- **Diversify.** To protect your wealth, don't keep it all in one pot. Mutual funds (refer to Chapter 10) are an ideally diversified, professionally managed investment vehicle to consider. And if you want your money to continue growing, consider the wealth-building investments — stocks, real estate, and small-business options — that we discuss in Part III of this book.

✔ **Make use of the opportunity.** Most people work their whole lives for a paycheque in order to pay a never-ending stream of monthly bills. Although we're not advocating a hedonistic lifestyle, why not take some extra time to travel, spend time with your family, and enjoy the hobbies you've long been putting off? And how about trying a new career that you'd find more fulfilling and that might make the world a better place? Many people have little flexibility. Don't waste it if you do.

Retiring

If you've spent the bulk of your adult life working, retiring can be a challenging life transition. Most Canadians have an idealized vision of how wonderful a retired life would be. No more irritating bosses and pressure of work deadlines. Unlimited time to travel, play, and lead the good life. Sounds good, huh? Well, the reality for most Canadians is far different, especially for those who don't plan ahead financially and otherwise.

Here are some tips to help you through retirement:

✔ **Plan both financially and personally.** Leaving behind a full-time job and career creates even bigger challenges, such as what to do with all your free time — the opposite problem that new parents have. You can get too much of a good thing, which is why planning for your time and activities in retirement is even more important than planning financially. If your focus during your working years is solely on your career and saving money, you may lack interests, friends, and the ability to know how to spend money once you do retire.

✔ **Take stock of your resources.** Many people worry and wonder if they have sufficient assets to cut back on work or retire completely, yet they haven't crunched any numbers to see where they stand. Sometimes in life ignorance can be blissful, but this is a case where ignorance might cause you to misunderstand how little or much you really have accumulated for retirement versus what you need. See Chapter 3.

✔ **Re-evaluate your insurance needs.** During your working years, you carried disability and perhaps some life insurance to protect you and your dependants should you not be able to earn an income. Once you have sufficient assets to retire, you won't need to retain insurance to protect your employment income any longer. On the other hand, as your assets have grown over the years, you may be underinsured with regard to liability insurance (refer to Chapter 18).

✔ **Decide on health care/living options.** Medical expenses in your retirement years, particularly the cost of nursing home care, can be daunting. Which course of action you take — supplemental insurance, buying into a retirement community, or not doing anything — depends upon your financial and personal situation. Early preparation increases your options. If you wait until you have major health problems, it may be too late to choose certain paths. See Chapter 17 for more details.

✔ **Decide what to do with your RRSP money.** When you're set to retire, you may have to elect what to do with your RRSP money. Selecting the right options is similar to choosing a good investment — different features carry different risks, benefits, and tax consequences. Read Chapter 11 for information on how to assess your different options for taking money out of your RRSP. Read Part III of this book to learn about investing.

✔ **Pick a pension option.** Pensions are structured by actuaries based on reasonable life expectancies. The younger your age when you start collecting your company pension and Canada Pension Plan (or Quebec Pension Plan) benefits, the less you'll get per month. Check to see if the amount of your monthly company pension stops increasing past a certain starting age. You obviously wouldn't want to delay access to your pension benefits past that age because you will receive no reward for waiting any longer, and you'll collect the benefit for fewer months.

If you know that you have a health problem that shortens your life expectancy, drawing your company pension and CPP benefits sooner is usually to your benefit. Should you plan to continue working in some capacity and earning a decent income once you leave your employer, waiting for higher pension benefits when you'll be in a lower tax bracket is probably wise.

As for your other choices that affect what amount your surviving spouse receives from your employer's pension plan should you die first, at one end of the spectrum you have the risky single life option, which pays benefits until you pass away and provides no benefits thereafter for your spouse. This option maximizes your monthly take while you are alive. Consider this option only if your spouse could do without this income. The least risky option and thus least financially rewarding while the pensioner is still living is the *100 percent joint and survivor option*, which pays your survivor the same amount that you received while still alive. The other joint and survivor options fall somewhere in between these two extremes and generally make sense for most couples who desire decent pensions early in retirement but want a reasonable amount to continue should the pensioner die first.

✔ **Get your estate in order.** Confronting your mortality is never a joy, but when you're considering retiring or are retired, getting your estate in order makes all the more sense. Learn about wills and trusts that might benefit you and your heirs. Also consider gifting if you have more than you need. You can't take it with you, and if you are worried about taxes that will be triggered by your death, gifting money to your heirs will reduce those taxes.

Chapter 22

Ten Things More Important than Money

● ●

*T*hroughout this book, we provide information and advice that should enable you to make the most of your money. Whether you have stuck with us since Chapter 1 or have simply skimmed a few chapters, you probably know that we take a holistic approach to money decisions.

Although we hope our financial advice serves you well, we also want to be sure that you remember the many things in life (we chose our ten favourite) that are far more important than the girth of your investment portfolio or the size of your latest paycheque. Too often in our capitalistic society, we place too much emphasis on financial success and status and too little importance on living with a higher purpose. We hope this chapter makes a small contribution to keeping you on the best path.

Family

In our culture, men especially and increasingly women see their primary role as "providing" financially for their families. Such a focus seems to permit people to feel comfortable with making sacrifices for the sake of their work and careers. We also seem to psychologically justify placing work before family because we've been taught the virtues of a strong work ethic.

Some employees rightfully fear that their bosses may not be sympathetic to the needs of their families, especially when those needs get in the way of getting the job done as efficiently as an impatient boss would like. However, others put their companies first because that's what peers do and because they don't want to rock the boat.

Your spouse, your parents, and your kids, of course, should come first. They're much more important than your next promotion, and you should treat them that way. Balance is key. Should your boss not respect or value the importance of family, then perhaps it's time to find a new boss. Just be sure that you have a sufficient emergency reserve (see Chapter 3).

Friends

The older some people get, the less time they seem to have for friends. People too busy climbing the career ladder may not even make time for friends.

So many items in our consumer-oriented society are disposable, and unfortunately, friends too often fall into that category. Friends aren't really friends as much as they are acquaintances who can further our careers, and once that function has passed, they're tossed aside.

What friends do you really care for? Do you have friends you can turn to in a time of need who can really listen and be there for you? Take the time to invest in your friendships, both old and new.

Your health

Stress, poor diet, lack of exercise, poor relationships within your family — all of these bad habits can have adverse personal health consequences. People neglect their health for different reasons. In some cases, as with money management, people lack the knowledge as to the keys to good personal health. Getting too caught up in one's career and working endless hours also often leads to neglect of one's health.

Some people don't fully realize what the downside may be to their neglect of their bodies. Worst case, of course, is your untimely demise. But plenty of people suffer from ongoing conditions that damage the body and can make them feel far less well than they could. Unless you believe in reincarnation, you only get one body — take care of it and treat it with the respect it deserves!

Kids

Investing in your children is absolutely one of the best investments you can make. Understanding how to relate to and care for kids can help make you a better and more fulfilled person. (And we think that understanding kids can help you better understand what makes grown-ups tick, too!)

Our future is our children. You should care about children even if you don't have any. Why? Do you care about the quality of our society? Have any concerns about crime? Do you care about the economy? How about entertainment and the arts?

All of these issues depend to a large extent on our nation's children and what kind of teenagers and adults our children someday become. We know that many parents struggle to balance the demands of work and raising kids. We think everyone benefits when parents find ways to work at their careers less and spend more time with their children. Find ways to make do with what money you have. When your children are grown, they won't remember — or appreciate — that by working harder at your career, you were able to buy them more computer software or Pokémon cards. They *will* remember — and won't appreciate — a lack of attention.

Your neighbours

Your neighbours can be sources of friendship, happiness, and comfort. Too often, we see people caught up in their daily routines neglecting their neighbours.

Of course, you may not want to get to know all your neighbours better. But give them a chance. Don't write them off because they aren't the same age, race, or occupation as you. Part of our coherence with our greater society comes from where we live, and our neighbours are an important piece of that connection. Don't miss out on that.

Appreciating what you do have

In our work as financial writers, we have the opportunity to interact with many people from all walks of life. Despite the overall level of affluence in our society, we continue to be struck by how many people focus upon and lament the material things they lack (a bigger house, more costly cars, and so on) rather than appreciating the material and nonmaterial things they do have.

Right now, make a list of at least ten things that you appreciate. Periodically (daily, weekly, or monthly), make a similar list. Our culture sometimes causes us to dwell on what we don't have (which is usually not nearly as important as what we do have).

Your reputation

What do you think of when we say William Jefferson Clinton, Ivan Boesky, or Michael Milken? All of these people would be deemed successful in a career and monetary sense, but is that what first came to your mind?

It can take a lifetime to build a reputation but only moments to lose it. The Tenth Commandment is, "You shall not covet." As people chase after more fame, power, money, and possessions, they often devalue and underinvest in relationships and breach the other commandments along the way.

Think of the people you most admire in your life. Although we're sure that none of them are perfect, we bet each has a superior reputation with you.

Education

Education is a lifelong process — it's not just about attending a fancy university and perhaps getting an advanced degree. Whether it's related to your career or a newfound hobby, there's always something to learn. As long as you have your mental capacities, you can keep learning and building on what you already know.

And, who knows, maybe someday you'll gain an understanding of the meaning of life. The older we get, the more we have to reflect upon and learn from.

Having fun

In the quest to earn more, save more, and invest smarter, some people get so caught up in society's money game that money becomes the purpose of their existence. Whether you call it an addiction or obsession, having such a financial focus will surely steer you from the good things in life. We've known plenty of people who realize too late in life that sacrificing personal relationships and one's health isn't worth any amount of financial success.

Therapists' offices are filled with unhappy people who spend too much time and energy chasing promotions and money. You've likely talked to people like this as well. Often, they seem to worry about having enough money, and when you tell them that they have "enough," the conversation usually turns to the personal things lacking in their lives.

Solving social problems

Although we live in a privileged and in many respects advanced country, we Canadians have a good deal of room for improvement. We have more than our fair share of problems, including poverty-stricken families, under-fed children, violence against women, and poor environmental practices.

Why not be part of the solution rather than part of the problem? You can find plenty of causes worthy of your volunteer time or donations, such as Big Brothers/Big Sisters, which partners adults with children for informal mentoring.

Glossary

• •

*T*he terms that appear in *italic type* throughout the book are defined in this glossary.

adjusted cost basis: For capital gains tax purposes, the adjusted cost basis is how Revenue Canada determines your profit or loss when you sell an asset such as a security. For an investment such as a mutual fund or stock, your cost basis is what you originally invested plus any reinvested money. For real estate, you arrive at the adjusted cost basis by adding the original purchase price to the cost of any capital improvements (expenditures that increase your property's value and life expectancy).

alternative minimum tax (AMT): The name given to a sort of shadow tax system that may cause you to pay a higher amount in income taxes than you otherwise would. The AMT was designed to prevent higher-income earners from lowering their tax bills too much through large deductions.

American Stock Exchange (AMEX): The second largest stock exchange in the United States, it typically lists mid-sized firms.

annuity: An investment that is essentially a contract backed by an insurance company and is frequently purchased for retirement purposes. Its main benefit is that it allows your money to compound and grow without taxation until withdrawal. Selling annuities is a lucrative source of income for insurance agents and "financial planners" who work on commission, so don't buy one of these until you're sure it makes sense for your situation.

asset allocation: When you invest your money, you need to decide how to proportion it between risky, growth-oriented investments (such as stocks) whose values fluctuate and more stable, income-producing investments (like bonds). How soon you will need the money and how tolerant you are of risk are two important determinants when deciding how to allocate your money.

audit: Revenue Canada examination of your financial records, often at the Revenue Canada offices, to substantiate your tax return. Among life's worst experiences.

bank prime rate: See **prime rate**.

bankruptcy: Legal action that puts a halt to creditors' collection actions against you. If you have a high proportion of consumer debt to annual income, it may be your best option.

bear market: A period when the stock market experiences a strong downward swing and is usually accompanied by and sometimes precedes an economic recession. Imagine a bear in hibernation, because this is what happens in a bear market: Investors hibernate, and the market falters. During a bear market, the value of stocks can decrease significantly. Usually the market must drop at least 20 percent to be considered a bear market.

beneficiaries: In the event of your death, the people to whom you desire to leave your assets or, in the case of life insurance or a pension plan, your benefits. For each retirement plan, you denote beneficiaries.

blue chip stock: The stock of the largest and most consistently profitable corporations. This term comes from poker, where the most valuable chips are blue. The list of these stocks is unofficial and changes.

bond: A loan investors make to a corporation or government. Bonds generally pay a set amount of interest on a regular basis. They are an appropriate investment vehicle for conservative investors who do not feel comfortable with the risk involved in investing in stocks and who want to receive a steady income. All bonds have a maturity date when the bond issuer must pay back at par (full) value the bond holders (lenders). Bonds should not be your primary long-term investment vehicle because they produce little real growth on your original investment after inflation is factored in.

bond rating: See **Standard & Poor's ratings** and **Moody's ratings**.

bond yield: How much a bond will yield to an investor depends on two important factors: creditworthiness of the bond's issuer and the maturity date of the bond. The better the rating a bond receives, the less risk involved and, thus, the lower the yield. As far as the maturity date is concerned, the longer you loan your money, the higher the risk (because it is more likely that rates will fluctuate) and the higher your yield generally will be. A yield is quoted as an annual percentage rate of return that a bond will produce if the bond makes its promised interest payments.

broker: An intermediary. When you buy a house, insurance, or stock, you will most likely do so through a broker. Most brokers are paid on commission, which creates a conflict of interest with their clients. The more the broker sells, the more he or she makes. But more is not necessarily better for you. Some insurance companies let you buy their policies directly, and many mutual fund families bypass stockbrokers. If you're going to work with a broker, a discount broker can help you save on commissions.

bull market: A period when the stock market experiences a strong upward swing, usually accompanied and driven by a growing economy and increasing corporate profits.

callable bond: A bond for which the lender can decide to pay the holder earlier than the previously agreed-upon maturity date. If interest rates are relatively high when a bond is issued, lenders may prefer issuing callable bonds because it gives them the flexibility to call back these bonds and issue new, lower-interest rate ones if interest rates decline. Callable bonds are risky for investors, because if interest rates decrease, the bond holder will get his investment money returned early and may have to reinvest his money at a lower interest rate.

capital gain: One way investors make money with an investment, such as stock. A capital gain is the profit from selling your stock at a higher price than the price for which it was purchased. For example, if you bought 50 shares of Rocky and Bullwinkle stock at $20 per share, and two years later you sold your shares when the price had risen to $25 per share, your profit or capital gain is $5 per share, or $250. If you held this Rocky and Bullwinkle stock outside of a tax-sheltered retirement plan, you would owe tax on this profit when you sold the stock.

capital gains distribution: Taxable distribution by a mutual fund or a real estate investment trust (REIT) created by securities that are sold within the fund or REIT at a profit.

cash value insurance: A type of life insurance that is extremely popular with insurance salespeople because it commands a high commission. In a cash value policy, you buy life insurance coverage but also get a savings-type account. Unless you are looking for ways to limit taxes payable on your death (if you are extremely wealthy, for example), avoid cash value insurance. The investment returns tend to be mediocre, and your contributions are not tax-deductible.

closed-end mutual fund: A mutual fund that decides upfront exactly how many shares it will issue to investors. Once all the shares are sold, an investor seeking to invest in the closed-end fund can only do so by purchasing shares from an existing investor. Shares of closed-end funds trade on the major stock exchanges and therefore can sell at either a discount if there are more sellers than buyers or at a premium if demand exceeds supply.

commercial paper: A short-term debt or IOU issued usually by larger, stable companies to help make their businesses grow and prosper. Creditworthy companies can sell this debt security directly to large investors and thus bypass borrowing money from bankers. Money market funds invest in soon-to-mature commercial paper.

commission: The percentage of the selling price of a house, stock, bond, or other investment that is paid to agents and brokers. Because most agents and brokers are paid by commission, understanding how the commission can influence their behaviour and recommendations is impor-

tant for investors and home buyers. Agents and brokers make money only when you make a purchase, and they make more money when you make a bigger purchase. Choose an agent carefully, and take your agent's advice with a grain of salt because this inherent conflict of interest can often set an agent's visions and goals at odds with your own.

commodity: A form of derivatives, a financial instrument whose value is derived from the performance of an underlying security such as a stock or bond. Raw materials (gold, wheat, sugar, and gasoline, for example) are commodities traded on the futures market.

common stock: Shares in a company that do not offer a guaranteed amount of dividend to investors; the amount of dividend distributions, if any, is at the discretion of company management. While they may or may not make money through dividends, common stock investors hope the stock price will appreciate as the company expands its operations and increases its profits. Common stock tends to offer you a better return (profit) than other investments, such as bonds or preferred stock. However, if the company falters, you could lose some or all of your original investment.

comparable market analysis (CMA): A written analysis, usually completed by a real estate agent, of similar houses currently being offered for sale and which have recently sold.

consumer debt: Debt on consumer items that depreciate in value over time. Credit card balances and auto loans are examples of consumer debt. This type of debt is bad for your financial health because it is high-interest and encourages you to live beyond your means.

Consumer Price Index (CPI): The Consumer Price Index reports price changes, on a monthly basis, in the cost of living for such items as food, housing, transportation, health care, entertainment, clothing, and other miscellaneous expenses. The CPI is used to adjust government benefits, and is used by many employers to determine cost-of-living increases in wages and pensions. An increase in prices is also known as *inflation.*

credit report: A credit report details your history of using credit and is the main report that a lender uses to determine whether or not to make you a loan. You must generally pay the lender to obtain this report.

debit card: Although they may look like credit cards, debit cards are different in one important way: When you use a debit card, the cost of the purchase is deducted from your checking account. Thus, a debit card gives you the convenience of a credit card without the danger of building up a mountain of consumer debt.

deductible: With insurance, the deductible is the amount of the loss that you pay if you file a claim. For example, say that your car sustains $800 of damage. If your deductible is $500, then the insurance will cover $300 and you'll pay $500 out of your own pocket for the repairs. The higher the deductible, the lower your insurance premiums and the less paperwork you will expose yourself to in filing claims (because small losses that are less than the deductible won't necessitate filing a claim). Take the highest deductibles that you can afford when selecting insurance.

deduction: An expense you may subtract from your income to lower your taxable income. Examples include child care expenses, business losses, and RRSP contributions.

derivative: An investment instrument whose value is derived from other securities. For example, an option to buy IBM stock does not have value in itself; the value is derived from the price of IBM's stock.

disability insurance: During your working years, you have a lot riding on your ability to earn an income. Without it, you would be in big trouble (unless a wealthy relative, wife, husband, or friend can support you). Disability insurance replaces a portion of your employment income in the unlikely event that you suffer a disability that keeps you from working.

discount broker: Unlike a full-service broker, a discount broker generally offers no investment advice and has employees who work on salary rather than on commission. Using a discount broker helps you avoid the conflict of interest that will inevitably come up with a so-called full-service broker. In addition to trading individual securities, most discount brokerage firms also offer no-load (commission-free) mutual funds.

diversification: You go out to eat Chinese food with four friends. The menu is a bit difficult to understand and you are not familiar with Chinese food. Is it prudent for all you to order the same dish? Probably not. If each person orders a different dish and you share the food, you have a much better chance of satisfying your palate. The same holds true when you invest your money. If you put all of your money into one type of investment, you're potentially setting yourself up for a big shock. If that investment collapses, so does your investment world. By spreading your money among different investments — bonds, Canadian stocks, international stocks, and so on — you'll ensure yourself a better chance of investing success and fewer sleepless nights.

dividend: Quotient, divisor, dividend? Forget elementary school math. With stock, the dividend is the portion of a company's profits paid to its shareholders. For example, if a company has an annual dividend of $2 per share and you own 100 shares, then your total dividend is $200. Usually, established and slower-growing companies pay dividends while smaller and faster-growing companies reinvest their profits for growth.

Dow Jones Industrial Average (DJIA): A widely followed stock market index comprising 30 large, actively traded U.S. company stocks. The stocks in the DJIA are selected by senior editors at *The Wall Street Journal.*

down payment: The part of the purchase price for a house that the buyer pays in cash, upfront, and does not finance with a mortgage. Generally, the larger the down payment, the better the deal that you can get on a mortgage. You can usually get access to the best mortgage programs with a down payment of at least 25 percent of the purchase price of a home.

earthquake insurance: Although the West Coast is often associated with earthquakes, other areas are also 'quake prone. An earthquake insurance rider (which usually comes with a deductible of 5 to 10 percent of the cost to rebuild the home) on a homeowner's policy pays to repair or rebuild your home if it is damaged in an earthquake. If you live in an area with earthquake risk, get earthquake insurance coverage!

Emerging Markets Index: The Emerging Markets Index is published by Morgan Stanley and tracks stock markets in developing countries. The main reason for investing in emerging markets is that these economies typically experience a higher rate of economic growth than developed markets. However, the potential for higher returns is coupled with greater risk.

equity: In the real estate world, this term refers to the difference between the market value of your home and what you owe on it. For example, if your home is worth $200,000 and you have an outstanding mortgage of $140,000, your equity is $60,000. Equity is also a synonym for stock.

estate: The value, at the time of your death, of your assets minus your loans and liabilities.

estate planning: The process of deciding where your assets will go when you die and structuring your assets so as to minimize likely taxes due upon your death.

financial assets: A property or investment, such as real estate or a stock, mutual fund, bond, and so on, which has value that could be realized if sold.

financial liabilities: Your outstanding loans and debts. To determine your net worth, you must subtract your financial liabilities from your financial assets.

financial planners: A motley crew that professes an ability to manage your money. Financial planners come with varying backgrounds and degrees: MBAs and Certified Financial Planners to name a few. A useful way to distinguish among this mixed bag of nuts is to determine whether the planners are commission-, fee-, or hourly-based.

fixed-rate mortgage: The granddaddy of all mortgages. You lock into an interest rate (for example, 8 percent), and it never changes during the life (term) of your mortgage. Your mortgage payment will be the same amount each and every month. If you become a cursing, frothing maniac when you miss your morning coffee or someone is five minutes late, then this certain payment mortgage might be for you!

flood insurance: "When the flood waters recede, the poor folk start from scratch" (Richard Wright). They start from scratch unless they have flood insurance. If there's even a remote chance that your area may flood, having flood insurance is prudent.

full-service broker: A broker who gives advice and charges a high commission relative to discount brokers. But this is not the biggest problem with full-service brokers. Because the brokers work on commission, they have a significant conflict of interest: namely, to advocate strategies that will be of financial benefit to them.

future: An obligation to buy or sell a commodity or security on a specific day for a preset price. When used by most individual investors, futures represent a short-term gamble on the short-term direction of the price of a commodity. Companies and farmers use futures contracts to hedge their risks of changing prices.

Guaranteed Investment Certificate (GIC): A specific term loan that you make to your banker. The maturity date for GICs ranges from a month up to several years. The interest paid on GICs is fully taxable, thus making CDs inappropriate for higher tax-bracket investors investing outside tax-sheltered retirement plans.

home equity: See **equity**.

home-equity loan: Technical jargon for what used to be called a second mortgage. With this type of loan, you borrow against the equity in your house. If used wisely, a home-equity loan can help pay off high-interest consumer debt or can be tapped for other short-term needs, such as a remodelling project. In contrast with consumer debt, mortgage debt is usually at a lower interest rate.

homeowner's insurance: Dwelling coverage that covers the cost of rebuilding your house in the event of fire or other calamity. The liability insurance portion of this policy protects you against lawsuits associated with your property. Another essential element is the personal property coverage, which pays to replace your damaged or stolen worldly possessions.

index: A security market index, such as the *Standard & Poor's 500 Index*, is a statistical composite that measures the performance of a particular type of security. Indexes exist for various stock and bond markets and are typically set at a round number such as 100 at a particular point in time. See **Dow Jones Industrial Average, Russell 2000, TSE 300 Index,** and **Wilshire 5000**.

inflation: The technical term for a rise in prices. Inflation usually occurs when there is too much money in circulation and not enough goods and services to spend it on. Due to this excess demand, prices rise. There is a link between inflation and interest rates: Interest rates must keep up with inflation or no one will invest in bonds issued by the government or corporations. When the interest rates on bonds are high, it usually reflects a high rate of inflation that will eat away at your return.

initial public offering (IPO): The first time a company offers stock to the investing public. An IPO typically occurs when a company wants to expand more rapidly and seeks additional money to support its growth. A number of studies have demonstrated that buying into IPOs in which the general public can participate produces subpar investment returns. A high level of IPO activity may indicate a cresting stock market as companies and their investment bankers rush to cash in on a "pricey" marketplace. IPO could stand for *It's Probably Overpriced*.

interest rate: What lenders charge you to use their money. The higher the interest rate, the higher the risk generally entailed in the loan. With bonds of a given maturity, a higher rate of interest means a lower quality of bond — one that is less likely to return you your money.

international stock markets: Stock markets outside of Canada account for a significant portion of the world stock market capitalization (value). Some specific stock indices track international markets (see **Morgan Stanley EAFE** and **Emerging Markets Index**). International investing is one way to diversify your portfolio and reduce your risk. In addition to the U.S., some of the foreign countries with major stock exchanges include Japan, Britain, France, Germany, and Canada.

junk bond: A bond rated Ba (Moody's) or BB (Standard & Poor) and lower. Historically, these bonds have had a 1 to 2 percent chance of default, which is not exactly "junky." Of course, the higher risk is accompanied by a higher interest rate.

leverage: Financial leverage affords its users a disproportionate amount of financial power relative to the amount of their own cash invested. In some circumstances, you can borrow up to 50 percent of a stock price and use all funds (both yours and those that you borrow) to make a purchase. You repay this so-called margin loan when you sell the stock. If the stock price were to rise, you would make money on what you invested plus what money you borrowed. While this sounds attractive, remember that leverage cuts both ways — when prices decline, you lose money not only on your investment but also on the money you borrowed.

limited partnership (LP): Often promoted in a way that promises high returns, broker-sold limited partnerships generally limit one thing: your investment return. Why? Because they are burdened with high commissions and management fees. Another problem is that they are typically not liquid for many years.

load mutual fund: a sales load is the commission paid to brokers who sell commission-based mutual funds. The commission typically ranges up to 6 percent. This commission is deducted from your investment money and thus reduces your returns.

marginal tax rate: The rate of income tax that you pay on the last dollars that you earn over the course of a year. Why the complicated distinction? Because all income is not treated equally: You pay less tax on your first dollars of earnings and more tax on the last dollars of your annual income. Knowing your marginal tax rate is helpful because you can analyze the tax implications of important personal financial decisions.

market capitalization: The value of all the outstanding stock of a company. It is the quoted price per share of a stock multiplied by the number of shares outstanding. Thus, if Rocky and Bullwinkle Corporation has 100 million shares of outstanding stock and the quoted price per share is $20, then the company has a market capitalization of $2 billion.

Moody's ratings: Moody's rating service measures and rates the credit (default) risks of various bonds. Moody's investigates the financial condition of a bond issuer. Its ratings use the following grading system, from highest to lowest: Aaa, Aa, A, Baa, Ba, B, Caa, Ca, C. Higher ratings imply a lower risk but also mean that the interest rate will be lower.

Morgan Stanley EAFE (Europe, Australia, Far East) index: The Morgan Stanley EAFE index tracks the performance of the more established countries' stock markets in Europe and Asia. This index is an important one for international-minded investors who want to follow the performance of overseas stock investments.

mortgage broker: Mortgage brokers buy mortgages wholesale from lenders and then mark the mortgages up (typically from 0.5 to 1 percent) and sell them to borrowers. A good mortgage broker is most helpful for people who will not shop around on their own for a mortgage or for people who have blemishes on their credit reports.

mortgage life insurance: Mortgage life insurance guarantees that the lender will receive its money in the event that you meet an untimely demise. Many people may try to convince you that you need this insurance to protect your dependants and loved ones. Mortgage life insurance is relatively expensive given the cost for the coverage provided. If you need life insurance, buy low-cost, high-quality term life insurance instead.

municipal bond: A loan that an investor makes to cities, towns, and states for public projects, such as building highways, parks, or cultural centres.

mutual fund: A portfolio of stocks, bonds, or other securities that is owned by numerous investors and managed by an investment company. See also **no-load mutual fund**.

National Association of Securities Dealers Automated Quotation (NASDAQ) system: An electronic network that allows brokers to trade from their offices all over the country. With NASDAQ, brokers buy and sell shares using constantly updated prices that appear on their computer screens.

negative amortization: Although it may sound like a description of the cause of dinosaur extinction, negative amortization occurs when your outstanding mortgage balance increases despite the fact that you're making the required monthly payments. Negative amortization occurs with adjustable-rate mortgages that cap the increase in your monthly payment but do not cap the interest rate. Therefore, your monthly payments do not cover all the interest that you actually owe.

net asset value (NAV): The dollar value of one share of a mutual fund. For a no-load fund, the market price is its NAV. For a load fund, the NAV is the "buy" price minus the commission.

New York Stock Exchange (NYSE): The largest stock exchange in the world in terms of total volume and value of shares traded. It lists companies that tend to be among the oldest, largest, and best-known companies.

no-load mutual fund: A mutual fund that does not come with a commission payment attached to it. Because of the lack of a load and generally lower management fees of these funds, they tend to have better returns than load funds. Some funds claim to be "no-load" but simply hide their sales commissions as an ongoing sales charge. You can avoid these funds by reading the prospectuses carefully and educating yourself.

open-end mutual fund: A mutual fund that issues as many shares as investors demand. These open-end funds do not generally limit the number of investors or amount of money in the fund. Some open-end funds have been known to close to new investors, but investors with existing shares can usually still buy more shares from the company.

option: The right to buy or sell a specific security (such as a stock) for a preset price during a specified period of time. Options differ from futures in that with an option, you pay a premium fee upfront and you can either exercise the option or let it expire. If the option expires worthless, you lose 100 percent of your original investment. Use of options is best left to companies as hedging tools. Investment managers may use options as a hedging tool to reduce the risk in their investment portfolio. Like with futures, when most individual investors buy an option, they are doing so as a short-term gamble, not as an investment. For example: You have an option to buy 100 shares of Rocky and Bullwinkle Co. stock at $20 per share in the next six months. You pay $3 per share upfront as the premium. During this time period, R&B's share price rises to $30 and you exercise your right to buy at $20. You then sell your shares at the market price of $30; you make a $10 profit per share, which is a return more than three times larger than your original investment.

pension: Pensions are a benefit offered by some employers. These plans generally pay you a monthly retirement income based upon your years of service with the employer.

performance: How do you judge an investment's performance? Traditionally, by looking at the historic rate of return. The longer the period over which these numbers are tallied, the more useful. Considered alone, these numbers are practically meaningless. You must also note how well a fund has performed in comparison to competitors with the same investment objectives. Beware of advertisements that tout the high returns of a mutual fund, because they may not be looking at risk-adjusted performance or may be promoting performance over a short time period. Keep in mind that high return statistics are usually coupled with high risk and that this year's star could turn out to be next year's crashing meteor.

preferred stock: Stock that offers a guaranteed amount of dividend to investors. Preferred stock dividends must be paid before any dividends are paid to the common stock shareholders. Although preferred stock reduces your risk as an investor (because of the more secure dividend and greater likelihood of getting your money back if the company fails), it usually also limits your reward if the company expands and increases its profits.

price/earnings (P/E) ratio: The current price of a stock divided by the current (or sometimes the projected) earnings per share of the issuing company. It's a widely used stock analysis statistic that helps an investor get an idea of how cheap or expensive a stock price is. In general, a relatively high P/E ratio indicates that investors feel that the company's earnings are likely to grow quickly.

prime rate: The rate of interest that major banks charge their most creditworthy corporate customers. Why should you care? Well, because the interest rates on various loans that you may be interested in are often based upon the prime rate. And, guess what — you pay a higher interest rate than those big corporations!

principal: No, not the big boss from elementary school who struck fear into the hearts of most eight-year-olds. The principal is the amount that you borrow for a loan. If you borrow $100,000, your principal is $100,000. Principal can also refer to the amount that you originally placed in an investment.

prospectus: Individual companies as well as mutual funds are required by securities regulators to issue a prospectus. For a company, the prospectus is a legal document presenting a detailed analysis of that company's financial history, its products and services, its management's background and experience, and the risks of investing in the company. For a mutual fund, a prospectus tells you about the fund's investment objectives, costs, risk, and performance history.

real estate investment trust (REIT): Real estate investment trusts are like a mutual fund of real estate investments. Such trusts invest in a collection of properties (from shopping centres to apartment buildings). REITs trade on the major stock exchanges. If you want to invest in real estate while avoiding the hassles inherent in owning property, real estate investment trusts may be the right choice for you.

refinance: Refinance is a fancy word for taking out a new mortgage loan (usually at a lower interest rate) to pay off an existing mortgage (generally at a higher interest rate). Refinancing is not automatic, nor is refinancing guaranteed. Refinancing can also be a hassle and expensive. Weigh the costs and benefits of refinancing carefully before proceeding.

Registered Retirement Income Fund (RRIF): A type of retirement savings account that allows your investments to grow tax-free. Unlike an RRSP, you cannot make annual contributions to an RRIF. Instead, you are required to withdraw at least a certain minimum amount each year, which is taxed as regular income.

Registered Retirement Savings Plan (RRSP): A type of retirement savings plan available to almost everybody who has earned some money either through a job or by being self-employed. Your contributions are usually exempt (yes!) from federal and provincial income taxes and compound without taxation over time.

return on investment: The percentage of profit that you make on an investment. If you put $1,000 into an investment, and one year later it's worth $1,100, you have made a profit of $100. Your return on investment is the profit ($100) divided by the initial investment ($1,000) — in this case, 10 percent.

reverse mortgage: A reverse mortgage enables elderly homeowners, typically those who are low on cash, to tap into their home's equity without selling their home or moving from it. Specifically, a lending institution makes a cheque out to you each month, and you can use the cheque as you want. This money is really a loan against the value of your home and thus is tax-free when you receive it. The downside of these loans is that they deplete your equity in your estate, the fees and interest rates tend to be on the high side, and some require repayment within a certain number of years.

Russell 2000: An index that tracks the returns of 2000 smaller-company U.S. stocks. Smaller-company stocks tend to be more volatile than larger-company stocks. If you invest in small-company stocks or stock funds, this is an appropriate benchmark to compare your performance to.

Securities and Exchange Commission (SEC): The federal agency that administers U.S. securities laws and regulates and monitors investment companies, brokers, and financial advisers.

Standard & Poor's (S&P) ratings: Standard & Poor's rating service is one of two services that measure and rate the risks in buying a bond. S&P's ratings use the following grading system, from highest to lowest: AAA, AA, A, BBB, BB, B, CCC, CC, C. See also **Moody's ratings**.

Standard & Poor's 500 Index: An index that measures the performance of 500 large-company U.S. stocks that account for about 80 percent of the total market value of all stocks traded in the U.S. If you invest in larger-company U.S. stock or stock funds, this is an appropriate benchmark to compare the performance of your investments to.

stock: Shares of ownership in a company. When a company "goes public," it issues shares of stock to the public (see also initial public offering). Many, but not all, stocks pay dividends — a distribution of a portion of company profits. In addition to dividends, the other way you make money investing in stock is via appreciation in the price of the stock, which normally results from growth in revenues and corporate profits. You can invest in stock by purchasing individual shares or by investing in a stock mutual fund that offers a diversified package of stocks.

Stripped (strip) bond: A bond that doesn't pay explicit interest during the term of the loan. Such bonds are purchased at a discounted price relative to the principal value paid at maturity. The interest-bearing coupons have been removed or stripped off. Thus, the interest is implicit in the discount.

term life insurance: If people are dependent upon your income for their living expenses, you may need this insurance. Term life insurance functions simply: You determine how much protection you would like and then pay an annual premium based on that amount. Although it is much less touted by insurance salespeople than cash value insurance, it is the best life insurance out there for the vast majority of people.

TSE 300 Index: This index measures the performance of 300 large-company Canadian stocks that trade on the Toronto Stock Exchange. If you invest in larger-company Canadian stock or stock funds, this is a good benchmark to compare the performance of your investments to.

Treasury bill: IOUs from the federal government that mature within a year.

underwriting: An insurance company's process for evaluating a person's likelihood of filing a claim on a particular type of insurance policy. If significant problems are discovered, an insurer will usually propose much higher rates or refuse to sell the insurance coverage.

will: A legal document ensuring that your wishes regarding your assets and care of your minor children are heeded when you die.

Wilshire 5000: Despite the name, this index actually tracks closer to 6000 companies of all sizes on major U.S. stock exchanges. If you invest in U.S. stock or stock funds of companies of all sizes, this is an appropriate benchmark.

Index

• F •

• **N** •